AMERICANS AND THEIR WEATHER

Americans and
Their Weather

WILLIAM B. MEYER

OXFORD
UNIVERSITY PRESS

2000

OXFORD

UNIVERSITY PRESS

Oxford   New York

Athens   Auckland   Bangkok   Bogotá   Buenos Aires   Calcutta
Cape Town   Chennai   Dar es Salaam   Delhi   Florence   Hong Kong   Istanbul
Karachi   Kuala Lumpur   Madrid   Melbourne   Mexico City   Mumbai
Nairobi   Paris   São Paulo   Singapore   Taipei   Tokyo   Toronto   Warsaw

and associated companies in
Berlin   Ibadan

Published by Oxford University Press, Inc.
198 Madison Avenue, New York, New York 10016

Oxford is a registered trademark of Oxford University Press.

Library of Congress Cataloging-in-Publication Data
Meyer, William B.
Americans and their weather / William B. Meyer.
p.   cm.
Includes bibliographical references and index.
ISBN 0-19-513182-7
1. United States—Climate—Social aspects.   2. Climatology—Social aspects.
3. Weather—Social aspects.   4. Nature—Effect of human beings on.
5. Climatic changes—Environmental aspects.   I. Title.
QC983.M455   2000
304.2′5′0973—dc 21   99-33193

1 3 5 7 9 8 6 4 2

Printed in the United States of America
on acid-free paper

To my parents and Anne and Andrei Bell,
who made it possible.

Preface

DIFFERENT READERS MAY expect quite different things from a book described as weather history. It is only fair to begin by saying in more detail what kind of a book this is and what it does and does not try to do. It is not weather history in one frequent sense of that term: a chronicle of meteorological events and the air-mass dynamics by which they developed and decayed. Its focus is not on the weather in its own right, but on what it has meant for American life. The conventional story of what weather has meant takes in chiefly great weather disasters, "weather events that changed the course of history," and the development of weather science and forecasting. All appear in this book, but not in the leading roles, for they leave out most of the ways in which the weather has mattered for Americans. At the same time, this book is not an example of another popular form of weather history— an attempt to show how the effects of weather and climate have shaped American life and activities, or national and regional development, or national and regional character—for they have not. The opposite is much closer to the truth. All of these things are what have continuously shaped and reshaped the effects of weather and climate. They have determined to what degree and in what ways any neutral physical phenomenon would represent a resource or a hazard for human purposes and pursuits. As they have changed, so has the meaning of every climatic feature and every weather event.

Climatic change as well as social change can alter the weather's meaning for society, as nobody today needs to be reminded. The possible effects of global warming are too widely discussed for anyone to be in danger of forgetting it. The danger lies elsewhere: in supposing that the effects of climatic change have been the whole history of climate-society relations to date or even the most important part of it. Research on "climate and history" has been dominated by the study of climate shifts and their impacts. Paradoxically, the less visible and less important sources of change—those in the climate itself—have gotten more attention than the social changes transforming weather-society relations in plain sight. So finally, this book is not weather history chiefly in the sense of a history of how the prevailing weather has shifted and with what results. Changing human activities have altered in many ways the significance of climates that have been far more stable than the societies occupying them have been. How they have done so is the book's topic.

So defined, the topic is a vast one. A book of this size cannot cover all of the significant and interesting relations between the weather and human activities. Readers and reviewers will certainly think of many that I have left out, but including them would have meant leaving out many that I do discuss. I have tried to select the most important and representative ones for coverage: the ways in which weather has mattered most at different times for American life.

Portions of this book draw on work supported by the National Oceanic and Atmospheric Administration Office of Global Programs (Grant No. NA46G P0494-02) and the Battelle Memorial Institute/ Pacific Northwest National Laboratories (Contract 280441-A-Q2). A number of passages from the text have appeared in William B. Meyer, "Nature and Society in New England: The Other Dimension," in *Boston and New England: Images and Encounters,* eds. Theodore S. Pikora and Stephen S. Young, NCGE Resource Publication No. 21 (Indiana, Penn.: National Council for Geographic Education, 1999). I have also had help and encouragement of various kinds from Karen Reeds, Mary Hartman, Susan Bryce, Sam Ratick, and Bill Turner.

Contents

AMERICANS AND THEIR WEATHER

Introduction

IN THE MID-1830s, the young Nathaniel Hawthorne sat reading "what once were newspapers"—a bound volume of New England gazettes ninety-odd years old. Comparing the daily life that they portrayed with his own, Hawthorne was struck by how different and how much more severe the weather appeared to have been in the past. "The cold was more piercing then, and lingered farther into the spring," he decided; "our fathers bore the brunt of more raging and pitiless elements than we"; "winter rushed upon them with fiercer storms than now—blocking up the narrow forest-paths, and overwhelming the roads."[1]

He was not alone in thinking so. Another resident of Salem, Dr. Edward Holyoke, had been of the same opinion.[2] In his later years, the doctor spoke as the classic authority on the weather, the Oldest Inhabitant. Born in 1728, he lived until 1829, the full span of the century that Hawthorne judged mostly at secondhand, and he had kept a daily temperature log for the better part of it. A newspaper in 1824 reported a general belief that the seasons were "more lamb-like" than in earlier times. An English visitor a few years later was frequently told that the climate was moderating.[3] Cold and snowstorms had grown less intense and less frequent: such had been, wrote John Chipman Gray in the 1850s, "and is perhaps still a prevailing impression among the inhabitants of New-England."[4]

All the same, that impression of the century gone by was wrong. Gray, who maintained that the winters had not changed, also tried to explain why intelligent observers could have supposed that they had. On one point, he granted, they were correct. Certainly the effects of the weather were not what they had once been. But there was no evidence that a shift in the weather was responsible. Holyoke's own records, analyzed after his death, did not bear out his belief that winter cold and storms had weakened in his lifetime.[5] As Gray pointed out, if the impact of weather on New Englanders had changed, it was because New England society had changed.

Though the cold and snowfall had not diminished, it might well seem that they had, for winters in colonial times "were more severely felt than any winter of the same severity would now be." "Our people are better clothed," Gray observed, "our dwellings better fortified against cold," and great snowfalls interfered less with travel than they once had. Thanks to a denser population, "our roads are far more quickly rendered passable after heavy storms," the snow "beaten down in a very few days."

So in some ways New Englanders had protected themselves better from the elements. If the winter of earlier times, as a later historian would put it, was indeed "different from the modern winter," it was "because of the devices that had softened its rigours."[6] But that, Gray continued, was not the whole story. Some other changes had had the opposite effect. They had increased the weather's importance and made it more, rather than less, of a nuisance than it had before. It was widely believed that summer droughts in New England had become more frequent. Again, the belief was an error that had a basis in fact. Dry spells had not grown more intense. Rather, Gray pointed out, "their effects have become of more consequence"; they caused more trouble thanks to changes in human activities.[7] Waterpower from the rivers ran the spindles and looms and lathes of the factories that sprang up and multiplied in the nineteenth-century Northeast. One result of industrialization, Gray noted, had been to amplify any drop in stream-flow into an economic and social crisis. Declines once too small to attract notice now commanded the attention of millowner and worker alike. The streams were watched with a new anxiety, and any dry spell was felt with a new acuteness. Even the average summer flow of the rivers was only about a tenth that of the wettest months, no small problem for mills trying to operate at a steady pace.[8] Every year had become a drought year.

Plainly, something had changed, for the weather had not affected New Englanders in the eighteenth century in the same way it affected them in the nineteenth. It was easy to suppose that what was different was the weather itself. Just so, rooms suddenly become hotter when we become upset or excited; just so, the adult rereading a book enjoyed in childhood invariably discovers that the book has changed. That the changes occurred elsewhere is a second thought.

Hawthorne had second thoughts on one point. When he published "Old News" in the *New-England Magazine* in 1835, he added a footnote qualifying his claim that lightning had fallen "oftener and deadlier" a century before. Perhaps, he ventured, it was the spread of lightning rods that had made the difference, not a weakening of thunderstorms themselves. Even here, though, not all change was for the better. The country roads of New England were already becoming infested with a new pest, "the lightning-rod man." Recounting terrible stories of thunderbolt strikes, he frightened many farmers and householders into buying devices that were not only overpriced, but were often so badly installed that they amplified rather than reduced the dangers of lightning: "instead of proving themselves faithful sentinels and guarding in the hour of peril, they have too often turned traitors, and invited the destruction which they promised to avert."[9]

Perhaps the metamorphoses in the weather's effects were not the reason, or the main reason, why so many New Englanders thought that their climate had grown different. Beliefs are rarely so simple to explain. But if Gray's examples do not prove the point he was making, they illustrate another and more important one: how changes in the weather's effects need not mean that the weather has changed.

Even when it has, that change is never by itself what matters. Knowing the weather's physical properties and how they have shifted is never enough to understand what they mean for those experiencing them. Any given change can have radically different results in different settings—the settings that at the same time, and to much larger net effect, determine and alter the consequences of stable and recurrent aspects of the weather.

One of the very shifts in climate that Hawthorne and Holyoke imagined had occurred in New England in the century leading up to the 1830s did take place in the century that followed: a small rise in mean temperatures.[10] The results were not what they would have been earlier. Most revolutionary-era New Englanders lived by farming, fishing, and sailing, all highly sensitive to the weather. They generally stood to gain if the length of the growing season increased, harbors froze later and less often, and winter storms at sea became less fierce. After 1830, the relative decline of these three sectors lessened the profit that the region could expect from a warming climate. Other changes increased the losses that a warming could bring. In 1934, a New Hampshire businessman could observe how "the 'northeaster,' so dreaded by coastal shipping, is rather a blessing to the skier, since it is a father to most of our heavier snows."[11] For winter sports, a long snowy season means a good year. A mild one interferes disastrously with business.

Even before the age of the ski resort, cold and snow had not been without their advantages. Ice cut from ponds for sale in the cities, a way of turning hard winters into hard cash, was just becoming an important article of trade in Hawthorne's New England. Throughout the progressively warmer late nineteenth century, milder winters and the "ice famines" that they could bring became a growing hazard for the booming ice business and for the urban populations that relied on it to keep food fresh in summer. In an era of horse-drawn vehicles and unpaved roads, a fall of snow, once it was beaten down, made getting about easy by sled or sleigh. Winter was the preferred time for hauling heavy loads and the season for speedy driving. A thaw or a snowless winter greatly hampered movement. First the railroad and then the automobile, the paved highway, and the airplane have changed snow from a resource into a pure hindrance for travel, and mechanical refrigeration has destroyed the natural ice trade entirely.

All of these developments and many others have determined what the effects would be of such warming as has occurred. They have also themselves transformed, in far more significant degree, the role in human life of a climate that has changed much less than the society inhabiting it has. The mid nineteenth to mid twentieth century warming is at most a footnote to New England weather history. During the same period, economic, social, and technological developments did vastly more to change the region's relations with its skies. Some other climatic shifts in other places, to be sure, have been of greater importance. Everywhere their effects have themselves depended on the evolution of society, though, and everywhere that evolution itself has repeatedly modified and transformed the meaning of weather and climate even if they have remained stable. The history of American weather to date is not principally the story of how the weather has changed, but of how Americans have changed.

Generally speaking, weather matters to people in two ways: as a help and a hindrance, as a resource and a hazard, as an opportunity and a constraint, as a source of gains and a source of losses. To what extent and in what ways it plays either role depend on the activities and wants with which it interacts.

Natural hazards, so called, are geophysical processes that threaten people or things that people value.[12] To call the weather or anything else a "natural hazard" is misleading if to do so suggests that it is hazardous by its nature. What can make it hazardous is its relation to human affairs. It is a danger or a hindrance only if people value things that it can damage or engage in pursuits that it can disrupt. At one extreme, the damage and disruption may involve massive loss of life and property. At the other, they may involve mere discomfort, weather as disamenity.

How much discomfort the weather causes anyone depends on that person's standard of comfort, and such standards vary greatly. One person's oppressive heat can be another's cozy warmth, one's bitter chill another's bracing freshness. So, too, the severer impacts of weather as hazard depend on more than simple exposure to a weather event. No two individuals, groups, or communities exposed to the same weather will ever be affected by it in precisely the same way. Some may be highly sensitive to it, others not at all. Among the former, some may be far better able than others to cope with the consequences. A drought will affect agriculture far more than it will affect most industries or services. Farmers who irrigate with groundwater will have less to fear than those who rely on rainfall, and they may gain if the loss of rain-fed crops drives prices higher. Of two nonirrigating farmers, one may have tools for coping—insurance, savings, off-farm employment, the support of an extended family—that the other lacks. All exposed to the same weather, they are vulnerable to it to different degrees; it is more of a hazard to some than to others, and to some it is no hazard at all.

Thus some recurrent weather event or some stable feature of the climate may become a hazard where it was not one before, or cease to be one, or become more or less of one with changes in society: in where people live, what they do, what they own, and how they arrange their relations to one another. The change can be as simple as a change in expectations. A higher standard of comfort makes the weather more of a disamenity than it was before. A higher standard of punctuality makes the same weather-related delays in travel more of a problem.

If weather is a hazard or a hindrance when it threatens anything people value, it is a resource when it is in any way useful. People benefit in a host of ways, often unwittingly, from sun, rain, wind, snow, heat, and cold. They may find the weather useful simply by finding it pleasant. But weather is an amenity, as it is a disamenity, not for its own qualities alone but also because of the standards by which it is judged. So too weather events and climatic patterns are—and are not—natural resources more generally in precisely the way they are—and are not—natural hazards. Just as the lives and livelihoods it affects are what make weather a hazard, they are what make it a resource. Without the defining elements of "human wants and human capabilities," the economist Erich Zimmermann pointed out, there are no resources in nature, only "neutral stuff." "The word 'resource' does not refer to a thing or a substance," Zimmermann observed, "but to a function which a thing or a substance may perform, or to an operation in which it may take part, namely, the function or operation of attaining a given end such as satisfying a want."[13]

It follows that natural resources, like natural hazards, change as human wants and the means of satisfying them change. They can appear and disappear without any alteration in the natural environment. Two developments made the warm climate of the American South a richer resource in the late eighteenth century than it had been before. The mechanization of spinning and weaving in Great Britain increased the demand for the cotton that could be grown in the South, and the invention of the cotton gin in the United States made it possible to increase the supply. The climate had not changed, but its usefulness had. Sugarcane can be grown in parts of the South, but the climates of those areas have long owed much of their value to tariffs and import restrictions on sugar produced overseas.

Weather as a resource has one great advantage over nonweather inputs that may be used in its place. By and large, it is free where many possible substitutes are not. Yet the tools or skills or the land needed to exploit it may be costly, and so may its frequent unreliability. Weather as a resource, perhaps even more than weather as a hazard, is likely to vary tremendously in its value and importance to those exposed to it. Some may use it intensively, many others in the same place not at all.

The more one focuses on climatic shifts as the source of past change in climate-society relations, the more one may tend to think of controlling the climate as the best way to improve what remains unsatisfactory in these relations today. The more attention, on the other hand, one pays to the social factors that have made neutral weather events into hazards or resources, the more aware one will be of other ways to make those events less dangerous or more valuable. Students of natural hazards beginning with the geographer Gilbert F. White in the 1940s have developed the concept of the "range of choice" in human adjustment to the environment.[14] Flood impacts, White stressed, can be lessened not only by controlling the water—by trying to regulate rainfall or streamflow—but by making human activities less exposed or vulnerable to it: by regulating floodplain development, for example, or by spreading losses through insurance. A similar range of choice exists where weather as a resource is concerned. Changing the weather itself is not the only or necessarily the most effective way to enhance its value.

Doubtless people would always prefer changing the weather to changing activities of theirs that conflict with it. But they cannot often hope to do so without changing other people's weather as well, yet any weather event is likely to be both hazard and resource for different people in many different ways. As ecological concern has spread, the likely subtle and unintended effects of trying to remodel something so basic to the environment have become a worrisome matter where they were not before. But even where clear and direct consequences alone are considered, there is no wind so ill that it blows no one any good. Hurricanes top all standard lists of American weather hazards. Even they provide benefits as well, though, and some provide more benefits than costs, replenishing water supplies and rejuvenating crops suffering from summer drought.[15] Hard winters meant suffering from the cold in nineteenth-century New England, most of all among the poor, but, as Hawthorne noted, "the coal-merchants rejoice." The best winter weather for the ice-cutter too was "just the opposite of the weather sought by the poor man,"[16] and if a mild winter meant less immediate hardship, it also meant a shortage of ice and hardship in the summer. Weather optimal for some crops will not be so for others in the same area. The humorist "Max Adeler," a contemporary of Mark Twain's and at one time nearly as popular, described a country neighbor so cheerful that he saw only the good in whatever weather happened to be prevailing, but to see the good he did not have to invent it. Was heavy rain falling? "It makes the corn jump an' cleans the sewers an' keeps the springs from gittin' too dry." Drought? "Moisture breeds fevers and ague, an' ruins yer boots. If there's anything I despise, it's to carry an umbrella." In a heat wave, he would say "Splendid! Splendid! Noble weather for the poor and for the ice companies and the washer-women! I never saw sich magnificent weather as this for drying clothes." Was it bitterly cold in winter? "It helps the coal trade an' gives us good skeetin'."[17] The activities helped or hindered have changed greatly since Adeler's time. The larger point remains valid.

The weather can be both hazard and resource even for the same people engaging in the same activity. Sunshine has become a valuable amenity because many people enjoy basking in it, and at the same time it is a hazard to their health. The large and rapid increase in skin cancer in the modern United States is the product of social trends that include more, and more irregular, exposure outdoors and a shift of population to lower and sunnier latitudes. Areas with cloudless skies, a hazard now eagerly sought, find them a rich resource for attracting tourism and settlement, and at the same time annual deaths in the United States resulting from exposure to the sun now exceed those from all weather hazards, conventionally defined, put together.

A few occurrences of a few of those hazards, a handful of famous disasters, account for much more than their share of what has been written about American weather history: 1816, "The Year Without a Summer"; the Galveston, Texas, hurricane of 1900; the northeastern blizzard of 1888 and hurricane of 1938; the Dust Bowl droughts of the 1930s on the Great Plains. To make weather history solely or even mainly the history of great weather disasters would be a narrowing of its scope as drastic and as unjustified as making it only the story of climate change and its effects. But these episodes are a part of the story, and their lessons hold true for weather history in a wider sense.

One of those lessons is that the category of weather disasters is itself—like those of weather hazards and resources—one to use with caution. There are disasters that do not involve the weather, but none are caused by it alone. September 8, 1900, was a day of calamity in Galveston not only because a hurricane struck but because a sizeable city had grown, force-fed by federal spending for harbor improvements but unprotected by any barriers against storm surges, on a low, flat coastal island in a climate prone to powerful storms, because most buildings were low and flimsy, because warnings of the storm were not rapidly or readily communicated, and because transportation was so slow and exposed that evacuation was hardly less risky than staying put. It was as much a land-use or a transportation disaster as it was a weather disaster. Most Galvestonians decided that it had been a disaster of political institutions. Fifteen years later they could judge themselves vindicated. The voters replaced their mayor and council after the 1900 hurricane by a novel system of government, a streamlined municipal commission. It set to work at once on a project that had long been considered but never begun: raising the city and building a protective sea wall. Another major hurricane that struck in 1915, after the work's completion, did vastly less destruction than the earlier storm had. The *Galveston Daily News* gave credit for the difference to the commission system, a "new form of government . . . a powerful instrument in the hands of the people for the management of their affairs."[18]

At the same time, the weather is also a factor in many disasters usually classified under other headings. The Great Chicago Fire of 1871 is not generally listed as a natural or a meteorological catastrophe. Yet it happened because of a severe summer and fall drought that had left the crowded city, built of wood down to its pavements and sidewalks, parched and highly flammable and because of a strong wind that spread the flames, while the means of fire fighting were primitive.[19] Identical weather in Chicago today would threaten no such catastrophe. On the other hand, drought and high winds in the mountains of southern California today are far more of a menace to life and property than they were a hundred years ago. Forest and brush fires mattered relatively little when the land was thinly settled. Today it is occupied by affluent suburbanites who favor wood construction for their houses, the highly combustible native brush for their yards, and narrow, winding streets that are hard for fire engines to negotiate. Population and property have moved straight into harm's way, making drought and wind immensely more destructive agents than in the past.[20]

A good way to see how a disaster involving the weather is never its doing alone is to ask, as in these cases, how the same weather's effects in the same place would have been different at some earlier or later time. Further examples would be easy to multiply. Many can be found in Blake McKelvey's *Snow and the Cities* (1995). It tells in engaging detail how the troubles and the opportunities caused by recurrent blizzards in American urban areas have endlessly metamorphosed over the past several centuries, how "the impact of similar storms . . . changed radically as the cities grew in size and technological complexity."[21] But it is not just exceptional storms or droughts that shed old meanings and take on new ones as human activities change. It is everyday weather as well, and to far greater net effect. Extreme events are involved in only a small part of weather-society interaction. As McKelvey traces the evolving impacts of urban blizzards, Bernard Mergen in *Snow in America* (1997) documents the more general transformation in the problems and possibilities of snow as a routine phenomenon, the ways in which social changes changed it "from resource to refuse to resource again" though its physical properties changed not at all.[22] Every weather event and every feature of the climate, whether as dramatic as a hurricane or as mundane as rain, clouds, fog, or sunshine, has repeatedly shifted over time as a help and a hindrance in American life.

It has done so in two ways. Much of weather history is the story of devices that have been conceived and adopted at least in part with the goal of dealing better with weather challenges and opportunities. Physical tools of this class would fill a gigantic museum—whose own walls, windows, roofing, and heating and cooling systems would be as much exhibits as anything else on display. They range from covered bridges, street paving, and storm sewers to skis, sleds, and sleighs, to snow shovels, snowplows, snow tires, and snowblowers to umbrellas, parasols, sunscreen lotions, and sunglasses. Social coping devices include such institutions as weather forecasting, disaster relief, and insurance reimbursement for losses suffered from adverse weather or income lost from seasonal unemployment due to low demand and layoffs in certain livelihoods at certain times of the year.

Much of weather history is the development and deployment of such coping tools. Few of them, though, belong to weather history alone. A closer look reveals that weather protection has by no means been the only consideration governing their use. Even television weather forecasting is watched partly for entertainment. Roofing is a matter of taste, tradition, style, and display as well as a shelter from the elements overhead. Much seasonal unemployment is determined by the social rather than the meteorological calendar. Clothing provides protection, but fashion dictates many clothing choices that worsen rather than temper the weather's effects. It turns out too that some coping measures—certain kinds of insurance or flood protection works are good examples—end up worsening the weather's effects by rewarding risky behavior or increasing people's sense of security more than they increase security itself.

Thus even in this sphere weather history is not a simple story of progress. Moreover, changes in activities not at all motivated by concern with the weather, yet incidentally altering its role, form a second major class of factors—possibly the more important of the two. They are much less likely than the changes of the first class to improve weather-society relations, though they can happen to do so just as readily as they can happen not to. Many devices have lessened the problems that automobiles have with the weather, but the ways in which the automobile itself is used, the rising demands of mobility, speed, and punctuality, are the dominant reasons why those problems came to exist.

Few major shifts in life have failed to register incidentally on Americans' relations with their weather, and by no means always for the better. The landmark dates in weather history are less the familiar ones specific to it—1816, 1888, 1900, 1938—than the familiar landmark dates of American social, political, and technological history. Even 1870, the founding date of a federal weather bureau, owes much of its importance to developments in other areas: to better communications allowing forecasts and storm warnings to be more rapidly distributed. Every change in American life that has made activities less flexible and schedules more imperative has made forecasts less useful.

To say that the weather only matters because of how societies organize their lives is far from saying that it necessarily matters little. They are the reasons why it can matter tremendously. It is equally far from saying that dealing with the problems that weather does pose in any given situation is a simple matter because solving the problem requires only a change in human wants or activities. Such things are not easily changed, and any different way of life will likely only mean different, not fewer, weather problems. Nor does it mean that those who suffer from the weather, even from foreseeable hazards, are necessarily to blame for their plight, for they may have had little choice in the face of other compelling reasons to act as they did.

Certainly, it makes little sense to condemn any change solely because it makes the weather either more of a nuisance or less of a resource. Such a change may still, overall, be for the better because the improvements that it brings in other areas more than outweigh these losses. Nor, for the same reason, is a change that improves weather-society relations necessarily an improvement overall. To assume that it must be is one form of what is called *climatic determinism,* a particularly dangerous temptation to annalists and analysts of weather and society. Climatic determinism here involves treating weather or climate as something that people should have regarded as supremely important, around whose presumed imperatives they should, if sensible, have shaped their lives.

This form of climatic determinism takes the weather as the key to what should be. Another form takes weather as the key to what actually is. The second form sees the weather and climate as having shaped people's lives whether they were aware of it or not. Such reasoning asserts that trait y follows from climate X as an effect follows its cause. A classic example is the assertion that a certain building style or style of clothing prevailed in a particular location because it was dictated by the weather. Another is the assertion that civilization (or manufacturing or some personality type or outlook or aptitude) appears in one area and not in another because the climate of the former stimulates it and that of the latter depresses it.

What these two distinct forms of climatic determinism share—apart from their tendency to exaggerate the weather's importance—is the assumption that the weather's human significance is determined by its physical characteristics. Both forms are often attacked for the supposed reactionary political implications of such a stance. Each is often accused of being "part of an ideology which rationalizes and naturalizes an existing social order" and a "resistance to social change," for being "a theory which operates to justify an existing social order and the vested interests connected with that order," for necessarily being "strongly politically conservative since, like its close relative and accomplice biological determinism, it presents human behavior as 'naturally given,' plays down the responsibility of the individual and collective for political behavior, and undermines the role of human agency in changing attitudes."[23]

If climatic determinism is true and such are its necessary implications, does it follow, as the argument suggests, that it should be ignored? But they are not its necessary implications, as many examples in the pages to follow will indicate. Climatic determinism can be made to support any leftist, centrist, or conservative stand on any political or social issue.[24] What is objectionable, rather, is that it is not true. One of the critics of the supposed reactionary tendencies of climatic determinism was on much stronger ground in lodging a second objection against it. "The same area and climate maintains itself through kaleidoscopic changes in economic and social life,"[25] he observed, evidence enough that there is something wrong with a thesis that would explain economic and social life as largely the climate's products. The explanation of architectural form as imposed by the environment, in the words of the folklorist Henry Glassie, "always seems to work in given situations, and it always falls apart when the architecture of different areas sharing similar environments is compared"—or when the same area is examined at two different periods. "When southern football was at the bottom of the heap, practice in the debilitating heat of the southern autumn was taken to explain the players' comparative lack of stamina," the sociologist Rupert Vance wrote in the 1930s. "Now that southerners hold their own or better in intersectional competition, such writers for the sporting press as George Trevor and Grantland Rice see reflections of the man building power of the climate."[26]

The other form of climatic determinism—which urges that activities in an area be made to conform to the natural environment, to what nature "intended" and be changed back, as is often said, from what "nature never intended"—is no sounder. For nature has no plans or intentions, and the environment never dictates anything, even for success or failure in certain activities, for the activities and what constitutes success and failure in them are themselves matters of human definition. There are innumerable different ways to inhabit the same climate. If there seem to be few, it is less the work of the climate than of commitments to particular ways of life that make some choices unthinkable and others seem to be necessities.

A defender of the thesis that weather is at least sometimes the sole and sufficient determinant of its social consequences offers an example meant to clinch the point. "When a man crouching in a ditch in the middle of an open field gets hit by a lightning bolt, the environmental influence is strictly a one-way street, with no reasonable alternatives and no conscious response."[27] But the example only shows that one factor can be mistaken for a sufficient cause, as the 1900 hurricane can be mistaken for that of the Galveston disaster, if the other necessary causes are taken for granted. The lightning in this case had the effects that it had only because a man was crouching unprotected in the ditch in its path. But the reasons why he was there at that moment, whatever they were, will never turn out to have been determined or imposed by the weather. The physical fact of a thunderstorm occurring never necessarily implies the presence of a victim exposed to its strike. Social changes affecting the exposure of Americans to lightning are apparent in the sharp (five- to ten-fold) decline in yearly fatal strikes per capita over the course of the past century. Exposed outdoor occupations, such as farming, ranching, and construction, are much less common than they were, and even they, by and large, enjoy better protection than before. At the same time, the decline in casualties would have been greater still but for the rise in outdoor recreation in the same period. Fewer deaths have occurred in fields and building sites, but a rising number on beaches, at sports events, and on pleasure boats in open water.[28]

Lightning's impacts have changed in many ways. A consistent climatic determinist, taking the weather itself to be the chief cause of the weather's effects, could only conclude that thunderstorms have changed radically in frequency, intensity, and place of occurrence. But they have not. Instead, their effects have differed from period to period because in each, they have encountered a different way of life—and so too has every other kind of weather.

Climates, Cultures, and Founding Myths

Colonies and Climates

The size, scope, and variety of changes in weather-society relations that history records are a great embarrassment to climatic determinism, for they have occurred without the weather itself becoming drastically different. But if determinism cannot account well for change, it surely holds more promise in explaining continuity. And indeed a pattern that goes back to the earliest years of Anglo-American settlement has long been a favorite illustration for climatic determinists of how environments shape societies. The Atlantic seaboard communities in the North and South of what is now the United States have for centuries differed markedly in their political culture and social structure. The environment has often been held responsible according to a general law supposedly governing such matters. Here as elsewhere, the enduring influence of heat made the South "traditional and conservative"; that of cold made the North "innovative and progressive."[1]

But it is conceding nothing to determinism to note that those contrasts do indeed have something to do with climate. They are merely related to it by another and far more tortuous pathway, time- and place-specific rather than universal, than the one suggested. The contrasts were not imposed by different climates molding originally similar groups of settlers and their descendants. Rather, the mixes of resources and hazards that different climates seemed to offer in one particular period attracted different kind of colonists and colonization, giving rise to different institutions and societies whose effects are still apparent. The contrasts between North and South do not bear out any timeless truth about climate-society relations, nor do they reflect anything that higher and lower latitudes always mean for their inhabitants. They reflect, rather, what those latitudes happened to mean in a certain time and place and social order, what they meant to the elites of Tudor and Stuart England.

Late-sixteenth-century England was not in an enviable position economically. It could feed and clothe itself, but its surplus productions for export were few and unimpressive. The most important of them was woollen cloth, which was not an article much in demand in the warmer Mediterranean countries that supplied England with many of its necessities and luxuries: wine, sugar, olive and other oils, citrus fruits, silks, and spices.[2] This state of affairs was made more distressing by the popularity of a set of doctrines known as mercantilism.[3] It held that the goal of trade was to increase the power of the state by increasing its wealth, measured by its stock of precious metals. A country could accumulate gold and silver directly by mining them or through trade by selling goods to other countries for hard currency. A large surplus of exports over imports was the mercantilist ideal. Countries that sold more than they bought amassed wealth and power at the expense of their trading partners. Unfortunate England had little to sell and much to buy.

Establishing overseas colonies in the lands recently explored by European navigators offered England new chances for bettering its position. But colonies, according to mercantilist doctrine, had to be chosen with care. They were most useful if they produced gold and silver for the mother country's treasury, if they created new markets for its products, or if they produced raw materials that it could ship, process, and sell overseas—especially ones that it had previously purchased from abroad. They were least desirable and a waste of resources if they only duplicated its own productions.

It was through these lenses that the English studied the possibilities offered by the nearest new lands open to them, those lying on the other side of the Atlantic. Themselves located closer to the pole than to the equator, and supposing agricultural productions to be governed by climate and climate in turn by latitude, the English looked for the greatest returns in the New World to lands far to their south. It was colonies in the parallels of the Mediterranean whose cultivation would best complement their own productions and make them more self-sufficient. As Richard Hakluyt, the most influential colonial promoter of the late Tudor period, put it, "[T]o conquer a countrey or province in climate & soile of Italie, Spaine, or the Islands from whence we receive our Wines & Oiles, and to man it, to plant it, and to keepe it . . . were a matter of great importance both in respect of the saving at home of our great treasure now yeerly going away, and in respect of the annoyance thereby growing to our enemies." He listed sugar, rice, salt, silk, oranges, lemons, figs, almonds, and pomegranates as other Mediterranean-latitude commodities that settlers in such a new land might "make it to yeeld, that England doth want or doth desire."[4]

Prized by the English in this relative sense, the lower latitudes were also judged ideal in an absolute sense. Hakluyt spoke of "the mines there of Golde . . . of Silver, Copper, Yron &c." as further attractions of southern colonies.[5] According to the geological thought of the time, precious metals grew and matured underground, at rates governed by the heat of the sun above. The sunnier and hotter the country, the more valuable its ores. Thus gold and silver were best sought—whether by mining them or by plundering the ships and towns of those who did—in the lands closest to the equator. Presumed rich in resources, the low latitudes were also seen as abounding in hazards. Ideal for English settlement from the mercantilist viewpoint, they had disadvantages of other sorts. Hot climates were presumed to be necessarily unhealthful and to be foreign to the character, ways, and constitutions of northern peoples.[6]

The English came late to New World colonization. They found much of the Americas preempted by the claims of other powers. They had a relatively open field—though challenged here and there by France, Holland, and Sweden—only in parts of the Caribbean and on the Atlantic seaboard north of Spanish Florida. As the English crown appropriated and divided up this territory, it was not by accident that one broad pattern emerged. Well-born sons of the gentry class settled, in Carville Earle's words, "in the optimal 'Mediterranean' colonies in the south"; these prize lands, which promised to grow the items most valued by the English because most unlike England's own, and which offered the best prospects for gold and silver, were developed chiefly by well-connected entrepreneurs affiliated with the Anglican church and the elite country families.[7] The drawbacks of a hot climate carried little weight with ambitious men eager to enrich themselves. They worried little about the dangers of laboring in the heat, for they had no intention of laboring themselves. On Virginia and later in seventeenth-century Carolina as on the West Indies, they imposed institutions and a social order that would shape the South's character for much longer to come. They molded a region "profoundly conservative in every sense—elitist, hierarchical, and strenuously hostile to social change," its citizens highly sensitive to infringement of their own liberty but little sensitive to the liberty of others.[8]

The north was settled mainly by seventeenth-century emigrants from the margins of English society who brought different ideals and institutions to America. Religious dissenters—Pilgrims, Puritans, and Quakers—colonized the lands that were poorer from the crown's point of view and whose inability to support olive trees and wine and sugar production quickly became clear. The northernmost major settlements during the early decades of colonization became known as "New England." The name, as Earle writes, "stood for an old England writ new, for a redundant region with dour prospects for improving the balance of English economic accounts . . . a land perceived as of marginal environmental worth" because it was too much like England itself.[9] Many of those who settled there would not have been averse, other things being equal, to a richer land, but they were better able to tolerate the north's disadvantages and even see them as attractions than the colonists of Virginia would have been. "For those bent on great fortunes, the northeastern coast of the New World had limited appeal. . . . Those emigrants who sought in the New World a *home* . . . chose this country precisely for its familiarity."[10] Eager to live as they had lived in England without the burdens of religious oppression, they thought less of finding a climate that would permit them to grow lucrative cash crops than of finding one similar to their own. Its mediocrity as a resource offered them the hope too of being left alone by the well-born and powerful. "If your place be not the best, it is better," the Plymouth Pilgrims were told by their London agents, paradoxically but correctly; "you shall be less envied and encroached upon; and such as are earthly minded will not settle too near your border."[11] There were many differences between and within the settlements of New England and the Middle Atlantic, but their political cultures were markedly more open to change, their political and social life less stratified and deferential, their ideal of liberty less restricted, than the lowland South's.[12]

The colonizers made their plans according to the climates that they expected. The ones that they actually encountered were full of surprises.[13] If the earliest European explorers of the New World had found America where they had hoped to find Asia, the early settlers found America where they had expected to find Europe duplicated. Latitude alone, they gradually discovered, did not govern climate. Eastern North America was colder on a yearly average than Western Europe in the same parallels, and with greater seasonal extremes of both heat and cold, with a drier air and more frequent and rapid fluctuations of dampness and drought. It was, in the words of the geographer Carl Sauer, "a lustier land to which the settlers had come, a land of hotter summers and colder winters, of brighter and hotter sun and more tempestuous rain."[14]

The differences, though seventeenth-century observers did not know it, were those to be expected between the west and east coasts of continents in the mid-latitudes. Great Britain, on the western side of the Atlantic, was made milder and wetter than the same latitudes in

North America by the tempering ocean influence carried by the prevailing westerly winds. The difference in climate, and especially the severe winters of the New World, meant that colonists could not raise many of the crops that they had wanted to and that they tried to. But even in coping with the weather itself it was only one of their handicaps, and one that mattered less than the differences to be expected between core metropolis and peripheral colony. The newly arrived settlers had come from a land rich in labor and capital to a land exceedingly poor in both, though rich in land and its resources beyond anything that they had known before.

As Captain John Smith wrote, the settlers at Jamestown, established by the Virginia Company in 1607, had no protection from the elements when they arrived save "Castles in the ayre"; "we had no houses to cover us, our Tents were rotten," and a fire during the first winter "destroyed the most of our apparel, lodging, and private provision."[15] They needed labor to build shelter, clear land, and tend crops, but they were even poorer in labor than their scanty numbers indicated, for many of them were gentlemen and servants who had come with no intention of doing such chores. Even those who had come to labor were accustomed to a high degree of idleness, having come from a densely settled land where work was rationed to make it go around.[16] Unrealistic expectations of quick wealth in a rich southern land made matters worse: "There was no talke, nor hope, nor worke, but dig gold, wash gold, refine gold, load gold," but none was found.[17] Exposure, hunger, and a pestilential location between salt water and fresh meant a tremendous death rate in the early years: severest in the first year, which reduced the initial population by two-thirds; severe again in the "Starving Time," the winter of 1609–10, when numbers dwindled from 180 to 100; and chronically severe in the hot months.[18]

The leader of the Pilgrims who in 1620 established the first English settlement in New England understood the nature of the weather problems that he and his companions faced. The first winter at Plymouth was so deadly for the colonists—only half survived it—as much because they had "no friends to welcome them nor inns to entertain or refresh their weatherbeaten bodies; no houses or much less towns to repair to, to seek for succour," he wrote, as because the weather itself was "sharp and violent, and subject to cruel and fierce storms."[19] Scanty harvests in the first years had to be supplemented by hunting, fishing, and foraging, by trade with the aborigines and with the few ships that passed, and by help from their English sponsors that usually fell far short of what they wanted. "The failure of a ship affected them as much, perhaps more, than the failure of a harvest would affect their descendants at the present time," wrote an early-nineteenth-century New Englander of the region's pioneers.[20] The same could have been said of most of the early seaboard colonies. All underwent the same trials as Jamestown and Plymouth in the first years, if not in such rigorous form, and all saw these hardships diminish as population and experience grew and regional trade developed. Everywhere the climate was unfamiliar and severe, but everywhere the growth of the ability to cope made it gradually less so.

Deluded by latitudinal analogies, colonists did have to waste much time and effort in trial and error discovering that the same latitudes did not everywhere possess the same climates. The Virginia settlers no more succeeded in raising the Mediterranean cash crops that they had planned to produce than they succeeded in finding gold and silver. The Carolina colony was the second Anglo-southern settlement within the present-day United States. Founded under a royal charter granted in 1683, it was meant, like Virginia, to duplicate the chief productions of the Mediterranean, but its orange trees and sugar cane and other experiments succumbed to frost.[21] But it was not climate alone that made the Mediterranean the center of production of all of its staples, and it was less climate than the persistent high cost of labor that caused some of them to fail in the New World. Silk production was pressed on many of the colonies by their mercantilist London sponsors and English governors well into the eighteenth century. Where sufficient bounties were offered, it was pursued with success. Once they were withdrawn, growing collapsed. What doomed it was not the cold, but the great shortage of hands in the colonies compared to the poor and densely peopled Mediterranean and Asian centers of silk production. The extreme laboriousness of the process made it the worst possible crop for eighteenth-century North America.[22]

In the end, the surprising differences in the American climate from what had been expected had little impact on the ways in which the colonies developed. The economy of the northern settlements rested on a mixed grain and livestock agriculture supplemented by fishing and seafaring and small manufactures. It differed more in detail—a larger role for maize and wheat, for example—than in character from that of England. The seaboard South indeed specialized, precisely as foreseen, in high-value cash crops for export, if not the same ones it was expected to grow at the outset. The Virginia colonists stumbled into precisely the great wealth that they had come seeking within a decade of the founding of Jamestown. Fortune presented them with a new staple, tobacco, for which Europe showed an insatiable appetite. Rice, by the end of the century, would become just such a lucrative export crop for Carolina as

tobacco was for the Chesapeake and sugar had become for the West Indies. Indigo and cotton would follow during the eighteenth century.
But because all were labor-intensive crops, if not so labor-intensive as
silk production, the South could only grow them if the problem of
labor shortage could be solved—itself a problem that many mistook, or
preferred to mistake, for a problem with the southern climate.

The South

In 1785, Thomas Jefferson assured a French acquaintance that "an ob-
serving traveller, without the aid of the quadrant may always know his
latitude by the character of the people among whom he finds himself."
He offered the American states as a case in point. Different climates
had made the peoples of the North and South strikingly different in
temperament. Northerners were "cool, sober, laborious," and so on,
southerners "fiery, voluptuary, indolent."[23]

Jefferson was not pioneering the idea. He was simply retailing an
error common to many Americans of the time: that the direct action of
the heat or the ease of subsistence in a warm country made lowland
southerners averse to work. When a federal constitution for the thirteen states was proposed in 1787 to replace the looser union of the Articles of Confederation, one of the arguments widely made against it was
that no single form of government or set of laws could suit the natives
of climates as different as South Carolina's and Georgia's at one extreme and New England's at the other, "the idle and dissolute inhabitants of the South" and "the sober and active people of the north."[24]

Those were the words of a northerner. To him and his section, the
idea had an obvious appeal. Northerners had good reason to hope and
claim that theirs was a more invigorating land, productive of health
and energy, long and bitterly cold though its winters might be. Where
"vertic suns intensely shine," wrote the revolutionary-era Connecticut
poet David Humphreys, "unbidden harvests deck the soil"; the sun's
rays "o'er the surface glow, / And embryon metals form and feed
below," but this wealth came at too high a price: "To drain their limbs
of strength the climate serves . . . By luxury loll'd in soft voluptuous
ease."[25] Yet the lowland southern gentry subscribed no less readily to
the idea. It bore out an image of themselves that they prized. The belief
that climate made the people of New England and the middle states
sober and energetic, southerners indolent and languid (and somehow,
at the same time, fiery and passionate) rested on a confusion between
the effects of climates and those of the English subcultures that had

been transplanted into them. A disdain for work, a show of idleness, and a touchy sense of honor were not imposed on lowland Southerners by the heat. They were part of a code of behavior brought from overseas and reinforced by the inequalities of wealth and power that it helped to create. Being indeed typical of the most prominent southerners, they were taken to characterize the region as a whole.[26]

But had all southerners been idle, patterns of livelihood would have been very different from what they were. If cold made northerners energetic and heat made southerners indolent, if a warm climate made living easy, then the contrast in latitudes, if it mattered at all, should have dictated one great difference between the crops that each section grew. Farming in the North should have been more labor-intensive than in the South. In fact, it was the South that specialized heavily in labor-demanding plantation staples and the North in grains that required less effort and attention. Within the South, too, labor should have been more intense in the cooler uplands than on the hotter seacoast. Again the opposite was true. The hunting, corn, and livestock economy that prevailed in the eighteenth-century southern backcountry was far less toilsome than the cash-crop regime of the steamy tidewater. There were good reasons why, but the fact that they prevailed showed how far the climate was from determining such matters.

Labor scarcity was the greatest obstacle confronting seventeenth-century Virginians in their efforts to profit from the growing and export of tobacco.[27] The cultivation of the leaf was an onerous business involving many painstaking operations. It proceeded from spring planting in soil that had to be carefully prepared, through the transplantation, tending, and weeding of the young shoots, to the fall tasks of cutting, curing, sweating, binding, and packing.[28] Rice late in the century captured the attention of lowland Carolinians looking for a profitable crop of their own. But its cultivation—first in upland fields, eventually in tidal wetlands irrigated with freshwater—was much more laborious than tobacco growing and in a climate of even hotter summers. On top of sowing, weeding, and harvesting, it demanded endless work to shore up the banks of the fields, clear the channels of silt, and repair damage done by floods and storms.[29]

Planters wished to grow these lucrative staples. Labor was reluctant in a land-rich, labor-scarce setting where easier and more rewarding work was easily found. If the South's opportunities were to be realized and the crops that would realize them be grown without exorbitant wages, then labor under legal compulsion was necessary. Tobacco plantations during the seventeenth century were increasingly worked by such labor, that of indentured servants and slaves of aboriginal and

African descent.[30] But it was the climate, not the level of wages, that their masters increasingly cited as the reason why labor must be forced labor: no one would work voluntarily in the heat or in a latitude so rich that subsistence took little effort. That it happened to be black slaves on whom the burden came chiefly to rest lent itself readily to an extension of the idea: that they were suited by their ancestry to labor in heat and humidity that whites of European descent could not stand. "The eighteenth century superstition that white men could not work in the fields in the South was never more than a superstition except as it served as a rationalized defense for slavery," but in that role it was one of the key ideas by which the planter class explained the region to itself and to others.[31] It justified a system of labor whose real origins lay elsewhere.

Agricultural history gives no support to the thesis that climate stamped the South as a land of laziness. No more does it support the myth that that climate was essentially a richer resource than the North's. Tastes and wants; world conditions of technology, politics, and demand and supply for particular items; and local conditions of labor supply were what gave the South's climate its value as a resource—a value that changed as those conditions did.

Such changes carried one staple crop from boom to bust in less than a hundred years though the climate became no more or less suited to growing it than before. The blue dye extracted from the indigo plant was a crucial input in early-eighteenth-century European textile manufacture. It was supplied at first mainly from the South American colonies of Spain and Portugal. Around mid-century, South Carolina planters, encouraged by mercantilist laws and bounties enacted in London, began growing and processing indigo on a large scale for English clothmakers. The new crop had several advantages from the planters's point of view. It commanded a high price, and the labor demands of processing, though heavy, fitted neatly into the periods of lighter work in the rice fields. The indigo boom spread to Georgia (also a center of rice cultivation), Louisiana, and the Spanish (briefly, English) settlements of East and West Florida. In all of these places, the boom was over, and indigo a minor and dwindling export, by late in the eighteenth century. Cheaper and better dye beginning to be produced under British rule in India captured the world market.[32]

Another warm-climate—and labor-demanding—crop became a highly profitable resource just as indigo was ceasing to be one.[33] Long-staple cotton had long been grown on the Carolina coast, largely by planters for their own domestic needs. Short-staple cotton, the only kind well suited to inland conditions, was little cultivated because of the difficulty of separating fibers from seeds. The invention of the cotton gin in 1793 greatly eased and quickened the process just as mechanization in the British textile industry was creating a far more intense demand for cotton fiber than had existed before. It was another crop that made heavy labor demands, and its rapid spread across the South created a booming new demand for slaves.

No less for cotton than for earlier crops, the climate was also a resource only so far as politics allowed. Much of its value depended on easy international trade in staple products. Selling chiefly in foreign markets, producers suffered from many interruptions of war or trade restrictions during the Revolution, the Napoleonic wars in Europe, and the War of 1812, which abruptly and drastically depressed the value of their crops. But restrictions on trade could become resources in their own right. Sugarcane, another labor-demanding and largely slave-grown crop, owed much of its early success in the lower Mississippi Valley to war-related declines in output elsewhere and a tariff-protected American market following the Louisiana Purchase in 1803.[34]

Crop choices defined certain kinds of weather as especially good or bad. Besides the vagaries of markets and politics, each lowland staple was sensitive to its own set of weather hazards: indigo and sugar especially to freezes, rice and sugar to floods and coastal storms, the tobacco crop to a succession of risks in the course of the year that made many Virginia planters as close and worried watchers of the weather as the scientifically minded Jefferson himself. The processing of many crops was also dependent on the weather. But levees gradually gave better protection from floods; water-powered mills became less sensitive to the weather when Mill acts, pioneered in the South, made it easier to flood the land of upstream neighbors for storage ponds; new tidal and steam-powered mills for processing rice and sugar were largely unaffected by dry seasons; and by the end of the eighteenth century, the air curing of tobacco in sheds and barns was being made faster and more regular by the heat and smoke of fires kindled underneath, especially in damp weather.[35]

That a warm climate made the tidewater South an inherently unhealthy land was a further myth, and one equally useful for the purposes of rationalization. Slaves of African descent were assumed to bear the heat and humidity better than whites whose ancestors had lived in colder climates. The ill-health of the region was real enough, but contrary to the myth, it was not severe only for whites. Though some slaves may indeed have possessed a greater degree of resistance to some of the region's diseases, it did not prevent them from dying at an appalling rate. But the high rates of death and sickness were the result of the activities that went on in the climate, not of the climate itself: a chapter in the region's history, not a fact of its geography.[36]

Outbreaks of yellow fever, worst in cities, were the most acute of the evils associated with the climate. The most chronic was the debilitating disorder, chiefly rural, known variously as the ague, fever and chills, and malaria, that appeared every year in late summer and early autumn. American and foreign observers supposed it to be the product of miasma, bad air poisoned by decay in the summer's heat. It was the product, in fact, as yellow fever was, of insect-borne pathogens that had been introduced by Europeans and had been foreign to the region before their arrival. Not unknown in the North, it was worst in the farthest south of the early colonies, Carolina, not simply because of its warmer climate but because the organization of agriculture and settlement around flooded, mosquito-breeding rice fields unwittingly promoted its spread.[37] It was quite deadly too on the Gulf Coast and in the West Indies.

In time, the rice planters, if they did not accurately gauge the cause of malaria, learned how to avoid its worst effects. They began using quinine as a remedy, locating their houses on protected sites distant from the sources of disease, avoiding the night air, and moving elsewhere during the fever season: to Charleston on the sandy and breezy coast, or as far north as Newport, Rhode Island, where they joined sugar planters fleeing the West Indies for the same reasons.[38] Near the Chesapeake, malaria was less severe than in South Carolina, but it was still a serious threat and greatly feared.[39] Many wealthy Virginians summered for reasons of health as well as comfort among the mountain springs in the west of the state. In the 1789–90 debate over the new national capital's location, northerners objected to a site so notoriously sickly as the banks of the Potomac.[40] When Jefferson became president in 1801, he observed that for forty years he had spent August and September away from the fever-ridden tidewater—where the new national capital had in fact been located—and had no intention of changing his habits; nor did he spend those months in Washington during eight years as president.[41] By getting the capital placed where they did, southerners, as if on purpose, discouraged the growth and the efficient operation of the central government that many of them distrusted.

The site chosen did have its advantages, notably a location on a navigable river. Roads were bad in all seasons, worst in the mire of spring and fall, and badly kept up throughout the South. Their maintenance was hardly encouraged by the localism and privatism especially marked in the region's culture. Those of Virginia were generally said to be better than elsewhere, but Jefferson's correspondence is filled with complaints about their condition in wet weather—"Heavy rains now falling will render the roads next to impassable"—and heartfelt relief at a "pleasant journey of fine weather and good roads."[42] The difficulties of land travel made water connections particularly important, but they had weather problems of their own. Rivers might fall too low for navigation in drought or be difficult to navigate as well as to ford when in flood. The Chesapeake region benefited from a wealth of rivers connecting to the ocean, and the bay was itself a busy highway, but those crossing took the risk of gusts and squalls and of delays when the wind failed.[43] A coastal or riverine location exposed towns to floods and storms. Low-lying Charleston and its environs were devastated by recurrent severe hurricanes.[44] New Orleans suffered even more. Politics in the early eighteenth century seemed to dictate the establishment of a French settlement on the low flatlands commanding the mouth of the Mississippi River, where climate and terrain seemed to veto it. Politics won, and floods from above, hurricanes from the Gulf, and fevers in the hot months became more destructive than before, having more around them to destroy.

The Louisiana colony did make some concessions to its environment. Levees begun almost as soon as New Orleans was founded offered some protection from high water. Though the heat was thought deadly and the death rate was indeed high, the settlers devised building forms with features that were at least well-suited to moderating a humid summer's extremes indoors. But tradition was not abandoned and entirely new houses designed for a new climate. Rather, some aspects of traditional design were retained and emphasized, and others were discarded. Here as elsewhere, the physical environment "served much less to cause the invention of a new element than to indicate which of a number of traditional possibilities should be chosen and, then, to reinforce the tradition of the chosen element."[45]

Not always did it even have that much of a role. The early domestic architecture of the Anglo-American South was not simply a generic English type but that of the English regions from which the settlers had come. The most distinctive features of the Virginia gentry house were those typical of architecture in that part of the British Isles—the West Country—from which the colony was initially settled.[46] A number of those features proved happily well-adapted to a warm and humid climate. The West Country chimney, placed at the house end and external to the frame, dispersed the kitchen fire's heat in the severe southern summer. Large rooms and high ceilings and "a passage generally through the middle of the house for an air-draught"—also of Old World origin—promoted coolness and ventilation.[47]

Some climatically useful elements, then, were retained, but climate was not always the reason. The central-passage design also served the strictly social purpose of distancing the family rooms from outsiders. Its evolution after the mid-1700s made the house less suited to thermal comfort in the summer heat and humidity, when a greater emphasis on privacy prompted many further changes that tended to lessen ventilation.[48] The high-ceilinged, central-hall, end-chimney gentry dwellings well-suited to coolness in the summer were also very chilly in the colder months. The mud-stopped log dwellings of the poorer folk in Virginia, Jefferson noted, were "warmer in winter . . . than the more expensive constructions of scantling and plank." They were also "cooler in summer," he wrote, and the double log cabin form that developed in the eighteenth-century uplands preserved the principle of the open sheltered central passageway—often called a "dog-run"—that lowland gentry houses were discarding.[49] Americans settling in New Orleans after the Louisiana Purchase of 1803, a visitor noted, "so inveterate is habit," refused to follow local designs well suited to the climate. They preferred instead to build the kinds of houses with which they were familiar: "red, staring brickwork, imbibing heat through the whole unshaded surface of the wall."[50]

In clothing and behavior as in architecture, there were many things done in other hot climates that climatic determinists would doubtless say had been imposed by the heat if the southern gentry had only adopted them. Many useful things were done, but the list of those that generally were not ranged from rising early in the cool of the morning and taking a siesta in the heat of the day to building—as the native peoples had done—separate dwellings for winter and summer to abstinence or moderation in the use of liquor in a climate whose extremes made excess especially dangerous. Regional culture made all three unthinkable. "Drunkenness may be called an endemic vice of Carolina," wrote the Charleston historian David Ramsay in the early nineteenth century—this observation would have applied equally well to the rest of the South—and he pointed out that clothing conformed no more rigorously to local conditions. When styles of dress, governed by English and French modes rather than by local needs, did happen to suit the hot southern summer, it was largely by chance, and "it rests with the fashion-makers in Europe to determine how long they shall be used in Carolina."[51]

Those who expected the differences in climate between America and Europe or between one region and another to impose differences in human life were as often as not disappointed. It was a Charleston physician, Dr. Lionel Chalmers, who in 1776 offered the fullest early

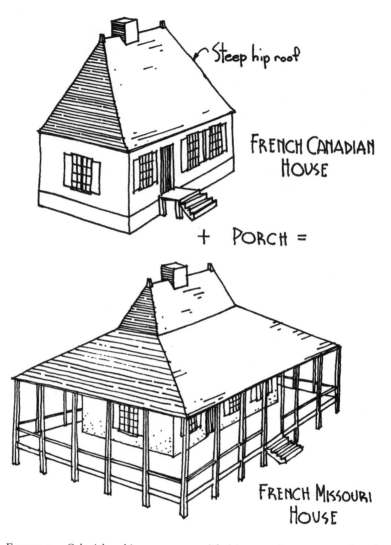

Steep hip roof

FRENCH CANADIAN HOUSE

+ PORCH =

FRENCH MISSOURI HOUSE

FIGURE 1.1. Colonial architecture was modified in new climates, not reshaped wholesale to fit them. French settlers's houses in the lower Mississippi Valley shared many features with those in French Canada.

explanation of the phenomenon now known as the urban heat island: the tendency for temperatures to be higher in cities than in the surrounding countryside.[52] The presumed direct connection between heat and ill-health made it especially troubling, given the already high summer temperatures. Jefferson as president urged his territorial governors in laying out or extending towns to reserve alternating squares of a grid pattern for trees and open space. Europeans, living under cloudy skies, could "build their town in a solid block with impunity," he judged, "but here a constant sun produces too great an accumulation of heat to permit that." The extremes of the American summer demanded a greater spread of "turf and trees." But the inconveniences of dispersing settlement and the seeming waste of building lots told too heavily against the plan. It was not employed in the extension of New Orleans; in the one southern case where it was tried, the new capital city of Jackson, Mississippi, it was quickly eroded, and the reserved lots turned to more productive uses.[53]

The North

Jefferson's vision of the leafy city fared no better in the North than in the South. Governor William Henry Harrison of the Indiana Territory laid out a new settlement that he named "Jeffersonville" on the proposed plan, but it was not long before the squares designated for green space were invaded by buildings.[54] Philadelphia in 1700 passed a law requiring inhabitants to plant trees so that the city "may be well shaded from the violence of the sun in the heat of the summer and thereby be rendered more healthy," but by late in the century, laws were being proposed to require their wholesale removal in cities including Philadelphia itself.[55] They took up precious space and obstructed movement, particularly of fire-fighting equipment. Their roots damaged streets and sidewalks, and many thought the dampness of their shade more harmful than the coolness was beneficial.

That it was beneficial, few doubted. Northern observers too understood that cities in summer were warmer than their environs and drew the conclusion that they must therefore be less healthy unless cooled by greenery or other means. Even in the temperate latitudes, wrote the Philadelphia physician Charles Caldwell, urbanization produced "an artificial torrid zone" with "all the fervours of a tropical climate," and it was not surprising that the unhealthiness of the tropics was the result.[56] Yet other concerns were more immediate than planting or maintaining trees. Benjamin Franklin could observe from Paris that the benefits of a cooling shade in summer would "amply compensate the loss of a house now and then by fire, if such should be the consequence," but not everyone took such a detached view.[57]

The need to satisfy other, conflicting wants never permitted Americans to obey all of the demands of the climate, whatever they might be thought to be. From some simple and ingenious experiments on the relations of colors to heat, Franklin showed "that black Cloaths are not so fit to wear in a hot Sunny Climate or Season as white ones," but the knowledge that it was so was not enough to make black and white uniform wear for winter and summer respectively. Colors had other meanings besides their thermal qualities, and clothes were not designed with the sole or the chief aim of snug protection from the elements, even—perhaps especially—among those best able to afford it. The extreme temperatures of the United States, wrote Connecticut's Timothy Dwight, "require modes of dressing very different from those, which are healthful in France and England." Yet in fact "we derive our modes of dress . . . from the inhabitants of milder and more equable climates." He had to admit that fashionable women of his own section, for example, wearing "few and thin garments in the severe season . . . dressed *à la Grecque* in the New England winter." Nor, as Philadelphia's Charles Brockden Brown noted, did Americans adapt themselves better to summer, going "amidst all these heats, clothed in cloth, flannel, and black fur hats," and his conclusion was much the same as Dwight's: "The truth is, that our manners do not accommodate themselves to the climate, either in winter or summer, but we follow, in most respects, the fashion of our ancestors, who came from the temperate atmosphere of Europe."[58]

In the North, Anglo-Americans also retained Old World models in the design of their houses. They made some changes that may have been responses to the climate: the replacement of thatched by shingled roofs, less likely to be ignited by sparks in the drier American air; more weatherboarding for insulation; larger fireplaces in which to burn more (and more plentiful) wood against the colder winters.[59] Prevailing design in the South placed the chimney outside the house frame; in New England, it was located at the house's center and its heat conserved. Yet this difference was not of New World origin. The contrasting patterns were typical of the English regions, the West Country and East Anglia, from which each part of North America had been chiefly settled.[60] They happened, in a sense, to suit the new climates overseas and were retained, but other traditions that were not suitable in the same sense were retained too.

In particular, Anglo-Americans balked at giving up the open fireplace as the chief means of space heating in winter. Providing chiefly radiant heat, it did little to warm a room beyond its immediate vicinity and was highly inefficient in its use of fuel. Most of the warmth that it produced went promptly up the chimney. Cold air from outside, colder by far than the air of an English winter, "whistled past every door and window towards the big fire-place to supply the tremendous draught."

Fires could not be kept up at night, and the typical New Englander well into the nineteenth century rose in the morning "in a room in which the cold air came through the cracks in the window. If the temperature were twenty degrees below zero outside, it was very little higher inside."[61] The chill was mitigated only modestly by bed hangings and warming pans and by the practice of sharing beds.[62]

Anglo-Americans were not unaware that closed heating stoves would have kept their houses far warmer with less fuel. Stoves were not unknown in the North, merely rare because they were generally disliked. German settlers even in the South found winters too cold without them, and the Germans in Pennsylvania used them too. They were not adapting more creatively than the Anglo-Americans to the challenge of colder winters. They had heated with stoves in Europe, and like the Anglo-Americans, they brought their customs with them across the Atlantic. Colonists who were accustomed instead to the English open fire disliked and feared the hot, stuffy, stale atmosphere that a closed stove produced and disliked losing the cheerful blaze of the fire more than they liked keeping warm. Franklin proposed a new fireplace design that would heat rooms better and more efficiently (itself improved upon by the Tory émigré Benjamin Thompson, Count Rumford), but he rejected the closed stove as too unpleasant to consider. Though it "warms a room very speedily and thoroughly with little Fuel," it offered "no Sight of the Fire" and produced an atmosphere "which is very disagreeable to those who are not accustomed to it."[63] Adopting only such palliatives as Franklin and Rumford offered, Anglo-American northerners clung to open fireplaces throughout the eighteenth century and into the nineteenth even as the depletion of fuelwood in the supply zones around the cities made them steadily more expensive.[64]

The high and rising cost of fuel was only one of the factors that made winter the most difficult season for the poor. Food was more expensive than at other times, and paid work was much harder to come by. For most of the year, North America remained labor-short compared to Europe. Many slaves and indentured servants were imported into the northern colonies to ease the problem, though they never formed nearly so large a share of the work force as in the South. In the northern winter, however, the shortage became a surplus. Agriculture, by far the commonest occupation, governed the economic calendar. Extra hands were needed chiefly for short spells of intense activity during the warmer months, for planting and haying and harvesting, in the North's mixed grain and livestock economy. Idled along with farm laborers in winter were workers in other trades subject to similar

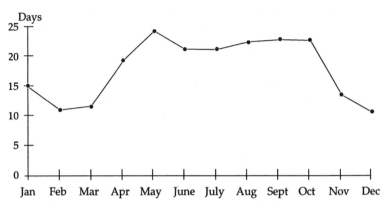

FIGURE 1.2. Work was scarce in the eighteenth-century Northern winter, as apparent in the average days worked per month by a laborer in the Hudson Valley of New York in the years 1789–91.

rhythms. Construction was hampered by the cold and dark; shipping was halted when rivers and harbors froze; and warfare, save for surprise maneuvers and irregular actions on the frontier, was heavily concentrated in the late spring, the summer, and the fall from the French and Indian wars through the Revolution and the War of 1812. Charity and relief were most in demand in winter and poorhouses fullest.[65] Municipal price controls helped curb winter hikes in the price of food and fuel and also to buffer the occasional impacts of short harvests.[66]

The seasonal slowness of business could be turned to profit. More than one nascent industry developed on the basis of cheap and plentiful winter labor. The coastal town of Lynn, Massachusetts, took its early steps toward becoming a shoemaking center on the off-season work of farm laborers and fishermen. The inhabitants of another town found useful work making nails in "a part of the year in which otherwise many of them would find little employment." Winter manufactures in the Connecticut Valley included "brooms, tools, and other woodware, or boots and shoes for home use or exchange." Wooden clocks were made largely with off-season labor.[67] Many of these trades drew on women's work, but it tended already to be seasonally steadier than men's, consisting to a greater degree of repetitive chores little altered by the outdoor changes of heat and cold.[68] Adjustments in the farm year also spread the burden of male work more evenly. Many tasks, such as the threshing of grain once it was harvested, were set aside for the slower season. Milk began to be available during more of the year and herds better-kept at the price of added effort once farmers dropped English custom and began to house and feed their cows in winter. The eventual result was a farm economy distinctly less seasonal than England's despite the earlier frosts and greater severity of the American winter.[69]

Cold had latent advantages as well as discomforts, and over time northerners began to exploit some of them. It helped to preserve perishable foods that could be stored in attics and unheated chambers. Storing other foods in cool cellars where they would neither freeze nor spoil also helped to make diet less skimpy and monotonous in the winter and spring. Butchering was concentrated in the late fall and early winter when natural forage ran out and when the cold ensured that the meat would not go bad while it cured. Farm households as far south as Virginia cut ice during the winter for use in refrigerating food during the warm months. It was especially helpful in keeping milk for processing into butter and cheese and in preserving them for sale.[70] In the early nineteenth century, one enterprising New Englander began shipping ice to the ports of the Caribbean, founding what was to become a major industry.[71]

Not too harsh but too mild a winter climate was a serious handicap on the roads of the Middle Atlantic. New England and upstate New York usually enjoyed snow cover uninterrupted for months. It greatly eased the hauling of heavy freight once colonists equipped themselves with the means of exploiting it. Deep snow briefly blocked the roads, but once beaten down, it offered an ideal surface for sled and sleigh traffic. The time when produce and wood could be most easily hauled to market was, conveniently, the time when the demands of work on the farm were lightest; the lighter burden of chores combined neatly with easier travel to make winter the prime season for sociability as well as freight movement. In winter in backcountry upstate New York in the 1790s, as James Fenimore Cooper recalled it, "the highways were thronged with sleighs" carrying new families to settle or hauling produce to a far-off market. "The village was alive with business," and many visits were paid locally and to more distant friends and relatives. "Immense is the value of this season," an upstate New York farmer wrote of winter; "logs for future buildings are easily drawn to the sawmill . . . grain is conveyed to the different landings on our small rivers, from whence in the spring small vessels carry it to the sea-port towns. . . . The constancy of this serenely cold weather is one of the greatest blessings which seldom fails us. More to the southward their winters are often interrupted by thaws and rains which are unfavourable to transportation." The middle states, Albert Gallatin likewise observed in 1808, those lying between thirty-six and forty-one degrees latitude, were less fortunate where transportation was concerned than those to their north. They could count on snow and frost to damage the roads each winter, but not on snow thick and steady enough to furnish unbroken sledding and sleighing.[72] But even cold weather without snow was welcome, for it froze the mud, albeit into a rutted and bumpy surface, and gave better support for a cart or carriage.

Snow and cold were prized because the roads were so bad in other seasons, especially in the dampness of spring and fall. Hard weather-proofed pavements were rare even in cities and even in Philadelphia and Boston, the cities best provided with them.[73] "A light rain coats the streets with mud," observed Timothy Dwight in Hartford, Connecticut, "and the wet season in the spring renders them in some places almost impassable"—a description that fitted most rural roads as well.[74] Such difficulties made carriage by river attractive when its own many weather handicaps did not make it impossible. "Nearly all the rivers which penetrated the interior were unsure, liable to be made dangerous by freshets, and both dangerous and impassable by drought; yet such as they were, these streams made the main paths of traffic."[75] Shipping was easier on tidal, coastal, and ocean waters, but the uncertainty and sometimes the violence of the wind that propelled it made it far from safe or punctual.

Seafaring trades were important in the Middle Atlantic, though proportionately less so than to the north. Profiting the most from the wind for freighting and fishing, New Englanders also suffered the most from it. Trading the land for the deck, they exchanged one set of weather risks for another. The privateers that preyed on enemy sail in wartime were built for the utmost in speed, but their generous spread of sail and high masts made them especially vulnerable to oversetting in rapidly shifting winds.[76] Wrecks took a high toll and markedly lowered life expectancy in the New England coastal towns engaged in fishing and marine trade.[77] Admitting the great usefulness of navigation in "supplying necessary provisions to a country in want, and thereby preventing famines, which were so frequent and destructive before the invention of the art," Franklin wondered on the occasion of his last sea voyage whether the shipping of mere luxuries justified "hazarding so many lives on the ocean."[78]

But shipping gained some new means of coping with the weather. A small marine insurance company opened in Philadelphia in 1793, a second three years later in New York. Lighthouses were built and maintained along the coast. The Massachusetts Humane Society, organized in 1786, erected huts along the coast to shelter shipwrecked mariners and later began to establish life-saving stations at hazardous points. The size of ships increased markedly around the end of the eighteenth century, and larger ships were less vulnerable to storms.[79] Franklin suggested some further measures for safety: a bell to ring when visibility was poor to avoid collisions among the growing number of ships at sea, pouring oil on rough seas to calm them, double planking of the hull, hoisting lightning conductors in times of storm.[80]

The last was a logical extension of another device that he had announced in the 1740s. A metal rod extending skyward above a building and properly connected to the ground, he showed, would harmlessly absorb strikes of lightning. By 1772, Franklin could report his lightning rods so common in the colonies that "numbers of them appear on private houses in every street of the principal towns, besides those on churches, public buildings, magazines of powder, and gentlemen's seats in the country."[81]

Franklin's device provided one example of how invention could lessen trouble with the weather. The steamboat provided another. There had been successful demonstrations of steam navigation before 1807, but it was Robert Fulton's voyage up the Hudson River from New York to Albany and back again in August of that year that marked the start of regular service. "I had a light breeze against me the whole way, both going and coming," he wrote to a friend; "I overtook many sloops and schooners beating to windward, and parted with them as if they had been at anchor."[82] Adopting steam did away with the unreliability of the wind as a hazard for transportation by abandoning it as a resource and substituting the cost of engine and fuel and the danger of explosions.

The weather was still of immense importance as hazard and resource to many spheres of life. Drought, rain, and frost were of central concern to agriculture, easily the dominant livelihood in eighteenth and early nineteenth century America, though their impacts depended on the farmer's crop choices and economic resources as well. The weather also controlled the grinding of grain and the sawing of wood, largely done by waterpower that ran short in droughts; all overseas and most interregional trade, entirely dependent on the wind for propulsion; and shorter-distance movement, sensitive to what the weather did to the roads or the rivers. The many obstacles to swift and reliable transportation and communication by road or sail or riverboat made business a thing of many delays and hazards and uncertainties and necessarily leisurely in pace.

Weather was relevant to so many activities and in so many ways, indeed, that the same conditions would help some while hurting others. The wife of Franklin's Poor Richard, sending the 1738 almanac to the printers, "scatter'd here and there, where I could find room, some *fair,* pleasant, sunshiny, &c. for the Good-women to dry their clothes in," balancing a male tendency to think chiefly of enough rain for the crops.[83] Clear weather was good for travel, except on sandy soils, where rain, on the contrary, made the ground firmer and travel easier. Different crops did well or badly with different amounts of rain, and wheat fared well in cold that damaged corn. An early frost hardened the roads but froze the rivers and damaged crops; a mild winter was good for comfort, but bad for ice gathering and freight hauling and food storage and for farmers selling wood to the cities. Mortality among blacks and whites in the urban North peaked in opposite times of the year—winter and spring against summer and fall. No season was inherently the deadliest; the differences were the result of group differences in living conditions and previous disease exposure interacting with the weather.[84]

"The Ruler of the Winds": *Weather and Climate Control*

Nowhere was it more obvious than in warfare, on land and at sea, that weather helping some at the same time hurt others. Spending many years in conflict with the aborigines, the French, and eventually the British, Americans had ample chances to notice how. The effects depended on the details of the situation, but even when the weather was such as to obstruct both sides from fighting—as when muddy roads prevented marching, or firearms and ammunition were wetted by a heavy rain—the halt was usually to one side's benefit over the other.

Historians who insist on the power of chance in human affairs are fond of citing interventions of this kind as demonstrating the difference that random factors can make. Seventeenth- and eighteenth-century Americans seeing weather events change the course of wars often saw purpose and design at work, not chance. New Englanders were more prone than most to do so. The Puritans looked for the hand of God in all manner of peacetime weather events, in lightning strikes, droughts, the rising and calming of storms at sea. They were just as ready to interpret rain that halted battles or made roads impassable for marching, fog that gave cover to maneuvers, or winds that sped or scattered fleets in the same way: as the work of divine providence.

That it was the side that they had to suppose was favored by heaven—their own—that often suffered did not shake their belief. If adverse weather came, they reasoned, it had been sent either to chastise them or to test their resolve. They were chastised and tested severely in

King Philip's War, the savage struggle between colonists and aborigines that raged in southeastern New England in 1675–76. The Puritan divine Increase Mather viewed its outbreak as his people's punishment and warning for their misdeeds. There were many early setbacks and defeats, several due to bad weather, Mather wrote, for "God saw that we were not yet fit for Deliverance, nor could Health be restored unto us except a great deal more Blood be first taken from us." Thereafter, the lesson having been taught, the skies had smiled upon them. At one key juncture, "the Lord in the nick of time sent Thunder and Rain, which caused the Enemy to turn back." A besieged house, set aflame, was saved by a providential shower. A summer drought threatening the colonists's crops in the middle of the struggle was broken by ample rains, which fell in Connecticut, moreover, not when a tribe had sought by its rituals to produce them, but only following the prayers of their Christian minister.[85]

The tendency to view the weather of war as other than a mere random factor was not limited to New Englanders, and it had not died out by the time of the American Revolution. When a northeast storm of wind and rain foiled his planned engagement with the British Army in Boston in March 1776, George Washington could not doubt "that this remarkable interposition of Providence is for some wise purpose," disappointed though he was to see a battle canceled that he had felt confident of winning.[86] Shifting breezes, fog, and rain several times allowed Washington's army to escape destruction during the New York campaign that summer and fall and were interpreted throughout America as timely aid sent by heaven. So was the sudden freeze that hardened the roads and allowed the Americans to maneuver to victory at Princeton in January 1777.[87] "To whom but the Ruler of the winds," asked Ezra Stiles, "shall we ascribe it that the British reinforcement, in the summer of 1777, was delayed on the ocean three months by contrary winds, until it was too late for . . . General Clinton to relieve the siege of Saratoga?"[88] That rain fell and the rivers rose just in time to cover an American army's escape after the Battle of Cowpens seemed no less a divine interposition.[89] The decisive campaign of the war at Yorktown offered a crowning example: "None but HE who sits king upon the floods, and holdeth the wind in his fists, could have so ordered the arrival and movements of the French fleet, as to defeat the British, and co-operate with the combined armies in the reduction of our enemies." "To everyone, who considers these things, the wonderful interposition of divine providence, in the capture of Cornwallis, must appear plain and obvious."[90]

But some Americans were already distancing themselves from such a reading of events. Some who still used the word *providence* in discussing the weather factor began using it in a sense closer to *luck* or *chance* than to deliberate intervention.[91] Prayer for rain in times of drought, the chief peacetime expression of a belief in special providences, remained common. But a small but influential and growing minority had shed that belief in favor of a Deism that expected no divine interventions and looked for help when it was needed to human effort alone. It acknowledged only general providence, not special interpositions. God had bestowed on mankind all of what it might need; it remained mankind's task to put that bounty to use.

One of the preachers of the new faith was Joel Barlow of Connecticut (1754–1812), a Deist in religion, a Jeffersonian in politics, sometime diplomat, enthusiastic eyewitness to the French Revolution, and self-appointed epic poet of the new United States. Barlow's writings lumped political oppression, revealed religion, and the natural environment together as allied obstacles to human progress, which depended on liberty, science, and a nature remolded according to human needs.[92] He held with his Puritan forbears that weather might be summoned when needed to suit human purposes, but he proposed to summon it by different means: not prayer but scientific weather control. The American of times to come, Barlow wrote, would "brew the soft shower" when one was needed, "rain and tempest all the skies" when "the Demon *Drought* begins his round," "fan autumnal fogs with vernal gales," "[l]ay the proud storm submissive at his feet." Ships would enjoy "stormless winds" managed to ensure their safety.[93]

As with weather, so with climate. The religiously orthodox foresaw an eventual millennium brought about by divine favor. "There will be no more unsuitable seasons or calamitous events, to prevent or destroy the fruits of the earth," predicted the Congregationalist minister Samuel Hopkins, "but every circumstance with regard to rains and the shining of the sun, heat and cold, will be so ordered, as to render the earth fertile, and succeed the labour of man in cultivating it."[94] Barlow too expected the seasons to be tamed, but by science and human effort. He expected human nature itself to benefit from the transformation. He was a convinced determinist who saw human beings as always molded by "climate . . . temperature and other local circumstances": "The soul, too, varying with the change of clime, / Feeble or fierce, groveling or sublime, / Forms with the body to a kindred plan, / And lives the same, a nation or a man."[95] He took the determinist's point of view to its natural conclusion. If the climate imposed an unsatisfactory state of society, matters must be mended by changing the climate, a step in the gradual self-perfection of humankind.

Orthodox religion, to Barlow's mind, could do nothing to help reach that goal. By discouraging scientific inquiry and preaching the inherent and irreparable sinfulness of man, it could do much to hinder human progress. British rule, for its part, had stunted the development that would allow Americans to subdue their environment. The intemperate climate, Barlow suggested in his most ambitious work, the epic poem *The Columbiad,* had been the natural enemy of the American cause in the Revolution. The spirits of "Flood" and "Frost" were bound to take sides with Britain, whose downfall meant their own eventual dethronement.[96] Freed from the constraints of imperial rule as from the superstitions of the church, Americans were freed to conquer the land and the atmosphere at the same time. Clearing the vast forest and cultivating the soils would warm and moderate the climate, as Barlow explained both in the verse of *The Columbiad* and in a lengthy prose footnote.[97]

He was only endorsing an idea widespread among his contemporaries.[98] As early as the seventeenth century, it was being said in the North American colonies that the removal of the forest was changing the climate or was likely to do so in the future. In the eighteenth and early nineteenth centuries the belief grew stronger. Few European visitors in the years following the Revolution failed to note its prevalence. Similar views, indeed, were common among Europeans who looked back on their own history and supposed that the clearing of the woods since classical times had lessened the cold of winter. So too, when once the forest was cut back to the proportions it now occupied in Europe, many Americans believed, the harsh seasons of the New World would give way to the moderate ones of the Old. Opening the ground to the warmth of the sun in winter would lessen the intensity and duration of cold, while cooling breezes would blow more freely in summer. Extremes that kept Americans from growing the crops grown at their latitudes in Europe would disappear. The United States would become self-sufficient in wine, "cotton will be produced in Pennsylvania, and oranges in Maryland," the people of Maine would "enjoy all that mild temperature of climate, and rich variety of the bounties of nature . . . of the most favored countries under the sun." The Hudson River, closed to navigation by ice for several months each year, would freeze only occasionally and for short periods.[99] In asking of Americans only the clearing that they wished to undertake in any event, it was the most appealing of prescriptions for climatic change.

Many of these theorists were radicals and Jeffersonians in politics and philosophy (they included Jefferson himself). They worried little about the possible impiety of trespassing on a realm so long and closely associated with divine intervention as the weather. The lightning rod, as just such a trespass, had made some conservatives uneasy. Franklin himself had been driven to protest that "the Thunder of Heaven is no more supernatural than the Rain, Hail or Sunshine of Heaven, against the Inconveniencies of which we guard by Roofs and Shades without Scruple."[100] But his device had other objections to confront. One critic suggested in the 1750s that the spread of lightning rods might, by draining electricity from the atmosphere into the earth, promote earthquakes, another in 1793 warned that it might be responsible for an increasing tendency to severe drought. Both drew the same general lesson against reckless tampering with God's earth: "by causes that are of human contrivance and altogether artificial . . . and which we could not have imagined or believed, before the introduction and use of them; we may bring on such irregularities, and such excessive degrees of drought, or rain, or other changes in the natural world, as may be very injurious both to health and vegetation."[101] There were critics too who argued that the clearing and cultivation that Barlow and others hoped would soften the American climate would instead make it harsher.[102]

Thus any intervention might have consequences, perhaps disastrous ones, that divine wisdom could have foreseen but that imperfect human wisdom could not. That was one objection to trying to remake the weather. That any change was likely to cause damage to some while helping others was a second. That the same weather shared by all was not equally beneficial to all was most obvious in war. But while hurt to some was precisely what made some kinds of weather providential on the battlefield, in ordinary life in a particular community it posed a more perplexing problem. So long as weather modification had been a religious matter, divine omniscience would take care of unforeseen consequences, and divine justice would look after the proper distribution of aid and harm. Weather magic such as the raising of tempests had troubled Puritan witch-hunters because it put the power to harm into unregenerate human hands. Barlow's science promised to do the same as the doctrine of the fall of man slowly gave way to the myth of progress. Once weather control changed from a religious to a secular responsibility, it required a deep faith in the moral and intellectual perfectibility of mankind to assume that the power would be used for the best. The "Sage of unknown name"[103] on whom Barlow called to devise the means of controlling the elements needed to be wise in more than science and technology to be sure of doing good.

Antebellum America

Antebellum Migration

In 1810, more than four in five Americans lived in one of the original thirteen seaboard states. Half a century later, though those states had grown considerably, they held less than half of the nation's population. The reason lay in the post-1815 rush of settlers beyond the Appalachians into the continental interior, "one of the great immigrations in the history of the western world."[1]

Chaotic though this movement was in many ways, it showed at least one orderly pattern. Individually these settlers followed many paths, but the typical ones moved due west, erring to the north or south only when their path was blocked by mountains or water or political boundaries or when they were pulled aside by the easier travel routes along navigable rivers. Most of the inhabitants of every inland state in 1860 came from the states to the east within its own latitudes. It was mostly New Englanders and upstate New Yorkers—themselves mostly of New England origin—who occupied the territories and states bordering on British North America. They left the central and southern parts of Ohio and Indiana and Illinois mainly to settlers from the middle states and the Chesapeake. The frontier of the Deep South was colonized from the far southern coastal states much more than from Virginia or North Carolina, states that furnished Kentucky and Tennessee and Missouri with the bulk of their inhabitants. "Ohio Fever" swept the rural Northeast after 1815, followed by "Michigan Fever" in the 1830s, but it was "Alabama Fever" and "Texas Fever" that gripped the southern states.

Modern research has documented what many Americans at the time spotted for themselves, what some who could agree on little else agreed was a constant truth of human behavior growing out of a basic law of climate-society relations.[2] "The great law that governs emigration," announced a Massachusetts congressman during an argument against the spread of slavery, "is this: that emigration follows the parallels of latitude." It was "a great law of emigration," "fixed and certain," echoed a Louisiana editor in a defense of the South and its institutions, "that people follow the parallels of latitude."[3] People were presumed to do so in order to avoid the change of climate that traveling north or south would have entailed. The Philadelphia political economist Henry C. Carey found proof in the data of the 1850 Census of "the simple law which governs the movements of men, who, in the process of peaceful emigration, are seeking improvements in their condition. Look where you may, you will see that such persons seek the nearest approach to the temperatures to which they have been accustomed."[4]

Such observers were wrong in thinking that the law was a universal one, but there were indeed good reasons for it to hold true in that time and place. Antebellum Americans feared discomfort and ill-health in novel climates: northerners the diseases of the southern summer, southerners the sharpness of the northern winter. That adjustment to any new climate involved a sickly and dangerous period of "seasoning" had been common wisdom in colonial times and remained so in the early nineteenth century. "Their migration to an atmosphere different from that they have been accustomed to breathe, must prove injurious to them," at least at first: so it still seemed to settlers and physicians alike.[5]

The popularity of this belief did much to discredit one proposal for a transfer of population eastward across the Atlantic. Facing a lively campaign for their assisted or coerced removal to Africa, many free black Americans claimed the climate in which they had grown up as their native environment, to which they were adapted and in which they had the right to remain. Tropical West Africa, their suggested destination, was impossibly unsuited "to the constitutions of emigrants from the New-England and Middle States." What the colonization movement, as it came to be called, proposed for the free black resident of the North was nothing less than "dragging him from health and safety in the most auspicious region in the world" where he had "taken so strong and just root" to "an uncongenial climate" located "in the torrid zone, beneath the scorching beams of a vertical sun." The basic argument was so much a matter of common wisdom that a southern defender of slavery could also make it in order to prove that African colonization was an inhumane and impossible alternative to maintaining the status quo. He pointed to "the deleterious effects of African climate . . . upon those accustomed to different latitudes," among them "the slave of our country, after the lapse of ages has completely inured him to our colder and more salubrious continent."[6]

Where westward migration was concerned, another factor probably mattered even more than worries about health in keeping settlers within the zones from which they came. Most Americans farmed for a livelihood. Their experience with crops was closely conditioned by climate. Though corn was grown everywhere, even it existed in many different strains adapted to the sunlight and warmth of particular latitudes, faring poorly if grown much to the north or south. The northern "flints" matured faster and suited a shorter growing season better than the southern family of "dent" corns. Cotton grew only under a southern sun. Wheat was raised with great success in the upper Mississippi Valley but not in the lower. The typical farmer, possessing many tools and skills that seemed to be what the economic historian Richard Steckel calls "latitude-specific," would not readily relocate to a climate where these would be of little use.[7] As the earliest European settlers of North America had done, antebellum pioneers used latitude as an index to climate and through it to conditions for agriculture. Farm journals routinely discussed the suitability of crops and practices in such terms. The fictional upstate New Yorker who exclaimed "there can't be any difference in the climate—the latitude's the same," the real Iowan who wrote that "we may reasonably expect the same Latitude to be characterized by the same phenomina [sic] generally"—both spoke for their age.[8]

Settlers had reasons for following the parallels that had nothing to do with climate or latitude as such. Straight west, other things being equal, was the shortest route to cheap land. Many of the seaboard states had had landholdings in the west demarcated by the extension of their boundaries, and their citizens had settled and continued to settle those areas by preference. A factor that by itself would have imposed a rough latitudinal zonation on movement was the great difference in labor institutions that had become essentially a difference between South and North. Southerners owning slaves, or hoping to own them some day, would not move northwest beyond slavery's legal limits, while many northerners avoided moving south into its domain.

If staying within similar climates, then, was not the sole cause for the "westering" tendency of migration, it was one of its consequences. Those settlers who did use latitude as an index to climate had better luck than the early settlers of the Atlantic coast had had. In neither case did it work perfectly, but it worked far better between the Appalachians and the Mississippi than it had two centuries earlier on the seaboard. By the 1850s, readings gathered by the Smithsonian Institution furnished the material for some crude climatic maps of the United States. The isothermals—contour lines of average temperatures—ran remarkably parallel to lines of latitude in the trans-Appalachian zone.[9]

Differences there were. The weather to the west, even on the same parallels, was "on a grander scale," as Donald Meinig writes. Trans-Appalachian pioneers found "greater seasonal extremes of heat and cold, and far more violent changes . . . spectacular thunderstorms, cloudbursts, hail, blizzards, or, most awesome of all, tornadoes."[10] The rivers rose faster in flood and shrank smaller in droughts. Easterners trying to discourage the outflux west dwelt lovingly on these contrasts. Hotter summers, fiercer storms, sudden floods—one prescribed such a *"change of climate"* to his neighbors as a swift and certain cure for the "Ohio fever."[11] Still, with the most important aspects of the climate, Meinig continues, "with the more general patterns of the seasons . . . experiences in the West were strongly reassuring." The aspects of climate most basic to a settler family's livelihood were much like the ones the settlers had known on the same parallels in the East.[12]

Yet even the same weather's significance could change greatly with the move west. The act of migrating itself meant greater exposure. The miseries of the open-air journey were especially great beyond the Mississippi, where shelter and help were scantiest and the weather fiercest. The overland Gold Rush migrants of the late 1840s crossing the Great Plains and the mountains encountered heat and cold, rain and drought and storm such as they had never seen before. The sea routes to California, too expensive for most, had their own perils: the storms of Cape Horn or the tropical fevers of the shortcut by land across the Isthmus of Panama.

On the trans-Appalachian frontier, which received most of the immigration of the period, weather extremes were not as severe, but the migrants still suffered much from exposure, and the hardships did not end when the journey did. Certainly pioneers enjoyed some advantages. "That luxury of luxuries in our northern winters," wrote a westerner in 1844, "a blazing wood fire," was more readily available than in the East. "Fuel, the supply of which furnishes elsewhere so painful a contrast between the comforts of the laboring class and their employers, is here to be had for the cutting."[13] Dwellers on the thinly settled frontier were richer than Easterners in land and its products, but they were far poorer in labor and its products. Roads were cruder; bridges were often lacking and could not soon be repaired if damaged by floods. The farmer and agricultural writer Solon Robinson, a New Englander transplanted to northern Indiana, warned newcomers of what they could expect. The West was not the East they knew, he observed, if only because there were fewer improvements in the land and fewer people to make them. Anyone surprised out of doors by a blizzard in the East could likely follow a road or other landmarks to shelter not too far distant. On the Indiana prairie, the nearest cabin might be miles away and might be impossible to locate even if it were much closer.[14]

Transportation

Frontier travel was especially difficult and dangerous, but even in the more thickly inhabited regions the roads were nowhere anything to boast of. Even in cities, a weatherproof pavement by the time of the Civil War was an exception to the rule.[15] The dust and bumpiness that made the rural roads unpleasant in July and August were welcome compared to the mud of spring and fall that made them nearly impassible. Northerners still welcomed snow as an aid to transportation, still exploited as much as they could the help that winter gave for carrying heavy goods. An upstate New York farm journal summed up the mild December of 1830 as "little snow, and no sleighing, which rendered it unfavorable for business. Travelling was for the most part very bad." Thereafter, however, snow had been abundant, making it "[f]or the traveller and business generally . . . one of our most favorable winters."[16] Stagecoaches set their record times in winter; sleighing and sledding as pastimes continued to offer the pleasure of speed in contrast to the slowness of movement in other seasons.[17]

Americans adapted their warmer-season vehicles to the bad roads. Carriages and wagons were built lighter, higher, and better-sprung than those that plied the smoother highways of Europe. Less was done to improve the roads themselves, for reasons as much political as technical. The paving methods that could have weatherproofed them required skilled and expensive labor: for laying a proper foundation, securing drainage, crushing stone for the pavement, and applying it to form an even and durable surface.[18] Throughout the period, though, the roads remained chiefly the responsibility of the individual townships or counties. They were usually maintained by means of a road tax, payable in cash or unskilled labor directed by an often unskilled supervisor. The consequences of these arrangements were described by a disgusted Ohioan in 1850: "Fifteen or twenty hands frequently labor away all day, at work which the next shower washes away, because of its injudicious application. . . . The two days labor which the law prescribes, is considered a penalty that has to be endured, and they seek its mitigation by working as little as possible. And those who let them off with the least amount of work, are considered the best supervisors, and are frequently elected on that account."[19] Traveling through the northern states in the early 1830s, Alexis de Tocqueville was as appalled as most foreign visitors by the state of the roads, yet they were the natural product of the localism of American life, the decentralization of authority, the distrust of the higher and more distant levels of government, that he admired.[20]

The United States acquired one well-surfaced highway built at federal expense: the National Road, running from the Maryland seaboard to the Midwestern prairie.[21] Aid for a countrywide network of roads on the same model had its vocal supporters in Congress led by Kentucky's Henry Clay. It also had opponents determined and numerous enough to prevent anything more of the sort from being done. They objected to federal funding for internal improvements as an encroachment by Washington on a domain clearly reserved to the states: "Let us have to wade through the mire of our roads, and brave the mighty floods of our streams, in the best way that we are able," declared a senator from Virginia in 1828, "yet we will not barter the Constitution of this land for any boon which we may be offered."[22] He and his allies prevailed, and by mid-century the National Road itself had been handed over piecemeal to the states through which it ran. Better and more weather-resistant roads awaited a time that did not see the centralization required to improve them as a worse evil than their unimproved state. There was a division of interests on the issue as well as one of philosophies.[23] Westerners wanted better roads to bring in new settlers and help them send their crops east. The commercial middle states were eager to cooperate. New England and the southern seaboard only stood to suffer by depopulation and agricultural competition. Whatever hindered out-migration and inland transportation was to them a help, roads more resistant to the weather a hazard. They naturally balked at paying for their own impoverishment.

Builders of private roads could, in theory, have laid and maintained good pavements and recouped the cost from tolls. Some did, but most turnpikes proved losing propositions for their builders.[24] The advent of other means of transportation deprived them of much business that might have helped to keep them solvent. What the historian George Rogers Taylor dubbed the transportation revolution between 1815 and 1860 did not take place on the roads and streets, which it essentially bypassed. It began with improvements in water hauling, by steamboat and canal.

Steamboats spread rapidly on rivers and coastal waters alike after 1815. Wherever they competed with sailing craft, they offered reliable service no longer dependent on the direction and strength of the breeze. Yet they remained very far from weatherproof. Safer than sailing craft in high winds, they were not invulnerable. The *Walk-in-the-*

Water, in 1818 the first steamer to be launched on the upper Great Lakes, in 1821 became the first of many to be wrecked in an autumn gale. Winter ice closed the lake ports to steam no less than to sailing vessels.

Steamboats plying unregulated inland streams suffered the most. The western rivers had two idle seasons in between two busy ones. Spring reopened traffic after the winter freeze, though high water and floating ice made it hazardous. Rivers sank so low in the summer heat that navigation ceased again. Farmers and businessmen waited anxiously for the "fall rise" that would carry the harvest to market. It usually came to the Ohio River by the beginning of October. Droughts could delay it as late as early December, causing general hardship, waste, loss, despair, and prayers for rain. "Produce accumulated at shipping points where it lay, often rotting, while scarcity and high prices ruled in the districts of consumption."[25]

Flatter hulls and lighter, high-pressure engines allowed western steamboats to operate in ever-shallower waters, even, it was said, "on a heavy dew."[26] Often, though, the rivers could not furnish even that. Interruptions, without growing longer, became a growing annoyance to merchants. Along the Ohio River by the 1840s, "[t]he attitude of passive acceptance of the situation and of thankfulness for navigable seasons when granted gave way to demands that something be done to end the intolerable burdens of the existing mode of transportation. The delay in the appearance of the fall rise in 1849 until early October aroused more complaint than many of the more extended delays of previous years."[27]

The solution, a prominent engineer argued, lay in bringing the river under control. Throughout the 1850s, Charles Ellet, Jr., promoted a plan for building a gigantic system of reservoirs on the Ohio's tributaries. They would accumulate water in wet seasons and release it in dry ones. By this means, Ellet claimed, and at a small cost compared to the benefits that would result, six feet of water, enough to float fully laden steamboats of medium size, could be assured year-round, and the channel would no longer freeze in winter.[28]

He proposed, in effect, to turn the river into a canal. New York's Erie Canal, begun in 1817 and completed in 1825, linked the Great Lakes and the West to the Hudson River and the Atlantic. Its success inspired an immediate burst of imitations elsewhere. For long-distance carriage of passengers and freight, canals had striking advantages over unregulated rivers as well as over rough and muddy roads. Feeder streams and overflow gates controlled the water level and mitigated the extremes of wet and dry seasons.

Floods, though, could breach the canal banks and stop traffic during weeks of repairs, wash out the towpath, or turn it to mud. Severe droughts could lower the water level enough to halt navigation.[29] Canals suffered most from winter cold. The New York system shut down completely, icebound, every December, not to reopen before April. An early freeze or a late spring stretched the idle period even longer. Only once in its antebellum history did the Erie stay open for longer than eight months.[30] In the Deep South, the water stayed ice-free year-round, but the South built few canals.

The solution to the problems of water traffic was found not in better controlling the flow of the rivers but in letting them alone, in shifting to a new mode of haulage by land, first tried in the United States in the 1820s, to which drought and ice were all but irrelevant. That railroads could run year-round counted for much in their favor. That they ran far faster than a horse-drawn canal boat, and that new rail lines could be readily extended to places where new navigable waterways could not, counted for more. But if it was not only the weather factor that allowed the railroads to snatch an ever-growing amount of business away from their established rivals in the years before the Civil War, their success in doing so greatly weakened the weather's grip on transportation.

The railroad itself had its troubles with the weather. Because low and level ground made the best routes, floods often meant washouts. Bridges could be felled by floods, ice, or violent storms. The railroad, finally, began the transformation of snow from movement's ally to its enemy. A blizzard could cover the tracks too thickly for a plow to clear, and a new hazard entered American life, "snow blockades" stranding trains for days in the stations or in the drifts between stations. When urban street railroads began to use salt to keep their tracks clear in winter, they ruined the streets for sleigh riding and sledge hauling.[31]

But on the whole, as the rail network spread and thickened, "distinctions that had once been crucial in dividing the days and months of the year . . . wet times from dry, hot times from cold, good weather from bad—gradually became less important to travel even if they did not disappear altogether." The seasons and the weather varied precisely as before, but with much less effect on the movement of people and goods. The temporary reversion to an older state of things during the Civil War only emphasized how much had changed. Rail lines were used when possible to move troops. But with marches across country, with artillery and supplies, still the standard means of maneuver, whole campaigns were crucially affected by the difference that wet or dry weather still made to the state of the roads. The breakdown of Union

FIGURE 2.1. The development of railroads made winter a difficult rather than a favored time for transportation. A Currier and Ives scene shows a train being dug out of a "snow blockade."

maneuvers in Virginia in the infamous "Mud March" of January 1863 was "so vividly ignominious that never again would the North or the South attempt a large-scale winter campaign in the east."[32] Fleets on the western rivers were equally at the mercy of high or low water.

If war inland by the 1860s still suffered from many of the handicaps that the weather had long imposed, war at sea was profoundly changed. The navies of North and South were largely steam-powered. Still vulnerable to violent storms, they were little affected by the lesser rises, falls, and shifts in the wind that had decided many naval battles in times past. Steam at sea had already begun to transform peacetime weather-society relations much as railroads did on land. In the summer of 1854, a British traveler embarked at Liverpool for the United States. He was Charles Weld, the much younger half-brother of Isaac Weld, who had journeyed through North America in the 1790s and published a book of his impressions. It was Charles's idea to describe how life in North America had changed in the sixty years since his sibling's visit. He had a striking change to record even before the New World came into sight. Isaac's vessel in 1795, baffled by unfavorable weather, had taken two months to cross the Atlantic. Traveling on a Cunard steamer, Charles had less than two weeks to admire "the almost marvellous skill and science which impels such a large ship across the Atlantic in defiance of adverse winds."[33] On a sailing ship, the wind was a constant preoccupation. To the steamship passenger, it no longer much mattered.

Steam's great asset was its reliability. The average westbound cross-ing by sail from England in the 1850s took more than a month. (The eastbound trip, favored by the winds and currents, was faster.) Given ideal weather, the crossing could be made in two weeks, but at the worst, it took ten weeks or more. Two weeks by mid-century was a slow crossing for a passenger steamer, ten days the record for speed.[34] Sail's great asset remained its cheapness, for the wind was a free re-source even though an unreliable one. Many early steamers carried sails for use when conditions permitted.

By the 1850s, westbound sailing packets themselves crossed the At-lantic in two-thirds the time that it had taken them in 1816.[35] Naviga-tion benefited from charts of prevailing winds and currents across the globe assembled by the navy oceanographer Matthew Fontaine Maury and from an evolution in American oceangoing vessels that took place between 1830 and 1860.[36] Ships's hulls became narrower and shallower, their bows sharper, their spread of sail greater, all making for speedier passages, though in reliability they remained no match for steam-powered craft.

Fast and reliable crossings were a luxury when ocean steamers first offered them. They quickly became a necessity for some purposes—carrying mail and passengers—and to them was sacrificed some of the increased safety in bad weather that steam also made possible. Charles Weld was preparing to return home in October 1854 when word ar-rived of the sinking of the American passenger liner *Arctic* and the loss of most of those on board.[37] The *Arctic* was one of the four steamships with which the New York-based Collins Line provided rapid and regular transatlantic service. It left Liverpool, England, on September 20, 1854. Entering dense fog as it approached the North American coast, it kept up full speed. Shortly after noon on the twenty-seventh, it collided in the mists with the smaller French steamer *Vesta* and sank less than five hours later. Of the *Arctic*'s more than four hundred pas-sengers and crew, eighty-six survived.[38]

A frequent first reaction was to blame bad weather for the catastro-phe. Within a day or two, it became clear that the loss of the ship and of so many lives had not been the work of fog alone. It was due, above all, to the fact that the *Arctic* had not slowed down in the fog nor even sounded signals to warn oncoming vessels. The Collins line installed steam fog-whistles on its remaining ships.[39] But it could not afford to have them slacken speed whenever visibility grew poor in the North Atlantic. Only pride in the way they outraced their British rivals kept Congress voting the heavy subsidies that kept the line afloat. All of the steamers followed "this practice of running at full speed through a dense fog," one newspaper observed. "That it must increase the chances of collisions everybody must see; but no one openly objects to it", for punctuality had become an imperative in its own right.[40]

Most vessels were still sailing craft, and most losses at sea involved these boats, in sinkings and accidents each too small for wide notice, though some—such as the wreck of the immigrant ship *New Era* off New Jersey in 1854—rivaled the *Arctic* disaster in loss of life. The rise of steam meant many things for safety at sea. Most were for the better. Though it made larger ships possible and hence larger disasters as well, the larger the ship and the less dependent on wind for propulsion, the safer it was in a storm.[41] Wind became less of a hazard than before, though collisions in fog became more of one, and the bells, whistles, and horns used as warning signals were often undependable.[42] Yet, as Civil War experience showed, fog could become a resource for shipping as well as a hazard. It was no small help to the many steam-powered blockade-runners trying to evade the northern watch off the chief Confederate ports.[43]

As steam made the open ocean—apart from fog—relatively less dangerous, the coast became relatively more so. But in the 1840s and 1850s the volunteer rescue efforts of shore dwellers in shipwrecks were supplemented by the creation of a federal life-saving service, and new equipment appeared that included improved life- and surfboats and mortars and rockets for attaching lifelines to vessels in distress.[44] Federal construction of harbors of refuge, protected basins where ships could sit out gales on the seacoast and the Great Lakes, began in the 1820s and 1830s and continued throughout the period despite growing southern opposition.[45] They were especially valuable on the Lakes, with their fierce storms, rocky coastline, and scarcity of naturally sheltered anchorages. Every antebellum Congress saw loud wrangling between Whigs and Republicans urging that more be built and Democrats suspicious that every so-called harbor of refuge was really a disguised project for helping local commerce or a mere grab for federal dollars.

Neither coastal improvements nor the life-saving service was of much help to the most weather-beset trade in the United States. The worst hazards for the New England fishing fleet lay beyond their aid, on the stormy and foggy fishing grounds of the North Atlantic. The losses it suffered were sometimes catastrophic for individual towns. An 1841 gale took fifty-seven lives from the single town of Truro, a storm five years later sixty-seven lives from Marblehead. The "Yankee Gale" that hit the New England mackerel fleet off Prince Edward Island in 1851 drowned three hundred men.[46]

Weather had always been a hazard, but two developments in the trade around mid-century made it worse. As railroads linked the fishing ports to distant markets and the fresh fish trade expanded, speed emerged as a new imperative: "The vessel once loaded with fish everything is made subordinate to the desire to reach home in as short time as possible," to beat other vessels and secure higher prices for the catch.[47] As a result, fishing schooners evolved in the same direction as other sailing ships, producing what became known as the clipper schooner. Longer, narrower, shallower, and with a greater spread of sail, it was notably faster than earlier models, but it was also more unstable, more liable to be capsized by strong and suddenly shifting winds. Moreover, much of the fishing once done from the schooner began to be done instead from dories launched from it. The new method increased the catch and speeded the voyage by harvesting a much wider expanse of sea, but the dories were easily lost in fog or upset in rough weather. The cost paid for the benefits of both developments was becoming apparent by 1861: sharply mounting losses of men and vessels.[48] "Excessive speed in every act seems to be the ruling passion" was Charles Weld's verdict on the United States.[49] It was one that by mid-century could be gratified as never before; accommodating life to the risks of the weather often proved to be a weaker passion.

The Telegraph

The time of Charles Weld's visit, the late summer of 1854, was unusually hot and dry in much of the eastern United States. Wheat fared badly in many places and corn worse. Low water in the rivers and canals hindered traffic. Water-powered mills had to curtail operations. Forest and brush fires were widespread. Prayers for rain were offered in cities and country alike.

The drought happened to take hold in northwestern Alabama shortly after an interstate telegraph line had been strung through the area. A preacher drew a connection between parched crops and the mysterious but plainly malign effects of the humming cable. "'They have robbed the atmosphere of its electricity, the rains are checked,'" he declared, "and so down went the posts by the dozen, and away went the wire by the mile, dragged by an angry and excited mob through Russellville, in triumphant avengement of their wrongs."[50] It was for nothing. The rioters had mistaken a chance correlation for cause and effect. The telegraph did not affect the weather. It did not need to, though, in order to affect the weather's significance.

Without making the weather more severe, the telegraph made it more of a hazard by giving it new chances for mischief. Samuel F. B. Morse in 1843 began work on the first intercity connection, between Washington and Baltimore, by laying the cable underground. But water seeped through the insulation, and the only remedy that Morse and his associates could find was to string the wires instead through the open air.[51] The change made their work easier. It took much less time and effort to stretch cables between poles or trees than to dig a trench in which to lay them and then fill it again. Repairs to damaged lines were also easier to make; but unfortunately damage itself became far more frequent, for the change had the drawback of exposing telegraph service to the full force and variety of the American weather. Many routine events began inflicting damage in new ways. Electrical storms and heavy fog disrupted the flow of signals. Lightning strikes could knock out connections and even electrocute operators. High winds snapped the wires; so did spells of heat and cold; heavy snow and sleet brought them down wholesale. Poles were uprooted by floods and felled by gales, especially the high masts set up to carry the wires across rivers. Charles Weld heard many complaints about the interruption of news through "the frequent displacement of the wire by storms."[52]

Better methods of insulation and wire stringing lessened some forms of interference. Others remained problems. They slowed but did not stop the spread of service. In 1860, the telegraph carried 5 million messages, a small fraction of the post office's 160–170 million letters but remarkable for so young and costly a means of communication.[53]

When Morse's invention was still a novelty, one writer sat in a room in Washington watching a group of men play chess by cable with another in Baltimore, "on an intensely dark night in December, with torrents of rain and storms of wind . . . the darkness, the rain and the wind being no impediment to instantaneous communication" nor even to the perfect comfort of the players.[54] The telegraph offered for the first time a means of sending messages without exposing a messenger to the risks and rigors of the route in between. In 1861, it connected California with the East Coast, something that railroads had yet to do and that the postal system did with difficulty. The arrival by sea in the 1850s of "the mail from California" was always a great event in New York and always liable to delay or worse from the hazards of the weather. The nation's greatest marine disaster of that decade was the sinking of the mail steamer *Central America* in a hurricane off Florida in 1857. The post from California, plus four hundred passengers and crew and a million and a half dollars in gold, went down with the ship.[55]

Workmen and engineers laying a submarine cable to span the Atlantic had to contend with the resistance of the weather, but once the cable was laid it was entirely weatherproof. The cable layers were harassed by storms at sea during the successive stages of work, but they persevered and by the summer of 1858 had linked Europe with America.[56] For the first time, independent of the weather on the Atlantic, near-instantaneous communication between the Old and the New World was possible. Though the link failed even as its completion was being celebrated, it would be reestablished permanently in 1866.

The telegraph brought another change of great potential importance. Once Americans had, as they liked to say, harnessed the lightning to carry their messages, for the first time news of a storm could easily outrun the storm itself. It was a fact advertised in 1856 in the hall of the Smithsonian Institution in Washington. For some years, the Smithsonian's director, Joseph Henry, and a government meteorologist named James Pollard Espy had been collecting daily weather data from locations across the country. Their observers took readings at specified times of day and mailed reports to the capital every month. Espy used them to analyze patterns of storm movement. As the wires spread, Henry established a second network. Telegraph operators were ordered to begin their mornings by sending Washington a report of the local weather. Henry had the results posted daily on a map showing current conditions across the United States. Black cards represented rain, brown indicated clouds, blue snow, and white clear skies.[57]

Even before the work of Espy and his contemporaries, Americans had formulated some crude but useful rules about how their storms behaved: that they tended for the most part to progress from west to east, coastal disturbances to advance along the seaboard from the southwest to the northeast. Espy, the meteorologist William Redfield, and others reconstructed in as much detail as they could amass the movements of many past storms with the aim of stating more precisely the rules by which they were governed.[58] "When we have fully learned the laws of storms," wrote Elias Loomis in 1848, "we shall be able to *predict* them," for such knowledge plus instantaneous telegraph reports of a storm's current whereabouts would make forecasts of its movement possible. Marine interests had evidently the most to gain. "If the navigator can anticipate the approach of a storm by 24 hours, this interval will be quite sufficient to place him beyond the reach of its fury"; captains warned of approaching severe weather would stay in port to avoid the storm and then benefit again by "promptly putting to sea with its closing winds."[59]

A government agency for forecasting foul weather found its champion in Matthew Fontaine Maury. During the 1850s, the self-taught navy oceanographer pushed the idea of having farmers, through the telegraph network, report to him on the weather as ship captains sent him their observations of the winds and currents. The data analyzed, storm warnings would then be wired from the capital to the threatened districts. Maury proposed to make every farmer-observer "a sentinel on the watch-tower . . . to admonish his fellow-labourers in the fields, as well as his co-labourers on the sea engaged in carrying his produce to distant markets, of approaching foul weather and consequent danger."[60]

A friendly senator drew up a bill to create such a service. Maury was to direct it. But the "Pathfinder of the Seas," as he was called, was the particular dislike of a circle of Washington scientists led by Joseph Henry of the Smithsonian and Alexander Dallas Bache of the Coastal Survey.[61] They thought him a national embarrassment, an amateur hopelessly at sea in the world of scientific research, competent perhaps to collect data but not to analyze it, a demagogue too quick to promise practical results, to appeal to the public for support, and to mix science with religion. Fueled by bureaucratic rivalry and philosophical conviction, their hostility boiled over when Maury, a naval officer untrained in meteorology, proposed to take charge of government studies of the weather on land. Certainly they understood from experience, as he did not, how far from simple it would be to predict the behavior of the weather. With a little trial and error, Maury supposed, "the laws that govern the course of storms would soon be so well known" that reliable warnings would be easy to develop. Those laws were rather, as Henry observed at a public discussion in 1856, a matter "of much complexity" and one best delegated to those best qualified to study it.[62]

The conflict stalled the project until the Civil War removed Maury from the scene—he seceded with his native Virginia—but likewise relegated the whole matter of a federal weather bureau to a peacetime future. Forecasting overall was not as slow to develop. Once the telegraph made it easier to guess at the weather to come, some private concerns— railroads and steamship lines—did not wait for government action to begin doing it for themselves, and some newspapers began doing it for their readers.[63] Henry in the late 1850s found a system as crude as any that Maury would have used good enough to meet some needs of his own. Taking it as a rule of thumb that the weather affecting Cincinnati in the morning would be in the capital around nightfall, he made it a policy to cancel the Smithsonian's evening lectures whenever the Ohio city reported rain.[64]

Henry and Bache had sound reasons to doubt Maury's credentials for the work he proposed to undertake. The effect of their opposition, all the same, was to stall a project that could have done much good even with Maury at its helm issuing imperfect warnings based on crude science. A storm in January 1857 swept north along the East Coast as many had done before it, wrecking dozens of ships with much loss of life. If a telegraphic weather service had been in existence, Maury pointed out, "New York and our shipping ports might have had from eighteen to twenty-four hours' warning in advance of this storm," and "timely warning" could have been given to "many whose lives such warning would have saved."[65] But Maury and others, in forecasting the effects that forecasts would have, themselves took for granted what remained to be shown: that the warnings would always be attended to and safety given priority over schedules. The very changes that made it easier to know what the weather would be made it harder, by tightening the timetables of business, to put the knowledge to use. If Atlantic steamships did not slow down even when fog surrounded them, if the fishing fleet embraced speed over safety in the form of the dory and the clipper schooner, just how much heed would warnings of storms have been paid?

Agriculture

Even before it came into wide use for forecasting the weather, the telegraph was already in regular service for softening some of the weather's effects. It long irked antebellum farmers that the dealers who bought their crops knew more than they themselves did about the state of the harvest and prices, and so generally got the better of their bargaining. When the Virginia agricultural reformer Edmund Ruffin established *The Farmers' Register* in 1833, he hoped to keep his readers better informed about crops and prices and foil the "crafty or lucky speculators" who traded on their ignorance.[66] A monthly journal, though, was a slow and clumsy way of spreading such information. Matthew Fontaine Maury in the 1850s offered a much quicker one through the telegraph. His national weather network was to give farmers not only warning of storms, but the latest word on prevailing prices.[67] The buyers, by the time Maury wrote, were using the wires already. Uncertainty about the harvest had meant wide speculative swings in prices. This price instability was greatly reduced by the flow of information through the telegraph and through the half-dozen specialized commodity exchanges that were in existence by 1861. The effects began to appear as early as the late 1840s: buying and selling went on within narrower limits; the ranges in prices diminished.[68]

The growth of the exchanges also made futures contracts easier to arrange. By setting the terms of sale before the crops were gathered, they transferred many of the risks of the harvest to the middleman. Consumers were better protected against short harvests raising prices and producers against large ones depressing them. The agents of the change were those whom Ruffin had denounced as greedy speculators, but in a calmer moment he understood their role better: "Their operations are more efficient than any other cause, to mitigate the evils of scarcity, and to prevent famine—and on the general average, even to reduce the prices of the provisions which they monopolize with the design of obtaining for them the highest possible prices."[69]

The telegraph and the exchanges, together with the transportation network of canals, steamboats, and railroads, created a national trading system better than ever able to move commodities where they were scarce. The more readily different regions were connected, the less impact poor crops here or there had on the consumer. This growing communications and transportation network meant an end to the kind of isolation described by Caroline Kirkland on the Michigan frontier, where "everything depends directly upon the operations of nature in their season." She recounted the effects of a fall drought. Livestock, even the family milk cow, had to be slaughtered because feed was scant and water low; the hides glutted the narrow local market; mills could not grind even the scarce grain that had been harvested because the streams were dry, but the isolation of the settlement made it hard to obtain flour from outside.[70] As transportation improved, such a state of affairs became steadily less typical of American life.

There were antebellum years of larger and smaller harvests, but none that was short or bountiful everywhere in a market the size of the entire country. In 1860, drought and heat damaged corn across the Deep South, but farmers supplied themselves from a northern surplus. More than one of them wondered, on the eve of secession, how wise it would be to sacrifice their access to such a large and reliable source of foodstuffs.[71] Southerners would indeed discover during the war what it was to live in an abruptly narrowed market. The cutoff of trade with the North and the blockade of the coast magnified the impacts of droughts and floods in major growing regions and made food supply a chronic problem for the Confederacy.[72]

If the farmer's market was increasingly national, it was also increasingly transatlantic, to a degree and in ways that created new risks and opportunities out of weather events. Early- and mid-nineteenth-century Western Europe was largely self-sufficient in grain. In bad years, however, it made up its shortfalls with large purchases from the United

States, an occasional windfall resource for American farmers that was never so rich as in the years following the War of 1812.

Those years are famous in weather history for a different reason: a legendary disaster. Yet the freak cold and drought that prevailed across most of the settled United States in the summer of 1816—most dramatic and most damaging in upper New York and New England, with frosts in June and August—was not per se a disaster for farmers. It did devastate the corn crop, on which many farmers depended. Hay for livestock feed also did quite badly. Fruits, berries, and root crops fared much better. So did small grains; the wheat crop was generally reported to be more abundant than usual.[73] Farmers who had relied on corn were left with little to sell or eat. Livestock farmers slaughtered the animals they could not feed, and beef and pork prices fell drastically throughout the fall and winter. Those of corn and wheat, on the other hand, rose higher than they would again—even without correcting for inflation—for the next century and a half.[74] Short supply accounted for corn's rise, high demand for wheat's. For Western Europe had also had a cold summer, with too much rather than too little rain, and an exceptionally scanty grain harvest. Its purchases during the fall, winter, and spring drove prices in America still higher and swelled the takings of those who had wheat to send abroad. With American governments in full retreat from the policies of food price regulation that had been accepted for centuries in Western political thought, calls for an embargo on grain shipments went unheeded by Congress.[75]

Nothing is better remembered about the famous cold summer than the mass exodus that it supposedly caused from the Northeast. To the extent that it was the weather that impelled farmers west between 1816 and 1818, it was not only their own, but Europe's as well, and they were pursuing opportunity as much as they were fleeing misfortune.[76] A second poor harvest in the Old World in 1817 kept wheat prices high, with predictable results. Sales of public lands in the West boomed and cultivation expanded. But bad weather overseas was a resource for American farmers having much in common with a hazard. High returns stimulated production that proved to be ruinous overproduction once the scarcity ended. European harvests returned to normal in 1818. Again able to feed itself, the Old World no longer needed to buy from America. The inflated wheat prices that had reigned for several years, farm income, and public land sales in the United States all dropped drastically, trade and westward migration slowed, and defaults spread, beginning several years of severe agricultural depression. Where all had been activity and prosperity two years before, a British visitor to the interior in 1820 saw farmers grazing their livestock on the fields of wheat that would no longer repay the cost of harvesting and shipping to market.[77]

The cycle of good and bad times was repeated a number of times in the antebellum period. Bad weather in Europe, plus the disruption of its trade by the Crimean War, made the middle 1850s a boom period for northern grain producers. A sudden drop in overseas demand in 1857 inaugurated several lean years for American farmers; another series of poor European harvests and renewed high demand for wheat began at the same time as the Civil War.[78] By contrast, the greatest southern plantation staple, cotton, enjoyed a much steadier demand because it had little foreign competition. When weather reduced output, prices rose to compensate. Secessionists trusted in cotton's indispensability to the mills of Europe to help the Confederacy win recognition and support overseas. The more general belief persisted that the South's climate was a rich resource by its nature. When competition for some of its products did develop, however, it stood revealed as less inherently lucrative, less a given of nature, and more one of human arrangements, than it was often thought to be. By the time of the Civil War, rice growing in the British colonies in South Asia was already cutting profits in lowland South Carolina, foreshadowing the fate that had overtaken indigo and awaited cotton.[79] Though the South's political philosophy rejected high tariffs, Louisiana sugar planters continued to enjoy substantial tariff protection and did all that they could to keep it in place.[80]

Antislavery northerners endorsed the thesis that nature had been especially generous to the South when doing so allowed them to convict that region of having spoiled its advantages. A congressman speaking in 1858 was engaged in this kind of reverse boosterism when he asserted that "Virginia had a position in advance of any of the States that are free, with a better soil and climate, and yet she has lagged behind in the march of prosperity. To what influence can you attribute your relative decadence, but to slavery?"[81] Many southerners continued to maintain a reverse boosterism of their own, insisting that the handicaps of heat, humidity, and disease made African slavery essential to the cultivation of a low-latitude soil and that the North did without it not from principle but because it did not need it. As the nation expanded toward the Pacific, slavery's future clearly depended on its ability to gain a foothold in the West. In the mid-1850s, Congress gave settlers the right to choose for themselves whether to allow slavery in the newly organized Kansas Territory. Many northerners and southerners insisted that climate inexorably prohibited or required bonded labor in Kansas, but both sides took the trouble to help nature along by trying to organize emigration from their sections to colonize the disputed ground. The South's efforts failed badly; the northern backers of the New England Emigrant Aid Company did somewhat better; yet the overwhelming majority of settlers came neither from the Deep South nor from New England, but from the states to the east—some of them slave, some free—within Kansas's own latitudes.[82]

By staying close to their latitudes of origin, most westward-moving American farmers avoided most of the problems of adapting their livelihoods to a new climate. Yet those who moved farthest west could not help experiencing a drastic change. Farmers reaching California finally found the true Mediterranean climate that the early colonial settlers had expected to find on the Atlantic seaboard. For a time it left them at a loss, but they soon assembled an agriculture that made use of its key features: mild winters and relatively little rainfall, concentrated in the winter. Fruit cultivation, especially grapes for wine, became a thriving industry by the time of the Civil War. Wheat growing flourished, as did livestock grazing on the grasslands.[83] The Latter-day Saints who settled in the basin of the Great Salt Lake in the late 1840s found what they sought: a land where they would be let alone. The price was its climate, with harsher temperatures and far less rainfall than they were used to. They pioneered irrigated farming, and their tight social structure proved well suited to the cooperative effort that made water management in a desert work smoothly. It also proved well suited to spreading the losses and mitigating the worst hardships caused by drought and frost in their first years in the Salt Lake Basin.[84]

Farmers who stayed in the East devised new ways to exploit familiar climates. They crossed varieties of corn to produce hybrids with useful characteristics. Northern New England shifted from the corn and wheat that the West could produce more cheaply to dairy, livestock, and potato farming. Land near large bodies of water proved safer from frost than other areas of similar latitude and elevation. Specialized fruit growing districts exploiting this natural protection developed around the Great Lakes, the Finger Lakes of upstate New York, on Long Island, along the Chesapeake, and on the Florida Peninsula.[85]

Agricultural weather lore was a mix of helpful rules and stubborn delusions, but even the latter were rarely worse than useless, and the former offered some hints about day-to-day variations. The behavior of animals, the phases of the moon, the way smoke rose from a chimney, and the form of the clouds were all used to guide times of planting and harvest.[86] Some of the most useful signs identified the directions and shifts of wind likely to precede rain. Thus armed, the farmer who possessed a wind vane received some help in foreseeing the weather. "The affluent farmer, who possesses a barometer," received more.[87]

Seemingly having far less than the windvane or the barometer to do with the weather, yet at least as useful in dealing with it, were some other devices that began to come into use on American farms in the 1840s and 1850s.[88] Before the invention of the horse-drawn mechanical reaper, wheat was harvested by hand-held implements. The work was done in an intensive burst of activity concentrated in the ten days during which the grain was ready but had not yet begun to deteriorate from the heat. Farmers paid high wages to assemble crews for the harvest; they suffered when bad weather delayed the work or damaged the crops. The horse-drawn rake greatly eased and speeded the gathering of the hay crop as the reaper did that of wheat. By allowing the same tasks to be done faster by fewer hands, mechanization "removed much of the danger of loss of crops arising from unfavorable weather conditions."[89]

Besides adapting their crops and their activities to the weather, farmers could control the weather to some small degree. Better drainage of fields lessened the risk of frost damage and winterkilling of wheat. Bonfires among fruit trees offered some protection against frost on chilly nights. The earlier confidence that deforestation would moderate the climate gave way to an increasing concern for preserving forests locally and regionally to keep the climate from becoming more severe. Rows of trees or shrubs or board fences could shelter fields from cold winds. Market gardeners near cities went much farther. Hothouses, sheltered from the cold by fences and trees or glass coverings and heated by steam pipes or fermenting manure, produced fruit, flowers, and vegetables for a much longer season than nearby farmlands enjoyed.[90]

Save in greenhouses, farm labor, slave or free, was not sheltered from the weather: nowhere less so than on the rice plantations of South Carolina, where there was work to be done in the flooded fields in both midsummer heat and the cold of January.[91] Nor, save in greenhouses, were crops sheltered either. Farmers who had done everything in their power remained substantially at the weather's mercy. The widening of the market lessened the chance that they would gain from higher prices what they lost from poor yields in a bad year. Untimely hail, wind, rain, cold, heat, humidity, drought, floods, thaws, and frosts were little less ruinous to a year's prospects than they had been in earlier generations.

Industry

In April 1837 Ralph Waldo Emerson recorded in his journal his relief "to learn that New England is to be the manufacturing country of America. I no longer suffer in the cold out of morbid sympathy for the farmer." Fluctuations in the weather, he supposed, a vital matter to agriculture, were all the same to the industrialist.[92] He was wrong. The rise of manufacturing did not so much make the weather irrelevant as make it matter in new ways.

It did not matter, to be sure, in one way that many supposed. That New England indeed led antebellum America in industrial development, and that the North overall far outpaced the South, seemed to some observers directly determined by climate. Jacob Bigelow, taking a professorship in applied science at Harvard in 1816, spoke in his inaugural lecture of the advantages that destined his region to success in industry. Chief among them was the harshness of the seasons. Not only did the difficulties of farming, its "yielding but a scanty harvest for a laborious cultivation," encourage other pursuits, but while idleness came naturally to those living in too easy an environment, the cold air of New England bred "vigour of body and activity of mind," priceless assets in technology and manufacturing.[93]

If Bigelow arrived at the correct answer—for the period, at any rate—to the question of where industry would flourish, it was not because his reasoning was impeccable. A single error would have led him astray from the conclusion that he wanted to reach. He committed two that offset each other. Had his premise been correct, and a severe climate been crucial to industrial success, he should have pointed to French Canada, more favored in this respect even than New England, as the destined core of the industrial revolution in North America, and Russia, rather than England, as its pioneer in Europe. He would have been wrong, because the premise itself was wrong.

But though the weather and climate did not govern the development of manufacturing in the way that Bigelow and others supposed, they had much to do with the industry of the period all the same. In turning to manufacturing for their livelihoods, northerners did, as Emerson observed, distance themselves from the chances of the elements that affected crops. Yet early- nineteenth-century manufacturing was sensitive to the weather in many other ways.[94]

By running their mills mostly on waterpower from streams, antebellum Americans gave the weather a great influence over their work. Evaporation in summer lowered the streams well below their yearly average volume. In the Northeast, the natural flow in July was only about a tenth that of March, the month when the rivers ran highest. In the trans-Appalachian West, where the climate was more extreme and natural reservoirs were fewer, many streams dried up entirely in mid-summer, and for long periods in years of drought.[95] When they ceased to run, so did the mills once reservoirs were exhausted. Whatever interfered with a steady supply of power lowered output while fixed costs went unrecouped, and workers lost their wages for the duration of any shutdown. As drought took on new terrors, so did heavy rain. Spells of high water, concentrated in the spring and fall, could stop waterwheels from turning as effectively as drought. And as mills and mill towns grew along the riverbanks, so too grew the amount of damage that a flood of any given size could do, not only to factories and dams, but to the communities around them.

Millowners attacked the problem of low water by enlarging their storage reservoirs, but in doing so many came into conflict with other users of the lakes and streams and with landowners on their banks.[96] Another response was to try to make the same amount of flow go farther. In the 1840s, closed turbines began to replace waterwheels as the means of capturing energy from falling water. They did so more efficiently, and they could operate, as waterwheels could not, in high water.[97] A third solution appealed to an increasing number of manufacturers. Mills that every spring were "greatly annoyed with too much water, compelling them to stop, and during the dry summer months, vice versa, too little to allow them to run" could switch to a prime mover that was independent of the weather and seasons.[98]

The extensive use of steam power in American manufacturing began in the 1830s. Like steam at sea, it had the advantage of reliability, the disadvantage of being more costly and complex to build, operate, and repair. But its use became steadily cheaper over time, especially as transportation improvements lessened the cost of coal as a fuel. Waterpower was still dominant in American industry by the time of the Civil War, and the advent of the turbine did much to slow its decline. Yet steam, insignificant in 1815 and dwarfed sixfold in total horsepower by water in 1840, was spreading rapidly; it served 35 percent of all manufacturing plants in 1860.[99]

Not everywhere, though, was energy supplied by the atmosphere traded for more reliable if costlier sources. At the Onondaga brine springs of New York State, by the time of the Civil War America's leading source of salt, the opposite occurred. Beginning in the late eighteenth century, the Onondaga producers had evaporated the brine over wood fires. As wood grew scarce, they began in the 1820s to use a second method: evaporation in open vats under the rays of the sun. They saved themselves the cost of fuel and gained a second advantage as well; the slower heat made "solar salt" a higher-quality article than the boiled product because impurities could be more thoroughly removed. The new method accounted for a steadily rising share of antebellum production even though it increased the problems of coping with the weather. Cool, wet summers, a gift to millowners in the same region, meant low output, and the rainstorm hazard required constant vigilance: "At the first symptoms of a shower all hands are immediately called to 'push on the covers,' and the temporary roof[s] . . . are passed on rollers over the crystallizing brine, to be removed the very instant the sun shines again."[100] The sun and the air and the winds continued to be used in drying such products as soap, glue, bricks, timber, paper, tanning bark, leather, tobacco, fruit, and fish, with the same interruptions by rainy weather but the same advantage of cheap and gentle evaporation. Women's work in farm households was less seasonal and less exposed to the weather than men's, but many of its key chores were much affected by the seasons and weather, notably that of drying clothes.

It was not only as a source of power that the weather had to be reckoned with. Some industries were highly sensitive to heat. Antebellum meat packing was a strictly seasonal business, running only from the end of autumn to the end of winter and often halted by warm spells for days or weeks. Early lager breweries had to close during the hot months, just when demand tended to be highest. Excesses of temperature interfered with baking, whether done in commercial houses or at home. Iron mills and glassworks idled their furnaces when outdoor and indoor heat combined reached the limits of the workers's endurance; a midsummer stoppage of a month or two became routine in both industries.[101]

Winter caused the most trouble in other areas. Textile mills required a warm and moist atmosphere for the best handling of the fibers. Dry cold made them brittle and easily broken during weaving. Brickyards and quarries closed for the winter because the cold interfered with the digging and handling of the clay and stone, sawmills because it froze the logs, masonry construction because it froze the mortar.[102]

With agriculture and construction together still accounting for most paid work, their parallel rhythms continued to lock the northern economy into a regular cycle of employment and wages. Demand and pay for casual labor were lowest and poverty and idleness most common in winter, labor markets tightest in summer.[103] Contractors responsible for canal digging, little of which could be done when the ground was frozen, had to import much of their work force rather than hire native employees at premium-season rates[104]—and the canals once open became one more sector busy in summer and idle in the cold months.

Because so many jobs failed to provide steady pay, transiency in search of work—both from trade to trade and from place to place— was common to an extraordinary degree. Winter employment was especially sought after. Midwestern farm laborers idled en masse after the harvest flooded into any trade that could accommodate them. Meat packing was one. Another was cutting wood in the forests for fuel and for timber; it could be hauled on the snow to a riverbank and then loaded or floated to the mill on the spring flood.[105] The rise of one new industry began to lessen the imbalance in seasonal labor demands by substituting machinery for manpower in agriculture, but it had to shoulder some of the remaining burden itself. The production of harvesters to satisfy demand peaked in June and July and dropped sharply thereafter. Their leading producer, the McCormick Company of Chicago, had to pay top wages in its busy period of spring and early summer to compete with construction for scarce labor.[106]

The gathering and sale of ice was another rising trade whose usefulness went far beyond the winter jobs in cutting that it created. Exports expanded tremendously, and domestic use as well. Brewers by the time of the Civil War were using ice and the coolness of deep underground cellars to prolong their operations into the summer. A few meat packers were beginning to use ice on a sizable scale for the same purpose.[107] As ice and the railroads extended the range of perishable foods, well-to-do urbanites began to enjoy a fresher and more varied diet. Gail Borden's invention of condensed milk created a product far less prone to spoilage in the heat than the original article.[108]

For even as they struggled to free their own operations from the weather, industries were turning out many new products that lessened the hold of the weather on American life and livelihood. Some soldiers early in the Civil War still used outmoded muskets and ammunition that a wetting made useless, but newer weapons made battle far less sensitive to rain than in the past. European-made pianos warped badly in the dry air and extreme temperatures of the United States; American manufacturers replaced the wooden frame with a cast-iron one unaffected by the state of the atmosphere. So simple a novelty of the period as the clothespin made it easier and safer to dry wash in the wind. The data gatherers of the 1860 Census counted twenty producers of lightning rods.[109] It was a small part of the growing sector of American trade devoted to defense against the weather. Clothing production was a large one, and while protection from the elements was only part of the rationale for most clothes, for one kind it was almost the sole one.

The manufacture of rubber garments suffered at first from the weather as few other industries did. Few others, once the problems were overcome, offered Americans more help in coping with the weather in their daily lives. A short boom in the production of waterproof rubber clothing and footwear in the early 1830s was checked by the discovery that such garments—popular in the milder temperatures of England—deteriorated quickly in the extremes of the American climate. They "became hard and brittle in cold weather, and in warm weather adhered together, often in a worthless mass."[110] The industry was revived later in the decade by the development of vulcanization. Blending sulfur with heated rubber created a substance resistant to winter cold and summer heat alike.

While spending the last two decades of his life fighting for his patent rights to vulcanization, the Connecticut inventor Charles Goodyear found time to write a two-volume book on *Gum-Elastic and Its Varieties* (1853). He devoted the first volume to a history of his researches, the second to hundreds of ideas for better living through vulcanized rubber. Among them were dozens illustrating the ways in which a single innovation in chemistry might lighten many of the burdens of the weather. Sailing charts for mariners made from rubber would keep their proportions in spite of heat and cold; rubber sails for ships would not stiffen and freeze in sleet as canvas ones did; rubber hammocks would let sailors sleep "warmer in cold weather, and cooler in hot weather than other hammocks"; inflatable rubber lifesaving equipment could lessen the toll from sinkings at sea. Shopkeepers could protect their entrances with rubber awnings; soldiers who had to sleep outdoors could do so comfortably in rubber tents. Goodyear offered farmers rubber covers to protect their crops, gathered up and left out in the fields, from wetting by rain. At home, rubber roofs would be durable and watertight, rubber mats could keep floors clean of tracked-in mud and water, rubber weather strips could seal drafty window and door frames against cold and driving rain, rubber feet on iron bedsteads would protect sleepers from electrocution in thunderstorms. On the road, rubber coverings would secure coaches and carriages and their drivers, passengers, and luggage from wet, rubber mailbags would keep letters dry in the rain.[111]

Goodyear's dream of the waterproof millennium was realized only in part. Yet enough of it came true to earn him no small place in the history of American weather. Rubber tents, blankets, and ponchos did much for the comfort of those northern soldiers in the Civil War lucky enough to be issued them. One enthusiast noted as early as 1853 that vulcanized clothing had transformed the experience of life outdoors: "[D]uring rainy weather, but more especially during a thaw, when the ground has been covered with snow, the best leather boots and shoes cannot resist the entrance of moisture"; rubber overshoes "resist moisture—they are impervious to wet, they keep the feet warm and dry when walking in the wet and cold"; they were, he concluded, one of the greatest advances in comfort that modern life enjoyed over earlier times.[112]

Clothing and Shelter

The response to rubber rain gear brought to light some of invention's limits as well as its potential for helping Americans deal with the weather. Fashionable society at mid-century "scorned rubber boots and waterproof cloaks" instead of embracing them.[113] They were uncomfortable in some ways, to be sure, air-tight and close, but they were less uncomfortable than footwear and clothing that could not keep out cold water. It was their virtues that counted most heavily against them. They were not accepted in fashion because of their too-naked usefulness.

"India-rubber shoes are a great blessing," one physician wrote, and "the prejudice of fashion against the India-rubber shoe" was to him and others only one more instance of a widespread form of stupidity.[114] Dress reformers—some from medical, some from moral, and some from feminist points of view—abounded in the antebellum United States.[115] They had no trouble showing that prevailing fashions in many ways failed the test of the weather and the seasons. If one accepted their premise—that clothing was "a protection and not a vehicle for displaying the person," a device merely for "keeping the body in a just temperature between heat and cold" and nothing more, affording "a covering to the body and a means of regulating its warmth"—then the need to redesign it along more rational lines was clear.[116]

Reformers understood that many, perhaps most Americans could not protect themselves well even by the standards of the time. Many went ill-clad because they could not do otherwise. It remained as difficult as it had been in the past for the poor, for those who lived on the frontier, for those who worked outdoors—farmhands free and slave, sailors, construction and railroad and canal laborers—to stay warm in winter, cool in summer, and dry in the rain and snow. Basic clothing, purchased or homemade, was a heavy charge on the average household. Toward the western margins of settlement, there was a chronic shortage of "articles which are indispensably necessary to comfortable existence, such as shoes, wearing apparel in general," wrote a New Englander after visiting Ohio in the early 1820s; the people were "in general but indifferently clothed, both in summer and winter," cash to buy garments being scarce and labor to make them equally so. Many Union and Confederate soldiers in the Civil War went shoeless even in cold weather, and many civilians, especially in the South, were little better off.[117]

What puzzled reformers was that others who could protect themselves better would not, that the well-to-do did not escape all of the discomforts of the weather that they easily could have escaped. Judging a complex matter by a single criterion, the doctrinaire among them insisted that suitability was the true test of beauty.[118] In fact, the more plainly any garment was shaped for use, the more likely it was to be found repellently graceless and ugly. The more plainly it failed to protect the wearer, the more fashionable it could become. Long skirts, an essential item of ladies's costume, could not have been worse suited to the snow and mud of the badly paved streets. To the dress reformer, they seemed a symptom of insanity, but they had a function and fulfilled it admirably; they announced that the wearer got around by carriage.[119] So did the avoidance of rubber footwear. So did the costume of "light dresses and short sleeves with only a shawl as covering," of "silk and kid slippers, even in cold northern winters" that left arms and feet and chest exposed even as other parts of the body were only too thickly covered at all seasons. A historian of Philadelphia who described American clothing as having been "ill-adapted to our climate" since colonial times could not have been farther from the truth when he blamed the problem on the persistence of English models in fashion, for by the time he wrote American styles had diverged in ways that made them even less suitable to the climate. English visitors, accustomed to dressing more heavily in their own milder winters, found the light American costume as appalling as American reformers did.[120]

Failing to keep its votaries warm in winter, modish attire did even less to keep them cool in summer. Clothes could be shed in hot weather, but only within limits that were quickly reached. Certainly upper-class antebellum attire became better adapted in a few ways to the warm season. Cotton garments to take the place of heavier woolens became more widely available. The 1850s saw the previous decade's dresses undergirded with heavy petticoats give way to airier hoop skirts. Light "country clothes" for wear at summer resorts, came into favor, though they were light only by comparison with what they replaced.[121] But with other changes occurring in the opposite direction, it would be rash to credit even these developments to anything but chance. The black stovepipe hat, which appeared around mid-century, was aptly named, "serving not only as a complete attraction for the rays of the sun, but as a reservoir of heated air," as well as being "liable to be blown off with every gust of wind." The dark broadcloth suit became standard gentleman's wear at all seasons around the same time. One reformer accurately called it "at the North no protection against the cold, nor is it indeed any more suitable at the South. It is too thin to be warm in the winter, and too black to be cool in the summer."[122]

An accessory as practical as the umbrella made its way into the wardrobe of fashion, but it had advantages that waterproof rubber garments lacked. It could be made of expensive materials, of silk and whalebone. It lent itself to fine workmanship and ornament and display. It was cumbersome enough to be useless for outdoor work and free of the suspicion of mere utility. It had, finally, a close kinship to the sunny-weather umbrella known as a parasol, whose usefulness was chiefly of the symbolic kind. In an age when the out-of-doors was the typical workplace, sun-burned or weather-beaten features were a mark of common status, a face and arms shielded from a tan a sign of distinction. When Walt Whitman in *Leaves of Grass* disparaged "those that keep out of the sun," it went well with his man-of-the-people persona. "Do not spoil your fine complexions by exposure to sun and wind," commanded the voice of fashion; use parasols, wear bonnets, mantillas, and capes (long sleeves and skirts went without saying); avoid the sunny side of the street in cities and open expanses in the country.[123] Doctors might protest as they protested against the scantiness of winter clothing, might urge more exposure to the sun as healthier; they went unheeded.[124]

The steady change of styles in a climate that itself changed little and the persistence of other features at odds with the apparent demands of the weather were reality's rebuke to a meteorological fundamentalism that made protection the sole test of merit. A call in 1856 for a distinctive national costume cited differences in climate as reason enough why Americans should not dress as Europeans did.[125] Yet what Americans wore, in its very maladaptations to the weather, was a truer and more revealing index to the national character than any designed according to climate would have been.

Meteorological fundamentalism was as prone to break out among architectural critics as among dress reformers, buildings being as much "for" shelter from the elements as clothes are "for" protection and as easy to write off as failures if they fail to provide it. Providing it, though, is a harder task for buildings than for clothing, which can more readily be changed to suit the weather and season. If American clothing was so imperfect a match with the elements, it is hardly surprising that the houses of the same period suited them no more closely.

The dwellings, like the clothes, of most Americans allowed much weather to penetrate through. Hard work in the fields in the first year left a pioneer family little chance to prepare shelter. "The material for finishing houses is scarce; labour is still more difficult to procure"; winter was apt to catch newcomers in "an unfinished log cabin, with all the cracks open, perhaps without door or windows, and but half a chimney, and sometimes without floor or fire-place."[126] There were other reasons as well that buildings could be ill-adapted, for architecture, like dress, has always had many other tasks to accomplish at the same time as protection.

The North American climate differed markedly from that of Western Europe, and in some ways North American buildings differed accordingly. When a Crystal Palace exposition building went up in New York City in 1853, based on the famous one erected in London two years before, its glass walls and roofs were not transparent but enameled, "our burning summer sun" making it impossible, in the architects's opinion, to imitate what had been—just barely—feasible in the milder climate of England.[127] But more revealing than what was done to adapt the building was the fact that the architects had chosen an English design to adapt. Despite the great differences in climate between the two regions, all of the fashionable antebellum house styles in the United States were closely derived from European forms. Architects and clients were less interested in distinguishing America's architecture from Europe's on climatic or any other grounds than they were in plundering the Old World past for their means of expression. Styles came and went chiefly on the strength of how they looked and what they suggested, and claims about the suitability of form to climate were more rationalizations than reasons.

The most popular high style for houses in the early decades of the century was the white colonnaded temple form of the Greek Revival. It had a number of advantages for the North American climate. It served, as Roger Kennedy writes, to "dignify porches and verandas," useful shade-givers in the summer heat, by giving them classical associations. Its white paint, mimicking marble, reflected the summer sun rather than absorbing it.[128] But critics objected that colonnades and verandas were out of place in a country with a long and cold winter, that the necessary fireplace or stove chimney was ludicrous in a temple form, that a more steeply pitched roof to shed the snow was essential, and that white paint, suitable for hazy Europe, was disagreeable—too stark and bright—in the drier, clearer air of the United States.[129] Two hallmarks of the Gothic Revival style that followed were indeed a much steeper roof and dark paint. Another law-giver of American architecture, another theorist with the true and only design in his pocket, though, condemned the Gothic cottage in turn as all wrong for the American climate. Its windows were too few and small to admit winter sun and summer breezes, and it created sweltering upper rooms by exposing "so much more roof that is necessary, and this so steep as to catch the full power of the sun." The extreme heat made "[a] roof nearly flat . . . greatly preferable to a steep one" in the United States. The critic's own design—the octagon house—was itself criticized not only for a too-flat roof but for too many large windows that would make it excessively cold in winter and hot in summer.[130]

A national style in a more extreme climate should have included more shade from deciduous trees than in England. Puzzled travelers wrote that the opposite seemed to be the case. Frontier cabins were generally sited in the middle of clearings and exposed to "the sweltering heat of an American August." Some supposed that with the habits of pioneers who had to clear land from the forest the settlers hated trees too much to preserve any even for their own benefit. Acuter observers realized that they had made a choice among evils. Wooden roofs rotted faster in the shade than in the sun, and falling limbs and trees were a serious hazard during violent storms.[131]

Thus even adaptations ideally matched to some aspects of the weather were ill-suited to coping with others. Even a steep roof to shed snow deprived the householder of the snow's insulation in winter. Such adaptations might also be ill-suited to meeting other demands, for shelter from the elements was far from the only purpose that architecture served. Its demands had always to be satisfied together with those of cost and convenience as well as those of style, status, and expression. The influential architect Andrew Jackson Downing insisted that houses must provide optimal shelter against their surroundings. He insisted as well that even perfect adaptation to the weather and climate was not enough. A dwelling "where the walls and roof are built only to defend the inmates against cold, and heat," he wrote, lacked beauty and produced a displeasing impression "of mere utility."[132] Weather being as diverse as it was, no one design could have passed Downing's first test, but he was right in supposing that it was not the only test a building had to meet.

Weather and Comfort: Coping with Cold

Before the 1820s, English travelers in the United States had suffered from the brutal outdoor cold of an American winter. Starting in that decade, they began to report a new form of discomfort, the brutal indoor heat of the same season. By mid-century, they complained about nothing more bitterly than "the extreme heat of the houses" in winter, their "close and suffocating rooms," "these terribly suffocating apartments," "oppressively hot."[133] Americans visiting the Old World had the opposite complaint to make. In the 1820s, James Fenimore Cooper could still praise the London indoors as remarkably cozy in winter. Two decades later, another American in the same city noticed that "the habit here is not to keep the houses very warm." By the 1860s, a third reported that an American wintering in England "is in a continual shiver. . . . No stranger can live for a week in an English house and not be ill from exposure."[134]

Western European homes had grown no chillier in those forty years. What had changed was the American domestic climate and the standard of comfort to which it gave rise. A drastic warming between 1815 and 1860 in the northern United States raised indoor winter temperatures far higher than they had been. Adopting new devices and new fuels for home heating had the effect, a largely unforeseen one, of giving Americans a taste for far warmer interiors than they had once found comfortable.

In 1815 and for some years thereafter, most Anglo-Americans, even in New England, still fed open fireplaces with wood to heat their homes; they still lost most of the heat that the fire produced; they still enjoyed winter temperatures, especially at night, that were little different from those outside. Franklin's and Rumford's hybrid fireplaces, half hearth and half stove, used fuel more economically. Franklin had balked at going farther and shutting up the fire in a closed stove. Noah Webster in 1817 exhorted his fellow New Englanders to take that step in order to save their forests from exhaustion and themselves from the poorhouse.[135] For wood prices during the early nineteenth century continued to rise steadily in the cities and in the countryside within their area of supply. As local stocks dwindled, the high cost of transportation severely limited the amount of fuel that could be brought from farther away. A chronic energy crisis set in. Convenience demanded a change as loudly as cost did. City residents, increasingly numerous, had far less space than did farmers in which to stack the quantities of wood that they required.[136]

German- and Swedish-Americans had long used closed wood-burning stoves that wasted very little heat. By the 1830s, Anglo-Americans in the northern states were widely adopting them.[137] As wood prices continued to rise, the price of coal fell until it became competitive. Particularly prized was anthracite, or hard coal. It had been little valued at first, so difficult was it to ignite and keep burning by ordinary methods. If made to burn, however, and it could be, it lasted far longer and gave off far more heat by volume than even the best grades of wood.

It took several developments to make anthracite available to city dwellers. Stoves had to be made over to handle the new fuel satisfactorily. First canals, then railroads had to link the mine fields of northeastern Pennsylvania to the cities.[138] The obstacles overcome, the annual output of anthracite—used for powering steam engines and for iron-working as well as for domestic heating—grew fivefold from 1825 to 1830 and again between 1830 and 1840; tenfold from 1840 to 1860.[139] Soft, or bituminous, coal predominated as a heating fuel in the western cities. Proximity to the mines offset its shortcomings: it had a lower heat content than anthracite, and it was dirtier to handle and to burn.[140]

Exceptionally efficient "air-tight stoves" further reduced the cost of heating with either form of coal or with wood. By mid-century, these stoves were reported to be in nearly universal use even among the poor in the cities of the northern and middle states and to be making rapid progress in the towns and countryside.[141] The results were not limited to the saving of labor, fuel, and forests, nor were they all as happy. Stove users ran the risk of accidents from burns to asphyxiation. The stove was a labor-saving device, as Ruth Schwartz Cowan observes, but the labor it saved was men's. Women's chores, which included frequent cleaning and blacking of the metal to prevent rust, increased. Hard coal mining—employing twenty-five thousand men by 1860—developed into one of the country's most dangerous and most exploited occupations, and soft coal miners were little better off.[142]

If the consequences of the change in heating methods were complex, the cause was not. "The fireplace has very generally gone out of use wherever fuel has been costly," George Geddes wrote in 1847, "and stoves of various kinds have taken its place." Anglo-Americans made the switch with reluctance and only under the spur that Geddes mentioned. "A fine, open, wood fire is undeniably the pleasantest mode of heating a room," wrote another upstate New Yorker. She regretted that as fuel prices kept rising, "wood must ere long give way to the black, dull coal; the generous open chimney to the close and stupid stove."[143] Economy—measured in the labor or in the money needed to acquire, store, and burn fuel—was the chief advantage that stoves pos-

FIGURE 2.2. The parlor of a mid-century Springfield, Illinois lawyer displays a sight common in the antebellum North: the fireplace closed and replaced by an air-tight stove.

sessed in Anglo-American eyes, the one that early promoters of stoves stressed above all others, and the one that their foes—who were many and vocal—conceded them.

To find the closed stove, so sensible and economical, an acceptable replacement for the hearth, Americans had to transform their standards of comfort in ways from which even their great apostle of sense and economy had recoiled. As Franklin had, they disliked losing the sight and glow of the fire. Lovers of fresh air, they disliked, as he had, the loss of ventilation that came with the change. The fireplace draft constantly pulled in air; the airtight stove merely gave off heat. Stove promoters exhorted Americans to change their tastes. Webster assured them in 1817 that with time they would get used to the close and stuffy atmosphere until in the end it would cease to seem close and stuffy: "the unpleasantness will yield to habit," he wrote. So too, another reformer promised, the taste for the glow of the open fire would vanish in time. "Habit, which created our desire for this, will soon remove the difficulty," he suggested. There was nothing inherently attractive, after all, in the sight of "blazing sticks, smoke and a heap of ashes."[144]

Those who felt the least pressure to save fuel showed the least interest in adjusting their tastes. The stove's economy counted for little in the South. It was still chiefly a rural society, and plantation-owner and yeoman farmer alike still had a relative plenty of wood within reach. Cities were smaller than in the North, fuel was less costly, and the milder winters required less of it. Even in the region's cities, stoves were few at mid-century. Open fireplaces remained the norm.[145]

Wealthy northerners could afford a compromise. Beginning in the 1830s, many bypassed stoves altogether to install central home heating.[146] They held onto their fireplaces but supplemented them with wood- or anthracite-fed furnaces, costlier than stoves but still far more fuel-efficient than the hearth and chimney. A system of conduits and registers circulated air warmed by a single cellar furnace to the common rooms used in the daytime. By opening and closing the registers, the householder could regulate the extremes of temperature. The circulation of heated air even added ventilation to that still provided by the fireplaces. Retaining fireplaces in the parlor meant keeping their pleasant glow. Retaining them as the sole means of heating in the bedrooms, as was often done, kept sleeping comfortable.

More elaborate systems of central heating used steam or water, circulated through pipes, to carry the furnace's heat upstairs. They warmed the house and the rooms more evenly than hot air did. They were costlier to install, though, and steam was noisy and hot water slow-acting. By the time of the Civil War, central heating was widespread in hotels and large institutional and factory buildings, but for domestic use it was still confined to the houses of the very wealthy. It took a blissfully unobservant observer, a rich Philadelphian, to describe it in 1859 as "now universal" for home heating.[147]

What was by then nearly universal among his fellows was a taste for warmer interiors. The new preference seems to have been less the cause than the result of the change in heating methods. Stoves and furnaces, adopted for economy's sake, also had a far greater heating power than the open fireplace. They could raise the indoor temperature much higher while burning less fuel. Using stoves, whose heat was hard to regulate, introduced, then accustomed, then addicted northerners to indoor winter temperatures exceeding any they had known before. The furnace had the same effect. Early hot-air central heating worked solely by the force of thermodynamics and required very hot air to work well. Stove promoters had had to struggle at first against what they called a rooted Anglo-American prejudice against the warm interiors that the new devices made possible and sometimes made unavoidable.[148] There were many early objections to stove and furnace heat as both uncomfortable and unhealthy. And far from conquering cold, some warned, it would make the cold worse by making Americans more sensitive to it: "[T]he occupants of such rooms become so enfeebled that they are in danger of freezing to death whenever they encounter such a blast as our ancestors would have considered only a healthy breeze."[149] These voices faded as the habit of warm interiors indeed took hold.

Regular exposure to stove heat in railroad cars did as much as anything to hasten the process of getting used to it. The car stove, to its credit, kept the passengers from freezing, no small feat in the northern winter, but it never warmed the car evenly. Passengers rushed to claim the choice seats, those at a middle distance from the stove. The latecomers had the often-noted choice between being refrigerated and being cooked. Most in time came to prefer the latter. A visitor from across the Atlantic on a mild day in 1849 opened a car window in search of relief from the stove's heat. "There was a general raising of collars and buttoning of coats, and slouching of hats, and shrinking and shrugging . . . I heard some saying; 'We shall all be frozen before we get to our journey's end.'"[150]

For the new technology had created an indoor environment in which English travelers felt extremely uncomfortable. If American interiors in 1815 had differed from those of England in winter, it was in being much colder because the American winter was colder. By the time of the Civil War, daytime winter temperatures above seventy degrees Fahrenheit were routine in houses in the northern United States, much higher than those that the English maintained with their open grates and fireplaces. A striking transatlantic change in climate had taken place, and English visitors recorded many perilous encounters with the new race of monsters, the dragons with their scorching breath that now infested every American home and hotel. After his 1842 tour of the States, Charles Dickens lashed out at the "accursed, suffocating, red-hot demon of a stove" that had pursued him wherever he went. Anthony Trollope, in 1861, with central heating gaining ground, was tormented again and again by "those damnable hot-air pipes" he everywhere encountered. By their agency, "from autumn till the end of spring all inhabited rooms are filled with the atmosphere of a hot oven."[151] Americans from the northern states who had once noticed nothing amiss when they had crossed the Atlantic began wondering why the houses on the other side were so poorly heated.

They wondered the same when they crossed the Mason-Dixon line. Because stoves were so slow to spread in the South, winter indoors there by the time of the Civil War was colder than in the North, just as it was severer in the mild climate of England than in the harsh one of New England. Frederick Law Olmsted warned northerners tempted to come South in winter for health or comfort that they would stay far warmer by staying home.[152] Traveling through the slave states in the 1850s, Olmsted suffered repeatedly from chilly drafts and lack of adequate heating. He repeatedly had trouble even in getting an inn room with a fireplace, and further trouble in getting a fire provided. The dwellings alike of slaves, of white small farmers, and of plantation owners, he found, were so badly insulated, with cracks in the walls and open windows common, that temperatures inside were little warmer than outdoors.[153] Olmsted escaped the cold only among the German settlers in Texas. Like their cousins in Pennsylvania, they had transplanted their well-insulated, stove-heated houses to the New World.[154]

With the shift in their standards of comfort, northerners had made themselves more comfortable than they had been before in stove-heated Russia, but if they complained of the room temperature there in winter, it was still of the heat, not the cold.[155] At the same time, they began to suffer dreadfully from the cold in a warmer southern land. Even English travelers in Italy, Dickens among them, complained like Americans in England that the rooms in wintertime were too chilly, the insulation poor, and the fires inadequate.[156] Americans complained no less. Reaching Rome in January 1858, Nathaniel Hawthorne recorded only bits of his first two weeks's impressions of the city because his fingers were too numb to hold a pen. The young Ohio writer William Dean Howells arrived in Venice as American consul in 1861 and found his lodgings "cruelly starved of the warmth which health demands." Howells expected his Italian friends to linger gratefully in his rooms and enjoy the cozy heat of the closed stove that he had installed. Instead, to his puzzlement, they "always avoided its vicinity when they came to see me, and most amusingly regarded my determination to be comfortable as part of the eccentricity inseparable from the Anglo-Saxon character." He could only suppose that they had some "absurd prejudice" against a proper room temperature.[157]

Evidently, the indoor climate had its global patterns just as the outdoor climate did. But that expectations and standards could also differ from place to place was the last possibility that most travelers were ready to entertain. They brought climatic determinism indoors; they assumed that a feeling of comfort or discomfort was dictated directly and simply by the temperature of the air. Few could free themselves of the belief that a pleasant indoor climate—however difficult it might be to provide in certain settings—was a human universal represented by their own preferences. Most ended up wondering why other people perversely kept themselves too cold or too hot even when they did not need to.

Weather and Health: Coping with Heat

If the victory won by stoves and furnaces over winter was an uneven one, more complete in the daytime than at night, for the well-to-do than for the poor, and in the North than in the South, and if it had its paradoxical side—by conquering the cold at home Americans had made themselves more sensitive to it abroad—it was judged a victory all the same. In 1852, a voice from Michigan could observe that "cold was once, and until a comparatively recent period, the greatest enemy of man; but he has now almost entirely overcome it. . . . Heat is now his greatest enemy, against which, as yet, he has found no effective protection." John W. Draper would put it more pithily a few years later. "In the infancy of humanity, cold was man's antagonist; his more perfect civilization struggles less successfully with heat."[158]

Civilization, in fact, had made the heat worse. Draper, a New Yorker by residence and a physician by training, was in a good position to know. As buildings and pavement replaced trees and open spaces, urban temperatures continued to rise above those in the surrounding countryside. Observers likened cities in the hot months to ovens or the biblical fiery furnace: apt analogies, save that many did not pass out of these furnaces alive.[159]

If summer heat was especially lethal in the largest cities, it was not only because the temperatures were highest there; the most vulnerable victims were concentrated there too: "[t]he longshoreman at his dock bearing and packing cargo, the laborer mixing mortar in the street, the hod-carrier climbing his ladder, the blacksmith at his anvil, the omnibus driver on his box, the teamster, hackman, pedestrian."[160] The northeastern heat wave of August 10–15, 1853, doubled the ordinary death rate for the week of its occurrence in New York City, the place hardest hit. Sunstroke claimed more than two hundred lives; at least a hundred additional deaths resulted from other complaints made fatal by the weather. Though all New Yorkers were exposed to the same weather, all did not suffer equally from it. Adult males, struck down at strenuous labor in the midday heat, accounted for more than their share of the casualties. So did recent Irish immigrants: ill-nourished and ill-acclimated, having recently arrived from a land of far milder summers.[161] Heat waves of similar strength affected the region in 1838, 1847, 1849, and 1854 with similar impact. Comparable extremes of cold were less of a hazard. The Northeast shivered in January 1857, January 1859, and February 1861 in temperatures as unusually low as those of 1853 were high, but they caused no comparable rise in mortality.[162]

Sunstroke was not the only affliction concentrated in the warm months. So were the most feared epidemic diseases: cholera, an intermittent but dreaded visitor from abroad, and yellow fever. But even in normal years summer was especially unhealthy. The routine toll exacted by the warm season far exceeded the occasional impacts of unusual heat waves or epidemic disease. By the 1850s, the month of highest mortality in the large cities of the North had shifted from October to August.[163]

Practically all of the new peak represented deaths of children between infancy and two years of age. They were three or four or five times as frequent every July and August as in the healthiest months.[164] Mainly to blame were gastrointestinal disorders, particularly the one known to doctors as cholera infantum and to the public as "the summer complaint." Its symptoms were diarrhea, thirst, vomiting, fever, and rapid emaciation, often ending fatally within a few days. Its causes, according to the medical theory of the time, were two: the direct action of the heat on the body and the poisoning of the system by the noxious gases of decaying filth.[165] Its cause in fact was bacterial infection through the tainting of water and the rapid spoiling of food and drink—especially milk—in the hot weather.

Summer sickness among the very young took far more lives and years of life than sunstroke during occasional heat waves or even cholera in its sporadic great epidemics. It was an annual heat-related urban disaster that because of its very regularity would not be remembered as one. As early as the 1820s, cholera infantum was blamed for several hundred deaths in Philadelphia alone every summer. The toll rose as the cities became larger and more crowded. It reached one to two thousand each summer in New York by mid-century.[166] The fact that cities were hotter than the countryside must have made some contribution to the toll. The fact that fresh food and milk and water were far harder to come by in the city must have mattered more. As well as intensifying the heat, urban growth had worsened its effects.

Doctors recognized removal to the country as the best defense against cholera infantum.[167] It was for health and comfort alike that affluent northerners every summer fled from "the burning, boiling, stifling atmosphere of the crowded city."[168] Mountain air, ocean breezes, and the coolness of woods or open country became precious natural assets to the resort trade. Well-to-do Bostonians took to the peninsula of Nahant during the hot months "for a breath of cool air and sight of the ocean"; perspiring New Yorkers headed for the island colony of Newport, for Long Branch, Cape May, and Absecon Beach on the Jersey shore, for the Catskill Mountains, for Saratoga, and a dozen other leafy spas upstate.[169] Nothing filled the guest registers faster than a hot spell. "The city is deserted by everyone who can afford to leave town," wrote a well-to-do Philadelphian during the torrid wave of July 1838. Leaving too, he found the summer resorts "crowded to overflowing," their guests "willing to sleep in barns, in entries, on the floor, anywhere for the sake of breathing a cooler and purer atmosphere . . . in town one would be surrounded by dust, noise & brick walls and immersed in a stifling atmosphere of 95."[170] Those who could afford such refuge could also protect themselves better in town. They could take their ease during the day and remain at home behind windows, blinds, and shutters closed to exclude the heat.[171] The same remedies were proposed as in earlier years to cool the city air outdoors: shade trees, fountains, parks, and open spaces.[172] Yet little ground could be spared for trees or open spaces, and urban growth and crowding overwhelmed such advances as were made.

Readings that represented a spell of unusual heat in the North were the ordinary summer temperatures in the slave states. Markedly hotter, the southern climate was not seen as worse for health and comfort in every respect. Respiratory ailments throughout the United States were more common in winter and in cold climates, for reasons including more time spent indoors in often ill-ventilated quarters. A secondary peak in northern urban mortality, concentrated among older adults, appeared every winter and was attributed to the enfeebling effect of the cold. Yet that the hot months and the low latitudes were inherently sicklier remained common wisdom. Just as many still supposed, in the face of mounting evidence to the contrary, that the climate made the South necessarily a wealthier land than the North, it was still widely imagined that a hotter climate necessarily meant greater ill-health: "[I]t is a tax, which those rich countries pay for other bounties, which nature has given them." Antebellum experience did nothing to change such beliefs. The better collection of statistics made it clear how unhealthy the slave states were. Samuel Forry's 1842 book *The Climate of the United States and Its Endemic Influences* documented death rates among military personnel three or four times as high at posts south of Washington, D.C., as north of it, and much higher in summer in the South than in winter. Wartime army experience did nothing either to refute the association of heat and ill-health. Disease felled many more soldiers between 1861 and 1865 than combat, and the concentration of malaria and gastrointestinal illness in the summer and early fall made the warm season the unhealthiest one for the Union armies during the Civil War.[173]

The supposed inherent dangers of the summer heat continued to furnish the planter class with one of its favorite justifications for slavery: that only blacks, because of their tropical ancestry, could work safely in the fields in the torrid season; that if slave labor were abolished, cotton and rice could not be cultivated in the South. Summer in fact was deadly for slaves as it was for their masters. The death rate peaked among adult plantation blacks in August.[174] Planters fared better because they could flee the lowlands in the summer and fall. Some went north. Others made do with the resorts of their own latitudes that offered cooler and fresher air. Virginians summered on Old Point Comfort on the ocean or in the mountain watering places in the west of the state. The grandees of the South Carolina low country migrated to the breezy seacoast as the heat approached, remaining there until "the first frosts of November, banishing all fear of the malarious atmosphere, give the signal to return." The merchants of New Orleans and the planters of the Deep South gathered along the Gulf at Biloxi, Pass Christian, Pascagoula, Ocean Springs, or in the resorts and springs of the uplands.[175]

Some southern physicians tried as best they could to dispute the claim that theirs was a naturally unhealthy region.[176] On the other hand, Dr. John Gorrie of Apalachicola, Florida, was a devoted regional patriot who did not hesitate to condemn the southern climate almost in toto.[177] Its unsafeness for summer residence led to the "annual absenteeism of the more valuable portions of a community," and "the disruption of social ties from migration" led to the disintegration and demoralization of society. And because the "oppressive heat" of the near-tropical zone sapped the energy of its inhabitants, ill-fitting them for success in commerce, the region faced a future of poverty and dependence, while the North grew rich at its expense.

Public health reformers, Gorrie observed, had settled for attacking the evils that seemed to be within their power to control.[178] They had urged that cities be kept cleaner; they had pushed for "the speedy removal of animal and vegetable putrefactive matter" before it rotted in the heat; but the annual return of summer sickliness even "where the most untiring efforts of cleanliness have been kept up" proved that the problem lay deeper. To an indirect attack on some of the climate's evils Gorrie preferred a direct attack on the climate itself. The high temperatures and humidity, as he saw it, were the real enemies, his weapon against them a machine to produce cold and dryness as the stove and the furnace produced heat. Those devices having revolutionized life in winter, the possibilities of space cooling in summer tantalized many inventors. John W. Draper declared an apparatus "which can cheaply and effectually force a supply of artificially cooled air in the summer . . . into dwelling-houses" to be a great national need.[179] Nobody who rose to the challenge of devising one matched the Florida doctor in ambition. He alone proposed to refrigerate the very outdoors.

Air mechanically compressed would grow warmer, Gorrie pointed out. If transferred at its new volume to a holding reservoir, it would release heat to the reservoir walls. It would also release some of its vapor as condensed water. Allowed to expand to its original volume, it would be cooler and drier than it had been before. To chill an entire city to any desired temperature, Gorrie wrote, and at the same time lower its humidity, one need only release into its streets and buildings a steady supply of compressed air, piped in from a coal-powered station on the outskirts whose own waste heat would dissipate into the air overhead. A medium-sized southern city, Gorrie thought, could keep its temperature below seventy-five degrees Fahrenheit all summer for a charge of about four dollars per household. The benefits he expected, beginning with the saving of life and health, would have justified a far larger expense.

Gorrie failed to interest backers even in the more modest schemes of his later years for manufacturing ice and cooling sickrooms. But his proposals, however farfetched, had the merit of taking some popular assumptions to their logical conclusion; he showed what the climatic determinism that many Americans professed came down to in practice. If heat itself was the enemy—if the southern summer was inherently unhealthy and debilitating—the region's future well-being required nothing less than what Gorrie proposed, changing the climate in areas where people lived while leaving the climate for agriculture unaltered; nor could summer mortality in northern cities have become any less deadly a hazard until means had been found to cool the air.

Reforming the Weather

Dr. Gorrie was far from the only American of his time to think that "adapting the atmosphere to our pleasures and wants," as he put it, made more sense than doing the opposite, that weather-society relations could best be harmonized by correcting the weather's behavior.[180] It was an age of reformers, Henry David Thoreau observed in 1843. Most, he wrote, wanted to reshape the world. Others aimed to "reform the globe itself," and for the same reasons. The reformers of society believed that cruelty, injustice, and waste grew out of human institutions that needed to be made over again. The earth, the other reformers claimed, inflicted the same evils on man, and the weather in particular, but it too could be reshaped for the better. "Let us not succumb to nature," Thoreau paraphrased them as saying. "We will marshal the clouds and restrain the tempests."[181]

The meteorologist James Pollard Espy figures in no histories of the "Age of Reform" that I have seen, but he was one of its most striking and representative figures: an abolitionist of storms, a liberator of mankind from the despotism of the elements, a geophysical temperance crusader ready to make the temperate zone finally live up to its name. Espy explained precisely how Americans could tame the weather, have showers or fair skies as they wished. He calculated the cost, a startlingly moderate figure. He offered benefits in return so immoderate that they defied calculation. By the means he suggested, Americans could be done with floods, droughts, high wind, excessive heat and cold, and all of the damage that they did to life and property.[182]

Luckier than some reformers, Espy had no trouble catching the public's attention. "Every body has heard of Professor Espy, the Storm King!" boomed one journal in 1845. "Few of our philosophers are better known to the public at large," observed another, "and few names, even among political men, have found of late a greater circulation."[183] Luckier again than many, Espy did not need to document abuses of which nobody was ignorant. Every newspaper, Thoreau himself allowed, brought word of fresh outrages committed by the weather: "shipwrecks and hurricanes," devastation on ocean and land alike,[184] and most Americans needed no newspaper to acquaint them with the weather's misdeeds.

Many do-gooders could be accused of meddling with things they knew nothing about; not so Espy. No American of the time knew more about the weather; he was a brilliant meteorologist with impeccable credentials to present. Joseph Henry, the first secretary of the Smithsonian Institution, and perhaps America's most distinguished scientist of the period, held Espy in high regard and supported his research for many years. The "Storm King," said the eminent French physicist Francois Arago, was to America what Newton was to England.[185]

Espy's chief contribution, his convective theory of rainfall, rested mainly on what he called the "self-sustaining power" that the process could develop once it had been set going. Air warmed at the ground rose; it expanded as it rose, and it cooled as it expanded. As it cooled, it lost some of its capacity for water vapor. The excess vapor condensed and fell as rain, and because condensation released heat, further rising, cooling, and condensation occurred. The updraft thus created pulled air inward from all sides at the ground and drew it aloft to continue the process. Large storm centers formed in this way were themselves carried along (from west to east in the United States) by the prevailing winds.[186]

Espy worked out this argument—a valuable contribution, especially useful in accounting for thunderstorms and hurricanes—in a series of articles and a book, *The Philosophy of Storms* (1841). Supposing—and here he erred—that he had laid his hand on the master switch that controlled all weather, Espy in the late 1830s began to speculate on how it might be manipulated for human benefit.[187] Rain, he suggested at first, could be artificially made to fall in times of drought. One need only generate enough heat at the earth's surface, and a storm would be set in motion. Espy marshaled many accounts from correspondents and the press to show that forest and brush fires in the eastern United States were often closely followed by showers. His thoughts on reforming the weather eventually took a grand and systematic form. Let timber lots be maintained in a belt from the Great Lakes to the Gulf along the western frontier, he proposed. When rain was needed, or even on some such regular schedule as the same morning every week, let some of those lots be set ablaze. On that day, a long curtain of showers would form and would sweep eastward across the states to the seaboard. Its passage would wring the air dry, and the skies would turn and remain fair in its wake. Gorrie had offered to cool cities for four dollars a household per annum. The yearly price tag for a weekly fire on Espy's plan would be half a cent per citizen.[188]

Plus, some might have added, the extinction of all of the weather's variety and unpredictability. If Thoreau nowhere mentioned Espy by name in his writings, perhaps it was because he could not bear to dwell on such a prospect. But objections conclusive to him would have weighed little among most Americans. When some raised cavils about what would be lost if Espy's plan were carried out as described—that almanac publishers, for instance, would be ruined and would demand compensation from the federal treasury—it was in a spirit more jocose than critical.[189]

It weighed much more heavily against the scheme that it seemed too good to be true. Joseph Henry, among others, thought it impractical and said so in print.[190] Espy could produce countless testimonials to his standing as a scientist; he could not overcome the suspicion that where weather control was concerned he was a crank with his head in the clouds. If Arago had likened him to Newton, Nathaniel Hawthorne, acquainted with many reformers but a skeptic himself, assigned Espy to different company: mingling in the "Hall of Fantasy" with a crowd of perpetual-motion enthusiasts. "The public at large think of him as a sort of madman," it was observed in the days of his first celebrity, "who fancies that he can produce artificial rain."[191] Twenty years of effort did not erase the disastrous first impression. Friends and admirers did their unavailing best to transmute Espy's image into that of the mis-prized genius ahead of his time: a Galileo, a Samuel F. B. Morse.[192] Only a few years before, one of them reminded Congress in 1848, Morse had been "hooted and scoffed at" when he proposed to send messages from city to city through a strand of wire.[193]

What Espy's harshest critics feared was not that the technique would fail to work. It was that the weather could be controlled and that the power to control it would be abused. Southerners were especially alert to such a danger. They might have been expected to be Espy's warmest supporters. Their region, entirely dependent on its agriculture, had much to gain from taming the elements, but they feared the national government even more than they feared storms and droughts and floods. Espy's plan presumed a benevolent state always acting for the common good. The southern theory of politics assumed a federal government always trying to expand its powers to use for selfish—mostly northern—ends. It was the last entity that antebellum southerners would have authorized to control the nation's very weather, when whoever controlled it might as he pleased "enshroud us in continual clouds" or change navigable rivers into "rocks and shoals and sand-bars." When Espy's project first came before Congress in 1838, one southerner expressed doubt that it would work, but he also "doubted very much whether, even if this thing was possible, it would be good policy to encourage the measure."[194] Liberation from the elements seemed a poor achievement if it meant falling under a different despotism as a result.

A northern congressman jovially warned his colleagues in 1848 that "this House had better keep on the right side of Professor Espy." The clerk recorded a burst of laughter, but with its reminder of the power that weather control would give some over others it was not a remark to amuse everyone. It came amid the efforts of a number of southern congressmen to deprive Espy of his salary in the Navy Department. The money supported his basic research, not his dreams of applying it, but it was his "trying to regulate the storms," his peddling "projects for the regulation of storms and the creation of rain," for "regulating storms, making rain, and taking general charge of the weather" that his foes emphasized in the debate.[195] To southerners he would remain for years a symbol and a warning. "[S]uppose that we were to have the power of regulating the clouds, that they should rain in this place or that place, according to some system of Espy," observed Senator Andrew P. Butler of South Carolina in 1854, "I would not trust such a power to this Congress . . . Congress would be sure to make it rain in some places while they would deny it to others." "The power which has been claimed by Mr. Espy, of raising a cloud here, and making rain fall there," Butler would add in 1856, "is a power which none but God can rule with justice. . . . As long as you leave it to the temptation of selfish man . . . [i]t will go to make the rich richer and the poor poorer."[196]

Elite southerners such as Butler, hypersensitive to any danger of federal encroachment on their way of life, saw chiefly the likelihood that the weather would be manipulated with deliberate intent to harm them. Some other critics saw the dilemmas that rainmaking could create even if it were used with the best of intentions. One of them was the Philadelphia writer Eliza Leslie. She offered the most searching analysis of what Espy's techniques might mean for society in an incisive little story, "The Rain King; or, a Glance at the Next Century," published in *Godey's Lady's Book* in 1842.[197]

Leslie set her narrative in an America ostensibly of 1942, but little different from her own time in its life and livelihoods, in which a descendant of the Espy family had perfected the means of weather control. The inventor, "the rain king," set up his works west of Philadelphia and opened an office downtown. Petitioners could ask for rain at a given time or object to rain requested by another. The balance of their requests was to determine the weather to come. As the first day of business began, crowds of people were waiting outside the office to register their wishes.

Though Leslie was no meteorologist, her tale showed a far better grasp of weather's human dimensions and of the pitfalls of weather control than anything Espy ever wrote. She understood, for one thing, how the diversity of human interests in the weather made control a doubtful project at best. To the rain king's confusion, cabmen came to apply for a permanent downpour, parasol makers for constant sunshine, umbrella makers for frequent sudden showers. Cabbage farmers wanted rain at that time of year, melon and hay farmers wanted dry weather; the merchants of nearby Burlington, New Jersey, asked for a storm to keep the townspeople from traveling to Philadelphia for their shopping. Leslie understood too how many people might vote for weather on the most trivial grounds. The more democratic the means of decision, the more the outcome would be swayed by a bewildering range of desires and the less likely it was to correspond to some rational ideal. One group of children in the story wanted stormy weather to gain a holiday from school; another group wanted fair weather to enjoy a scheduled school picnic; a young bride wanted rain to keep her new husband at home with her, a society lady the same to keep away some unwanted visitors. Leslie understood how the actual results for society even of perfectly controlled weather would not be identical with the ones hoped for. The inventor tallied a narrow majority for rain and brought it down as requested. But the cabmen caught cold from exposure; when the umbrella makers began to profit, their employees went on strike for higher wages; the young husband, too long alone with his wife, quarreled with her; and the people of Burlington decided to stay at home altogether rather than shop locally.

Leslie grasped, finally, how the weather's artificial origin would change the way people regarded it. Those who did not want rain were far more furious when the rain king made it fall than they would have been had it arrived on its own. "Natural rains had never occasioned anything worse than submissive regret to those who suffered inconvenience from them . . . these artificial rains were taken more in anger than in sorrow by all who did not want them." The rain king's technique brought him a flood of complaints rather than a shower of thanks. At the close of the story, he surrendered his title until he could resolve a problem that had never worried him before: how "to furnish any individual with exactly as much rain as will suit that individual's own particular purpose, without infringing on the convenience of his neighbour." Next to that challenge, the technical one he had already solved was nothing, and until it was solved, the way he had discovered to control the weather was worth much less than he had supposed. What Leslie succeeded in saying in a short parable, another writer of the time said in a single line: "[I]f every one had their own way about the weather, we should have no weather at all"—or worse, he might have added, every kind at once.[198]

THREE

Postbellum America

Postbellum Migration

One of the earliest historians of the Civil War saw it as a fundamental clash between the peoples of different latitudes. Climate had made the antebellum North and South distinct societies and natural enemies, John W. Draper argued, the one democratic and individualist, the other aristocratic and oligarchical. If such were the case, the future of the reunited states was hardly a bright one. But Draper saw no natural barriers to national unity that wise policy could not surmount. The restlessness and transience of American life that many deplored instead merited, in his view, every assistance possible. In particular, he wrote, Americans needed to be encouraged to move as freely across climatic zones as they already did within them. The tendency of North and South to congeal into hostile types of civilization could be frustrated, but only by an incessant mingling of people. Sectional discord was inevitable only if the natural law that "emigrants move on parallels of latitude" were left free to take its course.[1]

These patterns of emigration were left free, for the most part, but without the renewed strife that Draper feared. After the war as before it, few settlers relocating to new homes moved far to the north or south of their points of origin. As late as 1895, Henry Gannett, chief geographer to the U.S. Census, could still describe internal migration as "mainly conducted westward along parallels of latitude."[2] More often as time went on, it was supposed that race and not merely habit underlay the pattern, that climatic preferences were innate, different stocks of people staying in the latitudes of their forbears by the compulsion of biology. Thus, it was supposed, Anglo-Saxons preferred cooler lands than Americans of Mediterranean ancestry, while those of African descent preferred warmer climates than either.

Over time, though, latitude loosened its grip and exceptions to the rule multiplied. As the share of the population in farming declined, so did the strongest reason for migrants to stay within familiar climates.

Even by the time Gannett wrote, the tendency that he described, though still apparent, was weaker than it had been at mid-century.[3] It weakened because a preference for familiar climates was not a fixed human trait but one shaped by experience and wants, and capable of changing as these variables changed.

Yet the notion that migration always and everywhere tended to follow latitudinal or isothermal lines remained for decades a part of common geographical literacy. Arguing for the purchase of Alaska from Russia in 1868, one congressman pointed out that because people changing their homes were "very likely to seek a climate something like the climate they have left," the new territory would quickly be filled with desirable immigrants from the same latitudes in the north of Europe. Another invoked the law "that emigration is apt to follow the line of latitude in which it starts" in opposing the purchase. Populous parts of Russia lay in the same parallels, he pointed out, but settlement from them had been minimal, clear evidence that Alaska had other crippling defects that had frustrated the natural tendency of movement. Why should the United States annex the Caribbean republic of Santo Domingo, asked Senator Charles Sumner in 1870, when few Americans would want to settle there? "Sometimes it is insisted that emigrants will hurry in large numbers to this tropical island once annexed," Sumner said, "but this allegation forgets that, according to the testimony of History, peaceful emigration travels with the sun on parallels of latitude, and not on meridians of longitude, mainly following the isothermal lines, and not taking-off at right angles, whether North or South."[4]

A national controversy arose in the late 1870s over the forced transfer of aboriginal nations far southward or northward to the Indian Territory (now Oklahoma) in order to open their lands for white occupation. Critics objected that it imposed an abrupt, unnatural, and unhealthful change of climate on those being resettled. It violated "the natural laws of emigration moving in the same parallel of latitude." That objection proved to be the strongest argument available to the nations and their supporters in resisting removal and the one by which the policy was finally discredited. The secretary of the interior who had authorized and defended the most controversial of the transfers later admitted that "great mistakes have been committed," and he belatedly endorsed the principle that "it is not good policy to remove Indians accustomed to a northern climate to this southern country."[5]

Though it was voluntary where the Indian Territory removals were not, the black "Exodus" from the cotton states to Kansas in 1879 and 1880 was just as widely seen as showing the hazards of too great and rapid a change in latitude.[6] The end of Reconstruction in 1877 withdrew the last federal restraints on white dominance in the South. In the early spring of 1879 thousands of southern blacks began moving west and north out of the old slave states. Most headed for Kansas. The "Exodus" slowed during the winter but resumed in force the next spring. By then it had aroused much debate in Congress and the press. Southerners and northern Democrats saw behind it a plot to deprive the cotton belt of its labor and swell the Republican vote in marginal northern states. Republicans retorted that the Exodus was the predictable result of southern mistreatment of the black population.

Both sides agreed that the movement ran contrary to the natural tendency of migration. They drew different lessons from that conclusion. That the emigrants would relocate so improbably from the sunny Deep South to the bleak plains of Kansas proved to the Democrats that they had been tricked by propaganda, heartlessly deceived by outsiders as to the conditions that awaited them.[7] The fact that the "Exodusters" had undertaken such a drastic and painful change of climate proved to Republicans just how painful must have been their oppression at home. One New England senator likened their sufferings in the Kansas winter to those of the Pilgrims in their first year at Plymouth. A song celebrated the Exodusters's heroism with a different parallel from history: "Whence came these dusky legions, / Braving the wintry wind? / For our snow-bound, icy regions / These fleeing, dusky legions / Leave a summer-land behind. . . . They fly from the land that bore them, / As the Hebrews fled from Nile . . . From a serfdom base and vile."[8] Frederick Douglass sympathized with the Exodusters's motives but thought their migration north unwise. Urging would-be emigrants to remain in the South and fight for their rights there, he thought it foolish of them to disregard the great universal law of successful human migration: that it "proceeds not from North to South, not from heat to cold, but from East to West, and in climates to which the emigrants are more or less adapted and accustomed."[9]

Most of the Exodusters indeed found the change of climate a painful one, and their experiences did not encourage the mass of black southerners to follow.[10] They suffered from inadequate clothing and shelter in the winter cold; their skills lay in growing cotton and were of little value on the Great Plains. Better-off migrants to Kansas equally unfamiliar with the climate fared better, having more resources for coping with its surprises.

For even northern settlers on the Plains found many surprises awaiting them. Avoiding a change of latitude, they discovered, did not guarantee them an unchanged climate. Latitude had proved a reasonable guide to climate in the trans-Appalachian West. It was widely expected to do the same beyond the Mississippi.[11] It proved little more reliable than it had been in early colonial times along the eastern seaboard. Plains settlers, like the transatlantic pioneers of the seventeenth century, found heat and cold far more extreme than they had previously known: lengthy spells of summer temperatures exceeding a hundred degrees and of subzero cold in winter made more brutal by high winds, storms more sudden and violent, and tornadoes more frequent than to the east.

As on earlier frontiers, the increased hardship was not simply a matter of weather. The same weather was more dangerous on the thinly peopled Plains than in more populous rural districts to the east. The chances for nearby employment off the farm to balance the risks of harvest failure were fewer. Wood for fuel at least had been plentiful on earlier frontiers. It was scarce on the treeless Plains, though the dugout and sod houses many settlers built gave better shelter than the draftier "sawed houses" that most preferred to construct as soon as they could.[12]

But new stoves were devised that burned hay or corn cobs, until the

FIGURE 3.1. Two devices for coping with the climate of the Great Plains: a late nineteenth-century South Dakota sod house and windmill, photographed in the 1930s.

railroads made coal available at reasonable prices. Newcomers to the Plains would comment on "how terrible is the wind, the incessant wind that fills the air with dust, irritates the eye, and dins monotonously upon the ears." "'I would not talk that way about the wind,' replied the old settler, 'it is our best friend."[13] Surface water was scanty, but windmills helped farmers tap groundwater for domestic use and livestock. Anything, indeed, that made water easier to obtain was welcomed, for the most important change that settlers experienced as they moved west was not in temperature but in precipitation.

If immigrants from a desert had settled on the Great Plains, Walter Prescott Webb suggested, they would not have described the land as dry.[14] They would have had to find ways of coping with too much rainfall rather than too little. Because postbellum settlers came mostly from the humid East, they judged the rainfall deficient, not only on the Plains but in most of the United States beyond the Mississippi. Coastal Washington and Oregon were wetter than much of the Atlantic seaboard, and high in the mountains rain and snowfall were substantial, but the distinction between a more humid East and a drier West held generally true. In 1878, the government survey geologist John Wesley Powell identified the boundary between them as roughly the hundredth meridian of longitude, running approximately through the center of Nebraska. To the west, the average rainfall was less than twenty inches a year, too little, Powell presumed, for normal agriculture. Even in a sizable zone to the east, he thought, with a rainfall between twenty and twenty-eight inches, farming would be precarious at best.[15] In large areas of the Far West, the average rainfall, in the best informed opinion of the time, was less than ten inches. Evaporation, moreover, was high and rainfall highly variable from year to year.

By the time Powell wrote, farming had already spread farther west than he thought safe. It had been preceded onto the Plains along and beyond the hundredth meridian by open-range grazing. The stockmen, cowboys, and longhorns who expelled the aborigines and buffalo themselves lived under the threat of expulsion by farmers. The low and undependable rainfall was for them a nuisance—drought meant scanty grass and dry water holes—that was also a blessing of sorts. The less inviting the climate, the less stockmen needed to fear an influx of farmers fencing and plowing their best grasslands. The influx indeed came, for land was invitingly cheap and abundant on the central and western Plains. Those who settled there hoped for the most part to re-create the rain-fed corn and livestock agriculture or wheat growing that most had practiced in the east. A drier climate, when they recognized it, was a liability and a challenge to be overcome.

Water

If the West was indeed too dry, the most direct solution to the problem was to change the climate. The means suggested for doing so included planting forests and creating large lakes to moisten the air, for both were widely thought to be as much the causes as the consequences of a wet climate.[16] By the early 1870s, scattered rainfall records and the testimony of the older settlers suggested that the rainfall on the Plains was increasing already. Neither forest nor water surface had yet spread so far and fast that it could be credited with the change. The explanation that became most popular attributed it to the widespread breaking and cultivation of the tough prairie sod. Rain that had once run off into the streams now soaked into the broken ground, and its reevaporation increased humidity and precipitation. Thus agriculture itself could produce the very conditions that it needed. Charles Dana Wilber, a land promoter, gave this comforting idea its classic statement: "Rain," he declared, "follows the plow."[17]

Evidence that such a change was taking place accumulated for two decades after the Civil War, despite occasional droughts. Western railroads and state and territorial agencies actively promoted the idea in order to attract settlers. A number of government scientists lent their support to the belief that John Wesley Powell's boundary was not the fixed line he supposed it to be, that the "rainbelt" was moving west.[18] Other scientists, along with open-range grazing and irrigation interests, scoffed at the notion of a changing climate on the Plains. Powell himself was especially loud in deriding the idea, for it was his fixed conviction that "[n]othing that man can do will change the climate."[19] Equally loud were others who knew that such change would be for the worse for them: irrigation interests, who would see their investments made valueless; open-range stockmen threatened by an influx of farmers into their grasslands.

The harsh winters of 1885–86 and 1886–87 largely destroyed the open-range cattle industry as it had existed. Though they are remembered as brutally severe, in meteorological terms they were not unprecedented on the postbellum Plains. It was their effects that were worse because the industry was more vulnerable by the mid-1880s than in the past. With fencing by farmers and overstocking of the range, the land and the grass available for grazing had dwindled.[20] The weather savaged the farmers next, in a series of epic droughts that struck in the late 1880s and the early and mid-1890s and largely answered the question of whether the climate had been transformed.

If droughts could not be broken, still their impacts on farmers might be softened. It could not be done through private insurance. The climate was too poorly known for the chances of drought to be calculated, and Plains farmers were too much jointly at risk to bear one another's losses. Public or private aid might be extended instead to those hardest hit. Yet westerners were of two minds in times of crisis about asking for help from elsewhere or furnishing it themselves.[21] To acknowledge that the crops had failed was to admit that the rainfall was unreliable and discourage further settlement and investment. States providing aid were careful to insist that the dry spell that had occasioned it was a freak misfortune. "The soil and climate are excellent," ran one such formula, "and with proper assistance the citizens of these counties will be able to cultivate their farms."[22]

If a chronic shortage of water was the problem, emergency aid was no solution. No one supposed that charity would or should keep a large population living in an area too dry for its subsistence. If recurrent drought made successful farming on the Plains impossible, as some took the events of the period to mean, then the farmers were in the wrong place and should move elsewhere. Many did. Perhaps three hundred thousand settlers fled the region in the early and mid-1890s. Many counties west of Powell's line lost half or more of their population.[23]

Drought was not the only cause of the exodus. Its impacts on farmers were mingled disastrously with those of low crop prices, national economic crisis beginning in 1893, and mortgage debt made heavier by deflation. Still, the great outflow seemed to vindicate the arguments that Powell had long been making. His first thesis—less controversial by the early 1890s than it had once been—was that westerners would have to adapt to the climate rather than hope to change it. More controversial was what Powell assumed adaptation must mean. A small portion of the region, he announced, could grow crops under irrigation; the rest must return to rangeland grazing as its mainstay.[24]

To say so was to say that the region beyond the hundredth meridian could support only a scanty population. The conclusion did not appeal to westerners, and it proved less solid than Powell imagined, for not all farmers needed the twenty inches of rain a year that he thought indispensable. Wheat flourished on the Columbia River Plain in the inland Northwest on far less rainfall. There good soils and the ideal timing of the rains with respect to the crop season offset the scantiness of precipitation. The climate proved so little a handicap that many farmers were convinced that their efforts had changed it for the better.[25]

Growing different crops might turn the climate of other regions from a problem to an advantage for agriculture. One group of settlers who reached the Great Plains in the 1870s showed how. They were emigrants from Russia whose German forbears had lived for a century on the sub-humid Volga steppes. To Anglo-American farmers, the Plains climate was drier than normal. To the Russian Germans, it was normal. To it they brought a farming system that had served for generations in a similar environment. A diversity of crops lessened the risks of failure in any one of them, and staples such as hard winter wheat fared better on the plains than the corn or the wheat varieties that Americans from the Midwest tried to grow.[26] Once Anglo-Americans adopted hard winter wheat themselves, the central Plains climate changed from a hazard to a resource. It was more suited to the new crop than were wetter climates conventionally classified as superior for agriculture.[27]

Another set of adaptations allowed cultivation to expand, more precariously, on the northern central Plains into Montana, again far beyond the boundary that Powell had set. What came to be known as dry farming emphasized the long fallowing of land and the loosening of topsoil to build up moisture between a surface mulch and a compacted lower layer.[28] Dry farming, promoted by a coalition of scientists and commercial, farming, and railroad interests, promised to make the settler "practically independent of the clouds."[29]

The promise could not be kept in full, though, and the weather could still inflict severe losses. Dry farming overextended itself on the Northern Plains, incurring another disaster of drought and depopulation in the years around World War I. It was irrigation that offered the agreeable prospect of a western agriculture, even in areas too dry for dry farming, better buffered against drought than agriculture in the humid east was. A lively reclamation movement arose in the late 1880s and 1890s whose estimates of the West's irrigable area far exceeded Powell's. Guarantee what the weather would not—a steady supply of water—argued the reclamationists, and the latent natural advantages of the West—abundant land, more sunshine, richer soils—would come into their own.[30]

Irrigation had already served some as a hedge against the possible failure of the rainfall to increase. The area of Western cropland watered by private companies grew tenfold between 1870 and 1890 to more than 3 million acres.[31] California in 1887 pioneered the irrigation district, a public entity with the power to condemn land, issue bonds, and impose taxes for hydraulic works. Other states followed its example. The Reclamation Act, passed by Congress in 1902 after more than a decade of western campaigning, earmarked the proceeds from public land sales in the dry states for more irrigation projects, their cost in turn to be repaid by the settlers using their water. Though easterners wondered why irrigated farming was being force-fed when prices for eastern crops were low already, they wondered to no avail.[32]

Federal reclamation, on the whole, was not a success. By 1918, its ambitious projects still served only a small fraction of the West's irrigated land. There was already widespread dissatisfaction among project farmers with the management of the work, and many were having a far harder time than expected in beginning their repayments. Costs had proved much higher than the propagandists had forecast and income much lower.[33]

Conversely, private and district irrigation enterprises flourished, but it was with the clearest success of anyone that some other westerners stopped fighting aridity as a hazard or a constraint and embraced it as a resource for non-agricultural pursuits. No better remedy was known for tuberculosis, the leading cause of death in postbellum America, than relocation to a drier climate. Western states and territories, especially Colorado, California, Arizona, and New Mexico, had dry air in abundance, and they promoted it vigorously. Health-seekers, by one calculation, made up from a fifth to a quarter of the migration to the Southwest from 1870 to 1900. They were responsible for much of the postbellum growth in such California towns as Los Angeles, San Diego, San Bernardino, Santa Barbara, Redlands, and Palm Springs.[34]

By late in the century, the states and territories of the region were already actively shooing away the health-seekers whom they had once tried to attract.[35] Californians went so far as to discuss quarantining all incoming tuberculosis patients or barring them from the state outright. The presence of too many coughing consumptives, they now feared, would interfere with the marketing of the climate to the healthy immigrant. They were learning that they could sell dry air not just to a narrow clientele of "lungers" but to all of the United States as an amenity of life. Once the climate was viewed in this way, it was not the West that had too little water but the rest of the country that had too much.

In 1873, a Los Angeles booster named J. P. Widney had proposed that the city create an artificial lake in the nearby Colorado Desert in order to moisten the atmosphere and free the region from the curse of aridity.[36] A mere two decades later, there was more fear that Los Angeles might be blighted by the curse of humidity. In the summer and fall of 1891, heavy rainfall and flooding created the inland sea in question, and with rain continuing for some time, it seemed to be having the effects that Widney had promised. John Wesley Powell took the talk about "the new lake in the desert" to be more wishful thinking by that "class of publicists . . . who are forever presenting schemes for the amelioration of hard climatic conditions," but in fact the reaction in

Los Angeles was less rejoicing than dismay. Even Widney now admitted that the change would make the region "less agreeable for residence" though better for farming. If the climate were to become "more humid than heretofore," asked a newspaper, if the nights were to become "so close, humid, and oppressive that one could easily imagine himself in New York or Indiana," asked one concerned citizen, who would move to southern California? If the new lake meant more "moist, 'sticky' heat" in the summer, declared the *Los Angeles Times*, "we don't want it at any price."[37]

The growth of an urban West, though helped by the dryness of the climate, created the new challenge of meeting ever-growing demands of municipal water supply. Yet in some ways the challenge was easier met than in the East. The more apparent a scarcity of water, the more effort was likely to be invested in overcoming it. In cities as large as Oakland and Denver, competing companies waged "water wars," undercutting each other's prices to the point of sometimes providing service for free.[38] In Los Angeles—by the time of the First World War the largest city in the region—boosterist fears that shortage would throttle growth kept the city proposing and the voters approving measures that kept supplies far ahead of use.[39]

That the East received more reliable rainfall than the West and lost less of it to evaporation did not guarantee it a water supply adequate to its wants. A shortage is an excess of wants over supply. Water is scarce, not when there is too little by some absolute physical standard, but when there is less than would-be users would like to have. It can be scarcer where it is relatively abundant—if competing wants are high and numerous, as they were in the East—than in a drier region where wants are fewer or supply is more efficient. With an increase in demand, supplies can become scarcer and a region effectively more arid even without a shift to a drier climate.

Many easterners feared that just such a shift was taking place around them. The belief that the West could be moistened by forest planting had a darker side: areas now well-watered might become drier as a result of reckless clearing. Preservationists warned that the climate would deteriorate and rainfall diminish if the forests of the East were not protected.[40] In wet years, it could be a matter for jokes. Steady dampness, alternating with "plenty of drizzle, mist and fog," and "nine days of continuous rain," wrote a journalist in 1878, had led many to conclude that "the business of tree planting has been shockingly overdone."[41] In dry periods, it was cause for serious concern. In 1882, the governor of New York warned that crises lay ahead if logging in the Adirondack Mountains were not curtailed: "The rainfalls will diminish, the springs and streams fail," depriving mills and canal boats and cities of the water that they needed.[42]

Urban water crises indeed occurred, but the reason did not lie in a deteriorating climate. As the number of municipal waterworks grew rapidly, householders and businesses found many new uses to make of their new supplies. Several devices greatly increased the pressure of demand: the bathtub, the shower, and the water closet. Not only cleanliness, but health benefited greatly; typhoid fever and other water-borne diseases declined; urban cholera epidemics became a thing of the past.[43] Firefighters enjoyed a larger and more reliable water supply. The rise in water use was emphatically a change for the better, but in city-weather relations it created new problems. Populations and per capita consumption alike grew more rapidly than expected. Save along the Great Lakes and the largest rivers, supplies, without diminishing, became less and less adequate to the demands placed on them, and any drought of a given magnitude became more and more of a problem. As use neared the limits of existing supplies, any dry spell threatened cities with a new danger for which the new term "water famine" came into general use. Their menace arose most often in summer and early fall, when both consumption and evaporation losses were highest.

New York City was located in a far more humid climate than Los Angeles, but it was New York that water famines threatened again and again.[44] Numerous enlargements in the supply were overwhelmed by growth in use. A particularly severe drought set in during the summer of 1881, and by late October, only two weeks's supply remained in the reservoirs before the weather finally relented and refilled them. The late fall of 1891 saw the city helpless again before an approaching failure of the system, with only a week's supply left by mid-November, before rain averted a famine for the moment and the completion of an enlarged system put one off for somewhat longer.[45] Curbing consumption was a measure reserved for such emergencies, however; metering was confined to commercial users; the city's preferred response was always to increase the supply. An expansion dwarfing all of the previous ones was undertaken in the Catskill Mountains with the construction of the Ashokan Reservoir, begun in 1907 and completed in 1917, a decade marked by another series of recurring water crises.

Water in Excess: The Flood Hazard

If too little water was one of postbellum America's recurring problems, too much was another. Efforts to store water against dry seasons gave rise to the most violent floods of the period, for as dams grew larger and more numerous, so did dam collapses and the devastation that they caused. The first catastrophic reservoir flood in the United States occurred in 1874 in western Massachusetts. Heavy rain washed out a badly built power dam; the water it had impounded swept over the towns below, killing 143 people and destroying a million dollars's worth of property. The failure of a poorly maintained dam on the Conemaugh River above Johnstown, Pennsylvania, in a heavy downpour in 1889 claimed more than two thousand lives.[46]

These and smaller disasters of the same kind were rare and exceptional events. Far more frequent were floods that occurred when large rivers swelled over their banks. The worst of them for destructiveness and disruption had no precedents in the American past. The years between the Civil War and World War I saw many severe floods on the Mississippi, those of 1882 and 1912 surpassing the rest. Large parts of the Ohio River Valley in 1884, Kansas City in 1903, Pittsburgh in 1907, and Dayton in 1913 were submerged with heavy losses of life and property. Smaller but still damaging inundations elsewhere were numerous. As the geologist and conservationist W J McGee observed in 1891, society seemed to have made great strides during the nineteenth century in taming four of its ancient adversaries—fire, famine, war, and pestilence—but the fifth, floods, had, if anything, become more harmful than ever.[47]

Many supposed that if flood damage was increasing, floods them-

FIGURE 3.2. Thicker occupation of floodplains intensified losses from floods in postbellum cities. The Maumee River inundates Toledo, Ohio, in early 1883.

selves must have become larger and more frequent. Either, thanks to
forest cutting, the rain came in heavier bursts than in the past, or—a
more widespread belief—changes in the land had changed for the
worse what happened to the rain after it fell. Once, the argument went,
the protective forest cover had checked runoff and moderated the flow
of streams. With the forest gone, the water flowed promptly from the
hillslopes into the swollen channels, and the rivers rose higher and
faster than before. Conservationists urged that existing forests be protected and vanished ones replanted to guard lands downstream and
avoid worse disasters in the future.

Yet there was little solid evidence that floods were any higher or
more frequent than in former times. A bitter turn-of-the-century debate pitted forest conservationsts against engineers, hydrologists, and
meteorologists who assembled and analyzed long-term records of
flooding and streamflow to show that increased extremes were not apparent even where much deforestation had taken place.[48] They might
become so in the future, but times of extraordinarily high water in
great river systems remained largely the work of the weather. The engineers understood better than the advocates of reforesting did the
chief reason why damage was on the rise. "Care should be taken," one
of them observed, "not to ascribe to increasing flood heights or fre-
quencies losses which are due to Man's operations in placing property
in the way of floods." "It is true," another wrote to like effect, "that
floods produce greater disaster and suffering than in years past, but this
is due solely to the fact that the population in the overflow areas had increased, and many great industrial improvements have been built up
directly in the face of the fact that the ground occupied was subject to
serious overflow."[49]

No river has ever flooded the same town twice, and most postbellum urban land exposed to high water grew more crowded with people
and buildings from one flood to the next. Railroad builders preferred
the low grades of water-level routes. Industry was tied closely to the
railroads and the flat land of the floodplains. Factory employees, need-
ing to live close to their place of work, settled in the same low-lying
areas. It was the exposed floodplain, McGee noted, "on which the modern city is located, the flat lowland over which the engineer builds railways, the zone upon which population is massed."[50] Rapid industrial
growth in postbellum Kansas City created a railroad-factory-working-
class housing complex in the bottom lands that was devastated by high
water in the late spring of 1903. An even larger overflow in the same
area, the engineer Hiram M. Chittenden pointed out, had occurred in
1844. "The damage was insignificant, because there was little property

there"; in 1903 the damage was immense because of the development of the area in the intervening years.[51] Intensified use of exposed areas was not a trend limited to cities. Cotton cultivation in the lower Mississippi floodplain boomed in the late nineteenth century, thanks to favorable world prices and to railroad development, thereby multiplying the lives and the property at risk from the river.[52]

Engineers themselves were divided over the best means of flood protection. Some advocated clearing river outlets and straightening channels to speed discharge to the sea. Some favored upstream reservoirs to impound water in times of heavy rainfall. Others judged levees along the riverbanks the only feasible mode of protection. Most shared one conviction with one another and with most forestry advocates: that flood damage was best reduced by controlling the water's behavior.

Levees lining the streambanks were the means most widely used. They were built and maintained largely under state laws and paid for by assessments on the property they protected. They were never as strong or as high as those living behind them would have liked, and they were never adequate in the worst floods. Those who relied on them looked hungrily at the federal treasury for the means of making good their deficiencies. Resistance to centralization remained the political philosophy of the post-Reconstruction as of the antebellum South. When it came to federal help for flood control, though, the statesmen of the lower Mississippi basin were broad-minded enough to make an exception.[53]

When heavy spring rains in the upper basin produced disastrous floods downstream in the 1870s, the states affected called loudly for help from Washington in taming the boisterous river. Challenged to show that the federal government possessed any right to act in the matter, members of Congress from Louisiana used all of the arguments that on other occasions southerners were accustomed to denounce as sophistry. They found the needed authority in a striking number and variety of places in the Constitution. They found it in the federal responsibility for the postal service, which floods interrupted, just as they interrupted interstate commerce, which Congress had the authority to regulate; they found it in the command that the federal government provide for the "common defense." "Now, what is meant by 'common defense'? It means defense against an enemy too great and powerful for a state. . . . Defense from one is as imperative as from another, whether it be a foreign enemy or a national river which is making war upon our citizens."[54]

By means of such wordplay, as southerners themselves often had occasion to point out, there was no power that Congress could not be shown to possess. Northern newspapers charged the advocates of flood control with inconsistency and expressed the hope that in future no more would be heard from that region about strict construction of federal powers.[55] Some southerners from states beyond the river's reach held to their old views. Senator John Morgan of Alabama declared himself unwilling to tear down the Constitution in order to build up the levees.[56] Northerners, for their part, could assert the existence of broad national authority without having to favor its use in any particular case. Thinking the costs of flood control better charged on those who reaped the benefits than on the entire country, they succeeded in keeping the assigned task of the federal Mississippi River Commission, created in 1879, limited to improvements for navigation.[57]

Most of the debate concerned how overflows should be prevented and by whom. Only a few opponents of federal involvement went beyond the claim that Washington might not constitutionally straitjacket the river to assert that it physically could not do it. The Mississippi would "set at naught and laugh to scorn all efforts to confine or control it," predicted one senator; "excuse me," said another, "if I express a doubt whether the tinkering of man with that stream is going to do it any good."[58] The prevalent philosophy was that tinkering could do immense good. Over time, northerners became increasingly willing to make it a national project, and the work of the Mississippi River Commission more and more became flood control still thinly masked as navigation improvements. Losses were so large, suffering so great, and the disorganization of society so extreme after the worst floods that doing something seemed imperative. Protection seemed the only feasible measure to take. The alternative was regulating floodplain settlement and use, but postbellum Americans treated human migration and land use as ungovernable forces of nature that had to be accepted, the forces of nature themselves as subject to law and regulation.

On the former point, in the political and legal climate of the period, they were not wrong. There was no precedent for land-use control of the kind that would have been necessary to lessen flood damage. On the latter point they were not entirely wrong either. Flood protection measures were not futile. The Mississippi levees, though they failed in the greatest floods, held in smaller ones. The seawall erected after the disastrous 1900 Galveston hurricane prevented comparable death and destruction from high water during later storms. When in 1917 Congress passed the first measure explicitly putting the federal government into the business of controlling floods, on the Mississippi and Sacramento rivers, history as well as theory gave it some cause for confidence in the outcome.

Even before committing itself to flood control, Congress many times appropriated money for flood relief.[59] It first did so in the early 1880s, allocating several hundred thousand dollars to help sufferers along the Mississippi and Ohio rivers. The federal relief appropriation after the Mississippi flood of 1912 totaled a million and a half dollars. Such assistance was open to the same objections as national spending for flood control, and its growth responded to the same imperatives. Even its supporters freely admitted that it might well be unconstitutional, but they pronounced it unthinkable to stand by and not offer help after disasters of such size.[60]

But even the supporters of such appropriations meant only for them to supplement state aid and private giving, not to displace these traditional sources of relief after floods and other calamities. The most notable change in disaster assistance occurred outside of the government sector. In 1881, a national agency funded entirely by private donations assumed the task of providing succor following disasters. The United States Red Cross, under its founding president, Clara Barton, set itself the goal of restoring the life and livelihoods of the communities affected in as short a time as possible. Floods in 1882 and 1884 along the Mississippi and Ohio rivers first allowed the Red Cross to demonstrate its effectiveness.[61]

Thus physical protection from floods, and emergency aid when protection failed, improved, but only modest progress was possible so long as they remained the chief responses. As losses grew, there was no serious challenge to the main cause of their growth: the thicker settlement of areas exposed to high water. That losses rose does not mean that such settlement was not on the whole a profitable one. The costs of forgoing settlement would doubtless have been greater than the losses actually incurred, but they would have been experienced in a different and milder form than the death and suffering and disruption following great floods.

Forecasting the Weather

Beginning in the late 1870s, Americans had a new tool for coping with rising water: forecasts of flood heights issued by the Army Signal Service. Farmers given warning could move their livestock to safe ground. River towns and cities could raise and strengthen their levees, if they had any. But little else could be done with the official predictions that could not have been done already. The railroads and telegraph lines, the docks, warehouses, factories, and houses that encroached ever more thickly on floodplains could not be moved out of reach. Overall, the warnings were a minor factor among the postbellum trends altering flood losses. In that sense, they were like much of the forecasting that was made possible when a national weather service was created after the Civil War.

In 1870, an act of Congress made the Signal Service responsible for taking meteorological observations and issuing storm warnings on the Great Lakes and the seacoast. Its duties were extended in 1872 to collecting observations and issuing warnings and weather predictions for the United States generally. Over the next two decades the Signal Service also began to monitor streamflow, forecast floods and crop harvests, and conduct meteorological and climatological research. A reorganization of activities in 1891 created the United States Weather Bureau, a civilian office within the Department of Agriculture.[62]

The collection of data on the weather already past was valuable in its own right. As records accumulated, weather insurance became feasible, for risks could be better estimated; engineering and water supply works could be better adjusted to likely extremes. The service's short-term forecasts and warnings attracted much more public attention but did not do as much to weaken the weather's impacts as might have been hoped, less because they were often incorrect than because they were often of little use. Slow communications hampered efforts to get them in timely fashion to those at risk, and many of those at risk could do little even when warned well in advance of approaching threats. The possibility that the weather is a hazard mainly because it is a surprise received its first serious test in these years. Better foreknowledge proved in many places a help but nowhere a panacea.

High-wind warnings for ships were the service's earliest product. For a long time, they were its most useful one, not just because shipping was exceptionally sensitive to storms, but because forecasts of storms were exceptionally easy to transmit in good time to shipmasters. Large signal flags, red with a black center, hoisted near the docks and along the ocean and Great Lakes coasts gave plain notice of oncoming foul weather. Double flags warned of especially violent winds. The annual loss in tonnage and lives on the Great Lakes, where the data are most reliable, steadily diminished as a proportion of the total exposed after 1870, and the share of loss associated with bad weather itself dropped sharply.[63]

Warnings appeared and losses fell, but not necessarily as cause and effect, any more than the rise in flood losses after the appearance of flood warnings meant that the warnings had made matters worse. Many other factors tended in the same direction: the ongoing change to steam from sail and from wood to metal hulls, safer design of fishing schooners, better fog signals and separate steamer lanes to lessen the chances of collision, more lifeboats, the creation of more life-saving service stations and harbors of refuge and of canals that provided shortened and sheltered passages around coasts risky in storm and fog. When such factors are removed, as a careful study has shown, the results remain impressive. The dollar savings that can be credited to storm warnings on the Great Lakes alone in the 1870s and 1880s exceed severalfold the cost of all operations of the federal weather service during that period.[64]

Warnings, though, were useful only when they were heeded. They would have been even more effective had not shipmasters often been unwilling or unable to pay attention. Those away from land at the time of a storm remained unprotected, for the warnings could not reach them. But even captains given ample notice of bad weather often felt obliged to set out nonetheless. The pressure for regular operations imposed by business conditions increased the potential for conflict with the weather. "The mail steamers do not, of course, let any adverse forecasts prevent their sailing," observed a New York newspaper in 1898. "Their owners cannot afford to. These vessels are scheduled to leave port at a certain hour, and when that hour arrives the mail contracts, express business, and indeed the passengers themselves demand that the steamer shall proceed at the time agreed upon."[65] The same held true of many other carriers.

Usually they got away with it, but not always. Warnings assuredly prevented many disasters, but the worst ones that did occur were not the result of forecasting errors. The coastal passenger steamer *Portland* went to pieces with the loss of 176 lives in a great autumn gale off Cape Cod in 1898. Red flags were flying at the Boston docks hours before her departure, but the captain had preferred to take his chances with the weather rather than with the schedule.[66] The gale of November 1913 on the Great Lakes was announced days in advance with signals at all of the major ports, yet it claimed a dozen freighters and more than two hundred lives. Late fall, when the fiercest storms occurred, was also so close to the winter closing of navigation that time afloat was especially precious and warnings apt to be shrugged off. A bureau forecaster spoke for many in casting the blame for the storm's toll on "the gross neglect, carelessness and greed of shipowners who demand that their ships make as many trips as possible, regardless of weather."[67]

Agricultural interests—farmers, shippers, and commodity dealers—were helped chiefly by cold wave and frost warnings.[68] Fruit growers, alerted of an approaching frost, could take measures to protect their crops. Cranberry growers maintained reservoirs of water with which to flood the bogs and save the crop from frost. Citrus growers could deploy heaters to keep the trees from freezing and smudgepots to lessen radiational cooling. Tobacco, if ready, could be cut and stored in heated barns, sugarcane cut and stacked in windrows, protecting all but the top layer. Packers and shippers of perishable produce could hold it back in heated warehouses; market gardeners and florists around cities could heat their beds and greenhouses.

Yet getting the warnings to farmers in time to be of use was no easy task. The first means tried ranged from steam whistle blasts to postcards to flags bearing the cold wave symbol—white with a black square in the center—flown from trains passing through the threatened area. None proved satisfactory. "[B]efore this information has been brought to the farmer," the bureau's chief lamented in the early 1890s, "much time has been lost, and that, too, in a matter where time is of the utmost consequence." He saw no chance that communication would ever become swift enough to make the next-day forecasts as valuable in practice to farmers as they were in potential. "The delays in publication and transmission remaining constant, as they must," he wrote, the only hope for improvement lay in scientific advances that would make two-day forecasts reliable.[69]

Even when warnings were received, they were useful only within a narrow range of temperatures. Severe freezes in Florida during the winter of 1894–95 were immensely destructive, warnings or none, because they far exceeded the citrus growers's ability to protect their trees. They all but wiped out the state's orange groves, which were concentrated in the northern part of the state, and they prompted responses to the frost hazard more effective than taking emergency actions on the basis of short-term warnings: moving production southward, exploiting better the local frost protection offered by lakes and hills, and planting hardier varieties.[70]

Even perfect forecasting of hailstorms would scarcely have lessened their impacts, so little could be done to protect crops against them. The bureau's forecasts of heat waves were less useful than its cold-wave predictions, not because heat waves were less harmful but because there were fewer ways to soften their effects.[71] Losses of life and property from tornadoes, which the Weather Bureau did not attempt to predict, unmistakably increased. As with floods, some took the trend to mean that tornadoes themselves were becoming more common. As the bureau pointed out, it was rather the result of increased exposure. There were more people and towns and property than ever before in the regions where most tornadoes occurred, but apart from the building of tornado cellars there had been no corresponding increase in protection.[72]

The Gulf and Atlantic seaboards remained subject as before to severe coastal storms—hurricanes in the fall and northeasters in the winter and spring. The most deadly and destructive storms of the period were two hurricanes that landed in South Carolina and Louisiana in the fall of 1893 and a third that struck Galveston, Texas in 1900—the storm usually counted as the most lethal weather disaster in American history. That the Weather Bureau forecast them all—albeit, in 1900, underestimating the height of the storm surge—did not prevent them all from doing tremendous harm. Most of the loss of life in 1893 was on offshore islands out of reach of the warnings and most exposed to high wind and water. Galveston was on a low-lying barrier island from which a speedy escape for most residents was impossible. The growth of population and property in exposed areas did more to increase damage than storm warnings did to lessen it. But areas devastated by the severest storms after 1881—tornadoes as well as hurricanes—also benefited from the relief and reconstruction services of the Red Cross.[73]

The Weather Bureau had particularly bad luck in forecasting some major blizzards of the period. If anything embarrassed it more than the forecast of "slightly warmer, fair weather, followed by rain" for the day the great Northeastern blizzard of March 1888 began, it was the similar forecast with a similar aftermath volunteered by the head of the bureau for inauguration day in the capital in 1909.[74] But again, other trends did far more than good predictions could have done to change the effects of urban blizzards. Following major snowstorms, northeastern newspapers were quick to draw comparisons with earlier events and ask whether society was becoming more or less vulnerable. Pessimists rightly cited the tendency of people to reside ever farther from work, depend on transportation that snow blocked, and, unlike their rural forbears, live "hand to mouth," taking daily deliveries of necessities such as milk and coal and bread: "With the growing complexity of civilized life the greater is the dependence of man on appliances which are at the mercy of the elements." Optimists just as correctly pointed to the replacement of ferries by bridges, of streetcars by elevated railroads in the largest cities and their replacement in turn by subways, and of hand shoveling by mechanical snow clearance, while other improvements in the making seemed likely, as one editionalist put it, to "weather-proof" human life still further.[75] Both sides had a point. The impacts of snowstorms were becoming both greater and weaker, but forecasts were among the least of the factors responsible.

The Age of Electricity

Embarrassed by several great snowstorms that it had not predicted, the Weather Bureau suffered from them a second time over. Its operations depended heavily on the telegraph. They were all but shut down when heavy snow, ice, or high winds felled intra- and intercity wires. Interrupted too, with much greater loss and disruption, were other intensive users of telegraph communications: stock and commodity exchanges, fire and police signal systems. It was one more set of snowstorm impacts that even accurate forecasts did little to reduce.

What could have eliminated them was burying the telegraph lines out of the weather's reach. By the 1880s, there was already much agitation in New York and elsewhere to have the great skeins of wires that festooned the streets and spread over the lower rooftops banished to conduits running underground. Overhead telegraph wires were disliked chiefly for their ugliness and their interference with fire-fighting operations, but the havoc wrought by storms did nothing to weaken the call for a change. Its advocates pointed out how much recurring trouble would be avoided if communications were not left exposed to the elements. As proof that the change could be made, they pointed to Germany, where all intracity wires and the main intercity connections, eight thousand miles of them by the beginning of the 1880s, ran underground, making them "completely secure against the vagaries of the weather."[76] But the example itself suggested why a similar rebuilding of the American network was unlikely soon. The telegraph was a government concern in imperial Germany, and the priorities of the state dictated its management. First among them was ensuring its reliable operation against all of the mishaps, from storms to sabotage, that could befall it aboveground. In the United States, telegraphy was a private business, and burying the wires, the companies insisted, would be expensive far beyond any possible benefits.

Only the largest cities, notably New York and Chicago, succeeded in imposing the change. Even they remained liable to lose their long-distance connections so long as the cross-country links ran through the open air. East Coast storms in 1904 and 1909 had no less impact on intercity contact than those of the post–Civil War decades. Only in 1914 could signs of progress be seen. A just-completed underground wire, running the hundreds of miles from Washington to Boston through New York, kept cable links from breaking down entirely during an early March blizzard.[77]

The weather did not have to fell the cables to obstruct service, though better insulators and lightning arresters reduced interference by atmospheric electricity. "The wires and pole lines have been gradually improved," an expert wrote in 1907, "and telegrams are less delayed by the effect of storms than ever before. . . . [I]n the not distant future an interruption of communication by storms will be a rare occurrence."[78] It remained far from rare, and storms had long since begun to interrupt other services provided through overhead wires.

"If the present be termed the 'age of steam,'" one writer had observed in the mid nineteenth century, "the next should be called the 'age of electricity.'"[79] His prophecy was borne out in more ways than he could have imagined. Not only did one form of electrical communication, telegraph service, continue to expand in the postbellum decades, but a second, the telephone, came into being in 1876, and a third, wireless radio, appeared at the turn of the century. Thomas Edison's demonstration of electric lighting in 1879 was followed in three years by the first central stations for electrical power generation. They were followed in due course by the adoption of electricity for many new uses and by a phenomenal increase in the amount generated and the distances over which it was sent.

Earlier Americans, Franklin's pupils, had known electricity chiefly as lightning, as a mysterious but plainly potent element of the weather. It is not surprising, then, that as some had supposed that lightning rods and telegraph wires might disrupt the weather, others worried that the postbellum growth in electrical generation and transmission might do the same, intensifying droughts, storms, and floods. For their part, engineers as prominent as Edison himself spoke expansively if vaguely of how electricity would soon give mankind the means of changing the weather to its liking.[80] All were wrong, but as had happened with the telegraph, electricity's new uses did do much to change the weather's impacts.

The telephone had all of the telegraph's advantages for rapid long-distance communication with one of its own over the telegraph. It permitted direct speech from person to person without the need of an operator or the use of a signal code. It was telephone service, not better long-term forecasting, that finally solved the problem of getting frost warnings and other bulletins to farmers in time for them to be of use, a key reason why farmers were among its most numerous and enthusiastic early subscribers.[81]

But because the telephone industry largely followed telegraphy's example in running its wires aboveground, atmospheric electricity could scramble service, and storms could bring the wires down wholesale. Wireless telegraphy, as one turn of the century innovation was first called, offered a means of communication unaffected by any such impacts. Wireless also made it possible to communicate with ships at sea. They could relay information on conditions offshore, enriching the supply of data for forecasting; receive warnings of storms even without being in sight of land; and send calls for help when in distress. The difference that radio signals could make was dramatized in January 1909, when the passenger liners *Republic* and *Florida*, with a total of 1,650 people aboard, collided in thick fog in the Atlantic Ocean near Nantucket. Frantic messages by wireless brought help to the scene before the *Republic* sank; casualties were limited to a dozen deaths and injuries sustained in the collision itself.[82]

If electric power could have been transmitted by wireless means—a favorite dream of the period—many problems with the weather would have been avoided. Lacking the means of doing so, power companies exposed themselves to all of the weather impacts on the wires that afflicted the telegraph and telephone. Thomas Edison's original central generating station, opened in New York in 1882, distributed electricity to customers within a radius of a mile through buried wires.[83] Many later stations in New York and elsewhere followed older precedent by exploiting the cheapness of overhead lines. The loss of lighting until the lines were repaired was added to the possible consequences of a storm for those who had switched from gas to electricity. The ending of dangers of electrocution from electrical wires brought down by storms was added to the list of benefits that cities could expect by forcing their burial. The wires went underground in New York and Chicago as the telegraph lines did, but in smaller cities electrical transmission merely multiplied the variety of services vulnerable to the elements.

In the open country, the urban objections to overhead wires had less force, but another disadvantage had even more. The substitution of alternating for direct current in the 1890s made long-distance high-voltage transmission from source to customers a possibility, but disruption from lightning and atmospheric electricity could have been a disabling handicap. As transmission lines grew longer, exposure became greater, and it was met in the same way that it had been in telegraph service: through insulation and lightning arresters whose design and improvement remained a major focus of industry research throughout the period.[84]

Weather could interfere with the production as well as the distribution of current. Drought and seasonal low flows did much to lessen "hydromania," as it would be called, the early enthusiasm for massive generation of electricity from streamflow as the exploitation of a seemingly free resource.[85] Because water was unreliable, stations using it had to install coal-powered generators to guarantee supply to their customers. Nationally, hydropower settled into a secondary role. It supplemented coal where and when flow happened to be plentiful, and it imposed on utilities the cost of extra fuel consumption when flow fell below expectations.

Even utilities that generated all of their power from coal could not escape other effects on the demand side. The total demand at any time—chiefly for lighting in the early years—varied with the time of day, the day of the week, and the season of the year, and also with the brightness or cloudiness of the weather. Competing providers of light—natural and manufactured gas utilities and kerosene refiners—suffered from the same variations in demand, but they could store their products against the times of maximum use. The electric power business "had one vital technological attribute that made it fundamentally different from all other kinds: for all practical purposes, electricity could not be stored but had to be manufactured, sold, delivered, and consumed at the same instant."[86] The utilities had to have enough generating capacity to meet the peak demand when it came—expensive surplus capacity that was idle the rest of the time. The higher the ratio of the maximum to the minimum demand, the greater the inefficiency of operation.

Demand for electricity for lighting had a marked seasonal pattern. It swelled to a maximum in December and January, when days were darkest. It dwindled to its lowest in June and July. The "summer trough" or "summer slump" was for decades one of the great headaches of the electric utilities. They had to acquire the expensive capacity to meet peak winter demands and see it sit unused for the rest of the year. "Generally speaking," a trade journal noted in 1912, "the central-station business is a seasonal one. It is not in such bad case as the professional snow shoveler, or the vender of palm-leaf fans, but it is an unhappy fact that the ordinary central station sees its loads and its receipts begin to dwindle as the long days of summer come on. By reason of this the fixed charges, which are always with us, run high per unit of output and the situation becomes generally somewhat unsatisfactory."[87]

Weather, Climate, and the Economy

To lighten the burden of seasonal unevenness, the electric utilities, led most effectively by the Illinois power tycoon Samuel Insull, sought customers whose demands would peak in summer and help offset their own summer slump. None fit the bill so well as farmers, as Insull realized, for their activities peaked just when lighting demand was lowest: "The highest consumption comes in the middle of summer, which is the opposite time to the consumption in the adjacent towns." Combined into one system with urban areas, town and country could help to offset each other's seasonal peaks and troughs.[88] Yet the need to build transmission lines through areas where customers were few and far between made rural electrification too costly, for the time being, to be undertaken on a large scale. Most farm households were unable to tap affordable power that would have helped them in many ways, and the utilities failed to acquire a market still so large that it alone might have evened out seasonal demand on their services.

Although it was no longer the most common of American livelihoods, agriculture remained a large enough sector to impose its timetables on the economy as a whole. Interest rates were still markedly seasonal early in the twentieth century, and on the same pattern as before the Civil War. They peaked in spring and fall, in step with the major transactions and money demands of the crop year. The peaks were lower than they had been in earlier times.[89] Nonetheless, they aroused livelier concern than before. It came to be common wisdom that great financial panics, which could idle hundreds of thousands of workers, bankrupt companies by the dozen, and depress activity in many sectors for months or years, tended to occur in the seasons of tight money, and especially in the fall. It came too to be common wisdom that such panics, often likened to weather calamities and more costly than the worst of them, could be prevented by a centrally managed currency that would ease the economy through the times of danger. On its founding in 1913, the Federal Reserve System was given a mandate to ease the seasonality of interest rates, and it was successful from the beginning in doing so.[90]

Year by year, too, the size of the harvest still had much to do with the general level of national prosperity. Just what effect it had, though, and how it affected farmers's well-being, depended on other factors. Foreign demand was one of the most important, and it depended as before on the weather overseas. American wheat farmers enjoyed abundant output and good years from 1876 to 1881 when bad European harvests kept prices high. They then suffered from a slump in the 1880s when conditions in Europe improved. They enjoyed a brief boom in 1892 followed by low prices and hardship in 1893 as a result of a severe Russian drought and famine in the former year and a good harvest in the latter.[91] Some new financial instruments—insurance against hail and tornadoes—helped cushion farmers against loss from bad weather in ways that forecasts could not.[92] Some others—the expansion of the commodities exchanges and of futures contracts, aided by the Weather Bureau's crop reports—cushioned them further against the hazards of excessively good weather and the danger of low prices in a glutted market, and they also confined the price swings affecting consumers within a smaller range.[93]

Weather impacts on food supply were lessened off the farm as well. Postwar meat packing became steadily less concentrated in the winter months. The use of ice cut from the northern lakes allowed midwestern companies to extend their operations into months once too warm and to ship to eastern markets in refrigerated railroad cars. Ice cutting on the lakes and rivers of New York and New England supplied a booming demand from the cities of the Northeast. Cold storage smoothed out for consumers the once sharp seasonal variations in the price of butter, and the introduction of oleomargarine provided a substitute less prone to spoil in the heat.[94] Beginning in the 1870s, the use first of ice and then of mechanical refrigeration in railroad cars made possible the shipping of fruits and vegetables to the Northeast from lands of longer growing seasons.

One paradoxical result of this conquest of the climate was to increase climate's importance in agriculture. "The most striking effect of the refrigerator car on fruit and vegetable production," as a historian of cooling technology observes, "was the impetus it gave to regional specialization." As spoilage declined as a factor, natural conditions of climate and soil became more significant than distance to market in deciding what crops regions could profitably produce. Greenhouse growing in the northeast declined, and a new national map of agricultural specialization took shape by the time of the First World War: California and Florida producing oranges for the nation as a whole; California, the Pacific Northwest, and the Great Lakes, other fruits; Georgia, peaches; other parts of the South, tomatoes and strawberries.[95]

Other factors were vital to the new specialization. Irrigation in California was one of the most important. Among the consequences, one of the more dubious was the reversal of much of the progress made through mechanization in freeing labor from a heavily seasonal schedule. The rising fruit and vegetable regions required large amounts of labor for short periods of the year. Where many different crops were grown on different production schedules, as was the case in California, farm workers could migrate from one to the next and keep active for much of the season. More than ever, though, California was plagued by severe labor shortage in the warm months followed by massive idleness once harvesting had come to an end. Canneries were frantically busy after the harvest and quiet at other times. To keep labor costs down, growers resorted to seasonally or permanently imported labor, first from China and then from Japan.[96]

Though increasingly mechanized, even the grain farming sector still demanded a large labor force for a portion of the year, satisfied largely by migrant workers who were often jobless in the winter.[97] It also imposed a heavily seasonal pattern on labor demand both upstream—in farm equipment manufacture—and downstream—in the transporting and processing sectors. The railroads and ships and grain elevators by which grain traveled to market had their peak season of activity in the late fall, with a secondary one in late spring. And many other occupations besides those closely tied to agriculture remained subject to weather and seasonal influences. Work on most buildings and roads typically shut down for the winter throughout the country in the postbellum years. Most of the rebuilding of Chicago after the Great Fire of November 1871 did not begun until the following spring.[98] Though gas and electric lighting was most in demand in the winter, utility employment peaked in the summer, for most of it involved open-air construction work, the extension and repair of pipe and cable networks.[99] The off-seasons in construction meant idle times as well for makers of construction materials, of boards and paint and plaster.

But some crude means were developed and gradually improved to extend the possible season for construction and make winter work possible. Materials and foundations could be artificially heated; adding salt to mortar could lower its freezing point.[100] Construction was not the only trade to begin to free itself from its weather constraints. Mined and boiled salt largely expelled solar-evaporated brines from the market; the Onondaga works that had specialized in the latter were virtually abandoned by the end of the nineteenth century. "The universal adoption of artificial means of drying," it was observed of the glue industry in 1895, "has removed from the business the principal element of uncertainty, and, while these methods add somewhat to the direct expense of manufacturing, they prevent the great waste formerly caused by bad weather."[101] Similar words could have been written about papermaking, brickmaking, tanning, and wood seasoning. Crude devices to humidify the air in textile plants made fibers less brittle during weaving, though they also created a climate that was oppressive to work in. Northern sawmills began to operate year-round. In winter, they stored their logs in "hot ponds," heated reservoirs that kept the timber in condition for sawing despite subfreezing temperatures outdoors.[102]

By the turn of the century, cooling based on natural ice had already been superseded in some manufacturing trades—brewing and meat packing among them—by mechanical refrigeration. Indoor climate control became "air-conditioning" in a patent filed in 1906. Its author, Stuart Cramer, installed systems in southern textile factories to maintain the high level of atmospheric humidity that best suited the production process. The engineer Willis Carrier was the most prominent early apostle of air-conditioning, defined as the maintenance of desired indoor air conditions within a set range whatever the irregularities of the weather outside. It spread fastest in trades that used moisture-sensitive materials: not only textiles but baking and candy manufacturing, paper and printing, tobacco and explosives.[103]

The natural irregularities of streamflow were more than ever a problem for mills dependent on it for energy. "In these days of sharp competition," observed one authority in 1888, "the advantages of a fixed and steady power afforded by a steam engine over the uncertain and fluctuating power furnished by a natural stream are becoming more and more recognized."[104] As early as 1870, steam exceeded water in total horsepower for manufacturing nationally, exceeding it fivefold by 1899, and its growth further insulated production of many sorts from the weather. Following the Civil War, ice manufacture by steam power had grown rapidly in the South, and though the North relied for much longer on the natural article, by 1918 it too had largely made the shift.[105] The replacement of harvesting by manufacturing did away with shortages and "ice famines" caused by early thaws or mild seasons.

Demand for ice, however, remained far higher in summer than in winter. Manufacturing freed the business from none of the chronic headaches of a strongly seasonal trade: oppressive overhead costs, frequent price wars in off-peak times, accusations of price gouging in peak ones, and irregular employment in the form of massive winter layoffs. There and elsewhere, the influences of weather on production had been lessened, but newer influences were emerging to maintain or even increase seasonality in operations. The invention of new tools for coping with the weather had only enlarged the class of commodities that were in demand only at certain times of the year; so had other new devices, such as bicycles and automobiles, that were used more in some seasons than others. The tendency of postebellum business toward the ever finer tuning of production to demand magnified the effect on employment and output of any such seasonal fluctuations in sales.[106] Much of the progress made in lessening seasonal constraints on production was thereby thwarted.

As a result, a pattern of "alternating spells of hectic activity and idleness or underemployment" remained a fact of life for much of the

American labor force.[107] Many American workers could not count on regular year-round pay from the same job. Thanks to the schedules of work in agriculture, construction, and construction materials, winter in the economy overall was still the season of unemployment, summer the time of high wages as employers competed for scarce hands. Every field had its own distinctive calendar of activity, though, and in theory, workers could have taken advantage of the variety of schedules on which different sectors operated and shift from one to another. In practice, it was a difficult and unreliable expedient, especially given the overall surplus of labor in winter in the economy as a whole. And superimposed on the annual calendar of activity were all of the uncertainties of general good and bad times. Even where the resumption of work could be counted on, few workers "earned enough money when they were working to render them indifferent to the loss of two, three, or four months' wages."[108]

Uneven employment created some opportunities as well as difficulties. Workers in some highly seasonal trades may have enjoyed wage premiums covering the cost of living in the idle months and providing, in effect, a paid vacation of sorts.[109] Workers did not strike randomly throughout the year but at the times when a strike would have the most effect. Employers were especially vulnerable to such stoppages at the beginning of the busy season, when any shutdown threatened to stretch on well into it, and at the end, when work was being rushed to completion. Members of the building trades went on strike most often in the spring and fall. The overall pattern of strikes mirrored that of labor shortages in general, with a towering peak in spring when the economy's demand for workers was building to its maximum, and a second, smaller peak in the fall.[110] The higher cost of living in the winter further depressed any tendency toward strikes in that season.

The electric utilities also turned uneven schedules of work to advantage as a way of alleviating their summer slump. They sought off-peak users. They found them in brickyards and stone quarries, which, hampered by snow and freezing temperatures, still operated mainly during the summer. Breweries, outdoor amusement parks, and ice cream plants also had highly attractive calendars of energy consumption. One of the uses of power that the utilities most eagerly promoted, to the point that many smaller electric plants went into the business themselves, was ice manufacture, another ideal customer because its demands peaked sharply in summer. Summer resort areas could be combined in a single system with nearby areas of year-round residence to make cheaper power available to all.[111] More generally, as Samuel Insull argued, the advantages of even annual demand offered a powerful argument for large power systems, serving entire cities or metropolitan areas or even regions and serving within them as wide as possible a clientele.[112] The more diverse the customers, the less likely were sharp peaks and troughs in total demand. Even where lighting remained the chief customer, system expansion could reduce the proportional inefficiencies of seasonal peaking in use. By all of these means, the power companies lessened their own troubles with seasonally uneven demand; they also set other industries some useful examples of what could be done.

Clothing and Shelter

In few sectors of the economy were sales, production, and employment as seasonally uneven as in clothing. Garment manufacturers were as subject as electric power plants to a highly periodic pattern of demand for their output and—though for different reasons—equally unable to operate on an even schedule by producing in advance for storage. Frequent and unpredictable style changes made advance production of many kinds of apparel too risky a strategy. Much of the industry had a year divided into one or two busy seasons and one or two slow or entirely idle ones, periods of high demand for labor followed by layoffs and low wages.[113]

The spring and fall changes of fashion that kept employment so uneven had their ostensible purpose in adjustment to the changes of weather. Yet few of any year's innovations and changes had much to do with such adjustment. In the decades following the Civil War as before it, voices could be heard to insist that "[t]he object of clothing is chiefly the protection of the body from heat and cold" and that it should be judged chiefly by that standard. But it did not escape the economist Thorstein Veblen that this account of the matter fell quite short of explaining what people actually wore. He asserted, on the contrary, that display was and had always been the primary purpose of dress, comfort at most a secondary one: "[T]he greater part of the expenditure incurred by all classes for apparel is incurred for the sake of respectable appearance rather than for the protection of the person."[114]

For those who sought it, protection by means of clothing became cheaper. Mass production and distribution markedly lowered the cost of almost all articles of apparel throughout the late nineteenth century and early in the twentieth. The share of the ordinary household budget that clothing demanded shrank steadily, though there remained many—urban workers, farm laborers, and farm tenants—for whom adequate protection was still out of reach.[115] But, as in earlier years, they were not the only Americans who were poorly clothed in this sense. Style and protection, as Veblen pointed out, could be directly at odds. Because inadequate clothing could be a mark of status and distinction, "it is by no means an uncommon occurrence, in an inclement climate, for people to go ill clad in order to appear well dressed."[116]

The output of rubber wear, chiefly protective garments for wet weather, grew tremendously in the postbellum decades. Between 1880 and 1900, the industry's output increased fourfold in value and its payroll more than threefold.[117] Yet water-resistant garments, for all their usefulness, made slow headway among well-to-do Americans. It helped not at all that rubber and oilskins had become the routine rainy-weather garb of low-status work in the open air. They were worn by fishermen and sailors, by farmers and cowboys, by trolley conductors and policemen, by deliverymen and teamsters, by pestered and embarrassed children.[118] Selah Tarrant, the seedy charlatan in Henry James's *The Bostonians* (1886), is set apart at one blow from better-bred characters by the "waterproof" he is always wearing. When the genteel and affluent Annie Kilburn in William Dean Howells's 1888 novel of that name sees a young society gentleman coming up the walk to her house wearing a rubber coat, she mistakes him for a traveling salesman.[119]

Rubber outergarments had had advantages too great for them not to make progress, but their progress was slowed by those very advantages. For those who had a maid "ready to relieve them of their damp clothing," fashionable dress remained "more desirable than the waterproof," for it advertised wealth and status.[120] There was, a trade journal fumed, "one person, even in these advanced days of material progress, who does not wear rubbers upon a rainy day": the ultra-fashionable young man. "[F]or his feet, no matter how wet the day, he thinks the only proper covering is a pair of leather shoes" though they might "crack from heel to toe" after a few sessions in the rain. "This idea of walking through water without a pair of rubbers seems to have its fundamental reason in the young man's desire to publish to the world his ability to buy new shoes for every rainy day."[121] When rubber wear did begin to win acceptance, it was due "not alone to the need of something to protect from the weather, but fully as much to the progress made by manufacturers in bringing out new and attractive styles."[122] Above all, mackintoshes, blending rubber unobtrusively with fabric, benefited from the example of fashion in England, where they had long been accepted upper-class gear.

As some garments that were plainly useful in coping with the weather met resistance, some others that were plainly maladapted to it persisted. As nonwaterproof clothing advertised distinction, so did the thin shoes and garments, decried by American reformers and British visitors, that remained fashionable women's winter dress. Skirts long enough to drag through the mud and water and snow of the streets never ceased to be essential wear before World War I, despite many protests and many attempts to introduce alternative styles. A Boston dress reform club in 1891 proposed a rational outfit for rainy autumn days. A newspaper described it as "a short skirt made of waterproof cloth in dark colors, reaching but an inch or two below the knee, with heavy boots and long gaiters . . . the skirts will be kilted and hang heavy, so as not to be disarranged by the wind. . . . An ordinary hat, or better still a tarpaulin sailor hat, will complete what will certainly be a very novel costume."[123] It proved far too novel for its day and made no mark on the dress of its time. Upper-class men's wear remained, as one survivor recalled, "hellish in hot weather." The parasol was still a standard article among women of fashion, but not one among men, who, with their heavier and darker summer wear, could have used its protection more.[124]

"[T]here are fashions in architecture as there are in millinery," a popular late-nineteenth-century author observed, "and we cut our houses this way this year and that way the next."[125] Americans did so with almost as little reference as in clothing fashions to the bettering of shelter or protection. No more than clothing fashions were these shifts responses to climatic changes, nor were they steps in a steady progress toward greater suitability to the climate as it was.

As the march of fashionable house styles—Second Empire, Romanesque Revival, Stick, Shingle, Queen Anne, bungalow-type, and Colonial Revival—continued, it remained common practice to justify each as better suited than its predecessors to the American climate. Critics who liked complex and eclectic designs argued that the extreme variety of the American seasons demanded the utmost in complexity and eclecticism in the houses that gave shelter from them.[126] There was never a fashionable style in the United States fitting this prescription better than the Queen Anne, which peaked in popularity in the 1880s. Even the turret or tower that was one of its hallmarks, often derided as pointless excess, could be defended on functional grounds. "In hot weather," wrote one proponent of the style, "its efficiency as a ventilator is remarkable. In quiet summer nights an enjoyable air current is established through any room having an open window and an open door and passageways to the tower, the attic windows or ventilators of the tower being open." [127]

But justifications in terms of climate always ignored the disadvantages of the style in question, which advocates of competing styles never failed to emphasize. It was the task of the true architect "to evolve a dwelling-place which shall be suitable to the conditions of climate in which we live," one critic wrote, but the ornate Queen Anne–style roof seemed designed on purpose to fail all four tests of its suitability: "to keep rain-water out of a house," "to prevent the snow collecting on the roof of a house," "to keep the heat of summer out of the house," and "to keep the warmth generated by the consumption of coal within the house in winter."[128] These failings did not prevent the style from enjoying enormous popularity nationwide, nor is there any evidence that they were the reason for its eventual fall from favor.

A later high style was part of a drastic shift around the turn of the century from ornate and eclectic to simpler forms. The so-called Prairie house of which Frank Lloyd Wright was the foremost exponent had aspects that happened to suit the climate well and others that did not. For all of Wright's talk about the organic suitability of house to environment, where climate was concerned he put adaptation second to visual effect. The low-pitched roof of the Prairie house did little to shed the rain, and frequent leaks became a part of life for many wealthy clients. Wright's aversion to basements meant that the most useful element of genuine American prairie architecture—an excavated or earth-banked space preserving a moderate temperature at all seasons—was discarded, and his love of large windows and distaste for curtains and double panes magnified the chill of winter.[129]

The most frankly practical design of the period proved a dismal failure. Concrete, some theorists argued, was the ideal material for houses in the harsh American climate. It kept interiors "cooler in summer and warmer in winter" than other materials, and it was more resistant to the stress of the weather.[130] With electric lighting, the phonograph, and the motion picture behind him, Thomas Edison in the early 1900s set about trying to rehouse America in concrete; he lost a good deal of money overestimating the utilitarianism of the American public.[131] Shelter, like clothing, became easier to obtain and afford, while remaining primitive and inadequate for many Americans; but not all of its inadequacies were the result of lack of means to afford better.

Yet though well-to-do Americans did not put shelter above all other considerations in the design of their houses, as a matter of course they continued to enjoy better protection than poorer ones. Lower-class rural dwellings were apt to be worst-defended against the cold. It was in summer, on the other hand, that crowded and poorly ventilated city

FIGURE 3.3. Urban heat waves were worst for tenement dwellers in crowded cities: a summer "heated term" in New York City, 1882.

tenements became most intolerable, and their occupants sought relief outdoors at the price of other dangers. "With the first hot night in June," Jacob Riis wrote of the Lower East Side of Manhattan, "police dispatches, that record the killing of men and women by rolling off roofs and window-sills while asleep, announce that the time of greatest suffering among the poor is at hand."[132]

Coping with Heat and Cold

The cities still felt the heaviest impacts of heat waves, and the larger the city, the more marked the increase in mortality at such times. Some ten thousand deaths nationally, most of them in the cities of the upper Midwest, were credited to the hot spell of July 1901. In New York City, this heat wave caused four hundred fatal heatstrokes and several hundred other deaths, well short of the excess mortality of nearly a thousand in Manhattan alone from the heat during the first half of August 1896.[133] The unprecedented temperatures of the first two weeks of July 1911 took more lives than any of the more famous weather disasters that have ever struck New England.[134]

The total impact of comparable heat waves increased as the cities grew. Opinions differed as to whether the proportional toll was rising or falling. The New York public health crusader Dr. Stephen Smith judged the hazard to be growing if only because urban congestion was making the heat more intense. If nothing were done, he warned, "the day would not seem to be far distant when the resident, especially if he is a laborer, will remain in the city and pursue his work during the summer at the constant risk of his life," and he and many others proposed more trees and more open spaces in the city to combat the heat island effect.[135] Increasing numbers of the well-to-do sought cooler air by moving outside of the city and commuting by train to work. Many others fled elsewhere during the hot months. The summer resort trade flourished in favored localities among those disinclined to "stay and fry through our summers in the city" and able to afford a prolonged absence.[136]

The relative few who could summer in the country were fleeing not simply the worst heat spells but the steady discomfort and danger of the season in town. Summer remained the chief dying time in postbellum urban America. Gastrointestinal illness among infants and very young children—what the physician-poet Oliver Wendell Holmes described as "the vast wave of infantile disease which flows in upon all our great cities with the growing heats of July" remained chiefly responsible.[137] Deaths from this cause were most numerous in the hottest summers, but they were high every year.[138]

The dangers of heat seemed amply demonstrated on the map as well as on the calendar. Warm climates had not lost their reputation as being inherently less healthy than colder ones. Disease wrecked a French attempt to dig a canal across the tropical Isthmus of Panama in the 1880s. It proved far more deadly than combat to American troops in the Spanish-American War, fought largely in the low latitudes of the Caribbean and the Philippines at the century's close.

Yet if any climatic zone could have been called inherently hostile to human life, it was not the tropics. A single winter without artificial aids, the sociologist Lester Frank Ward observed, "would suffice to sweep the entire population north or south of the thirtieth parallel off the face of the earth."[139] The hazards of cold were downplayed because much had already been done to overcome them, and ways were found to overcome those associated with heat as well. The United States was able to govern the lands that it acquired in the war and to embark shortly thereafter on the digging of the Panama Canal without being prevented by the yellow fever and malaria that had so plagued the French. It did so thanks to medical advances that proved that the fevers and general ill-health of low latitudes were not, as had long been supposed, inseparable from their climate, but were biologically transmitted and could be combated successfully by sanitary means even though the climate might remain just as it had been. By 1910, the death rate among Americans working in the Canal Zone was lower than that of any state in the Union.[140]

The summer urban mortality peak proved just as ephemeral. By the turn of the century, it had begun to subside dramatically. By the time of World War I, the overall summer peak in city deaths had virtually disappeared, and that among infants less than two years old had been much reduced. It had been the product not of the heat per se but of milk, food, and water gone bad in the heat. These deaths were lessened by changes that did not cool the summer climate but rather neutralized its effects: by cleaner city water supplies, better-quality milk made available in cities by better refrigeration, transportation, and public health regulation, and improved nutrition.[141]

Other advances in various ways reduced the discomforts of summer indoors by lessening inadvertent space heating. Pressing clothes had long been a trying task in summer: "The heavy flatirons were heated over a very hot fire, and the combined temperatures of fire and irons on a July day called for grim endurance."[142] Electric irons gave off far less unnecessary heat. Gas and electric cooking stoves produced less waste heat than ones fed with wood and coal; electric lighting produced less than gas. The electric fan did more for hot-weather comfort than any small gadget previously available. By the turn of the century, it was cheap enough to be available to many Americans, and because it consumed off-peak summer power, its spread was strongly encouraged by the utilities. By the time of World War I, a few experiments had been made in adapting industrial temperature and humidity control to domestic space cooling in the homes of the very wealthy.

Space heating in winter was already well developed, too well for some tastes. Even an occasional American voice was raised against "the artificial and unwholesome climate indoors which the furnace-maker has created," with entire dwellings, even the bedrooms, "heated up to 70 degrees, and often to 75 degrees for six months in the year." More than one English traveler found Yankee indoor warmth a pleasant change from conditions at home.[143] They remained exceptions to the rule that in America "a newly arrived Englishman suffers . . . from the prevailing taste for hot rooms," while "an American visitor complains of the temperature which suits the English." Theodore Dreiser, "having heard something of English fires and English warmth," was not surprised to find the indoors "cold as a sepulcher" and the natives satisfied with the fire in the grate "if the four or five coals huddled together are managing to keep themselves warm by glowing." Spending the winter of 1882–83 in London, Elizabeth Cady Stanton rebelled against the indoor chill and obtained a stove to provide her quarters with "[t]he delightful summer heat we, in America, enjoy in the coldest seasons." Finding her English friends unwilling to do the same, even when they had felt the stove's warmth for themselves, she concluded that they were simply less open-minded than Americans, irrationally resistant to change even at the expense of their own comfort and well-being. Visiting from England, Max Beerbohm complained that American hotels were "stifling hot"; Rudyard Kipling found them "triply over-heated"; they reminded Ellen Terry of the forcing rooms used in England for ripening pineapples. "And their private houses!," she continued. "How the dear people can stand the overwhelming heat of them, I don't know!"[144]

English visitors saw conditions mostly in the settings where upper- and middle-class Americans lived and where the central heating that they deplored was increasingly the rule. Hot-air systems remained the cheapest to install and operate; hot water provided the most even and fine-tuned heat and steam the most powerful; some communities experimented with centrally generated steam piped into individual buildings. That electric space heating could offer cleaner, finer-tuned, and more convenient service than any was recognized at an early stage.[145] The conversion of coal to electricity being far less efficient than burning coal directly for heat, however, it promised to be very expensive; and the coincidence of peak demand with the winter peak in lighting demand made it doubly impracticable.

But even to switch to furnace heating was to be freed from many burdens, to say "good-bye stoves, good-bye coal scuttles, good-bye pokers, good-bye ash-sifters, good-bye stove dust," and good-bye to all of the chores that they entailed.[146] Stoves remained cheaper, but also less comfortable, dirtier, harder to control, more demanding of labor, and poorer in providing ventilation than central heating. They remained the standard heating device among the northern urban poor and most rural householders. In the milder climates, the stove still lagged well behind the open wood fire. Health-seekers in postbellum southern California complained bitterly about the indoor chill that they had to endure. An open fireplace was the most they could hope to find in the way of heating apparatus. Only recently, a 1914 guidebook to California reported, had the larger resort hotels begun to heed their guests's demand for steam-heated rooms.[147] Harriet Beecher Stowe after the Civil War urged northerners to come to Florida for the winter but warned them to bring plenty of warm clothes. They would be exchanging their homes, furnace-heated to seventy degrees or higher, for "the open fire on the hearth" and "a much lower temperature."[148]

For the lower classes in northern cities, the cost of heating fuel could be a heavy one. Many families used scrap wood scavenged from the streets—discarded boxes and fragments of demolished buildings.[149] Kerosene, oil, and gas were in use here and there, but whether stove- or furnace-heated, most town dwellings and public buildings by the turn of the century burned coal: anthracite in the Northeast, smoky soft coal in the Midwest closer to the bituminous fields. Coal of one kind or the other had also made deep inroads in rural America at wood's expense, and the increasing dependence on coal meant an increasing vulnerability to any interruptions in its supply.

Most anthracite came from a few fields in northeastern Pennsylvania. The pattern lent itself to concentrated ownership of the supply and of the railroads that carried it to market. Several early combinations turned the industry into a near-monopoly, restricting supply and raising prices. Each held together for a few years and then fell apart, but a more durable arrangement came into being in the late 1890s.[150] Anthracite miners responded by forming an effective combination of their own. They were among the worst-off members of the American work force: their labor intermittent, hazardous, and wretchedly paid, they and their families wretchedly housed and slaves to their debts at the company store. By the turn of the century, the United Mine Workers, under a vigorous new president, was agitating for higher wages and safer conditions against mine and railroad owners unwilling even to recognize the union. The news that a strike had stopped anthracite production in May 1902 aroused fears of a heatless winter in the Northeast.

By mid-October, the mines were still idle, and anthracite in New York City was selling for twenty dollars a ton, four times its normal fall price. Substitute fuels climbed in price and flowed northeastward from their usual markets, creating shortages elsewhere. Fear came close to panic as winter approached. President Theodore Roosevelt felt obliged to act in view of "the urgency and terrible nature of the catastrophe impending over a large portion of our population in the form of a winter coal famine."[151] His threat to seize the mines brought the owners to a settlement in mid-October. Mining resumed promptly, but too late to make up the year's shortfall in production. Prices for all heating fuels dropped from their speculation-inflated peaks, but they remained high and houses chilly throughout the winter. The strike's aftershocks included half-a-dozen outbreaks of a new form of social disorder. Trains carrying coal were stopped in towns through which they passed by mobs led by leading citizens—two ministers, two bank presidents, and a policeman in one case—and forced to hand over or sell their cargo.[152]

The fragility of the fuel supply system was revealed again in the winter of 1917–18. Under the stress of government management for wartime freight priorities, the railroads failed to deliver cities their accustomed supplies of coal for a winter that proved to be an exceptionally harsh one. Suffering from the cold, higher death rates, and extensive industrial and office shutdowns were the consequences. A second such winter, in the opinion of experts, was avoided only by the end of fighting in November.[153]

A century before, winter room temperatures in the United States had depended mainly on the weather outside. Technology had broken the weather's grip, but it had not brought temperatures under the full control of the householder. It had made them dependent instead on household income, on the pricing strategies of the coal and railroad companies, on labor relations in the mine fields, on international peace, and on the orderly workings of the freight system. All were steadier than the thermometer outdoors, but as events showed, they were not as reliable as consumers might have wished.

Transportation

War-related disruptions in freight were the principal cause of the coal crisis of 1917–18, but the weather was no help. The severity of the winter—the coldest on official record in much of the Northeast—not only made the coal shortage that developed in December more uncomfortable to live through, it worsened the shortage itself by making fuel at once more in demand and harder to transport. Much of Boston's coal was brought in by sea, but the harbor froze for the first time in many years. Ice in New York harbor likewise obstructed barges, sinking several, and more than once had to be dynamited to open a path for shipping.

It was one more reminder, if one more had been needed, of how much less reliable water transportation could be than rail in winter, as it could be, for different reasons, in spring, summer, or fall. That disadvantage and others by 1918 had relegated it to a minor role in American freight carriage. On the Erie Canal, the yearly tonnage of freight peaked in 1880 and declined thereafter, despite the removal of all tolls in 1882. The absolute annual tonnage carried by boat on the lower Mississippi likewise began to fall around 1880. The percentage of total freight that traveled inland by water declined sharply. Only on the Great Lakes, with their traffic in ore and timber, and the Ohio River, with its heavy flow of soft coal, did barge and steamboat hauling continue to prosper.[154]

The sensitivity of the waterways to the weather, the seasonal closings and uncertainties of operation that winter or low water imposed on many of them, represented one reason for rail's growing domination of the freight business. The most important reason lay elsewhere. Water hauling might be cheaper per mile, but there were other costs that such a comparison failed to include. The denser the rail network became, the more easily railroads could carry freight from origin to destination without the heavy expense and wear and tear of unloading and reloading. Branch rail lines that made such uninterrupted carriage possible were far more readily constructed than were branch canals or navigable channels.[155] The length of active railroads grew steadily throughout the period. River and harbor improvement bills turned into the "annual scramble for the contents of the Treasury" that an antebellum Democratic president had warned of, but they did little to alter the patterns of transportation in the United States.[156]

One effect of the trend away from water was to insulate the flow of goods and people from natural fluctuations. In one sector this trend was particularly dramatic. When the Pennsylvania oil fields had been opened around the time of the Civil War, much of their production was sent to market by river, with great delays and much loss from high and low water and ice. The postbellum years saw the development of pipelines that freed crude oil movement from almost all serious weather interruptions. Rail had more problems than pipelines, if fewer than river transportation, in coping with the weather. The tracks remained highly vulnerable to flooding, and snow blockades remained a problem even in the East. New lines running through the mountains of the West were often buried under much heavier snowfalls. Weather-related accidents took a ghastly toll of life and limb among railroad brakemen, whose trade rivaled anthracite mining and the marine fisheries for danger and was most hazardous in winter. To set the hand-operated brakes, still in general use, one on each car, brakemen had to walk along the top of the moving train. In snowy or icy weather that made their footing insecure, it was work "attended with danger at every step."[157]

But innovations lessened many of these worries. The air brake, which came into general use by the end of the century, abolished the dangers of braking by hand.[158] New rotary snowplows sliced through drifts far more effectively than earlier models had pushed through them. Railroads protected long stretches of their lines in the western mountains with fences and even wooden sheds to keep off the snow. The Southern Pacific alone built thirty-two miles of shed on its route through the Sierra Nevada.[159]

As the railroad and pipeline networks spread and waterway traffic ebbed, road traffic and the roads themselves saw little change for decades after the Civil War. Even in the cities of the Northeast, hard-surfaced streets were still rarer than unpaved ones.[160] The country ways remained a national embarrassment. Few were much better than they had been before the war, "soft earth roads," as two authorities described then in 1894, that thanks to the weather became "impassible for heavy loads during a considerable part of the year."[161]

The roads remained largely the domain of local governments, which controlled the labor, usually unskilled, that citizens were required to contribute to road maintenance and the tax money that they could pay instead. Localities guarded these powers jealously against higher-level efforts to take them away. And bad as the roads might be, many farmers preferred coping with them as they were to paying the heavy cost of surfacing them better.[162] Neighborhood control over roads was strong in cities, too. Abutting owners typically paid much or all of the cost of paving or other street improvements in assessments on their property, and they typically held a veto power over any improvements proposed. They often resisted hard surfacing, fearing both its expense and the disruption of life by the heavier and faster traffic that it would attract.[163]

Two inventions made the defects of the roads less tolerable than before. The first was the bicycle, a particular craze of the 1880s. Cyclists, organized as the League of American Wheelmen, launched the "good roads movement," a national crusade for a network of hard-surfaced, weatherproofed routes. Their magazine *Good Roads* regaled readers with picture after picture of muddy and rutted lanes and vehicles stalled or abandoned in them; with calculations of the loss incurred by farmers and the nation as a whole from bad roads; with didactic verse and fiction on the same theme; with descriptions of new devices for surfacing; and with a far-ranging catalogue of the blessings that hard paving would bestow.[164]

The second invention appeared in the 1890s. Nothing slowed the spread of the horseless carriage more than the fact that "the American who buys an automobile finds himself with this great difficulty: he has nowhere to use it. He must pick and choose between bad roads and worse."[165] Only in the summer could drivers hope to find roads free at least from mud and snow. Even in summer, they were not spared dust clouds and mud-brewing rainstorms, and even in summer the roads preserved the ruts and bumps they had acquired at other times.

If the automobile and the roads were ill-suited to one another, two remedies were available. The automobile could be adapted to the roads as the American carriage and wagon had long been. This solution reached its classic form in Henry Ford's Model T. With its flexible construction, its strong, light vanadium steel frame, its powerful engine, and its body lifted high off the ground, it was designed, Ford wrote, to drive if necessary "through sand and mud, through slush, snow, and water, up hills, across fields and roadless plains."[166] Its popularity was immediate and immense.

Or the roads could be improved. By the turn of the century the automobilists had taken control of the good roads movement. The cause was already making headway. Beginning in the early 1890s, one state after another replaced or supplemented local control over road repair with centralized funding and supervision. Widespread rural opposition was either overridden or bought off by generous state spending. Congress in 1893 created a national Office of Road Inquiry to collect and disseminate facts on better methods of surfacing.[167] The year 1912 saw federal appropriations for postal roads to aid rural free delivery, which the Post Office had been allowed to waive where the roads were too bad. In 1916, a large appropriation for road improvements marked a full federal entry into the field.

Progress had been slow. Of more than 2 million miles of rural road in the United States in 1904, hardly more than 5 percent had surfacing of any kind. Ten years later, the length of surfaced road had not even doubled.[168] In *Main Street*, Sinclair Lewis made Gopher Prairie, Minnesota, the epitome of everything unattractive about small-town America in the early twentieth century, and he did not spare the thoroughfare that gave the book its title. It was "a black swamp from curb to curb" in spring, hard to cross even on foot, and once again a "muddy expanse" in September; in summer, a mass of "powdery dust"; in winter, when automobiles were put into storage and replaced with horse-drawn sleighs and cutters, all hard-frozen ruts underneath the snow that hid it from view.[169]

Bad roads were far from the automobile's only problem with the weather. Driver and passengers in the open car were exposed to all conditions and extremes: cold, heat, rain, snow, wind, dust. Starting and restarting were difficult in cold weather. The internal combustion engine required a cooling system, but the water-circulating systems that came to predominate were liable to freeze and crack. They had to be drained when the car sat idle, even overnight, in winter. And even progress in road surfacing only substituted one set of problems for another. The smooth tires of early automobiles slipped and skidded alarmingly on smooth pavements, prompting the introduction around 1908 of the earliest treaded tires and the use of tire chains in snow.[170] The better the pavement and the faster cars could drive, the greater became the hazard of collisions when fog, rain, or snow reduced visibility—especially of collisions with the other, slower-moving traffic still sharing the roads, with pedestrians, carriages, and wagons, with recreational sledders in winter.

Poor visibility was the worst of the many weather hazards faced by another high-speed novelty in transportation that followed soon after the automobile. The earliest airplanes were immensely vulnerable in many ways to the elements. Their worst handicap was their near-helplessness in conditions as frequent and unavoidable as cloud and fog, for pilots's sense of direction and elevation proved to be unreliable without visual cues. The frequency of crashes under such conditions cast a dark shadow over their future as a reliable means of moving people, mail, and freight. It was the chief reason why the airship, or blimp, though slow and itself vulnerable to wind and storms, was still generally accorded a major or even the dominant role in commercial air travel in early twentieth-century predictions of the future.[171]

The Climate of Utopia

Ten years before Kitty Hawk, one writer relegated artificial rainmaking and "its twin absurdity, the flying machine" to the category of dreams that would never come true.[172] Others foresaw both as equally certain to be elements of life in the progressive times to come. American literature has never seen such a torrent of utopian fictions as flowed from the presses near the end of the nineteenth century. One novel after another described worlds in which technical and organizational wonders had solved the besetting problems of the present. In many of them, society's problems with the weather had indeed been solved by rainmaking and other contrivances for weather control.[173] Typical inhabitants of utopia were William Dean Howells's Altrurians, who had had "climates to change, and seasons to modify, a whole system of meteorology to readjust" in order to make the world the paradise it could be.[174]

Many of the projects for transforming climates that Howells and others worked into their novels were variants of ones that had been proposed and discussed in the postbellum American press. Some involved the diversion of ocean and atmospheric currents.[175] Others looked to the creation of bodies of water in arid zones to moisten their climates through evaporation.[176] When writers of fiction brought such projects into their work, to be sure, it was not always in a reverent or prophetic spirit. At the end of *The American Claimant* (1892), Mark Twain had his self-deluded confidence man Colonel Sellers planning to market a scheme for climate control (through the manipulation of sunspots) to the governments of Europe. When in 1912 the New York engineer Carroll Livingston Riker proposed yet again that the ocean currents of the Atlantic be rearranged to moderate the northern climate, an admirer wrote innocently that "[t]here was a time when a project of this sort would have met with ridicule," and events showed that the time was not yet past.[177]

Such schemes remained mostly talk. Once, though, the talk became unusually earnest, when control of the skies for a time seemed within reach. For several years in the early 1890s, the federal government conducted tests of a means for making rain though loud explosions. The early claims of success issued by the experimenters prompted much discussion of what lay ahead if the method proved reliable.

It had first been proposed in a small book, *War and the Weather*, published in 1871 by the Wisconsin civil engineer Edward Powers.[178] An enormous amount has been written about the nature and meaning of the American Civil War; but Powers's interpretation, put forward only a few years after the event, remains the most original ever proposed. In effect if not in intention, he wrote, what had seemed to be a great conflict had in fact been a great collaborative effort. The opposing sides thought that they were fighting over the fate of the Union; they had actually been working together to unveil the means of controlling the weather. On many occasions when they exchanged heavy fire, the opposing armies, without knowing it, had been jointly conducting "a scientific experiment for the artificial production of rain."[179]

For rain, Powers pointed out, had fallen copiously in the aftermath
of many of the war's battles and bombardments, as in those of many
earlier conflicts. Powers larded his book with the testimony of veterans
who reported "a general impression," as one former general and future
president wrote, "that the atmospheric disturbance, caused by heavy
cannonading, hastened or created showers."[180] It followed that rain
could be made artificially in times of drought, not by means of Espy's
forest fires, but by the production of a thunderous clamor. The proposal quickly sank from view, but it was revived around 1890 when
Powers published a second edition of this book. Western droughts and
the support of an influential Illinois senator combined to earn the
method a series of tests at federal expense.[181] Expeditions sent to Texas
under the command of one Major Robert Dyrenforth spent weeks ex-
ploding large quantities of gunpowder, dynamite, and other noisemak-
ers and watching the skies anxiously for results.

FIGURE 3.4. Federal experiments in rainmaking were a gift to cartoonists, who
raised in humorous form issues that were of serious concern to others.

Public discussion dealt mostly with the technical side of the matter. Could noise produce rain? And had it, in the initial experiments, actually done so? Scientists, almost without exception, answered no to both questions. They and their supporters in the press denounced the tests as a farce and a national embarrassment all too typical of the way in which the government of the United States treated such matters. Harvard's Robert DeCourcy Ward, a young climatologist at the time, would recall the Dyrenforth experiments with a shudder as "a most humiliating experience" that "did much to discredit us in the eyes of European scientific men." To the Russian philosopher N. F. Fyodorov, on the other hand, what put the savants and governments of Europe to shame was their failure to follow America's lead in trying to develop a technique that could save millions of lives from famine. What disgraced America itself was the stingy and narrow way in which it had approached the task.[182]

Most commentators took it for granted that a technique that could "avert the disaster of droughts and reclaim large tracts of land hitherto regarded as little better than desert" would bring only good if it could only be developed.[183] As in Espy's time, though, some were clearheaded enough to ask what problems might arise if Americans acquired the power to make rain at will. Problems aplenty could be foreseen as soon as that question was posed, enough to make some view "with anything but unmixed feelings the present march of science." It was plain on a little reflection that almost any interference with rainfall would hurt some while it helped others. "Shall White, in order to save his corn, cause a pour-down that ruins Black's wheat and oats?" The question led straight to another: "[W]hen it is settled that rain can be caused at any time, who will decide that rain is necessary or desirable?"[184] Rainmaking plainly could not be left in private hands so long as the rain could not be limited to a landowner's own property. It would have to be managed by some government bureau if it were to be used for the greater good. But such management, some argued, would rather guarantee that weather control, like every other government power, would be used to benefit already favored classes and sections and the party in office: "[T]here is no end to the possible abuses that might result from getting the rains under the control of politicians." Americans would discover that they had merely traded the caprices of the weather for "the capricious favor of Government employees."[185]

As in Espy's time, southerners faced the hardest questions. The 1892 debate in Congress over funding the rainmaking experiments for another year was conducted mostly within their ranks, and they argued mainly over the desirability rather than the feasibility of the technique. They felt equally the advantages that weather control offered—most of them could have spoken, as one did, of "my constituents, who are agricultural people"—and several aspects that they found particularly repugnant. They worried that already some sections were unfairly benefiting from federal interference, and others were being hurt. Which states, one of them wondered aloud, had lost the rain that the experimenters claimed to have brought down in West Texas? They worried about a future when "[g]overnment agents might bring down rain on any man's land who would agree to support the Administration and discriminate against those who are not in favor of the Administration." They had other concerns as well. One denied that the federal government had the constitutional authority to engage in such experiments, another warned against "foisting upon the people of this country an expensive bureau of the Government," such as weather control would surely require; yet another questioned the wisdom and the propriety of interfering with "the providence of God."[186]

The evident failure of the tests by the end of their second year quieted the debate. Glib commercial rainmakers went on making the rounds of the West but on the whole were not taken seriously. But the questions that had been brought up remained certain to arise should any better means of weather control be discovered—other than the means employed by one American of the time. He alone learned how to do the seemingly impossible: to make rain to his own perfect contentment and that of his neighbors as well. He was the western poet Joaquin Miller, who settled in the late nineteenth century at "The Hights," a mountain estate overlooking Oakland, California. In the cabin he used for writing, Miller entertained visitors by singing an Indian rain song; as he came to the end, drops would begin to patter, then roar, on the roof. When alone and at work, finding that the sound helped him to write, he made a practice of summoning down a shower. To favored guests, Miller would reveal his secret: a perforated water pipe running through the foliage over the roof and controlled by a faucet hidden in the cabin. "I can turn on the spigot and sit in my own individual shower," he told Hamlin Garland.[187]

No other way of manufacturing weather would have done so well. Miller knew it himself. In a utopian novel of his own, published in 1893, he had looked askance at the "supreme selfishness" of a colony of dryland settlers who prayed for rain to water their corn, even knowing that it would destroy their neighbors's much larger crop of figs. He also wrote about weather control—"rain whenever it is needed, but never when it is not needed"—in his ideal future society.[188] He had the sense, though, to realize that that was where this power belonged. If utopia and weather control did go naturally together, it was not because the latter was essential to the former. Weather control, rather, required utopia, for no society short of a perfectly just and harmonious one was sure to use that power for the better.

FOUR

Modernizing America

Migration North and South

As late as 1911, a leading American geographer could confidently assert that blacks in the United States would always live chiefly in "the warm, moist air of the Gulf and South Atlantic states," "where they find the heat and moisture in which they thrive"; nature decreed that few would ever settle and fewer survive in the North because they could not withstand the cold.[1] Events, though, were contradicting this blend of racial and climatic determinism. Black migration from the South to the colder states was already substantial. It intensified dramatically during World War I. A boom in labor demand in industry, along with a near-cessation of the immigration from Europe that had once filled it, drew black and white southerners alike in unheard-of numbers to the manufacturing cities of the North.[2]

The black exodus to Kansas in 1879 and 1880 had briefly looked as if it would become just such a mass interregional movement of population. But the pioneer Exodusters had suffered from the drastic change in climate, most of all because it affected their livelihoods in farming. Their skills, which lay in cotton growing, were useless in Kansas, and their experience did little to encourage others to follow. The great northward migration of the early twentieth century was a migration not to new farmlands but to the cities for factory and service employment. The difference in climate between southern origin and northern destination did not matter much to it.

White southern farmers, fearing the loss of cheap labor, warned departing blacks that they would find the winters of the North too bitter to endure.[3] The new exodus proceeded all the same, and it discredited in the process the long-held idea that either race or habit always imposed a latitudinal pattern on human movement. The change in climate from South to North did mean discomfort or worse for many who undertook it. They suffered especially from the unaccustomed cold that few could afford stoves and fuel to ward off—though they had suffered too from inadequate shelter and clothing in the southern winter. But the chief constraint on migration to novel climates had broken down. By the early twentieth century, lines of latitude no longer channeled settlement as they once had done. The reluctance of farmers to leave familiar climates had been a powerful constraint on the overall patterns of movement. It mattered less and less as fewer Americans earned their living from the soil.

If the new northward migration was not hindered by climatic differences, a new southward flow of more affluent Americans was positively aided by them. Having weakened as a constraint on movement, climate in another way became more of a force in propelling it. The greatest change in American climate as a resource in the early twentieth century was the striking rise in its value as an amenity, the greatest change in its influence on migration its shift from a factor in production to one of consumption. The boosterism of the nineteenth century had emphasized, truly or falsely, the similarities of the place being promoted to the place from which the buyer came. The promotion of post-Civil War California and Florida, offering a change of climate for pleasant living seasonally or year-round, had not failed, but attracted only modest numbers of immigrants from colder and cloudier sections. The years following World War I saw the first mass movements in American history of people who were seeking agreeable weather for daily life.

One of the most colorful episodes of a colorful decade was the Florida boom of the 1920s. More than anything else, it was a carnival of climatic boosterism. "[A]n October snowstorm in any of the Northern states is not only good for a column on the front page of almost any Florida paper," wrote Kenneth Roberts after a visit to Miami, "but frequently also for a long editorial of compassion and brotherly love, in which are concealed a few digs at the snow belt."[4] Developers and promoters garnished the map with such names as Sun City, Sunniland, Sunnyland, and Sunylan. Places that had names already adopted mottoes to convey the same message of winter warmth. Key West promoted itself as "The Southernmost City in these United States." St. Petersburg was both "The Sunshine City" and "The Tropical Wonderland." Fort Myers was the "Real Tropical Part of Florida" and "Truly a Tropical City." Homestead was "The Heart of the Florida Tropics." Vero Beach was "Where the Tropics Begin." The entire state was "the only tropical state in our forty-eight."[5]

Not long before, such slogans would have done more to deter settlement than to attract it. The tropics and near-tropics had been identified in the North with almost everything undesirable, above all with disease, but also with listlessness, poverty, and stagnation. Now, southeastern Florida was growing at a startling pace, and the climate seemed to be the chief underlying reason for its growth. If true, it presented a puzzle. As the newspaper editor Frank Stockbridge wrote in 1925, the influx of people was unprecedented, yet the climate was no different from what it had always been. What had changed, Stockbridge pointed out, were the conditions that determined its value and significance. If agriculture's decline as a livelihood was one, there were many others. These factors had made the climate a resource that it had not been before, turning the small but lively winter influx that a few towns in Florida had enjoyed in the late nineteenth century into a mass phenomenon by the 1920s and bringing many people to settle year-round.

The growing affluence of the American population, Stockbridge wrote, meant greater opportunities than before for leisure, travel, and recreation. Railroad development had made the state more accessible to the North. So, more recently, had paved roads and the spread of the automobile. Mechanized earth-moving had made it easier to turn sandbars into islands and drain wetlands for sale and development. Public health advances had purged the state of the malaria and yellow fever that had scared many earlier northerners away. They had dispelled the long-standing assumption that a warm land was necessarily an unhealthy one. On the contrary, proclaimed the chief organ of the boom, "an epidemic in Florida is hardly possible on account of the climate and the fresh air the people get. Epidemics spring up where men are herded together in unsanitary conditions and forced to stay indoors, cooped up by the cold weather outside, forced to breathe the same air a number of times, weakened constitutionally by the ravages of cold and fog."[6]

Florida real estate prices, insanely inflated by the beginning of 1926, sagged and then collapsed during the spring and summer.[7] But there was no mass departure even when the frantic land speculation came to an end. Florida kept most of the settlers it had gained and continued to gain more. Dade County, the center of the boom, grew by 250 percent during the decade 1920–1930 and a 1,000 percent in the period 1920–1950.[8]

Another state did even better. Movement to California in the 1920s, though less colorfully promoted than the Florida boom, was far greater in absolute terms, "the largest internal migration in the history of the American people."[9] The entire state grew from a population of 3.4 million in 1920 to 5.7 million a decade later, largely as a result of in-migration, and the south grew much faster than the north.

As with Florida, climate—heavily promoted by such boosterist organizations as San Diego's Year-Round Club, founded in 1921—

accounted for a large share of the increase.[10] California and Florida each had some assets that the other did not—the latter's proximity to the East, coastal California's cooler summers and lower humidity. As competitors in the same market, each did its best to play up its own advantages and denigrate its rival. A snowfall in California, wrote Kenneth Roberts, "causes Florida newspapers to spread loud and exultant headlines entirely across their front pages, declaring excitedly: 'NO LIVES LOST IN CALIFORNIA BLIZZARD.'"[11] Their assets overall were so similar, though, that if the name of the state were omitted from its propaganda, it was observed, one could not easily tell which of the two was being described.[12] California benefited from the same improved transportation, rise in affluence, and rise in leisure time that aided Florida and likewise from agriculture's decline as the chief occupation of migrating Americans. They did not move to California for its similarity in climate to their place of origin, because the climate was unlike any found elsewhere in the United States. Boosters of San Diego pointed out that it was unique not only in the country but in the world, "the ONLY PLACE on the globe" with the winter temperatures of Florida and the Mediterranean and the summer of Scandinavia.[13]

The value of California's climate depended heavily on other factors, and climate itself was far from the only reason for the state's phenomenal growth. It was clearly a major one, though, and all the more clearly so because the models, laws, and assumptions used to account for migration on other grounds failed entirely to predict the great southwestward flow of people. "The greatest single movement in the entire history of the country, one of the greatest in the world," one geographer wrote in 1934, had been the migration to California since the war, but it was of such a novel character that it left him at a loss. "Since the movement is abnormal in most respects," he wrote, "it is inconceivable that it will continue."[14]

Outdoors and Indoors

If the sunnier states exerted a new pull on migration during the early twentieth century, it was in part because of new attitudes toward the sun. As late as the first years after World War I, a beauty advisor could still class a tan as an affliction, to be prevented by "wearing a broad-brimmed hat," applying creams and powders for protection, and "avoiding all unnecessary exposure of the skin to sunlight." "One must be tanned" had become the inexorable rule only a decade later.[15] Costume and outdoor behavior shifted from reducing to increasing exposure, and the parasol as an aid to beauty gave way to the ultraviolet lamp, as well-to-do Americans metamorphosed with remarkable speed from a shade- to a sun-loving species.

Doctors and medical popularizers for the most part applauded.[16] Yet medical advice in earlier times had not persuaded Americans to spend more time in the sun, and it is unlikely that it was responsible for the shift when it occurred. The reasons, rather, were sociological and symbolic. Farming had ceased to be the standard occupation; work for most Americans had shifted indoors. "Our present-day civilization keeps many of us out of the sun for most of every day," wrote a journalist in 1929, and once exposure was no longer routine or easy, it came to be prized: "[A] dark skin color became a sign of higher status, as it was associated with not having to work and with having a preponderance of leisure time in which to relax or participate in sports."[17]

An increase in exposed skin was part of a larger revolution in American dress. Women's long skirts, ineffectively attacked by reformers for most of a century, went the way of the parasol. Hemlines rose from the ground to the knees, even as the better street paving demanded by the spread of the automobile was making long skirts less of a liability than they had ever been before. Sartorial rationalists praised the lighter and scantier clothes that made up the "flapper" look of the twenties as less oppressive in summer than earlier modes.[18] At the same time, they found "the scantiness of apparel worn by many women . . . during the winter months" more mismatched than ever with the cold.[19]

It was in the hot season, on the other hand, that men's heavier garments seemed worst-adapted for comfort or health. The social critic Stuart Chase compared the Middle American businessman, with his "mandatory coat in summer," unfavorably to the Central American villager on the score of sensible dress.[20] Reformers called for the abolition of the wool suit and the hat as obligatory wear and for the legalization of skimpy casual clothes in public places. In some ways, men's costume indeed became lighter, but the change was not in every way a rational one. Heavy winter wool and flannel underwear lost ground, a change facilitated by the spread of central heating.[21] American men increasingly relied on coal rather than clothes for warmth indoors; they were less protected than before from the cold outdoors where protection was most needed.

As advertising accelerated fashion's continuous changes, new styles took hold regardless of regional climate and often persisted regardless of season. Thanks to publicity campaigns, one business consultant bragged, "We have seen 'summer furs' worn in the hottest days and the thinnest hosiery and the most fragile short-vamp shoes in winter. Woolen sweater waists have been made a summer item of every-day wear, although sweaters were formerly worn in winter almost exclusively."[22] With some old maladaptations still apparent and with new ones emerging, critics had as much cause as ever to complain that fashion took precedence over good sense, to lament that "the purpose of clothes has got mixed up with a lot of ideas about adornment, sexual attraction and modesty" and that such elements of "habit and foolishness" had disastrously perverted dress from its proper function: "to make the body relatively immune to changes of temperature."[23]

If that remained the theory of clothing, a paper published in 1941 emphasized how little it had to do with the practice. Standard costume proved to be less a means of adapting to temperature than a means by which satisfactory adaptation was made impossible. Study groups of men and women were asked to come to a research laboratory wearing their normal indoor attire. Women thus clothed reported feeling comfortable when the room temperature was 76 Fahrenheit; men, whose garments were severalfold heavier, preferred a temperature of 71.5 Fahrenheit. Women felt too cold at the latter temperature and men too hot at the former, and an intermediate level satisfied neither.[24] And to English visitors, either level remained excessively hot and a senseless outrage against human comfort.[25]

Insist as some might that "the first function of a house is to shelter from the weather" and that dwelling forms should differ as regional climates did, architectural styles like dress fashions flourished and decayed as national phenomena.[26] Spanish Mission and Spanish Colonial designs multiplied in the North and East, while Californians built Colonial Revival and Cape Cod houses equally unrelated to the conditions around them. The Russian-born sociologist Pitirim Sorokin observed that "over an immense area with the most different climate and other conditions, one sees practically similar types of houses in the East and the West, in the North and the South. The variations in houses in the different parts of the country rarely surpass those between different houses in the same city or neighborhood."[27]

But a style ill-suited to the climate could more easily than ever be insulated against its rigors. Old expedients for windows—double panes in winter and curtains and shutters in summer—remained available. Glass wool and other new insulating materials could make walls less drafty and reduce heat loss; so could the spreading use of plywood as a building material that did not expand and contract with changes in the atmosphere.

As the means of insulation advanced, so did the machinery of space heating. Anthracite, the fuel on which much of the Northeast depended, became increasingly expensive. After the 1902 strike and the 1918 wartime railroad snarl, it bore the taint of unreliability as well. Events of the 1920s did nothing to make it more attractive on either score. Two more strikes again interrupted the winter supply to the cities of the Northeast, while the wage settlements that ended them further raised hard coal's retail price. In the winter of 1922–23, anthracite users had to cope with a 40 percent shortfall in the usual supply; indoor cold and discomfort were widespread. The impact in 1925–26 was still greater.[28]

The strikes shocked many consumers into switching to other fuels that they would soon have found more attractive in any case. Coal, especially soft coal, retained an advantage in cost, but all other considerations were on the side of its rivals. Both oil and natural gas were far cleaner fuels to handle and burn. Both, gas in particular, demanded much less labor and attention than coal did for domestic use. New houses were increasingly designed for gas or oil heating, coal furnaces in the cellars of existing homes scrapped in its favor. Improved design and aggressive promotion of oil burners raised the number of American households using them for heat from some twelve thousand to nearly half a million during the 1920s.[29] Natural gas heating spread more patchily, for its use in any locality had to await a pipeline connection to a place of supply and the laying of a local network for distribution.[30] At the end of the 1930s, most American households—18.5 million—still used coal. Wood was still more widely used than coal in the southern and western states. Gas already heated 4 million households, however, and oil 3 million.[31]

The very well-to-do by that time could enjoy moderate temperatures indoors year-round whatever the temperatures outside. Air-conditioning in the 1920s took its first real steps outside of the industrial world into the realm of climate control—mostly in offices and service establishments—for human comfort. Residential air-conditioning, however, was slow to develop. Technically it was available to anyone who had electricity. "Out of 22,000,000 wired homes in the U.S.," though, a survey in 1938 discovered, "less than 0.25 per cent can yet boast so much as an air-conditioned room."[32] It was not yet clear that much demand existed, at least at the high price that prevailed. Widely affordable cooling units had yet to be devised, save for the crude evaporative devices known as "swamp busters" that worked well in the dry heat of the Southwest.[33]

"I see one-third of a nation ill-housed, ill-clad," said Franklin Roosevelt on taking office in 1933. Some of this state of affairs was the work of the Depression, but the words would have been true even earlier. Central heating itself remained limited to the upper stratum of society. Nationwide, more dwelling units in 1940 still lacked furnaces than had them: 20 million against 14 million. Even in the northern states, only three out of five units had furnaces. In the "Middletown" of the sociologists Robert and Helen Lynd, more than half of the households as late as the mid-1930s were still stove-heated.[34] Only a tenth of American farm households enjoyed central heating. It was virtually unknown in the rural South and West, but even in New England only a third of farmhouses had furnaces, and even in the North Central states, only a fifth. Stove heat itself had yet to reach parts of the country. In the Ozark Highlands, a well-to-do farm family might rely on two open fireplaces to heat the entire ill-insulated house; a poor one, on a single fireplace. The makeshift "Hoovervilles" created by the Depression were comparable in their wretchedness as shelter to the living quarters of many migrant farm workers even in the 1920s.

Conveniences that reduced exposure to the weather were just as unevenly distributed. In Middletown, one in five families in the mid-1930s still used unheated outdoor privies. On American farms, the chief difference was between families that had privies—fewer than 10 percent had indoor plumbing—and those that had no facilities at all.[35] Until the New Deal launched large-scale rural electrification, the horrors of hot weather in much of the countryside still included cooking, canning, and weekly ironing that required the help of a blazing wood or coal fire.[36]

Even many Americans who had previously enjoyed a sheltered existence were introduced by World War II to a severity of heat and cold and wind and precipitation unprecedented in previous conflicts. The global range of the conflict and the very increase in the ability to fight and maneuver in spite of conditions that had once been prohibitive meant greater exposure. "In earlier wars, the generals planned their campaigns to begin when the weather would not be a serious detriment. In World War II, however, the fighting took place at any time, regardless of intense cold and deep snow, sodden, half-frozen earth, burning desert sunshine, or humid tropical heat."[37]

There was discomfort too on the home front. Fuel was rationed, and winter indoor temperatures dropped to levels more typical of England. Oil at first was scarcer than coal, for much of it was transported by tankers that were vulnerable to submarine attack. Washington encouraged homeowners to switch from oil to coal in order to avoid a crisis in the supply of heating fuel—only for strikes, transportation tie-ups, and the demands of other uses to create wintertime shortages of coal as well.[38] Householders were assured that their health and even comfort need not suffer in chillier quarters, for foreign experience showed that the body adjusted readily to "at least 10 degrees below what we in the United States consider the standard temperatures for dwelling houses"; they were urged to dress more warmly ("Wear a sweater and win the war!," ran one such exhortation).[39] A widespread new interest in insulation and passive solar heating as ways of eking out scarce fuel underlined how many such opportunities had been neglected before the war.

Scientific research conducted for the armed forces on the thermal qualities of clothing offered a vision of a happier and more efficient future when protection from the weather would have been reduced to a science. Inefficiency in adapting clothes to climates had been tolerated even in the quite recent past, wrote two of its guiding spirits; fashion had unaccountably remained "the primary consideration among so-called civilized peoples in their choice of clothing." Yet "in the modern competitive world the increasing emphasis placed on efficiency has made such liberties less and less allowable," and the systematic study of comfort would show what kinds of clothing any weather required.[40] The wind chill index, developed during the war, was a further product of the same line of work devoted to stating in precise quantitative terms what temperature meant for comfort. An early critic paid tribute to its rough usefulness as a guide to the weather's severity. He pointed out, though, something that too often went unnoticed when science approached such issues: that even the best-crafted formulae for predicting comfort from physical variables alone could be of only modest use. The stubborn fact remained that "differences . . . above all in mental attitude, make one person feel comfortable when another finds the weather unbearable."[41]

Transportation

The automobile during the 1920s and 1930s became what the passenger train had become, a mobile piece of the indoors. Most American automobiles in 1920 were open to the weather. By 1930, closed cars predominated, and interior space heating became possible. The first systems, economical but slow, used waste heat from the engine-cooling apparatus. The late 1930s brought the first gasoline-burning car heaters, which could produce results within as many seconds as their predecessors had taken minutes. Air-conditioning reached passenger trains in the early 1930s; the first air-conditioned cars were on the market by the end of the decade.[42] The best American models by 1940 were as comfortably sheltered and climate-controlled as the best American homes. English visitors disapproved as they disapproved of Americans's stifling and underventilated dwellings and wondered at "their description of an hour's drive in a car with all the windows closed and the heater turned on, as 'getting a little fresh air.'"[43]

A slew of inventions in one way or another lessened other difficulties that drivers had with the weather. Antifreeze solutions were introduced in the 1920s to lower the freezing point of the cooling fluid and prevent cracking on cold days or nights. The powered windshield wiper was first installed in 1924, the windshield defroster in the 1930s.[44] Another worry for motorists and another advantage for rail that diminished was the old problem of muddy roads in spring and fall. Testimony to the progress that had been made came in 1927 when Henry Ford withdrew the Model T from the market. Designed so effectively for the era of bad roads, it had suffered from the progress of paving—though Ford's action dismayed many who lived in areas that progress had yet to reach.[45]

By then, the private automobile had become central to American life. The Lynds in *Middletown* recorded a remark by a lower-class mother that would become famous: "'We'd rather do without clothes than give up the car.'"[46] Thanks to their greater flexibility, automobiles displaced other means of getting around; they offered personal trans-

FIGURE 4.1. The muddy seasons on unpaved roads remained a widespread problem for drivers in the 1930s.

portation from door to door that was faster and less exposed than travel by horse or bicycle or on foot, that was bound by no set schedule and broken by no intermediate waits for connections.

These advantages outweighed not only their high cost but their problems with the weather, which were distinctly greater than those facing rail travel and which, despite the progress that was made, grew larger in some ways. With the triumph of the horseless carriage came the demise of the horse-drawn sleigh, and snow changed from a resource for movement to a problem of ever-growing proportions. The multiplication of automobiles clogged the streets and made them harder to plow; it also fostered suburbanization that lengthened the trip to work and heightened the difficulty of completing it in bad weather. "The motorized urban society," writes a historian of snow in America's cities, "was becoming more rather than less sensitive to wintertime storms. . . . Moderate storms of four to six inches, once taken in stride by most cities, became major hazards."[47] Not only did the automobile make the lower latitudes more accessible to northerners for vacations or longer stays, but it made sunny and snowless regions vastly more attractive. The development of Florida, promoters declared, "has enabled many an ardent motorist to enjoy his machine during the winter months"; California's dry climate had much to do with its reputation as "kinder to the automobilist than any state in the Union."[48]

Rail remained the dominant means of inland freight hauling, but the nationwide length of track in use peaked between the world wars and began a slow decline. Motor trucking advanced in tandem with the automobile. It benefited from the spread of paved highways and carried an increasing amount of the nation's freight—especially short hauls and such commodities as perishable farm produce. Though costlier, it had the same advantage in flexibility over rail that rail had held over water and that travel by car had over the train, and it shared all of the car's problems with the weather.

The shipping of ore, timber, grain, and other commodities on the Great Lakes was still competitive in an open market, the Ohio River was still a great highway for soft coal, and federal efforts modestly increased freight traffic on the Mississippi and the Sacramento.[49] Otherwise, river and canal traffic continued to lose ground in the 1920s to faster and more reliable carriage by rail and truck. It did not help that by then only sizeable barges could compete in most places with land hauling, and the larger the barges and the more depth that they required, the more of an obstacle dry seasons and low water became. Charles Ellet had proposed in the mid nineteenth century to keep the Ohio River open for steamboat traffic with a six-foot channel, but it took a nine-foot channel, completed by the federal government in 1929 after two decades of work, to keep the Ohio an active freight route.[50]

It did not help either that the winter closing of navigation in the North, with all of the uncertainty as to when it would occur each year, was less and less tolerable under what a team of transportation economists called "the increasing emphasis on regular schedules in business activity." The annual but variable freeze was one of the chief handicaps of New York State's Barge Canal, the enlargement of the Erie opened in 1918, and one of the reasons why it never came close to attracting the amount of traffic for which it had been designed. It never even matched the Erie's mid-nineteenth-century peak, though its operation toll-free at the state's expense—as the federal government maintained the Ohio channel—was a substantial subsidy to shippers.[51]

The wind at sea disappeared as a resource for transportation just as snow did on land. Sail entered its final decline in the 1920s. A frenzy of building to meet wartime needs had left, when peace returned, a vastly oversized fleet of merchant vessels of which the wooden sailing ships were the first to be scrapped. By the mid-1930s, a mere fifteen commercial sailing vessels were still active along the Atlantic coast, and not a single schooner still plied the Great Lakes.[52] The wind became chiefly a recreational resource—and hazard—as pleasure sailing grew in popularity. Fog remained a more serious concern for merchant shipping. As in the past, it could close a major port until it lifted. It was not a handicap to all vessels, though. Like any aspect of the weather, it was only a help or a hindrance according to what people wanted to do. It proved as useful to the marine arm of a booming new sector of the economy between 1920 and 1933 as it had been to southern blockade-runners during the Civil War. A veteran of the Prohibition-era Coast Guard recalled how rumrunners "preferred to do business in thick weather, in fog, rain and blizzards. The dirtier the weather the better they liked it."[53]

Fog was only a minor nuisance for airships, which had a brief vogue during the twenties and thirties but suffered from their slowness and their acute vulnerability to violent wind. Fog and clouds, on the other hand, were the worst of the weather hazards—adverse winds and icing were others—that for years held back the airplane from developing into a safe and dependable mode of travel. So long as pilots navigated by eye, anything that reduced visibility remained a serious hazard during take-off, flight, and landing alike. Disorientation and the inability to maintain altitude and direction without visual guidance produced many crashes in post-1918 as in prewar flying.[54] At the beginning of the 1930s, nearly 20 percent of scheduled air trips were either canceled or not completed, largely because of weather conditions. To the unreliability of service—devaluing its chief asset, its speed—was added the discomfort of flight through low-level turbulence.[55] Airsickness was a problem throughout a flight so long as planes were confined to altitudes of some five thousand to six thousand feet.

Research in the 1920s overcame the most serious obstacles to safe navigation through fog and cloud. Work supported by the Guggenheim Fund expanded and refined the collection of tools that eventually merged into the technique of "blind flying," replacing the pilot's senses with instruments as the chief means of guidance when visibility was poor. The key elements were gyroscopic devices to maintain stability, the altimeter to maintain height above the ground, and a network of radio beacons to guide planes across country and bring them to a safe landing. Demonstrations gradually won over pilots who were at first reluctant to trust instruments over their own—albeit proven undependable—sense of position and direction.[56]

Radio beams were still subject to interruption from static and interference, landings in fog risky, and high winds and icing serious hazards. Yet the 1930s saw a sharp decline in losses and disruptions from the weather, a drop in flight cancellations and delays, and a great rise in commercial air travel's popularity.[57] Flight improved in comfort as well. The closed fuselage having replaced the open one, the heated cabin became possible. Smooth high-altitude flight in pressurized cabins began on commercial routes in 1940.[58]

The Guggenheim Fund also supported better weather forecasting and warnings for aviation. It sponsored trial work on meteorological observations in California along the heavily traveled Los Angeles-San Francisco air route, giving pilots better information about conditions both before take-off and, by radio, while en route. The Weather Bureau took up similar work and benefited in turn from the greater volume and range of weather observations that flight generated. The bureau's transfer in 1940 from the Agriculture to the Commerce Department confirmed the rising importance of its new responsibilities compared to its older ones.[59]

The expansion of radio broadcasting was a change almost as dramatic in American life between the wars as the spread of the automobile. The suspicion was voiced in the 1920s and 1930s that radio, as lightning rods, the telegraph, and electricity in turn had been suspected of doing, was altering and disrupting the weather.[60] Again, it was not, but like each of these earlier technologies the radio did substantially alter what the weather meant to Americans. Most of all, it eased the speedy dissemination of up-to-date forecasts and warnings. Regular weather broadcasts and crop price reports targeted to rural audiences proliferated from the early 1920s onward.[61] Urban listeners likewise gained easier access than before to current forecasts.

A shakeup in the personnel and direction of the Weather Bureau in the 1930s improved forecasting with the introduction of sophisticated European-developed means of analysis in terms of air masses and fronts. Those techniques did much for the military's forecasting capability in the Second World War, though the record compiled was a mixed one. It included successful prediction of conditions before the North Africa landings of November 1942 and D-Day in 1944 and an erroneous forecast of smooth weather before the invasion of Sicily in 1943. But even flawless forecasting was of little help in reducing many weather constraints and impacts.[62] Army campaigns were still much affected by the state of roads and the ground. Wind had long since been dethroned from its commanding importance in naval operations, and mattered chiefly as a hazard when it rose to hurricane strength. The greatly expanded use of aircraft for bombing, reconnaissance, and supply, on the other hand, made cloud and fog far more of a problem than in the past. The wartime development of radar as an aid to blind flying not dependent on ground-based radio beacons would prove to be of immeasurable benefit to air flight, civilian as well as military, after the war.[63]

Such promise of future benefits offered something to offset the hardships of having weather broadcasts curtailed for security reasons. Less than a week after Pearl Harbor, the bureau placed drastic restrictions on the information henceforth to be published, particularly data on wind direction, cloudiness, and frontal movements, all potentially useful for enemy air operations. Radio broadcasts were confined to severe weather warnings; newspaper weather maps were discontinued; and ordinary forecasts were limited to temperature ranges for the following day.[64] "Meteorologically we are living in 1800" was one newspaper's assessment of the new regime—which would have been true, though, only if the provision of forecasts had been the one and only change in weather-society relations to take place since that time.[65]

Business

Shortly before the war, the editors of *Fortune* magazine imagined what would happen in American life if weather forecasters were to go on strike. There would be "losses in the millions" for farmers, shippers, and construction companies deprived of cold-wave forecasts; disasters on the Great Lakes and in the air in the absence of storm warnings, with a suspension of marine insurance and a halt to commercial aviation; disruption of the futures markets, deprived of data on conditions just past; disruption of retailing and recreation from their "inability to plan a day's business"; people would be at a loss to allot their time; the makers and sellers of barometers alone would profit hugely.[66]

If all of these and other calamities did not occur when weather information was restricted in wartime, part of the reason was that the restrictions were not absolute. Businesses were given access to certain kinds of information if they could prove them vital to their activities and their activities vital to the war effort. Severe weather warnings were still communicated to the public as before. But though not misplaced, the emphasis on forecasts as a means of coping with the weather was not complete either. There was much that business could not do to adjust operations to forecasts even when they were available and dependable, much else that it could do to soften impacts and exploit opportunities in other ways. Many important shifts in the weather's economic role had taken place that had nothing to do with better predictions of the weather to come.

As the passing of the horse-drawn sleigh destroyed snow's usefulness in one way, new winter sports made it useful in another. The opening of Averell Harriman's Sun Valley in Idaho in 1936 inaugurated the era of the large ski resort furnished with new devices to move skiers to the top of the slope.[67] But the growing popularity of this and other forms of outdoor recreation also made weather fluctuations costly and disruptive in new ways. Forecasts could do little to help; moving some activities indoors could do much. Enclosed, artificially frozen skating and hockey rinks and indoor tennis courts could operate whatever the weather outside.[68]

Insurance offered open-air businesses another way to stabilize their income. Policies against rain were introduced to the United States only around 1919. Forty companies were providing them by the mid-1920s. They covered losses incurred not only by activities that went on outdoors but by indoor ones that suffered when the weather discouraged the journey to attend: "races, county fairs, baseball and football games and aviation meetings, seaside and riverside hotels . . . exhibits, pageants, fetes, moving pictures, concerts, flower shows, garden parties, athletic contests and the like."[69] They depended heavily on the data collected by the Weather Bureau for calculating probabilities and premiums, but they provided another and surer route around weather problems than use of the bureau's forecasts. In 1921, desiring snow for a scene in the picture he was filming, the movie director D. W. Griffith had an insurance policy written to pay him twenty-five thousand dollars if none fell at the set before work was scheduled to end. It was the first time, an executive observed, that a policy had been issued against the failure of a storm to occur.[70]

Minimal weather interference with outdoor filming was one of southern California's great assets for the movie industry, one that rose in value as films grew longer, budgets larger, schedules tighter, and losses from any interference higher. The possible costs of waiting for nature to provide any desired weather effects rose as well, and directors, including Griffith himself, increasingly preferred making them artificially to filming them in action. Weather needed as background could be simulated by a growing arsenal of devices. "The studio chief engineer," gushed a trade journal as early as 1926, "is a veritable tri-god, combining all the virtues of Helios, the sun god; Pluvius, god of rain, and Thor, lord of thunder." The artificial fog, snow, and thunderstorms long produced on theater stages were supplemented by wind machines, scale-model miniatures ("typhoons in bathtubs," wrote Aldous Huxley, who saw some in use on a visit to Hollywood), trick photography of various kinds, even refrigerated sets with ice- and snow-making devices.[71]

Air-conditioning adapted to the needs of production in particular industries continued to spread. Firms whose work could not be moved indoors developed other tools for coping with the weather. A federal report issued in 1924 did much to dispel what was left of the notion that a winter shutdown in construction was inescapable. Though concrete foundations and shells could not be laid unprotected in cold weather, the concrete could be heated while being mixed and kept warm while setting by small oil- or coke-fired "salamander" stoves distributed around it. The building site could be sheltered from wind and snow by canvas tarpaulins, allowing even exterior work to proceed in all but the severest weather. Stoves could keep the building frame warm enough for such interior tasks as plumbing installation, plastering, and tiling, or the building's heating system could be installed at once and run while indoor work was going on.[72]

These measures were not costless. Some construction jobs, such as road work, were still not feasible in the northern winter. Small tasks—building single-family homes, for example—likewise remained concentrated in the frost-free months. The more technical progress that was made, moreover, the clearer it became that not all of the reasons for seasonality in construction lay on the supply side of the business. Custom in the trade and seasonal peaks and troughs of demand proved less easy to overcome than climatic constraints had.[73]

Much of what held true in the building sector proved to hold true in industry and trade generally. Employment in the United States became more even across the year during the 1920s, and so did strikes.[74] But economic theorists, business and labor consultants, and government officials took a closer interest than before in the puzzle of why the seasonal unevennesses with which businessmen had long had to grapple persisted to the extent that they did. By and large, they discovered what the economist Simon Kuznets noted in a comprehensive review in 1933. Not only in construction, Kuznets wrote, but in many other trades, seasonal operation with all of its inefficient idling of capital and labor was less than ever something imposed directly by weather constraints on production. Such constraints had been greatly weakened by advances ranging from factory air-conditioning—"artificial hot and cold air have made manageable some of the manufacturing operations which had been well nigh impossible during extremes of temperature"—to the replacement of waterway hauling of inputs and outputs by year-round rail transportation. Yet seasonality imposed by demand, by consumer habits and preferences, Kuznets found, was becoming more marked a feature of the economy than ever before.[75]

Some seasonal patterns, such as the pre-Christmas buying boom, were not directly related to the weather. Sales of ice remained an extreme example of one that was. Most of the industry's work force was laid off with the drop in business in winter, while manufacturing capacity sat idle. Mechanical refrigeration gradually settled the matter by making the ice-box obsolete.[76] But many new goods were introduced that were likewise in far greater demand at some seasons than at others. Automobile sales were much higher in the spring than they were in the fall and winter, and gasoline sales peaked with the driving season.[77] Summer static interfered with radio reception and the appeal of the outdoors with listening. Radio sales and production, as a result, were heavily seasonal. The industry laid off nearly half of its workers every spring.[78]

As economic depression made unemployment the major issue of the 1930s, the size of the seasonal work force was an obstacle to one of the remedies proposed.[79] If its members were included in a program of unemployment insurance, their off-season benefits alone seemed likely to exhaust the entire fund every year. If they were not included, then a large share of the work force was left unprotected. The Social Security Act of 1935 resolved the matter by letting each state define the program's scope. The result was a patchwork that nonetheless began to buffer labor against some forms of seasonal layoffs.

More desirable still from most points of view would have been to make employment steadier year-round. The electric utilities had set many examples for lessening the losses inherent in seasonally uneven operation that other enterprises could imitate. To make consumption more even across the year, they had merged power systems, uniting users and regions with different schedules of demand. They had charged premium rates for peak power users; they had aggressively promoted new uses for their product that would raise off-peak sales. As early as 1921, Samuel Insull's Commonwealth Edison of Chicago had so successfully dealt with its summer slump that the six warmest and brightest months, April through September, accounted for fully 47 percent of its yearly output.[80]

In the same spirit, some manufacturing firms cultivated overseas markets in climates with seasonal peaks of demand different from those at home in order to smooth their schedules of production. Others diversified their output by adding "filler" products at the times when demand for their chief offerings was slack. International Harvester's plants had been idle for three months every year when farm machinery sales were low. They began using those months to make other items, from truck bodies to knife grinders. Diversification buffered weather-related as well as seasonal swings in demand affecting rubber goods factories. A severe winter lessened tire sales, but it increased the sales of rubber boots and outerwear, while a mild winter had the opposite effects.[81] Department stores were less sensitive than individual specialty stores to the seasons and the weather not only because they offered shoppers better shelter from the elements, but because they offered a wider range of products. Buying would be active in winter-type goods even when slack in summer-type ones and vice versa.[82]

At the same time that it was overcoming many of the weather's constraints on production, the motion picture industry became better insulated on the distribution side. Early picture houses had become so uncomfortably hot in summer that attendance regularly slumped, and many closed for the season altogether. Cooling systems were first installed in the mid-1920s. Within a decade, they served a majority of the nation's movie theaters. "Almost immediately, the 'summer slump' was turned into a bonanza."[83] A once slack or even idle time became the peak season of attendance; the losses from excess capacity across the year were greatly reduced; and heat waves became as much of an asset to the industry as they had previously been a liability.

Some companies followed utility and coal company precedent by charging lower rates and cutting prices in the slow season, though at the risk of lowering profits at other times. Some firms established off-season contests or quotas among their salesmen to stimulate their energy and ingenuity.[84] Others found that advertising could create demand for their products at times of the year when it had not existed. Sales of raisins and dates peaked in the winter when fresh fruits were scarce, but producers successfully pushed their use in warm-weather salads and desserts. Uninstructed Americans through the early 1920s had drunk Coca-Cola chiefly in the summer. A heavy campaign of advertising featuring scenes of winter sports taught them that "Thirst Knows No Season," and demand became strong year-round.[85] The power of fashion was apparent in the heavy seasonality still typical of garment manufacture.[86] "If fur manufacturers could educate the feminine public into wearing furs in the summer," reasoned another manufacturer, "if felt and silk hats were becoming a summer as well as a winter necessity, surely our sweaters could be made popular in warm weather and eliminate the summer slump."[87]

The automobile industry's seasonal peaks and troughs in the 1920s were in some measure self-inflicted, the unforeseen result of its own attempts at harnessing fashion to increase its sales. General Motors early in the decade pioneered the introduction of new styles every spring in order to raise demand. The price that carmakers paid was to worsen an already serious seasonal imbalance in sales, which already peaked in the spring. In the 1930s, in an attempt to even out employment by setting fashion and weather at odds, the industry shifted to fall as the time for new models, a time less well suited than spring to the buyers but far more convenient to the industry.[88]

The electrical utilities themselves offered not only a model for others trying to cope with the problems of seasonal demand but an unfolding cautionary tale against an overdose of the remedy. By the 1930s, they were in headlong pursuit of the power load that air-conditioning promised to bring. They enthusiastically boosted the new technology in every sphere of American life. Utility leaders saw it as their chance to erase the summer slump once and for all. A few urged caution, fearing that one problem was about to be replaced by another. "As a result of decades of promotional effort," wrote one, "the summer load of many systems has been built up to a point where it approximates the winter load in magnitude. When an executive sees this newcomer, air-conditioning, threatening to build up a large summer peak he cannot be blamed for tearing his hair."[89]

Agriculture

Though the seasonality of trade and work was a problem in sectors of the American economy as up-to-date as radio, automobiles, and motion pictures, it remained most marked in agriculture. It became steadily more so in California, which continued to shift from its early concentration on wheat and livestock toward an impressive variety of mostly high-value and labor-intensive fruits and vegetables sold across the nation. Irrigation and flood control were essential to the shift; so were freezing, canning, refrigerated transportation, and storage; and so were labor arrangements that helped growers solve the problem of finding a large work force willing to work for modest wages for very short periods at harvest time. They had previously found one in Chinese and Japanese pickers. They found another in the 1920s in Mexicans and Filipinos who moved annually across the state harvesting one crop region after another.[90] "The unique nature of California agriculture," wrote the young John Steinbeck, "requires that these migrants exist, and requires that they move about. Peaches and grapes, hops and cotton cannot be harvested by a resident population of laborers . . . a large peach orchard which requires the work of 20 men the year round will need as many as 2000 for the brief time of picking and packing. And if the migration of the 2000 should not occur, if it should be delayed even a week, the crop will rot and be lost."[91]

He exaggerated California's uniqueness. The same challenges faced fruit and vegetable growers in the East.[92] Those raising vegetables and sugarcane in the drained mucklands of the Everglades; apples, berries, and hops in the Pacific Northwest; truck crops in New Jersey; onions in Ohio; tomatoes in Indiana; orchard crops in the Great Lakes states; and strawberries in the lower Mississippi Valley among others had benefited from the same new circumstances expanding the range of their produce but had the same difficulties finding workers. The California case was the largest and most striking, though, and it attracted the most attention, both for its scale and for its great financial success: a success in exploiting a Mediterranean climate that attracted observers from the Mediterranean itself, eager to repeat it at home.[93]

Labor arrangements were not all that the growers needed to make a resource out of the climate. They benefited from the expansion and improvement of federal frost warnings, from better means of frost protection, and from government quarantines on pests. Marketing arrangements overseen by agricultural cooperatives were freed from most antitrust restrictions by the Capper-Volstead Act of 1922.[94] Sugar growers enjoyed much more drastic restraints on competition. Federal policies beginning in the 1930s shut all but a few foreign sources out of the American market.[95] Western farmers on federal reclamation projects continued to receive a substantial subsidy in the form of extensions and cancellations of repayment requirements. Observers in the 1920s raised the question, not for the first time, of why money was thus being spent to subsidize production in an already pathologically overproducing sector with chronically depressed prices.[96]

For the 1920s, on the whole, were not a prosperous but a dismal decade in American agriculture. Events drastically devalued two of its largest crops. Great Plains farmers had exploited their climate by raising wheat in years that had richly rewarded such a specialization. Prices during the First World War had risen sharply and encouraged farmers to expand their operations. Peace brought a drop in demand and the revival of farming elsewhere. American farmers planted more wheat to make up for falling prices and thereby worsened the glut, worsened too by generally good weather, that kept their incomes depressed.[97] Cotton farmers of the Southeast had prospered like wheat growers during the war. Prices peaked in 1919, then plummeted in the early 1920s and remained low throughout the decade. The depression that followed the stock market crash of October 1929 soon spread worldwide. One of its early results was a further abrupt decline in demand for wheat and cotton alike. The latter in 1931 brought less than a third what it had the year before the crash.[98]

In the Depression years, a clear distinction between natural and economic disasters proved even less easy than usual to maintain. Severe drought in the summer of 1930 withered cash and subsistence crops across much of the South. Resulting hunger and want confronted the Red Cross with a challenge far larger than any it had handled before and under circumstances more difficult than usual. The nationwide economic slowdown had taxed the resources of its donors just as the need for help was greater than it had ever been. It also magnified the impacts of harvest failure in the cotton belt, where hard times had already stretched resources thin and where the stagnant economy made off-farm work impossible to find, while less food than usual could be gathered from gardens and forests and rivers than in years of normal rainfall. In Appalachia, the slump that had begun to affect the coal industry in the early 1920s cut employment in the mines. Many families had had to return to subsistence farming on a poor soil, a living so precarious at best that the added impact of the drought threatened them with starvation.[99]

By the winter of 1930–31, depression, as well as intensifying the impacts of the drought, had created nationwide poverty entirely unrelated to weather shocks. The Red Cross was the acknowledged agency for helping Americans left destitute by disaster. The needs even of the rural drought-affected region alone, though, were larger than anything the Red Cross had ever had to meet. Though urged by President

Hoover and others to take on the tasks of drought and unemployment relief, it declined to enter the latter field on its own. Hoover and the lame-duck Republican majority in Congress, for their part, were unwilling to establish a federal dole or to endow the Red Cross with public money for either task. They clung to the principle that the remedy for hard times lay in self-help aided by private giving. The only measures that Congress did adopt and Hoover accepted offered farmers loans to feed their livestock and plant the next season's crops. Because collateral was required, the loans could help only those who had assets to provide it, as sharecroppers and tenant farmers typically did not.[100]

The Red Cross's drought relief efforts—it aided two and a half million families in all, was supporting half a million in February 1931, and undoubtedly prevented many deaths from hunger and disease—also exposed some of the weaknesses of its favored mode of operation.[101] It had always insisted on working through local committees with the goal of reestablishing as quickly as possible the preexisting way of life in the affected area. That policy had much to be said for it. At the same time, the local committees did not necessarily represent the interests of most residents or of the most needy. Those of Appalachian Kentucky, Tennessee, and West Virginia "viewed the drought as an act of Providence that would rid the mountains of the poor," especially of ex-miners who had gone back to subsistence farming, and they acted accordingly.[102] The planter-dominated committees that administered relief in the cotton belt kept rations for the destitute low during the fall picking season to avoid driving up the price of labor and the standard of living at that crucial time of year, then raised them to keep the workforce fed and settled during the idle season. The very systems of livelihood that the Red Cross sought to restore had had much to do with the fact that some of the hardest-hit victims were so vulnerable to the drought to begin with.

So too the Great Plains droughts of the 1930s known collectively as the Dust Bowl were not the same crisis for all farmers in the region affected.[103] They brought opportunities to those who could take advantage of them. Wealthier farmers could expand their holdings and employ labor at distress wages. The fact that the Dust Bowl, like the southern drought of 1930–31, coincided with the Great Depression meant that its impacts on those hardest-hit were more severe than they would have been a decade earlier.

The dry years on the Plains in the 1890s, likewise worsened by global depression and deflation, had also impoverished many farmers across the region. They had driven out a larger share of the population, in fact, than the meteorologically harsher droughts of the 1930s did.[104]

For the fact that the Dust Bowl coincided with the New Deal meant that federal aid was forthcoming as it had not been before. Power in Congress changed hands in the 1930 election and the White House two years later. A new regime was installed that was far less averse than Hoover's to vigorous federal measures for relief.

One of these measures was emergency aid to disaster sufferers. The rule so staunchly defended by Hoover, that handouts must be avoided and that even crisis needs must be met chiefly through private effort and charity, was abandoned. Though the Red Cross continued to operate as before, Washington gradually assumed ultimate responsibility for seeing to it that basic needs were met during emergencies of any sort. Aid to farmers under the New Deal took forms as varied as food assistance, government loans, cattle purchases, feed grain subsidies, and public works employment.

Some early New Dealers had more radical measures in mind. They saw the basic problem of the Plains as the overextension of farming into a climate too unreliable to support it. Their solution, harking back to John Wesley Powell, was to return large areas of cropland to grass for grazing and resettle the farm population elsewhere. But such efforts met stiff resistance in the region itself, and policy turned instead to helping farmers cope with the climate as it was.[105] Federal money built water storage and distribution works, from large irrigation projects to small local and farm-level systems, that offered emergency relief jobs and promised to make agriculture permanently less vulnerable to drought.[106] Private hail and tornado insurance had long existed, but a section of the Agricultural Adjustment Act of 1938 instituted the first durable program of drought protection through all-risk crop insurance. Limited for a trial period to wheat but extended within a few years to cotton, it was supported by subsidies to cover the program's operating expenses and by regular appropriations that proved necessary to cover the excess of claims over premiums. Opponents of the program warned that it would require such help every year. It would also, they predicted, encourage the farming of risky and marginal areas by farmers who would reap the benefits of good years and trust to insurance in the bad ones—and indeed it signaled the end of the earlier focus on discouraging "marginal" settlement.[107]

But historically, drought and other hazards cutting yields had been only one of the weather risks in farming. A second had been unusually good weather, which raised output so high that prices and incomes collapsed. Henry A. Wallace, secretary of agriculture during the New Deal and a farmer, farm journalist, and crop breeder himself, well understood both concerns. When Wallace described the severe drought year of 1934 as more a blessing than a disaster, he meant that by bringing down output, it had done much to erase the accumulated surpluses that for years had kept American farm incomes depressed.[108] Overproduction and low prices in the 1920s had been not merely occasional but chronic, driving farmers to plant more and thereby further worsen their common plight.

The New Deal response was the Agricultural Adjustment Acts of 1933 and 1938. These bills contained measures to stabilize both farmer income and national food supply against what Wallace called two opposite kinds of disaster, "extreme swings due to tricky weather" whether too bad or too good.[109] The danger of excessive harvests would be averted, and the added goal of soil conservation promoted, by acreage limitations that farmers would be paid to accept and by government loans that would help them store crop surpluses. Such storage would buffer consumers against high prices in bad years, while crop insurance would protect producers.

The two acts channeled federal dollars chiefly to landowners, especially large ones. They did little for smallholders, and even less for sharecroppers, tenant farmers, and farm laborers.[110] Indeed, the placing of restrictions on acreage rather than output prompted cotton growers in particular to intensify and mechanize their operations, getting more output from the same area, and discharge many of their tenants and sharecroppers. This expulsion from the land formed the chief source of the great 1930s migration of "Okies" and other poor southerners seeking work in California. By swelling the labor force, it was in turn a boon to that state's cotton and produce growers—until the coming of war made labor scarce again and prompted the government to arrange the admission of Mexican farmworkers in large numbers.[111]

In the public mind, the "Okies" were promptly and mistakenly labeled as refugees from the dry years on the grain-farming Plains. "The plight of the migrants," wrote Carey McWilliams in 1942, "was characterized as a 'natural catastrophe'—'a tragedy of the dust bowl'—and the migrants themselves became 'refugees from drought,'" though very few were.[112] Most were from the cotton states; most refugees from the Dust Bowl went elsewhere. The misunderstanding has not gone away, and even historians who take pains to correct it have been saddled nonetheless with the very term "Dust Bowl migration," to denote the influx to California, that reflects and reinforces it.[113] That influx was indeed a flight from a weather-related agricultural upheaval, but it was not the one commonly supposed. Most migrants to California were victims less of the direct effects of bad weather than of measures taken for protection against good weather.

Floods and Storms

Rising federal involvement in flood management was as striking a trend of the 1920s and 1930s as the growth of agricultural programs. Only in 1917 had Washington overtly entered the war against inundations, and then only on two rivers—the Mississippi and the Sacramento—judged to be of national importance. The strategy remained the one favored earlier: keeping the river within its channel by more and higher and stronger levees along the banks. Local and state levee authorities who could demonstrate a certain level of expenditure could for the first time receive federal help.

This approach did well enough in its first major test, the Mississippi River flood of 1922. In the spring of 1927, however, heavy rains and snowmelt filled the channel with more water than it had ever had to carry since the first Europeans had settled along its banks. Despite frantic efforts to shore them up, the levees broke in more than a hundred places from Illinois to the Gulf of Mexico. Seventeen million acres in seven states were submerged, along with 160,000 homes, mostly in Louisiana, Arkansas, and Mississippi.[114]

Not least of the casualties was the "levees-only" policy. The federal flood protection act of 1928 ensured that the Mississippi levees would be rebuilt and raised further, but other tools were to be tried as well: upstream reservoirs for floodwater storage, cutoffs of river meanders to move water through the valley faster, and floodways and spillways, branch channels along the river's path whose outlets could be opened in emergencies to draw off excess volume. The act, moreover, made flood control on the Mississippi the responsibility principally of Washington. Local contributions were no longer a condition for federal help.[115] Similar measures transformed the basin of the Sacramento River, once subject to frequent overflows, into a rich rice, fruit, and vegetable growing region, and even navigation on the newly tamed channel boomed.[116]

Engineering solutions, meant to prevent floods from occurring, remained the core of policy. The federal government in earlier floods had made small cash contributions for emergency relief. In 1927, it left the provision of food, clothing, and shelter entirely to private charity and the states, though Secretary of Commerce Herbert Hoover did provide many services to facilitate aid work and economic recovery. Relief was administered chiefly by the Red Cross. It earned much applause for the way in which it met so large a challenge. But the flood, as the drought of 1930–31 would do, also illustrated more clearly than ever some of the problems with the Red Cross's long-preferred approach: that of working closely with local leaders to restore the previous order as soon as possible. The most powerful figures of the lower Mississippi's rural floodplain were the cotton planters of the Yazoo Delta. They had every interest in seeing aid limited and administered in a way that would not fundamentally alter the economy nor deprive them of cheap labor.[117]

Hoover as president remained unwilling to commit the federal government to emergency relief, whether for unemployment or for natural disasters. His stance was one of the factors that brought Franklin Roosevelt and the New Deal to power in Washington in 1933 and led to a much enlarged federal relief role. Enlarged too was the federal role in building flood protection works. New Deal planners saw their construction as a means of reducing unemployment and stimulating economic recovery in the short term that would also leave a useful legacy to the future. A federal act of 1936 declared flood control on rivers throughout the Union to be a national concern and a proper field for federal spending. It defined any project as an acceptable one if its total benefits exceeded its total costs. A second act in 1938 made the program more purely a federal responsibility by doing away with a requirement for state and local contributions.[118] Flood control, along with power generation and navigation, was also a key part of the activities of the Tennessee Valley Authority, organized separately under the New Deal.

Control works proliferated on America's rivers: levees, dams, storage reservoirs, channel improvements, and spillways. On the Tennessee and elsewhere, hydroelectric power generation was made a part of many projects. As irrigation water, relief aid, and crop insurance were meant to do with droughts, the combination of emergency assistance and engineering works was meant to rob floods of much of their power to harm and make rivers more useful in other ways. Undoubtedly it did. It did other things as well. By expanding the sphere of federal action from two of America's rivers to all of them, the new policy introduced a pork barrel element in decision-making about projects. It encouraged the agencies charged with flood control to justify more projects though dubious cost-benefit calculations in order to increase their appropriations.[119] It imposed gains and losses unequally, displacing many upstream communities to build reservoirs for the sake of ones downstream and far distant. A critic wrote of the TVA's dams that "in order to achieve flood control, they would have to create a permanent flood in the valley itself," evicting many people and destroying many landmarks. Their undoubted benefits would be purchased by "harms, inflicted upon a sizable and innocent minority."[120]

As Congress got deeper into the business of regulating rivers, there remained a few voices to urge a different course of action, to reiterate

FIGURE 4.2. The Tennessee Valley Authority's Norris Dam, one of many that helped even out streamflow in the interests of flood control, navigation, and electric power generation.

"the self-evident fact . . . that flood waters cause damage only to the extent that value is placed in their path. Therefore, such damages can be minimized not merely by reducing the height or frequency of floods, but by reducing the occupancy and values of areas subject to floods." The policy being pursued, of raising protection works and re-building after every flood, might indeed raise damage in the future.

Ought not the replanning as well as the reconstruction of flooded areas be considered as an alternative, the critics asked, and ought not property owners in them pay assessments to lighten the burden imposed on others?[121]

These points were developed in detail in the first important assessment of federal flood control policy, that of a young geographer named Gilbert F. White in the University of Chicago Ph.D. dissertation that he completed in 1942.[122] White catalogued a wide range of possible tools for dealing with the flood hazard. Recent policy, he observed, had selected a few and disregarded the others. It emphasized protection by flood control works and loss-sharing through emergency relief. It largely ignored policies by which to discourage floodplain occupation and development, the chief process that gave floods their potential for harm. White too pointed out that the measures favored—"protecting the occupants of floodplains against flood, of aiding them when they suffer flood loss"—might have the effect of encouraging development in areas that could never be protected perfectly. Against all intentions, they might in the end increase rather than lessen flood losses. Insurance, a means of coping not yet seriously tried, might soften impacts by spreading them, but unless premiums were calculated to reflect actual risks, it too might promote rather than reduce damage.

White's larger point was that "Floods are 'acts of God,' but flood losses are largely acts of man." It held true of all extreme weather events and indeed of all weather phenomena. Coastal storms continued to occur as before, but their human significance continued to change as human activities did. The damage done by the great New England hurricane of 1938 differed in countless ways from that done by other storms in the past. The Red Cross had help in its relief work from New Deal programs such as the Works Progress Administration and the Farm Security Administration, and the depressed economy meant that labor for repairs and rebuilding was cheap and plentiful. In Hartford, Connecticut, and Springfield, Massachusetts, protective works built after the New England floods of 1936 made the rise of the Connecticut River much less damaging than it would otherwise have been. The toll on the wooden sailing fleet of earlier times would have been catastrophic; as it was, merchant shipping suffered less than small recreational craft, which were more numerous than ever before. Coastal summer and year-round homes, which had also proliferated, accounted for the greater part of the buildings leveled or damaged. The storm downed thousands of miles of power lines, and affluent households dependent on modern electric devices were deprived for weeks of basic comforts. The Yale archaeologist A. V. Kidder pointed out that modernization had in many ways magnified the hurricane's impact: "Think what happened to those of us in New England who lived in the most specialized of modern homes. The electric current failed and we had no heat, no light, no water, no ice. But the farmer continued happily to sit by his stove, and read by his lamp, and pump from his well."[123]

Not every modern device, though, had made life more vulnerable. Highway and track washouts, bridge failures, and felled trees blocked road and rail travel for many days. But the newest means of transportation, air service, resumed the morning after the hurricane passed. It did a tremendous business among impatient travelers, and it also made possible the rapid shipment of medical and other emergency supplies. Forest destruction in north-central Massachusetts was extensive, but the economic loss that it represented was far smaller than it would have been fifteen years earlier. The region's timber had been valuable at that time for making wooden boxes. A shift in techniques had made it all but worthless by 1938.[124]

Three disastrous hurricanes struck Florida in 1926, 1928, and 1935.[125] One of the factors that made the first particularly damaging was the great land boom. Though it had already collapsed by September when the storm struck, it had swelled the population of the low-lying, hurricane-prone coastal strip of the Miami area and covered it with hasty and shoddy construction. Yet because the boom had deflated, the buildings destroyed were worth far less and the economic loss was much lower than if the same storm had arrived a year earlier. Inland agricultural development, on the other hand, did much to magnify the loss in both 1926 and 1928. Drainage efforts in the Everglades, after many reverses, had created a rich truck farming area on the shore of Lake Okeechobee where the exposed population had previously been small. High winds spread the lake's rain-swollen waters over farm workers' settlements, and at least two thousand lives were lost in 1928. Most of the four hundred who perished in the 1935 hurricane were World War I veterans in federal relief camps working on the new Overseas Highway between Key West and the mainland and helplessly exposed to the high storm surge. Each disaster was not the work of the timeless forces of nature but was very much an event of its own day. So was the most damaging storm of the war years, a typhoon that sank three American destroyers in the South Pacific, damaged many other ships, and took almost eight hundred lives in December 1944. The loss was the combined result of the weather, of ship design, of disregard of weather warnings, and, above all, of the military considerations that had placed the fleet in the storm's path.[126]

Weather and Climate Control

If they could have used weather control as a weapon of combat, the strategists who ended the Second World War by using the atomic bomb would doubtless not have hesitated. If they could have dealt with floods and droughts not by building dams and distributing relief, but by controlling the rainfall, New Deal planners would surely have done so. They worried hardly at all about the extent of their authority; it was the power to intervene in the heavens that science told them they lacked. American meteorologists and climatologists of the time insisted that human activity could have no more than small and local effects on the weather, and they tolerated no dissent from that belief.

Scientists did not deny that the climate of the farm or the building or the city block was much changed from its original state and might be changed further. Walls and windbreaks gave crops some protection against harsh and desiccating winds, while screens and stoves and smudgepots and flooding of fields protected others against frost. Enclosing spaces with walls and roofs gave shelter from rain and snow and wind and made artificial heating and cooling possible. A few kinds of fog might be dispersed one day by means yet to be devised.

There was "no hope, however, of our ever being able to bring about any but local modifications."[127] On that point, American weather scientists were unyielding. Rain could not be produced, they insisted, not by any of the favored methods of the past, not by any others that could be devised. Cannonading the sky and erecting metal rods to draw off its electricity, both long practiced in Europe, were two means equally useless for preventing hailstorms. Tornadoes could not be dissipated by explosions. Fog could never be dispersed more than briefly over small areas. Planting forests would not bring rain to dry lands nor soften harsh summers and winters. Projects grander still—diverting ocean currents and flooding deserts—scientists dismissed with a wink and a shrug.

Their predecessors had said much the same at the turn of the century, but not with the same success in cowing the public. Americans in the years between the wars took the lesson more submissively and talked back much less than their forbears had done. When they still proposed or tried to change the weather, the means on which most of them relied were frankly supernatural ones. The commercial rainmakers who had flourished in earlier times were few and inconspicuous in the droughts of the 1930s. Rain was desperately short on many occasions, but prayer was the only form of summoning a shower still frequently tried. Even that more than ever came under attack as unscientific, for liberal theologians found it an embarrassing anachronism. The leading Protestant modernist of the time, Dr. Harry Emerson Fosdick, declared: "No imaginable connection exists . . . between man's inward spiritual state and a rainstorm . . . Evidently this still needs to be said in this benighted and uncivilized country. The crude, obsolete supernaturalism which prays for rain is a standing reproach to our religion."[128]

Conservatives and fundamentalists disagreed, but with all of the possible means of weather control in headlong retreat, all of the questions awakened in the past about its possible injustices and inequities slept quietly throughout the period. The endlessly repeated denial that weather control was possible was a lullaby in their ears. There was little reason to worry about whether or not it was desirable or what abuses it might engender. Only in a work of fiction, and of light fantasy at that, did such questions arise. Only there, when the means of making rain were perfected, did the devout oppose its use, as a trespass on the realm of the Creator; did clashing ideals split the ranks of its defenders into those preferring "independent rains, pure democracy, every man his own rain agent," others "cooperative rains freely arranged," and still others "standardization, enforced acquiescence, regulated rains of regularized intensity and duration, all weather originating with a Rain Bureau which should operate from the capital"; and were county-level Rain Boards eventually adopted as a compromise.[129]

Weather scientists would take on even a popular president who dared hint that the climate could be modified. In 1934, Franklin D. Roosevelt outlined a program of tree planting on the Great Plains to form a vast regional "Shelterbelt." Geographers found Roosevelt's reference to "ameliorating drought conditions" as the Shelterbelt's chief purpose highly suspect.[130] The forester Raphael Zon, one of the new project's directors, hastened to set matters straight. He himself had long spoken of tree planting in the West as a means of regulating rainfall across all of the United States. By 1934, he was as good as apologizing for those earlier views. It was only "popular imagination and newspaper publicity," Zon assured the critics, that had turned the Shelterbelt into a "grandiose plan of changing the climate of the entire plains region." It would have some climatic benefits, he said, but strictly local ones. It would protect the crops and livestock of the abutting landowners "against the desiccating winds of summer and the cold blizzards of winter." With the possibility of anything more, Zon declared himself not concerned.[131]

The onslaught against the loose talk about the Shelterbelt repeated John Wesley Powell's campaign against "rain follows the plow" half a century earlier. As Powell's had, his successors's claims about human impotence to affect the weather rested on some unproven assumptions about the way things were. The key assumption was that the weather operated on a scale dwarfing any human forces that could ever impinge upon it. Powell had drawn a simple and sweeping conclusion: "Nothing that man can do will change the climate." His successors' message was more nuanced but essentially the same: "The most, and the best, that man can ever hope to do is to deal with a very small part of it, over a very limited space at best."[132]

The message was not altogether correct, but many errors have their uses, and this one had more than most. The lesson that could be drawn from it was an immensely valuable one: that if Americans wished to lessen their losses from the weather, they would do better to adapt their activities to avoid damage and disruption than to dream of changing the weather itself. The things that could be done to reduce flood losses, as Gilbert White showed, ranged far beyond trying to confine rivers within their banks; no more did their inability to control the weather mean that Americans had to sit passively and fatalistically beneath it. They could in many ways adjust the things that they did and the locations in which they did them to make the weather less harmful and more useful—if that was what they most wanted to do.

This view of climate-society relations emphasized the key independent role of human activity in deciding what effects the weather would have. In that sense, it turned on its head another approach, that of environmental determinism, which explained human behavior, culture, and institutions as shaped by the effects of the weather or climate or other elements of the biophysical surroundings. Yale's Ellsworth Huntington (1876–1947) was the most influential representative in the academic world, in popular periodicals, and on public library shelves of geography as a science of society built on such a determinism.[133] In works from *Civilization and Climate* (1915) to *Mainsprings of Civilization* (1945), Huntington asserted the great importance of weather and climate in human life and the objective superiority of some parts of the earth and times of the year over others. Most favored, as he saw it, were the temperate latitudes, the seasons of spring and fall, and regions experiencing frequent change in temperature and barometric pressure from passing frontal storms. Warm and humid climates, on the other hand, fostered laziness, poverty, social inequality, political instability, violent crime, and sexual immorality. The world map of civilization had always closely resembled that of climate, Huntington asserted, and he tried to link the great epochs in human history, the flowering and decline of past civilizations, to climatic changes, particularly shifts in the prevailing tracks of storms.

If climate were indeed such a controlling factor, then human progress required that it itself be brought under human control—a depressing thought, Huntington granted, given what science said about that possibility. "We cannot change the climate," he observed, "so why ascribe to it such great effects merely to destroy hope in some and moral responsibility in others?" Apart from waiting for a natural shift and hoping that it would be for the better, he had only two "ways of overcoming the handicaps of climate" to suggest. One was to move activities indoors as much as possible and control the indoor climate better, adjusting winter space heating more precisely to the objective ideal and developing an equal capability for space cooling in the hot season. The other was to substitute a change of climate for a climatic change. Massive migrations could be arranged to bring working people from the less favored zones during the less favored seasons to settings more conducive to human energy: "In the future," Huntington wrote, "we may expect that such interchanges will take place on a scale to stagger the imagination."[134]

Second only to Huntington as a promoter of determinism was the medical researcher Clarence A. Mills, best known for a 1942 book whose title summed up its point of view: *Climate Makes the Man.* Mills went so far as to blame the Great Depression on a series of unusually warm and stormless seasons that had sapped human energy. He dismissed the New Deal and all other proposals for reviving the economy as useless. When the weather rebounded, he wrote in 1934, business would follow. Until that happened, government spending to stimulate recovery was a "useless wasting of national resources," for it could do nothing "to counteract the depressive effect of the weather."[135]

Not everything that climatic determinists wrote was climatic determinism. Huntington himself rejected the label. He pointed out that he never claimed that climate determined everything. Yet to claim that it determines anything, as he often did, is determinism still. As time went on, he found fewer colleagues to agree with him. Briefly influential in the social sciences, his approach was rapidly losing ground by the 1920s. Critics within geography—Berkeley's Carl Sauer, Isaiah Bowman of the American Geographical Society and Johns Hopkins, Preston James of the University of Michigan—exposed its fatal weaknesses. It erred in giving climate and other environmental factors a greater importance in human life than the evidence warranted. It erred more fundamentally as to what kind of factors they were. It all too readily took their role to be something fixed and independent of society, when the facts, as James wrote, showed that "the significance of the elements of the environment is determined by the nature of the people. . . . No climate . . . should be described as inherently favorable or unfavorable except in terms of specific human cultures."[136]

The critics knew better than to dismiss the environment as an element in human life simply because Huntington and others had exaggerated and oversimplified its role. The environment could matter greatly, they understood, but only because of what people did, wanted to do, and were able to do, none of which the environment itself ever determined and all of which shifted over time in ways that continually made the environment matter differently. "The geographical elements of the environment are fixed only in the narrow and special sense of the word," Bowman wrote. "As soon as we give them human associations they are as changeful as humankind itself. That is why modern geography has so definitely steered away from determinism. . . . The physical world changes constantly in its *meaning* to man."[137]

Since 1945: New Amenities, New Hazards

Migration

If the average citizen's surroundings defined the national climate, then the United States grew markedly warmer and drier in the postwar decades. Migration continued to carry the center of population west and began pulling it southward as well. The growth of what came to be called the Sunbelt at the "Snowbelt's" expense passed a landmark in the early 1960s when California replaced New York as the most populous state. Another landmark was established in the early 1990s when Texas moved ahead of New York.

In popular discussion, it was taken for granted that finding a change of climate was one of the motives for relocating as well as one of the results. It was not until 1954, though, that an American social scientist first seriously considered the possibility.[1] The twentieth-century flow of Americans to the West Coast, the geographer Edward L. Ullman observed in that year, had no precedent in world history. It could not be explained by the theories of settlement that had worked well in the past, for a substantial share of it represented something entirely new, "the first large-scale in-migration to be drawn by the lure of a pleasant climate."

If it was the first of its kind, it was unlikely to be the last. For a set of changes in American society, Ullman suggested, had transformed the economic role of climate. The key changes included a growth in the numbers of pensioned retirees; an increase in trade and service employment, much more "footloose" than agriculture or manufacturing was; developments in technology making manufacturing itself more footloose; and a great increase in mobility brought about by the automobile and the highway. All in one way or another had weakened the bonds of place and made Americans far freer than before to choose where to live.

Whatever qualities made life in any spot particularly pleasant thus attracted migration more than in the past. Ullman grouped such qualities together as "amenities." They ranged from mountains to beaches to cultural attractions, but climate appeared to be the most important, not least because it was key to the enjoyment of many of the rest. Ullman did not suppose that all Americans desired the same climate. For most people, in this as in other respects, "where one was born and lives is the best place in the world, no matter how forsaken a hole it may appear to an outsider." But in a country the size of the United States, those who wanted a change could still be quite numerous and quite important in net patterns of migration. And there was, Ullman suggested, a standard by which to identify the areas that would appeal to most of them. They would seek an outdoor climate similar to the one that most maintained when the climate was under their control, that is, inside their homes: a year-round temperature of about seventy degrees Fahrenheit, and no precipitation.

This ideal was best represented in the continental United States by coastal California. The next best approximation was found along Florida's southeastern shore, its summer heat tempered by constant breezes from the Atlantic Ocean. The desert Southwest, the Gulf and South Atlantic coasts, and the Pacific Northwest enjoyed more blurred versions of the optimum climate as Ullman saw it.

This optimum had little to do with the needs of agriculture, nor did it have much to do with livelihood in general. It was defined on other grounds entirely. It was optimal for thermal comfort according to the prevailing national standard in such matters. It was also the ideal climate for outdoor recreation—independently defined by the economist Marion Clawson as "one where it never rained, was always pleasantly warm but not hot, was always mildly sunny, was never too humid, had only gentle breezes"[2]—for driving, increasingly the chief outdoor activity in the United States, and for keeping heating and cooling costs low. Postwar California had profited greatly from its natural resources, another geographer wrote in 1959, but they were largely resources of a new kind: exploited by consumers, not by producers.[3]

A popular *Places Rated Almanac* first appeared in 1981 and went into a fifth edition in 1997. Its authors had no doubts about the importance of climate: "It decides what we'll wear, when we vacation, whether we'll work outside—even how much we pay to keep the indoors comfortable."[4] Climate earned eighty-three pages in the 1997 edition, against twenty-five devoted to "Jobs," twenty-nine to "Cost of Living," forty-four to "Education," and twenty-one to "Crime." The almanac's criteria for a good climate were quite close to those that Ullman had identified. They were mildness, the absence of extreme temperatures, winds, and humidity; brightness, the prevalence of sunny days; and stability, or a low degree of storminess and a narrow range of seasonal temperature variation.

The almanac ranked the 351 metropolitan areas in the United States and Canada on these three criteria. Nine of the ten most attractive were in California; the rest of the top fifty were in California, Florida, Oregon, Washington, Texas, Arizona, and British Columbia. The one addition to the list of areas that Ullman had named as the most highly favored ones, Hawaii (Honolulu ranked in the almanac's top ten), only bore out his point that the value of climate changes with society and technology. When Ullman was writing in 1954, Hawaii had been difficult to reach; within a few years, it was readily accessible by jet air service. Its addition to the list also underlined the shift in evaluations that had taken place. In 1898, when Congress was debating the annexation of the islands, one opponent had pointed to their disagreeable seasons—or lack of seasons—as an argument for leaving them alone: their "absence of extreme cold and intense heat results in a warm sameness that is enervating in the extreme." Little did he know that a century later it would be thought a description of the ideal. "One period's asset is another's liability and vice versa," as Ullman would write in another context.[5]

Places Rated does not directly show how important a pleasant climate is to Americans today. It shows only how important the authors of a commercial publication striving to give Americans what they want think one is. But that itself is suggestive, and in fact the authors do not seem to have erred in their emphasis. Academic research on migration has not paid strong or consistent attention to climate as a factor. Ullman's article, though widely read, inspired little further research. Few studies of migration in the United States through recent years have attempted to weigh the possible role of amenities, climate included. Yet the exceptions generally bear out both Ullman's claims for climate as a significant factor and his description of the features that most attract population: moderate temperatures at all seasons, low humidity, little wind, and no snow.[6]

Climate's dominant role in a second phenomenon, seasonal migration, is well established. Since the end of World War II, the numbers of "snowbirds," northern retirees spending part of the winter in warmer climates, have grown enormously. By the time of the 1980 census, nonpermanent residence in the United States was heavily concentrated in winter in four states: Florida, California, Arizona, and Texas. By the late 1980s, some seventy-five thousand retirees from Minnesota alone spent periods in winter averaging eleven weeks out of state, almost all in lower latitudes. In interviews, "the overwhelming explanation for having chosen a seasonal migratory life-style was the desire to escape severe Snowbelt winters."[7]

Large-scale seasonal migration tends, among its other effects, to unbalance the economies of both source and destination regions. For both, it means too much labor and infrastructure at some times of the year and too little at others. Oceanside summer resort areas in the north, with milder temperatures and other attractions, experience the same unevenness in use. Cape Cod, Martha's Vineyard, and Nantucket are overwhelmed by visitors and spending during the warm months, with severe overcrowding and a shortage of labor that disappear altogether in the winter.

Growth itself can produce disamenities eventually outweighing the amenities that spawned them. Climate's value can be reduced as well as enhanced by changes in other spheres of life. The value of amenities, even of ones such as climate themselves largely unchanged by development, is never fixed or absolute but depends on other factors. A close look at the late-twentieth-century California economy showed that the state's leading source of income was not agriculture or industry but real estate transactions; "[T]he primary business of California has been the selling of pieces of California to people willing to pay ever larger amounts for the privilege of living in one of the finest climates on earth."[8] By the 1990s, though, growth for the first time showed signs of eroding its own base, not by damaging the climate but by raising the cost of enjoying it. The state registered a net out-migration during much of the decade. Most of it went to places in the inland West sharing California's dry climate (if not the moderate temperatures of its coastal sections), but less costly, crowded, and stressful to live in. And these places, in turn, as a result of this influx, became more like the California that the emigrants were fleeing.[9]

Indoors and Outdoors

If the national climate were measured not by conditions in the open air but by those in which people spent most of their time, that of the postwar United States became far milder and more uniform than before. Indoor winter temperatures, forced down by wartime fuel rationing, rebounded when peace arrived. Central heating, thermostatically controlled, changed from a luxury to something widely taken for granted. Coal faded rapidly as a fuel, and oil more slowly in favor of cleaner and more convenient substitutes. By the 1990s, gas was used to heat half of the nation's households, electricity half of the remainder.[10]

Electric heating benefited from the spread of electric-powered space cooling. The design and marketing of small, affordable units for room use brought air-conditioning within the reach of many American households. In 1960, one in eight enjoyed it. Only ten years later, more than one in three did. As a result, a problem was solved that had troubled the electric power companies since their birth in the late nineteenth century—the surplus of winter over summer demand. By the late 1950s, the spread of air-conditioning in many areas, particularly in the South, was shifting the residential peak demand to the hot months.[11] Once it no longer consumed peak-season power, electric heating became a practical possibility, all the more as the phenomenal growth of air-conditioning in the 1960s replaced the previous nation-wide pattern of a single winter peak in power use with a new one. Consumption reached a maximum every year and set its new daily records in July and August. When use began to strain generating capacity in the late 1960s, it was in summer that blackouts and brownouts began to occur. A secondary peak continued to occur in the midwinter months, with troughs in the spring and fall.[12] The pattern was the result of all variations in use combined, but it chiefly reflected the variable demands of indoor climate control: of keeping homes at nearly the same temperature year-round, the informal national standard of seventy to seventy-five degrees Fahrenheit.

It was, some believed, more than merely a national standard. Laboratory research on thermal comfort developed in close association with the heating and air-conditioning industry. It dealt purely with physical variables: air temperature, radiant heat, humidity, air movement, and the clothing and activity level of the human subject. Its key method was the chamber study, which collected reports of comfort and discomfort under different sets of conditions. The result was an influential set of standards, graphs, and equations identifying a climate close to that of most American homes as the human optimum.[13]

Chamber-study research assumed that an objective ideal could be found and sought to define it by eliminating many of the factors—above all, experience and expectations—that had much to do with whether people actually felt comfortable or not in any particular setting. It represented the last academic stronghold of an outright climatic determinism, the last field where it remained not only respectable but routine to assume that the weather's human meaning was a function of the weather alone. But when human variables were restored to the study of thermal comfort, quite different results emerged. When people were studied in their everyday settings rather than in the artificial environment of the research chamber, the range of temperatures judged comfortable expanded enormously. Differences in habit and custom made many subjects not only accept but prefer conditions that chamber-study researchers had declared far too hot or cold.[14]

What field studies eventually showed, history could have taught, and so could travel writing. Postwar visitors from abroad still failed to greet American indoor temperatures as the ideal that they were denied at home. They shared the assumption guiding chamber studies of thermal comfort, that there was such a thing as a single correct indoor climate; they disagreed only as to what it was. Russian émigrés in the novels of Vladimir Nabokov found houses in the American Northeast chilly and drafty and the vaunted central heating "a farce," "the tepid exhalations of a throbbing and groaning basement furnace . . . transmitted to the rooms with the faintness of a moribund's last breath."[15] English travelers continued to find the same houses hot and stuffy. Evelyn Waugh visited America several times in the late 1940s and returned to England bewildered. "They heat their rooms to 75 degrees," he reported, "then they nail the windows down so that you suffocate."[16] A compatriot of his told Americans that they warmed their houses to a ridiculous and uncomfortable degree in order to "conceal from the members of the family the hollow emptiness of their personal relationships" and to "compensate for the warmth which is lacking in American life. American central heating is an attempt to make this artificial external warmth a substitute for the natural internal emotion which died out in pioneer days." An American writing in the 1980s explained the English fondness for "shivering in drafty houses" as a product of several national traits: puritanism, masochism, and simple lunacy.[17]

Room temperature differences around the world have narrowed. England experienced a marked indoor warming, amounting to some two degrees Fahrenheit per decade from the 1940s to the 1970s, that has brought it closer to the American standard.[18] The convergence could be seen as bearing out the claims made by the science of thermal comfort: with advances in technology and affluence, people have been able to create conditions ever closer to the objective and universal ideal. It may, on the other hand, be less the vindication of that science than its own doing, a case of a self-fulfilling prophecy. As critics have shown, people adjust to a wide range of conditions and come to prefer the ones to which they have adjusted. More and more, it is the ones prescribed for them on the basis of controlled chamber studies to which they are exposed and acclimated. "[B]uilding designers treat comfort as a purely physiological matter, because that is how it has been defined by thermal comfort researchers. That narrow definition in turn encourages the production of buildings equipped with air-conditioning and other high-tech systems designed to meet these supposedly natural needs," in the process making them the ones that people prefer and expect.[19]

The increasing uniformity of indoor climates has had its benefits. One is a greater freedom of movement. Changes of residence from one country to another entail far less discomfort and require far less adjustment than they once did. So do vacations overseas; so, within the United States, do seasonal and permanent migration. The spread of central heating largely did away with the indoor chill that had long surprised northerners wintering in the lower latitudes, and air-conditioning provided relief from the summer heat. It may not be by chance that the beginnings of net in-migration to the South, the reversal of a century-long trend, coincided with the rise of air conditioner use as a mass phenomenon.[20]

Some national trends in architecture and construction also benefited from air-conditioning and central heating. Many common house features that had aided in passive climate control disappeared or became less common: interior and exterior shutters, interior doors and partitions, vestibules, small and recessed windows, and thick walls.[21] One of the most striking changes in postwar construction was the greatly expanded use of glass, increasing the potential for excessive heat gain in summer and loss in winter.[22] Its use reached an extreme in the International Style skyscraper, with its vast expanses of windows facing in every direction. Only powerful air-conditioning and heating systems made such designs possible in the American setting.

Yet it was not true, James Marston Fitch observed in 1961, though it seemed to be widely believed, that climate had ceased to matter in architectural design because it had been conquered by technology.[23] The laws of thermodynamics had not been repealed. Modern styles, Fitch pointed out, made climate matter more than ever. They amplified its effects in both summer and winter, adding to the burden that heating and cooling systems had to carry. But so long as the energy to run those systems remained cheap and plentiful, the burden was not a heavy one.

It became much heavier during the 1970s. The coal crises of the early twentieth century were repeated in crises in the supply of oil, natural gas, and electricity, in dramatic price increases, and in several cold winters of acute shortage. One response was to adjust indoor temperatures. In the energy crisis of 1973–74, Americans were urged from the White House to lower their thermostats to sixty-eight degrees in the daytime in winter in order to lessen fuel consumption. In a second crisis later in the decade, they were urged to maintain levels of sixty-five degrees in winter and eighty in summer. The exhortations themselves had little apparent effect.[24] Higher energy prices pressed Americans more effectively in the same direction. The prevailing domestic winter temperature by the mid-1980s had slipped just below seventy degrees Fahrenheit.[25]

The higher cost of energy aroused a new interest in ways to supplement mechanical climate control, which had been eagerly discussed during wartime fuel crises but neglected at other times. There was a revival of attention to underground or earth-banked houses, to more careful solar orientation, to the use of light colors in hot regions to reflect sunshine away and of trees to provide shade, to new kinds of glass and windows that reduced heat gain and loss. Governments and utilities promoted insulation and other measures that would quickly pay back their cost in energy conserved. In doing so, however, they learned that consumers would not necessarily adopt even devices that saved money with no loss of comfort or added effort. A host of considerations— from trust in the messenger to the social meaning of saving and spending—entered into a decision about whether to adopt a conservation measure.[26]

Nor was there as much resort as there might have been to another expedient. High winter room temperatures in the United States, one commentator asserted in January 1977, were an adaptation to dress, which was itself an independent variable rather than a response to climate. They went along with the light clothing that Americans more than ever liked to wear. A change in costume would be a necessary and sufficient condition for a change in indoor climate and the energy savings that it would bring. "The task is to start making Americans start wearing long, heavy, winter underwear. Once that occurs, thermostats will be set back spontaneously without oratory from Washington."[27]

But the shift that he urged—to clothing as a means of keeping warm—ran counter to the dominant trend, which was toward lighter costume and was taken for granted in the prevailing standards for indoor temperatures. Norms and laws that had forbidden scanty dress in many public settings were steadily eroded. As a result, late-twentieth-century American costume was better adapted in some ways to the climate than earlier dress had been. In other senses, it was worse adapted. It was less oppressive in summer heat outdoors; it encouraged higher thermostat settings inside in winter. Leaving more skin exposed, it offered less protection than ever against the sun. A tan remained part of an attractive appearance, to be sought by artificial means if it could not be obtained naturally despite the heightened danger of skin cancer. The average annual mortality traceable to sun exposure increased sharply during the postwar decades, with costume and behavior change and southward migration among the chief reasons. Today it exceeds loss

"It seems to me the winters are colder than they used to be."

FIGURE 5.1. As with earlier fashions, the popularity of miniskirts in the 1960s did more to shape the experience of the weather than the weather did to shape it.

of life from all weather hazards conventionally defined—coastal storms, floods, tornadoes, lightning, blizzards, heat waves—put together.[28]

Inadequate protection from other aspects of the weather was likewise more than ever a matter of choice rather than necessity. Clothing's share in the cost of living further declined.[29] A materials revolution in dress created the possibility of better protection from the weather. Improved insulated and waterproof fabrics were developed and widely worn. It was still an open question, however, as to whether protection was the reason for their popularity, or whether what was valued was rather the look of functionalism.[30] Fashion went on changing in other ways that it would be ludicrous to attribute to climatic changes, even to indoor ones. Even laundry had less than ever to do with the weather, as the postwar rise and rapid spread of the clothes dryer displaced the outdoor clothesline. For all that, weather remained the favored American rationalization for wearing one thing rather than another.[31] This durable bit of environmental determinism also remained the favored folk explanation for why people in other countries and climates dressed as they did—but it had little to say about why foreigners and Americans over time dressed ever more alike.[32]

Transportation

Indoor climate control improved in the automobile as in the home, making conditions more uniform and imposing some of the same costs in energy. By the 1990s, the overwhelming majority of new American cars were equipped with air-conditioning—at the price of markedly lessening their fuel efficiency in summer. Their glass and metal construction was as ideal as that of the International Style skyscraper for passive heating in summer and heat loss in winter, equally dependent on energy-expensive technologies for maintaining a uniform temperature. It was also, as the nation's fleet of cars grew, one of the chief factors—as the expanded use of glass in buildings was another—making the damage done by hailstorms far greater than in the past. In the nineteenth century hail had been a hazard chiefly to crops. Late twentieth-century damage, heaviest in cities and a heavy share of it borne by windows and windshields, has run in some cases to hundreds of millions of dollars and in one case to two billion from a single storm.[33]

The problem of mud that had most annoyed the earliest drivers had largely disappeared. The goals of the good roads movement had been achieved, but at a price far beyond the mere cost of smoothing and surfacing. Pavements permitting high-speed driving had been "weather-proofed" only in one sense. Certain kinds of weather became far more dangerous; highways were slippery when wet or icy and dangerous when visibility was poor. Automobile accidents occurred at a much higher rate in rain, snow, and fog than in fair weather.[34] The sudden onset of poor visibility or slippery pavement on a busy highway began to produce large pileups involving many dozens of cars.[35] Fog by the 1980s was involved in some five hundred traffic deaths per year, wet weather and slippery pavement in ten times that number.[36] A slew of innovations, from improved tires to improved windshield wipers,[37] only palliated the hazard created by new patterns of activity: the higher standards of punctuality and speed and the massive suburbanization, exurbanization, and long-distance travel that the car had fostered. Some experts look forward to devices such as automatic alert systems to warn drivers of dangerous conditions.[38] It remains to be seen whether reliance on them might not on the whole dull the driver's sense of risk at least as much as assist it.

More driving and more urgency about it made snow—neutral stuff that had once been a help to transportation—more of a problem. Snowstorms reduced traffic much less on weekdays and at commuting rush hours than at off-peak travel times: hardly a surprising fact, but a sign of how little forecasting by itself could do to lessen some hazards.[39] In the face of other pressures, much travel could not be adjusted to bad weather that was predicted or actually occurring, and the result when it occurred was frequent chaos and sometimes worse. Most deaths attributed to blizzards are automobile-related: heart attacks from the exertion of shoveling driveways, exposure and carbon monoxide poisoning in snowbound cars.

Motorized plowing could remove snow more quickly than ever, but it was a costly way for cities to handle the problem. Maintaining a fleet of plows sufficient to deal with major storms required a large capital investment that sat idle for nearly the entire year. Having "thousands of new kilometers of streets to maintain and millions of new automobile owners to propitiate," postwar local governments relied more than ever on salt as a cheap way of keeping pavements clear.[40] The amount of salt applied to streets in the United States rose tenfold between 1950 and 1970, and new records for its use were set in the mid-1990s.[41] But its apparent cheapness was an illusion. The cost of buying and spreading the salt itself was exceeded roughly tenfold by the measurable damage that it inflicted: corrosion of cars and infrastructure, pollution of water supplies, killing of vegetation.[42] The total costs of its use, as best they could be calculated, at least equaled the benefits.[43] Salt lessened one weather problem only by creating problems of equal magnitude elsewhere.

In some thinly settled northern areas, the snowmobile again made snow a help rather than a handicap to winter transportation. In most places it was useful only for recreation, and fleeing wet and wintry climates altogether remained for most Americans the surest solution to the problems that they posed. The snowless latitudes seemed to be as ideal for an automobile-dependent society as the snowiest ones had been for the horse-drawn conveyances and unimproved roads of the eighteenth century. The Sunbelt climate was exploited as an aid to driving, and to suburban sprawl and low-density development. As a result, it became a hazard in a new and unexpected way; "the combination of heavy automobile traffic and copious sunlight" proved to be a particularly unhealthy one.[44] The problem first became evident in the 1940s in southern California, when the clear skies and surrounding mountains that the region's boosters liked to promote turned out to have some drawbacks never before suspected. The nitrogen oxides released from automobile combustion systems combined with sunlight to brew ozone, a highly reactive gas. Its effects included damage to vegetation, cracking of automobile tires, and headaches and eye and respiratory irritation. Ozone smog appeared in metropolitan areas across the country, but it occurred chiefly during dry and sunny weather and remained worst in dry and sunny regions and enclosed basins. Nowhere was it nearly so acute as in the Los Angeles area, where a new division of the year, the "smog season," began every May and continued through the summer, and where the excess of ozone over national air quality standards by the early 1990s inflicted several billion dollars' worth of health damage every year.[45]

The effects of weather on movement were more often than not the incidental results of choices made without reference to the weather. By no means all or even most northern migration to the Sunbelt was made for the sake of the climate, but new relations to the climate were among the consequences. The ease of moving oil and natural gas by pipeline and of messages by satellite had the effect of insulating those sectors from much disruption. The convenience of transmitting electricity through open-air wires kept disruption by wind, snow, and ice chronic, and it became steadily more costly and troublesome as dependence on electricity grew. Rail was in 1945 and remained a half-century later the least weather-sensitive major form of freight hauling, of long-distance travel, and of short-distance commuting. That fact did not keep it from fading rapidly in all three roles in the postwar years. The triumph of the automobile, favored by the speed, flexibility, and independence that it offered in a society that prized all three, incidentally meant more inconvenience from the weather. What business the trains did not lose to the road, they lost to the skies, and one of the consequences of air travel's explosive rise in popularity was the same increase in weather worries.

As with cars, innovations lessened some problems. Air travel became more comfortable as high-altitude flight above turbulence became routine and as heating, cooling, and cabin compression improved. It became distinctly safer and more reliable than before as the introduction of radar coupled with ground control after World War II reduced the risks of bad-weather flying. Delays and groundings due to poor visibility decreased dramatically in the 1950s and continued to drop thereafter.[46] The wind gusts, heavy rain, and hail associated with thunderstorms remained serious hazards, but the radar devices pioneered during World War II gave pilots and ground controllers a tool to identify and steer clear of them. The phenomenon of sudden downdrafts—powerful and destabilizing vertical gusts of wind associated with severe storms—epitomized the kind of weather that had been insignificant and unnoticed, in no way a hazard to human life, until new activities began exposing lives and property to its effects. This phenomenon, was investigated in detail after being implicated in a number of large plane crashes in the 1960s and early 1970s. The new technology of Doppler radar helped pilots and ground controllers to spot and evade danger areas: an episode rightly cited as a model of atmospheric research usefully applied to human problems.[47]

Though less of a hazard than before, bad weather—high wind, icing, poor visibility—remained a leading cause of serious air accidents and the chief cause of small-plane crashes, especially coupled with risk-taking and disregard of precautions. It also remained by far the chief source of flight postponements and cancellations and the losses to airlines and their customers that resulted from them.[48] The increase in the number of planes and flights multiplied older problems. Tighter scheduling and more congestion on the ground magnified the effects of any delays in takeoffs and landings. The annual cost of delays and disruptions to the airlines by the late 1990s was estimated at $2.5 billion and increasing steadily.[49]

Radar, in theory, was a great help to marine navigation. It was much more reliable and precise than sonic signaling in fog and rain. By allowing ships to keep track of one another's positions, it could all but do away with collisions in times of low visibility. Yet after several decades of experience, the risk analyst Charles Perrow pointed to radar's use as a prime example of the limits of technological solutions to safety problems. From a review of the accident record, he judged that at best, for all its promise in making things better, it had perhaps not made them worse: "The collision rate did not go down with radar. In particular, collisions between ships where at least one had radar did not go down; they may have gone up." Injected into a situation where speed was greatly valued, it merely meant that captains behaved less cautiously. The pressures of regular and rapid operations in business made them less tolerant than ever of delays and slowdowns for safety's sake, and "excessive speed in poor weather," Perrow observed, remained a serious hazard as before.[50]

Government policies that halted the decline of inland water carriage helped in other ways to keep the weather a powerful source of interference. The Army Corps of Engineers and other federal agencies maintained and extended on many routes the minimum nine-foot channel depth essential for modern barge traffic. River and canal freight continued to benefit from heavy indirect subsidies in the form of dredging, water flow management, and the development of new navigational channels. Aided by all of these measures, and for the most part not required to pay for them, waterway navigation rebounded. Economic trends that increased shipments of oil, grain, coal, and iron ore, all prime commodities for carriage by water, were a further reason for the recovery of this sector and so was the appeal of barge transportation in an era, after 1973, of rising energy costs. Cargo carried on the Mississippi River system grew from 8 million tons in 1950 to 100 million by 1980.[51] The channel improvements undertaken by TVA greatly boosted commerce on the Tennessee River. The Great Lakes remained a busy highway of trade, and the opening of the St. Lawrence Seaway in 1959 connected them to the ocean with a channel adequate for medium-sized freighters.

Traffic on the seaway was disappointing from the start, though, and one of the reasons was the climate. The Lakes and the seaway both continued to suffer from the winter closing and from the yearly uncertainty as to when it would take place. During the 1970s, Lakes shipping for the first time operated with only brief winter interruptions under a program run by the Army Corps of Engineers and the Coast Guard. But if the experiment proved that the winter freeze need not remain the bar to December-through-April operations that it had always been, it proved too that the change could cost more than it was worth and for reasons that in earlier times would have counted for little. The gains from "year-round shipping" proved to be modest; the drawbacks lay not so much in the cost of ice-breaking and other measures as in the new concerns of shoreline residents and activists about damage to the environment.[52] Proposals in Congress for making the seaway a year-round route were stopped by strong opposition from communities along its banks.[53]

The rise in water traffic kept the costs of drought for transportation high. Navigation on the lower Mississippi was particularly vulnerable, for it lacked the system of dams and locks that helped to maintain the channel depth on the upper river. The hot and dry summer of 1988 stranded hundreds of barges below St. Louis. Losses were heavy; much freight was diverted to the railroads; filling the Mississippi with water from the Great Lakes was proposed but strongly resisted by the lakes states and Canada.[54]

Barges moved freely on the Missouri River during the same summer. A nine-foot-deep navigation channel was maintained that year as in others by releases from the huge upstream reservoirs that had been built in the postwar decades. Technically the Missouri's management for navigation was a great success, just as the year-round shipping program on the Great Lakes had been. Managed only by nature, the channel had never been much more than barely useable for short periods even by light-draft steamboats drawing a few feet of water. Managed for multiple purposes under the federal government's 1945 Pick-Sloan Project, it permitted barge travel during six to eight months of every year. Why it was being so managed was less clear. There was not in 1988, nor had there ever been, nearly as much traffic on the channel as it had been planned to accommodate. It was not built and maintained to meet an evident demand, nor did one develop. In 1953, one analyst observed that a 1,000-percent increase in traffic would be needed to make benefits truly balance costs, and freight on the river increased scarcely at all in the decades that followed.[55]

Water

Dry regions are different from wet ones; they have less water. Or do they? As matters stood in the early 1990s, a shift to a drier climate in the Missouri River Basin would have made water more plentiful for its chief users: irrigation, recreation, and municipal supply systems. A study explored the likely results if the Dust Bowl drought conditions of the 1930s were to become the region's permanent climate.[56] Such a change would have made the continuance of the federal navigation program on the river impossibly difficult. Its abandonment would have freed more flow for other uses than the climatic shift would have taken away. It would also have greatly increased the net regional returns from water use, for the returns from navigation were small for the amount it required.

More water in a drier climate is a paradox only if the weather and climate alone are assumed to make water scarce or plentiful. These factors are never irrelevant where so weather-sensitive a resource is concerned, but they are never all that counts. Wants and management always matter as well. A change in either can work the same results as a change in climate; both can change with a changing climate to amplify or offset its effects, and both change much more often and more profoundly on their own than the climate does.

The Missouri's managers made the river navigable by giving navigation priority over other activities. The victory was an expensive one, not only because the dams, reservoirs, locks, and channel dredging needed for barge traffic cost money—unrecouped by any tolls or fees—but also because managing the flow of water to ensure a nine-foot channel withheld much of it from other uses. A half-century after the federal plan for developing the Missouri was adopted, serious discussion began of phasing out navigation altogether.[57] Advocates of the change used arguments that had been advanced fifty years earlier and some new ones as well. Irrigated farming could have made more profitable use of water from the system's huge upstream reservoirs than barge traffic did. Boating and fishing on the reservoirs had unexpectedly become mainstays of a thriving new recreational sector—larger in economic terms by the 1990s than navigation, and harmed by the massive summer drawdowns that kept the channel full. By altering the natural pattern of peaks and troughs, the control of flows also disrupted the river as habitat. The plants, fish, and other wildlife that lived in and along the Missouri had not been a concern to many people in the past, but with time they became more of one. On another carefully controlled river, the Tennessee, reservoir drawdowns affecting recreation, shoreline properties, and ecological processes became a source of rising irritation as amenities and environment came to matter more. The new summer peak in electricity demand associated with air-conditioning, moreover, scheduled times of low water when shorefronts were in most active use.[58]

Water's shifting character as a resource can be seen most strikingly in the new value placed on its absence. Now that rain affects most Americans most directly as a nuisance, hampering driving and the enjoyment of the outdoors, drought more than ever is accounted fine weather, and climates once considered ideal are now thought too wet. A pair of studies done at the national scale, plus a third within a small region—the Olympic Peninsula of Washington State, containing a range of conditions from temperate rain forest to semidesert—have arrived at similar figures for the value that Americans attach to living in a dry climate. Houses on the average fetch some three hundred dollars less for every extra inch of annual rainfall in their locality.[59] This preference adds up to a huge net transfer of wealth from the humid East to the arid West, produced by changes in tastes and wants since the time when scanty precipitation was more liability than asset.

Even the contented inhabitants of deserts and semi-deserts, though, still expect water to pour regularly from the tap if not from the sky. As population flowed to cities in drier regions, water supply crises should have become more frequent as a result. Yet the largest and most numerous crises in the postwar decades, as in the late nineteenth century, were not in the West. The New York supply system, having expanded into the Catskill Mountains early in the century, reached another crisis in the 1920s and turned to the Delaware River, an interstate stream whose flow was eventually divided by the states involved and the courts.[60] Drought produced a municipal emergency in 1949–50. Crisis measures lasting for the better part of a year included restrictions on baths and showers, car washing, lawn and garden watering, ice skating, swimming and wading pools, dishwashing, and drinking fountains; the declaration of "dry days" for special conservation efforts; and regular prayers for rain ordered by the Catholic archdiocese. New additions to the supply fell short of daily use again during several years of regional drought in the early and mid-1960s, and the customary emergency restrictions were again imposed.

With the new system complete, another severe drought in 1970 caused the city's water managers little concern. The margin of supply was more than adequate to absorb the shortfall, and no crisis was experienced. After a decade of rising demand, a similar drought in 1980–81 had far more impact; it created the next in New York's long series of water emergencies. Storage at the low point, in February 1981, dropped to a level comparable to the worst recorded during the dry period of the 1960s.[61]

What was different by then was that the possibilities for further expansion of supply seemed at an end. As a result, the city in the 1980s turned instead to the measures for demand management that it had long resisted: an expansion of domestic metering and an increase in rates. It was late even among northeastern cities in adopting them, but not otherwise untypical of a region where complacency had long prevailed and conservation measures had rarely been taken until action was forced by an imminent breakdown of supply.[62]

The largest western city had long followed a different policy. A representative of Los Angeles took advantage of the 1960s drought to pay a visit to New York. His purpose was to entice water-dependent industries to the semiarid West with the promise—and not an inaccurate one—of a cheaper and more reliable supply.[63] Southern California had an average annual rainfall less than half of downstate New York's and much less reliable, but it was New York that was beset by one drought crisis after another. As a way of coping with a drier climate, Los Angeles had routinely made many adaptations, such as metering, monitoring of leaks, and acquisition of new sources well in advance of demand, long before they were standard practice in the East. In the 1930s, the city expanded its holdings to the Mono Lake Basin, north of the Owens Valley, and to the Colorado River several hundred miles away—the latter an arrangement bolstering resources beyond demand to the point of financial embarrassment for the city.[64]

Other cities in southern California, the Southwest, and the drier zone in general were much less fortunate. They had obtained no such large and dependable supply, in part because Los Angeles had taken so much of what there was. When severe droughts seemed to threaten the adequacy of their supplies and the future growth on which they counted, many found the idea of continental-scale water transfers, of drawing on the water of the Great Lakes or the Mississippi to meet their needs, a compelling one. The proposed source regions, though, did not see matters that way. And in fact the West did not need to go nearly so far afield to meet its water needs, unless those needs were defined as enough for all activities that anyone wanted to undertake—in which case there was no region in the United States, whatever its climate, that did not suffer from a shortage. Irrigation was by far the West's chief consumer of water. There was enough to grow large quantities of such relatively low-value irrigated crops as pasture grass, alfalfa, rice, corn, and cotton. Half or more of the water in many western states was used to grow such crops, often with crude and wasteful methods.[65] Much of the water was supplied far below cost by federal and state reclamation programs.

If those crops had been grown elsewhere where rain was more plentiful and the western water used to grow them had been devoted instead to other purposes, a large financial gain would have resulted. That fact has inspired many proposals for ending federal irrigation subsidies and for promoting the transfer of western water to higher-value uses. Making it easier for water rights to be bought and sold would allow market incentives to push them into the most profitable employments and would encourage the more efficient use of what water remained in agriculture. The severe drought that affected California between 1986 and 1991 showed that such shortage as actually arose was not the result of an absolute lack of the quantity of water required for human existence, or even the amount required for a quite affluent level of existence. A state Drought Water Bank was set up in 1991 to buy water rights from farmers for emergency transfer to domestic use, and it had no difficulty obtaining all that it wanted.[66]

But if the case for water marketing is unanswerable on the grounds of economic efficiency, there are many other objections to its free and unregulated use.[67] Two of the strongest are the same objections that had long been made against the Los Angeles system but that have received more attention in the post-1970 climate of opinion than they had gotten before: the social and ecological impacts of cities's demands on their water supply regions. Los Angeles's massive withdrawals of land and water brutally and permanently stunted the economic development of the once-promising Owens Valley. They drastically lowered the level of Mono Lake, severely damaging a unique natural environment.[68] The large-scale transfer of water to urban use that water marketing promised threatened both the environments of the places of origin and the economic survival of the communities that had grown up around existing water uses. Sales to the Drought Water Bank were voluntary between the seller and the buyer. They nonetheless aroused much antagonism among third parties, left out of the transactions and denied any gains from them, who stood to lose from sizeable reallocations and the restructuring that they must bring.[69] Farmers who own water rights can sell them, but farm machinery suppliers lose from the change and gain nothing in return. Water transfers have much in common with rainmaking as a means of augmenting supplies; the technical difficulties are not so worrisome as the social ones.

Agriculture

Severe droughts continued to occur on the postwar Great Plains, but even where irrigation was not in general use, their impacts on the region continued to diminish. That of the 1950s was second in intensity only to the 1930s Dust Bowl among ones recorded since the time of European settlement. Yet the Dust Bowl itself had caused less upheaval than some milder earlier droughts, and the dry years of the 1950s passed over the Plains with scarcely a ripple to be seen in overall statistics of wealth and well-being. Out-migration, which had been massive in the 1890s and substantial during the Dust Bowl, was minimal. Farm income showed no marked decline and farm foreclosures no marked increase.[70]

If drought's impacts, on the Plains as elsewhere, were softened, it was not chiefly because crop output itself was insulated from the weather. There was no apparent lessening over time in the proportion of Plains wheat crops lost to droughts of similar severity. Though modern hybrid grains give far higher yields than earlier ones, the percentage decline in yield in dry years is apparently about equal to that experienced with earlier varieties.[71] Hail is as physically destructive to crops as ever and more destructive economically because high-yielding varieties produce more for it to destroy. The variations in crop yields from one year to the next still chiefly reflect variations in the weather.[72]

The decline in drought's social impact on the Plains, and in the weather's on American farmers generally, stemmed more from social than from technical arrangements. Among the most important were two policies pioneered in the 1930s during the New Deal and continued by Democratic and Republican congresses alike after the war. Federal disaster relief aid during the droughts of the 1950s included loans, feed and grain assistance, and special commodity purchases from ranchers and farmers.[73] The federal crop insurance program was revived in 1944 after a year's suspension. Initially limited to wheat and cotton, it expanded steadily in scope. By the 1980s, it was authorized to sell policies on any agricultural commodity. Subsidies continued to cover excesses of losses over premiums when they occurred.[74]

In some ways, however, insurance and disaster aid worked at cross purposes. The growth of emergency relief appropriations discouraged farmers from making insurance their chief defense against bad weather. Participation in the crop insurance program never rose to the levels expected, and one reason was the natural reluctance of farmers to pay premiums for coverage when severe losses were typically followed by multibillion dollar appropriations aiding the insured and the uninsured alike. Subsidized crop insurance itself encouraged risky and uneconomical behavior at taxpayer expense, allowing farmers to cultivate marginal lands and reap benefits while passing on losses through their policy coverage.[75] It is not clear that the total losses from droughts of comparable severity on the Plains have declined. A greater share of the cost may simply have been transferred elsewhere and borne outside the region, exported via Washington to the United States as a whole.

Insurance and disaster relief, however useful to some, are selective in their coverage. They do little to reduce the impact of bad years on migrant farm workers, whose jobs remain among the most economically as well as physically weather-exposed in the United States. Drought or freezes damaging crops mean less demand for labor, and weather-related variations in the time of harvest add another uncertainty to the search for work. As fresh fruits and vegetables became more important in agricultural output, the demand for short-term farm labor has remained strong. Poverty in areas from which migrants came combined with liberal immigration policies to keep wages low and to discourage mechanization.[76] Unemployment benefits, food stamps, and other forms of public assistance shifted much of the cost of supporting the seasonally migrant work force from employers to the government.[77]

Not every federal program meant to aid agriculture necessarily has that effect. Weather forecasting may mean losses rather than gains for farmers, the paradoxical conclusion reached by two economists who examined the matter.[78] Both found that at least in the short run, improved predictions would lower profits rather than increase them. Farmers using the forecasts would adjust their operations in order to lessen weather damage to their crops. The result would be an increase in total production of the commodities involved. When the amount of most farm commodities put on the market increases, prices tend to fall proportionately more. Critics of national weather forecasting who see it as a subsidy by the rest of society to farmers may have the matter exactly backward; it is society that benefits from its consequences through cheaper food production and farmers who suffer economically.

But the hazards of lower-than-expected weather losses that better forecasts could intensify were themselves lessened by the continuation of another set of federal policies. New Deal measures to protect farmers against falling prices caused by good weather and too-bountiful harvests were maintained and elaborated after the war. Deficiency payments, commodity purchases, subsidized acreage restrictions, and other measures further reduced year-by-year variations in food prices and farm income due to the weather beyond what another means of adaptation, the commodity futures market, already did.

Still other policies helped to make the climate of producing regions in the United States more valuable a resource than it would have been in an unrestricted international market. Tariffs and import restrictions protected many homegrown commodities from foreign competition. The sugarcane and sugar beet growing regions of the United States retained control over much of the domestic market thanks to strict limits on imports of sugar produced more cheaply overseas. Other products suffered more from the development of competitive growing regions elsewhere in the world. The cotton grown in irrigated fields on the southern Great Plains was a more valuable commodity in the 1950s and 1960s than it was by the 1990s, when competition from cotton produced overseas, along with the rising cost of pumping groundwater from a declining aquifer, cut severely into profits.[79] The days were long past when the southeast could think itself naturally wealthy because it could grow cotton. No less than ever, climate's richness as a resource for agriculture depends, beyond the physical properties of the climate, on economics, policy, and technology and can change as they do. A climate where a certain plant can be successfully grown to maturity remains only part of what was needed for its profitable production.

Policy and competition also had much to do with the impact of shorter-term weather events on consumers and producers. In 1972, a poor harvest in the Soviet Union was followed by shortage and higher prices in the world grain market. But though much was said at the time about the weather as cause and higher prices as effect, the episode was as much the work of American government policy as of the weather in the Soviet Union. Comparable Soviet harvest shortfalls had occurred in other years with no such consequences. They were produced in 1972 by an American offer to sell large quantities of grain to the Soviet Union at fixed and highly favorable prices, an offer whose acceptance in full seriously destabilized the world market.[80] Severe freezes in the 1960s and 1970s severely reduced Florida's output of oranges, but because few other sources of supply were available, increased prices for the oranges that were harvested meant that the loss was borne more by consumers than by producers as a class. But the higher prices stimulated Brazil to enter orange production for foreign markets, in which it was aided by the growing cheapness of refrigerated transportation. The results were apparent when damaging freezes again hit Florida in the 1980s. Prices rose by much less than in the 1960s, to the benefit of American consumers but to the loss of producers.[81]

Agriculture's output fluctuates more with the weather than does that of any other major sector of the U.S. economy. The location of agricultural activity still has more to do with climate than that of most other activities. But the map of agricultural production in the United States and farm losses and profits year by year now have as much to do with the political climate as with the physical. The impacts on American farmers of droughts in 1983 and 1988 were magnified, for instance, by federal financial policies and their consequences. A strong dollar and high interest rates discouraged exports and increased the burden of farm debt.[82]

The net effect of policy since the New Deal has been to lessen the role of weather and climate in farming.[83] But much of agriculture's vulnerability to the weather has been displaced rather than overcome; it has been transferred from the weather to the policies that mediate its effects on farmers. Many of the policies specifically designed to stabilize farm income, particularly the ones that require large subsidies, have shown signs of fragility. In the 1980s and 1990s efforts were made in Washington to abolish almost every federal program significantly modifying the impact of the weather and climate on agriculture. Farm subsidy payments, the Weather Bureau's frost forecasting services, irrigation subsidies through federal reclamation projects, subsidized multiple-peril crop insurance, tariff and import quota protection for farm products, and mammoth agricultural disaster relief bills all came under attack, and though most survive, their future remains unpredictable; none is certain to survive unmodified in the future.

Work and Play

Manufacturing today is much less affected than agriculture by the weather, but not because it is inherently the less sensitive of the two. Many manufacturing processes are now vastly more intolerant of small variations in the atmosphere than any form of agriculture has ever been. They can be carried on only because they have been protected as never before. Early indoor climate control in industry was concentrated in fields such as textiles, paper and printing, and food processing where the use of water-absorbent materials made humidity regulation useful. By the 1950s, precision processes that could stand only the tiniest shifts in conditions were making many more industries dependent on air conditioning: "manufacture of bearings, scientific and control instruments, meters, electronic tubes and devices, test gauges, optical products, photographic equipment, precision gears, and many machined products whose dimensions are kept within small tolerances," as a standard air-conditioning treatise itemized them.[84] Many industries, from pharmaceuticals to computers, now demand some degree of climate control not only for the production but for the storage and use of their products.

Climate control cannot ward off all weather disruptions affecting industry. Many kinds of food processing still cannot operate year-round because their raw material supplies remain seasonal.[85] Outdoor production is still exposed to the weather and sensitive to its variations, from offshore oil extraction (severe storms) to raisin drying (rainfall). Weather considerations remain particularly strong in outdoor construction, affecting the speed, volume, and timing of house building.[86] Construction has also remained one of the more seasonal sectors of the economy, with a persistent winter trough in activity. But the cyclical changes of weather have not been the sole factor in keeping the work year unbalanced. A 1970s survey found that mobile home manufacturing, an industry carried on entirely indoors, was fully as seasonal, and on the same schedule, as conventional housing construction. Evidently more powerful than the inclement weather of the cold months in idling many workers was a highly seasonal pattern of demand.[87]

Many other "seasons of business" also reflect variations in demand that hinder steady operation.[88] If overall seasonal fluctuations in employment have continued to fall, and they have, part of the reason lies in the loss of jobs in many of the areas where demand has remained most uneven.[89] In some, mechanization reduced the labor force affected by busy and slack times. In others, labor-intensive production moved overseas and transferred the seasonal peaks and troughs of work with it. Both were major factors in the apparel industry, long perhaps the most strikingly seasonal of American manufacturing sectors.

The postwar decline of manufacturing employment and the rise of the service sector altered in many ways the relations of work to weather. Much service employment is little affected by the seasons or affected in ways that have nothing to do with their meteorological characteristics. Such cannot be said of retailing, though, which is also quite sensitive to the day-to-day effects of inclement conditions.[90] No means of lessening those effects has proven more successful than enclosing shopping entirely from the elements. The principle of protection under one roof had already worked to the advantage of department stores. It was extended to clusters of stores in 1954 when the developer Victor Gruen opened his Southdale shopping complex in Minneapolis, the first large retail center entirely enclosed and artificially heated and cooled inside. A promotional leaflet pointed out the advantages of the design. "Weather records show that in Minnesota there are only 126 'ideal weather shopping days.'" On average every year, 125 days were spoiled by sub-freezing temperatures, 14 by temperatures of 90 degrees or above, and one hundred by rain. "But in Southdale Center *every day will be a perfect shopping day!* Special heating, lighting, and airconditioning will keep the weather always 'fair and mild.'"[91] Such facilities, which soon became known as shopping malls, were an immediate success financially and with critics and commentators. By 1976, no open shopping centers of any substantial size were being built in the United States, and existing ones were being widely enclosed.[92]

But extreme weather was not in every way an adversary. Carefully excluded in some forms, it was eventually brought back in others to help fight a worse threat: boredom. Ever more lifelike and spectacular weather effects succeeded one another on the screens of the movie theater complexes embedded in the typical mall. A new standard in this realm, doubtless itself soon to be surpassed, was set in the computer-enhanced tornado scenes of the 1996 film *Twister.* Pioneered at roughly the same time was the so-called "entertainment mall," whose offerings included simulated wilderness excursions in various climatic zones and artificial storms of thunder and lightning.[93]

While shopping grew more and more difficult to distinguish from entertainment and recreation, the latter became of increasing economic importance as demand for both grew. In the first postwar years, county fairs remained the best customers for rain insurance, but football games already accounted for a large and rising share of business.[94] In time, many sports teams, as well as buying policies, sought coverage in a more literal sense and joined the retreat indoors begun by basketball, hockey, and tennis. Houston's Astrodome, opened in 1965, was the first of many large stadiums with a roof that permitted play regardless of conditions outside and a climate control system for audience comfort.[95] Even sports that had to remain outdoors found ways other than insurance to reduce their vulnerability to the weather. Ski areas suffered from snow-poor winters but were not without remedies. Snowmaking first became part of their arsenal in the 1950s and was in nearly universal use by the 1990s. It makes possible large investments by resort developers that the uncertainties of natural snow would not have allowed—at the cost in many places of depleting streamflow diverted to the slopes, to the detriment of the environment and downstream water users.[96]

For all their costs and side effects, such measures offer sports and recreation interests more help in dealing with the weather than forecasts could. Indeed, the outdoor recreation sector is not necessarily helped by more accurate prediction at all. Its chief problem with the weather and seasons is the uneven use of facilities—overcrowding in fair weather with little use at other times. The problem can only be worsened by better public knowledge of what the weather will be like.[97]

What eventually became by far the most popular national pastime offered not only up-to-date weather forecasts but indoor entertainment without even a journey outside. Television viewing became the chief means of coping with spare time when the weather was less than ideal. Though—indeed, because—it is entirely shielded from the weather, it varies regularly with conditions outside. Viewing follows a recurrent seasonal cycle with further short-term weather variations: highest when days are short, the air cold, and precipitation frequent, and the value of advertising time varies seasonally as a result.[98]

A warm and sunny climate less disruptive of outdoor activities than a cold and wet one has become of growing value as tourism's importance has increased. The role of weather and climate in tourism has been little studied, possibly because it is so plain as to be taken for granted.[99] If academic research neglects it, however, business does not. The regions that have been most vocal and successful in exploiting their climates as a lure to settlement have attracted short-term visitors as well. It was not by chance that Disneyland and Disney World were built where outdoor conditions seemed optimal year-round. The sunshine of Florida and California draws many visitors from Canada and Europe as well as from other states. Annual income from tourism in Hawaii first exceeded income from agriculture in the 1960s and exceeded it threefold by 1980. On the island of Maui, resort development focused on the low-rainfall leeward coast and avoided the wetter areas that had been the most actively used for cultivation. "The lack of rainfall that inhibited historic settlement and economic enterprise . . . became an advantage in the race to attract tourists."[100]

Vacation havens enjoying mild, dry, and sunny climates have profited from many of the same changes in society that have promoted amenity migration. The rise in the share of the work force receiving paid vacations has also greatly increased the value for tourism of such favored areas. At the same time, a shift to a tourist economy has created some new difficulties and challenges. Such an economy is usually a highly seasonal one, with high unemployment in certain parts of the year and uneven use of facilities. The need to build enough capacity for peak season loads contributes to the problem of overdevelopment that in many locales has eroded the ecological and human quality of life. A shift to year-round tourism, on the other hand, though more efficient, is sometimes deplored by permanent residents as destroying the peace and quiet of the "off-season."[101]

The seasonality of much travel and tourism also imposes an uneven pattern of demand on related sectors, notably transportation. The summer peak in leisure means a peak in desire for airline flight. Accommodating it would oblige airlines to maintain levels of equipment that would lie idle at other times of the year: a less acute problem than aviation's other troubles with the weather, but financially almost as worrisome. Most airlines have preferred to try evening out demand by aggressive pricing policies encouraging off-peak travel. Some have benefited in addition from the offsetting growth of winter vacation travel from colder to warmer climates. Travel on the highways is also seasonally uneven and for the same reasons. The total miles driven peak in summer, thanks to most people's preference for warm-weather vacations and pleasure driving. An ideal pattern from the point of view of safety, it also means the overuse of road capacity at busy times—the times, unfortunately, when most road repair work has to be done—and its underemployment at others. With gasoline demand following the same pattern, refiners are obliged to produce extra quantities for storage in anticipation of the summer peak in use, which they cannot do without added costs. In consequence, retail prices typically rise in the spring and peak during the summer, much to the dissatisfaction of motorists who naturally dislike paying more for fuel just when they want to use more of it.[102]

The seasonality of the entire economy once depended mainly on the interaction of the weather with the activities of agriculture. It now depends chiefly on uneven patterns of consumer and labor behavior. It stems more than anything from two factors. The first is the late fall rise in demand associated with the Christmas holidays, the second the prevalent scheduling of leisure, the great uniformity in the choice of summer as the time for long paid vacations. Followed through a single year, economic activity in the United States grows to a peak in the fourth quarter (October–December) and slumps in the first (January–March). A second pronounced slump in employment, output, and activity occurs every year during the midsummer months of July and August.[103]

The summer lull is nowhere more uniform than in education. It remains one of the most rigidly seasonal of activities in the United States. This summer lull continues despite the evident inefficiency of idling, for several months every year, facilities that are often inadequate and that could be made less so by being used in overlapping shifts year-round. Closing schools in summer has the further effect of reinforcing the tendency for family vacations to be taken in that season and for economic activity generally to slow. The customary school year is often referred to as a survival from agrarian times when children needed to be free to help in the fields during summer. That alone would not account for its persistence long after the demise of agriculture as a major sector of employment, and in its own right it is a questionable version of history. The typical rural school up to the time of the Civil War had two terms yearly, one in winter and one in summer.[104] The single long summer vacation became a uniform rule at all levels only as farming was losing its dominant position among American livelihoods. Proposals for a change to year-round operation have been made in many places and adopted in a few, including several big-city school systems under severe fiscal pressures. The opposition that has stymied them elsewhere evidently has much less to do with nostalgic attachment to a relic of the past than with a powerful modern factor. Parents, students, and teachers prefer the warmer months as the time for idleness and freedom and tend to view any proposal to change the calendar as "an assault on the idea of summer itself."[105]

The regular seasonal pattern in the economy as a whole is further varied every year by weather-related irregularities mostly associated with the cost of energy. The energy costs from extreme heat or cold are the most visible impact of weather on the overall level of economic activity from week to week. Every form of energy has its own seasonal calendar. Natural gas use shows a winter peak about twice the consumption in the lowest summer month; electricity displays summer and winter peaks and spring and fall troughs. Heating oil is in vastly greater demand in winter than in summer and has to be stored in large quantities beforehand.[106] But demand cannot be exactly forecast. An unusually cold winter means higher than normal consumption of oil, gas, and electricity and less than usual of gasoline; an unusually hot summer, exceptionally high electricity demand; rainy weather, a slow gasoline market. Energy suppliers can in theory get much benefit from forecasts of seasonal patterns in planning their inventories, but in practice it seems that few use them, for their short-term flexibility and their tolerance for error are small.[107]

The more severe the heat and cold, for the most part, the healthier the standard indices of overall activity suggest the economy to be. An unusually heavy demand for cooling or heating means a more than ordinarily lively level of spending. Though plainly bad economically for many people, severe weather is demonstrably good for others, for somebody gets the extra money that is spent countering its effects. Matters have only been muddled further in the 1990s by the development of "weather futures," financial instruments used by some as hedges against the energy and other costs of unexpected weather and by others as instruments of speculation. In perhaps more ways than ever, the climate for business is only good or bad depending on whose point of view is taken—one person's weather hazard representing another's resource.

Weather and Climate Hazards

As Americans' appreciation of natural amenities grew, not only did the climates of different areas become more or less valuable as resources, but lives and property were exposed in new ways to certain kinds of severe weather. Suburbanization lengthened time spent on the roads and increased sensitivity to rain, fog, ice, and snow. Scenery and climate drew affluent residents and expensive homes to the suburban mountains of southern California, a land of intense and fast-moving brushfires in times of drought and high wind and landslides following heavy rains. By the late 1970s, flash floods had begun causing noticeably more death and damage nationally than in the past. "Increased use of mountainous areas for recreation and canyons for house building," it became apparent, "has greatly increased the potential for disaster," not least because recreational use was greatest in summer when the chief triggering events of flash floods, severe thunderstorms, were most numerous.[108]

Above all, shorefront development magnified the perils of wind and high water. Construction along the Great Lakes exposed more houses than before to flooding and wave damage. Counties on the Atlantic and Gulf coasts, rich in scenery, sand, water, ocean views, and climate, acquired a growing share of postwar national totals of population and property value.[109] The trend increased exposure to hurricanes and other coastal storms. Actual loss did not in every way increase. Deaths from hurricanes fell rather than rose. They had been much greater at the beginning of the twentieth century than they were toward the close. Some coping tools more than offset the increased risk to life, such as better and more widely disseminated forecasts and speedier means of evacuation. But the largest hurricanes by the 1990s caused property damage far greater than comparable storms had inflicted in the past. Direct losses from Hurricane Andrew's passage through South Florida in 1992 exceeded $30 billion.[110] "The rapid rise in hurricane-related damages has led many to mistakenly conclude that severe hurricanes have become more frequent in recent decades," an expert noted in

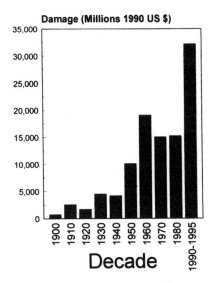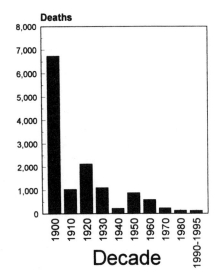

FIGURE 5.2. The changing character of hurricane losses: deaths per decade have declined though the exposed population has grown, while monetary losses, even adjusted, have risen sharply.

1997. They did more damage, rather, because areas exposed to them had been intensively developed.[111]

Even sharply rising losses from coastal settlement are not necessarily rising net losses. Against them must be set the possibly larger gains in satisfaction from moving to the seashore that would have been forgone—at the same time that the loss would have been averted—if the move had not taken place. So must whatever reduction in hazard exposure—whether from heartland tornadoes or from northern blizzards—that the move also entailed. Nor are losses the simple product of the move per se. A great deal of the damage done by Andrew would have been avoided if building codes in southern Florida had been better enforced. Large areas of substandard construction bore much of the storm damage. Even the most encouraging trend, the decline in storm deaths, on the other hand, may mask a rising potential for greater disaster should a severe storm directly hit a major city. As population has grown, the highways have become less adequate to handle a rapid mass evacuation of residents from a threatened area.[112]

Hazards and amenities do not always go together. The West Coast, heavily developed like the East and for the same reasons, is much less vulnerable to coastal storms. The hazards of snow have been reduced by amenity-seeking migration to the South and West. Suburban growth, typically to higher ground than the central city, has removed many households from the reach of floods. It has also lessened the impact of heat waves, which have only recently been recognized as the most lethal of American weather hazards, conventionally defined. Excessive heat in the summer of 1988, by an expert assessment, claimed between five thousand and ten thousand lives across the United States. More than five hundred deaths were directly attributed to a short but severe hot spell in July 1995 in the worst-affected place, Chicago, and some two hundred more were recorded in excess of usual mortality levels.[113] Deaths from extreme heat are markedly higher in central cities than elsewhere.[114] They have become concentrated among the elderly, the poor, and racial minorities, who are less likely to enjoy protection by air-conditioning and freedom from physical exertion, and more likely to live in the hottest neighborhoods. The widespread use of air-conditioning by more affluent households has undoubtedly reduced heat mortality. It may also have created new possibilities for large-scale disaster should power systems fail to meet the record demands now routinely recorded on the hottest summer days.

Postwar federal flood policy remained a mix of physical protection through water control works and crisis relief—increasingly made available for other disasters as well—when they failed. The purpose of the first was to forestall suffering by preventing inundations; of the second, to ease it by spreading the losses that floods inflicted. But protection works themselves were not least among the reasons for continued urban development in the exposed floodplain. The U.S. Army Corps of Engineers, their chief builder and proponent, on occasion was quick to admit and even proclaim the fact. In 1950, a corps representative took local officials and journalists on a boat tour of the Kansas City riverbanks to show what "booming industrial growth" it had drawn to the lowlands with its improvements. "Statistics bear out the claim," Henry C. Hart wrote a few years later, referring to damage figures from the great inundation of 1951 that submerged those very lowlands. "The area flooded was no greater than in 1844 or 1903," the previous great floods in the area, but the industrial development encouraged by the levees meant that the damage was far higher. Property values in the exposed area had tripled between the 1930s, when federal flood control began, and 1951.[115]

A study published in 1958 suggested that the Kansas City experience was not an isolated case. A University of Chicago research team led by Gilbert F. White found that nationwide damage from floods, as best it could be calculated, had grown, not declined, during the twenty years since the federal government had entered the flood control business and begun spending large sums annually on protective works. Rising expenditures had been accompanied by rising losses, not because floods had become more frequent or more severe, but because development in areas prone to floods had outstripped flood control. The very increase in protection and disaster aid had been one factor encouraging expansion into such still-risky settings.[116]

These findings helped to guide a restructuring of federal policy in the 1960s. One of the new tools for coping that it introduced was insurance. White had warned in the 1940s that insurance by itself might worsen losses by reducing personal risks. The National Flood Insurance Plan of 1968 made eligibility for coverage—similar in financing to that offered under federal crop insurance—conditional on community land-use planning and damage mitigation efforts, and it incorporated steps to discourage new construction or rebuilding in floodplains. Lax enforcement and the relaxation of many of the provisions of the law by Congress, however, weakened the effect of these safeguards, and in the end insurance as it was administered may have further encouraged risky development.[117] It remained true in the 1990s as it had been earlier that "the single most effective approach to hazard reduction, land use planning with hazards in mind" had "received less attention than any other adjustment" in federal and state policy.[118] Annual flood losses have continued to rise.[119]

No federal policy for hazard reduction has been kept up longer than the provision of weather forecasts and storm and flood warnings. Forecasts increased modestly in accuracy in the postwar decades, but a more important change lay in the way that they became much more easily and rapidly communicated than in the past. Thanks to radio and television broadcasts, a cable television channel devoted exclusively to the weather, and the World Wide Web, they are far more accessible than ever before.

The explosion in weather information and the rise in its accuracy undoubtedly mean a lessening, all else being equal, in acute weather hazards. There is more time to prepare or evacuate threatened areas, to suspend exposed outdoor activities, to prepare emergency postdisaster services. In the 1940s, the Weather Bureau, building on wartime experience, for the first time took on the task of issuing tornado alerts. These warnings are undoubtedly among the chief reasons why proportional loss of life from tornadoes has steadily declined, but they have owed much of their effectiveness to the collateral development of improved communications.[120] Many forms of simple weather inconvenience that came as more of a surprise in earlier times have surely been lessened as well.

But short-term weather forecasts can do little or nothing to help avert many other weather-related problems—tornado damage to fixed property, for instance. The more accurate they became, the less doubt remained on that point. Severe East Coast winter storms in February 1978 and March 1993 were predicted almost to perfection days in advance and were quite destructive all the same; so was Hurricane Andrew. The notion that perfectly forecast weather would be perfectly harmless, and that better forecasting is the key to progress has never been more convincingly refuted than in the past few years.

Moreover, very little is known about how and how much people actually use forecasts to lessen damage and disruption. Tremendous effort invested in predicting the weather for the general public has been accompanied by scarcely any inquiry beyond lone case studies and anecdotal accounts into how the predictions are employed.[121] The best investigation remains a survey, conducted in New England in the early 1970s, of how people decided whether or not to make a trip to the beach in summer. It reached conclusions not quite consistent with the assumption that people would understand a weather prediction and adjust their plans to conform to it. Many subjects in the study, rather, adjusted their understanding of the prediction to make it conform to their plans. Forecasts did affect beachgoing, but unevenly. Those who had the least flexibility in their arrangements were the least likely to interpret any particular forecast to mean that adverse weather was likely to occur.[122]

It was a finding, as its author, Robert L. A. Adams, pointed out, quite consistent with findings about response to other atmospheric hazards. The relation of knowledge to action among the New England beachgoers closely resembled, on a different time scale, the way in which homeowners living in low-lying, storm-prone coasts and on floodplains, and farmers living in frost- or drought-prone farming regions behaved. All had little flexibility in their location or activities; all, when asked in surveys, tended to underestimate substantially both the frequency and the severity of hazard events. As with recreation seekers contemplating a beach trip, their understanding was shaped by the circumstances in which they found themselves. Their perceptions of hazards, Adams suggested, were not independent variables but "attempts to justify their particular commitments to hazard-prone locations."[123] They behaved toward the climates that they inhabited, with their records of weather past, as Adams's subjects behaved toward short-term weather forecasts. Floods in floodplains and storms along the Gulf and Atlantic coasts should not have taken anyone by surprise. Such recurrent events, even before daily forecasts, were unpredicted only in the sense that their precise date of recurrence was not known; their whole history predicted their return again and again. It was less weather considerations than other factors entirely that determined how much damage they would inflict when they arrived.

It is not even clear that the explosion in weather information and media coverage has meant a better public understanding of weather and its role as a hazard. Understanding any phenomenon requires an appreciation of its relative as well as its absolute importance. Because weather disasters as conventionally defined—storms, floods, heat waves—are treated in the media as news in a way that other phenomena also inflicting losses are not, they come to seem more important than they are and the others less. Prevailing criteria of significance on network news broadcasts decree that "the winter breakdowns of tenement furnaces" are not nearly as newsworthy as more dramatic weather-related events even if impacts are equal.[124] Apparently because tornadoes are reported in the news out of proportion to their actual importance among causes of death, subjects interviewed in the 1970s tended to overestimate the risk of death from them roughly tenfold.[125]

Media coverage of the weather only tends to narrow an already blinkered focus on certain types of loss from the way in which activities interact with the weather. The usual list of American weather hazards consists of severe storms and extreme temperatures, but it does not include the most lethal modern ones. As soon as exposure to sunshine is recognized as a weather hazard, it can no longer be maintained, as it often is, that losses of life from the weather have diminished. Losses of life in storms are far smaller than those resulting from wet pavements and poor visibility on highways. The new attention given to heat-wave impacts obscures the fact that winter in the United States is now the peak season for deaths, though not for all groups, and for reasons that remain unclear. The very means used for defense against the cold are a significant source of impact. Carbon monoxide poisoning from faulty space heaters—rarely listed among the hazards of weather-society interactions—takes more lives on average each year in the United States than lightning does.[126] As stoves and furnaces have given way to other methods of heating, however, the risk of building fires has greatly diminished. These are only examples. The full importance of American weather as hazard has always depended on the human practices and purposes common at any time and place. It will never be documented accurately until the image of weather hazards as severe storms gives way to a wider understanding of how life and weather interact.

Weather Modification

On November 13, 1946, a small shower of snowflakes fell from a cloudbank near the New York-Massachusetts border. To all appearances, it was the most minor and mundane of weather events. Ordinarily it would hardly have been noticed and would instantly have been forgotten. In fact, it has a secure place in weather history, for in its time it had wider repercussions than many a blizzard or hurricane. What made this event so important was the fact that it had been made artificially. Vincent Schaefer of the General Electric Corporation and a colleague, the Nobel chemistry laureate Irving Langmuir, had for some time been looking for ways to stimulate precipitation. Adding silver iodide particles to supercooled clouds, they discovered, would provide nuclei around which droplets or snowflakes might form. Following laboratory trials, Schaefer successfully seeded the famous cloud from an airplane with silver iodide.[127]

The researchers were quick to announce their results. Langmuir followed with many boisterous claims about what could be done in the future to control the elements.[128] The support of his name and prestige helped to make weather modification, as it came to be called, seem suddenly a credible possibility after many years in the shade. Congress encouraged the Weather Bureau, long its chief foe, to become involved in the research and trials already being pursued by other institutions. The next few decades were a lively period of speculation, experiments, and attempts at practical application. Rainfall and snowpack enhancement for the benefit of agriculture and hydropower generation led the way, but hail prevention, hurricane suppression, fog dispersal, and other possibilities also received much attention.

Among these possibilities, fog dispersal at airports stood out in two ways. Its successes were clear and generally admitted, and it brought few side effects harmful to other parties. But even it could claim only modest success, for warm fogs, by far the most common type, remained difficult to disperse; and even it produced some unwelcome results: occasional sudden snow squalls—hazards to driving—in communities downwind.[129] Virtually every other form of modification stirred up lively controversy on both counts, with scientific skepticism as to whether it was having any effect on the weather accompanied by public fears that it was having or would have a harmful effect.

The largest single effort in the field, Project Cirrus—a collaboration between General Electric and several federal agencies—established the breadth and depth of controversy large-scale weather modification would stir up more conclusively than it settled any questions of science and technology. A Caribbean hurricane that Project Cirrus seeded experimentally in 1947 promptly shifted course and headed for land, striking the Gulf coast and doing substantial damage. Whether the seeding had caused the course change was impossible to say. Langmuir, his enthusiasm outrunning his prudence, claimed that it had, evoking threats of lawsuits against General Electric by those who had suffered harm.[130]

Many of the worries jolted awake by the cacophony of talk about weather control were the same ones that had been roused by James Pollard Espy's projects and by the federal rainmaking experiments of the 1890s. The diversity of activities and interests still meant that almost any change brought about for the benefit of some would bring loss to others, who naturally disliked being sacrificed, even to a greater good. New York City hired a cloud seeder to replenish its upstate reservoirs during the drought of 1949–50. More than one official opposed the action for fear of liability claims. The city was indeed taken to court by Catskill hotel owners who claiming that rain had reduced their business, and by upstate residents alleging damage to crops, recreation, and roads and buildings. A devastating flood and dam washout followed cloud seeding operations by a utility company in northern California in the mid-1950s. The ensuing lawsuits were in the courts for most of the next ten years. Even a procedure as seemingly innocuous as hail suppression met stiff resistance. It was challenged during the 1950s droughts by Texas ranchers who feared that it might lessen precipitation needed for their grasslands. Orchard owners in Pennsylvania—a state that had given counties the option of banning weather modification activities within their limits—hired a hail suppression expert in the 1960s and came into angry conflict with farmers suspicious that his activities were causing or worsening drought.[131]

Snow suppression promised to make driving easier, but at the expense of skiing and hydropower generation. Snowpack enhancement promised to do the opposite. In an aggressively litigious society, the most certain outcome that scientific experimenters and speculative private rainmakers alike could expect to produce by their actions was a deluge of legal actions. Private operators fell into the impossible position of having to claim success in order to collect fees and deny it to escape liability. Weather being legally a "public good" in which no property rights were recognized, they could not force free riders to pay for any benefits that they produced, but they could be held accountable for any damage that a jury might decide they had caused.

There were other reasons, new since Espy's time, to feel doubts about the future of weather control. Following such works as Rachel Carson's *Silent Spring,* as well as many well-publicized cases of localized environmental disaster, Americans were more conscious than in the past that dismaying surprises might be the result of even seemingly simple and beneficial interventions in a system as complicated as the natural world. For example, the Great Plains were commonly supposed to suffer from deficient rainfall, but as the historian James C. Malin pointed out, a shift to the rainfall levels typical of the East would have disastrously worsened rates of soil erosion.[132]

It was apparent as it had been in the past that if highly reliable means of changing the weather were developed, their private use would not long be permitted. Only the government, and presumably only the federal government, could bring order into a chaos of uncoordinated private weathermaking, take precautions against unwelcome surprises, and weigh different interests and long-term environmental effects in order to decide what the weather should be. But though government was able in theory to balance interests and act for the larger good, experience by no means testified that it would do so.[133].

Thus some of the key questions regarding the future of weather control concerned its social rather than its technical dimensions. Yet funders of government and private sector research devoted their resources almost entirely to the question of how physical techniques could be improved and their performance verified. The social side of weather modification was not initially given any significant part in the research program. An observer might have wondered, and some did, why large sums were being spent to develop means without some attempt to answer two questions about ends: Would the use of these techniques even be permitted, and if so, to whose benefit would they be used?

The biases of the research funders were in part to blame. They viewed the key questions that needed to be settled as ones of technology and atmospheric physics. The attitudes of social scientists themselves, however, had quite as much to do with the neglect of the human side of the question. By the 1950s and 1960s, American geographers, sociologists, and political scientists had all but officially decided that the environment in general and weather and climate in particular were of no great importance in human affairs and could safely be ignored. Part of the reason for the trend may have lain in the evident advances of technology that indeed seemed to make the environment ever less of a factor in human life, part in a doctrinaire insistence that social phenomena be treated solely in terms of other social phenomena, and part in a revulsion against the earlier excesses and oversimplifications of environmental determinism and the biological and racial determinism with which Ellsworth Huntington and others had mingled it. "The reaction against determinism was led by geographers who realized that people are not mere passive actors on the natural stage," recalled one distinguished scholar of the postwar generation, "but as so often happens, they went to extremes, and anyone who even dared mention the environment was immediately accused of determinism."[134]

Yet environmental research in American academia probably suffered more from incidental habitat loss than from deliberate hunting. The pioneers of the social sciences in the United States wanted them established as autonomous fields of study. They had university teaching, training, and research and funding in "the social sciences" sharply distinguished and organized and governed separately from those in "the natural sciences," and both in turn from those in "the humanities." Their success in doing so did much to discourage any research dealing with the subject matter of more than one of these realms. Nature-society relations as a result became a subject without an academic home, a stateless person in a world of sovereign disciplines. Geography had united a large earth science with a large social science component, but it split into two subfields, physical and human geography, which had increasingly little to do with each other. American geographers, the Berkeley professor Erhard Rostlund observed in 1956, had been partitioned into those who studied the natural world and those who studied the human. As a result, "the question of whether or not there is a significant relation between nature and culture has been left out";[135] it had become nobody's business. A 1968 review of geographical research on the relations of society to weather and climate was largely a catalogue of work still waiting to be done. It found few studies of the role of weather variations in agriculture; of the relations of weather to transportation, to energy production and demand, to the manufacturing, retail, and service sectors, or, Edward Ullman's pioneering speculations apart, to migration and regional development.[136]

Yet a few geographers and other social scientists had retained an interest in human-environment relations, and they willingly turned their attention to the lively, though small and ill-funded, research field that came to be called "the human dimensions of weather modification." But the phrase, as two contributors to a 1966 book by that title suggested, was an unfortunate one.[137] It set out a program of applied research for which the basic research had never been done. A better way to shed light on what cloud seeding offered or threatened for society was to do the neglected basic research first—"to ignore weather modification probabilities at the outset" and ask instead, belatedly, what roles the weather played in human activities. Then one could determine what weather modification might mean for those activities, what it could offer, what other means of reaching the same goals might be available, and how valuable or dangerous modification might be to society. But using the same framework, one could also assess how any number of social changes might affect weather-society relations. Even to clarify the issues raised by cloud seeding and hail suppression, it made much more sense to study the human dimensions of weather than to study the human dimensions of weather modification. To phrase the topic in the latter form was to accept in advance one framing of the issue. To consider weather modification by itself as a solution was to already cast the weather itself as the problem, just as to define floods as a problem of water rising too high had been to view dams as the logical response.[138]

Widespread interest in weather modification declined as much because of social and political obstacles as because the results of technical trials and research were unpromising. Haphazard and scattered private activity, under various forms of regulation, continued, but it faded as a practical prospect for helping Americans cope with the elements on any substantial scale, although its history while it had lasted taught several lessons. It showed how little the social sciences knew about the role of weather and climate in human affairs and hence how little they could say about what difference a change in either might make. It revealed how valuable such knowledge might be for making important choices, and how inadequate even a well-developed technical, natural-science understanding of the physical bases of change was to a full understanding of the potential and the hazards involved. Finally, such activity made clear how deeply ingrained remains a kind of environmental determinism that focuses above all on environmental change as the key source of change in nature-society relations. Much more attention and concern were focused on what altering the weather might mean for Americans than on the many—and in many respects more important—ways in which social change might and did alter the weather's effects.

It was not long before all of these lessons were repeated. As interest in rainmaking faded, scientific and popular concern grew over a new way in which changes in the weather might threaten human activities. This time it was inadvertent rather than deliberate change: global warming caused by rising concentrations in the atmosphere of gases released from fossil fuel combustion and other processes. Just as earlier research had been imprisoned within the framework of the "human dimensions of weather modification," there is now a lively field of study in the social sciences known as the "human dimensions of climate change." The relations of society to climate are no more a focus of research than ever before, but study of the relations of society to climatic change is flourishing. The more things have changed in some respects, the more they have stayed the same in others.[139]

Conclusion

THE POSSIBLE EFFECTS of a greenhouse warming are part of America's weather future rather than its weather history. Climatic change may for the first time become as important a factor in American life as climate has long been. But, like climate, it will never be a factor that operates by itself. How climatic change matters will always depend upon how society has evolved and continue to evolve, just as will the significance of those aspects of climate that remain the same

There has been major climatic change, but in another sense entirely. American weather over the centuries has repeatedly and in many different ways become much better and worse, milder and harsher, more generous and more stingy, but not because its own patterns have changed much. For words such as *better* and *worse* are terms of human assessment. They do not describe some fixed and inherent quality of the weather; they mean only that its qualities are better or worse for what someone wishes to do. As the things people have done and wished to do have changed, so has the "goodness" or the "badness" of the weather. The peak seasons of mortality in different places and for different groups have shifted repeatedly. New modes of transportation have turned snow from a resource to an obstacle and made fog, clouds, hail, rain, and downdrafts hazards in new ways that new devices in turn have moderated and mitigated. Aridity, once a serious constraint, is now a lucrative asset in the real estate market. Today's comfortable indoor temperatures would have seemed far too hot to Americans of the early nineteenth century. Summer seems as naturally the time for leisure as winter once did. The list could go on for many pages. The belief, widespread throughout American history, that the climate itself is not the same as it used to be is a projection onto the climate of the rapid changes of American life.

These changes have been so many and varied that their net effect has not simply been to make the weather more or less important. In the early 1970s, as he was winding up a three-volume study of the American experience since colonial times, the historian Daniel Boorstin paused to consider the American experience of weather and how it had changed.[1] He saw every reason to suppose that weather and climate caused less trouble than ever before. Certainly in "a nation that every year held a smaller proportion of farmers, where fewer livelihoods depended on rainfall or frosts," and "where people were increasingly accustomed to central heating, air conditioning, humidifying, and dehumidifying," it should have been so. Assuredly, much of the weather's impact on American life has weakened, and there are others besides Boorstin who maintain plausibly that it has done so overall.[2] But there are others too who maintain on plausible grounds that the United States is becoming "increasingly vulnerable to natural hazards," not less so.[3] Those on one side of the debate can emphasize the tools and institutions that have been developed and adopted to lessen existing weather impacts, those on the other can stress the changes in life and livelihood that have created new ones. The same holds for weather as a resource. The shift away from farming has helped make climate less important in production while the rise in affluence and leisure time has helped to make it more important as an amenity.

Boorstin himself acknowledged that, in at least one sense, the weather appeared to matter ever more, not less. Though it was a minor factor in American life compared with what it had been, he observed, Americans seemed not to have noticed. Instead of ignoring it, as they were freer than ever to do, they showed "a new and widespread interest in the weather" and an "awakened interest in the weather-to-come." Perhaps it was for new practical reasons; perhaps it was, as Boorstin himself suggested, because in the weather, "Americans hoped to find a residual stock of the unrepeatable and the unpredictable. . . . In a world of prefabricated, packaged, predictable, repeatable experience, the fickleness and mystery of the weather had taken on a new piquancy."[4] If so, it is far from the first new role that the weather has assumed in the course of American history, nor will it by any means be the last.

Notes

INTRODUCTION

1. Nathaniel Hawthorne, "Old News" (1835) in *Tales and Sketches* (New York: The Library of America, 1982), 253–54.

2. *A Meteorological Journal from the Year 1786 to the Year 1829, Inclusive, by Edward A. Holyoke, M.D., A.A.S., with a Preface by Enoch Hale, M.D., A.A.S.*, Memoirs of the American Academy of Arts and Sciences, n.s. 1 (1833), 114–15.

3. *Providence Gazette*, Feb. 4, 1824; Harriet Martineau, *Retrospect of Western Travel*, vol. 2 (New York: Harper & Brothers, 1838), 186.

4. John Chipman Gray, "On the Climate of New-England," in *Essays: Agricultural and Literary* (Boston: Little, Brown, 1856), 176.

5. Holyoke and Hale, *A Meteorological Journal*, 115–16.

6. Van Wyck Brooks, *The Flowering of New England, 1815–1865* (New York: E. P. Dutton, 1936), 407.

7. Gray, "On the Climate of New-England," 177–78.

8. Theodore Steinberg, *Nature Incorporated: Industrialization and the Waters of New England* (New York: Cambridge University Press, 1991), 21, 104, 106; Louis C. Hunter, *A History of Industrial Power in the United States, 1780–1930*, vol. 1, *Waterpower in the Age of the Steam Engine* (Charlottesville: University Press of Virginia, 1979), 126.

9. Hawthorne, *Tales and Sketches*, 1486, note to 254.9; Earl W. Hayter, *The Troubled Farmer: Rural Adjustment to Industrialism, 1850–1900* (De Kalb: Northern Illinois University Press, 1968), 198–208; Lucius Lyon, *A Treatise on Lightning Conductors* (New York: George P. Putnam, 1853), v–vi.

10. H. E. Landsberg, "Two Centuries of New England Climate," *Weatherwise* 20 (1969), 52–57; John H. Conover, "Are New England Winters Getting Milder?-II," *Weatherwise* 20 (1969), 58–61.

11. Quoted in E. B. John Allen, "The Development of New Hampshire Skiing, 1870's–1940," *Historical New Hampshire* 36 (1981), 28.

12. For a definition of natural hazards along these lines and a discussion of what it implies, see Ian Burton, Robert W. Kates, and Gilbert F. White, *The Environment as Hazard*, 2d ed. (New York: Guilford Press, 1993).

13. Erich W. Zimmermann, *World Resources and Industries: A Functional Appraisal of Agricultural and Industrial Materials*, rev. ed. (New York: Harper & Brothers, 1951), 7, 8, 10. See also the work of James C. Malin,

e.g., *The Contriving Brain and the Skillful Hand in the United States* (Lawrence, Kan.: the author, 1955).

14. For a review of the concept, see Robert W. Kates, "Human Adjustment," in Susan Hanson, ed., *Ten Geographic Ideas That Changed the World* (New Brunswick, N.J.: Rutgers University Press, 1997), 87–107.

15. A. L. Sugg, "Beneficial Effects of the Tropical Cyclone," *Journal of Applied Meteorology* 7 (1968), 39–45.

16. Nathaniel Hawthorne, "Snow-flakes" (1838) in *Tales and Sketches* (New York: The Library of America, 1982), 595; *Hunt's Merchants Magazine* 33 (1855), 169.

17. "Max Adeler" (Charles Heber Clark), *Out of the Hurly-Burly; or, Life in an Odd Corner* (1874; Philadelphia: P. Garrett, 1888), 289–92.

18. David G. McComb, *Galveston: A History* (Austin: University of Texas Press, 1986), 121–49; Bradley R. Rice, "The Galveston Plan of City Government by Commission: The Birth of a Progressive Idea," *Southwestern Historical Quarterly* 78 (1975), 365–408; Harold M. Hyman, "I. H. Kempner and the Galveston Commission Government," *The Houston Review* 10 (1988), 57–85; *Galveston Daily News*, Aug. 29, 1915, 4.

19. Robert Cromie, *The Great Chicago Fire* (New York: McGraw-Hill, 1958), 5–6, 9–12; Donald L. Miller, *City of the Century: The Epic of Chicago and the Making of America* (New York: Simon & Schuster, 1996), 143–58.

20. Mike Davis, "The Case for Letting Malibu Burn," *Environmental History Review* 19, no. 2 (1995), 1–36; Stephen J. Pyne, *Fire in America: A Cultural History of Wildland and Rural Fire* (Princeton, N.J.: Princeton University Press, 1982), 405–6; Sandra Sutphen, "California Wildfires: How Integrated Emergency Management Succeeds and Fails," in Richard T. Sylvis and William L. Waugh, eds., *Disaster Management in the U.S. and Canada,* 2nd ed. (Springfield, Ill.: Charles C. Thomas, 1996), 183–84.

21. Blake McKelvey, *Snow in the Cities: A History of America's Urban Response* (Rochester, N.Y.: University of Rochester Press, 1995), xv.

22. Bernard Mergen, *Snow in America* (Washington, D.C.: Smithsonian Institution Press, 1997), 241.

23. Edgar T. Thompson, "The Climatic Theory of the Plantation," *Agricultural History* 15 (1941), 60; Simon Shackley and Brian Wynne, "Viewpoint: Climate Reductionism," *Weather* 49 (1994), 110.

24. The best discussion of environmental determinism's political significance is Mark Bassin, "Geographical Determinism in Fin-de-Siecle Marxism: Georgii Plekhanov and the Environmental Basis of Russian History," *Annals of the Association of American Geographers* 82 (1992), 3–22.

25. Thompson, "The Climatic Theory of the Plantation," 55.

26. Henry Glassie, *Folk Housing in Middle Virginia* (Knoxville: University of Tennessee Press, 1975), 189; Rupert Vance, *Human Geography of the South: A Study in Regional Resources and Human Adequacy*, 2d ed. (Chapel Hill: University of North Carolina Press, 1935), 361.

27. John E. Chappell, Jr., "Commentary: Harlan Barrows and Environmentalism," *Annals of the Association of American Geographers* 61 (1971), 199.

28. For the turn of the century, see Alfred J. Henry, *Loss of Life in the United States From Lightning*, Bulletin No. 30, United State Department of

Agriculture, Weather Bureau (Washington, D.C.: Government Printing Office, 1901). I add to contemporary figures the correction factor proposed by R. E. Lopez et al., "The Underreporting of Lightning Injuries and Deaths in Colorado," *Bulletin of the American Meteorological Society* 74 (1993), 2171–78. On recreation-associated deaths, see Ferdinand H. Zegel, "Lightning Deaths in the United States: A Seven-Year Survey from 1959 to 1965," *Weatherwise* 20 (1969), 168–73, 179; and H. Michael Mogil, Marjorie Rush, and Mary Kutka, "Lightning—A Preliminary Reassessment," *Weatherwise* 30 (1977), 192–99.

CHAPTER I

1. A. Cash Koeniger, "Climate and Southern Distinctiveness," *Journal of Southern History* 54 (1988), 24; for a review and rebuttal of earlier versions of the claim, see William A. Foran, "Southern Legend: Climate or Climate of Opinion?," in Daniel W. Hollis, ed., *The Proceedings of the South Carolina Historical Association 1956* (Columbia: South Carolina Historical Association, 1957), 6–22.

2. Lawrence Stone, "Elizabethan Overseas Trade," *Economic History Review*, 2d ser., 2 (1949), 30–56.

3. The relationship of English mercantilism to North American colonization is reviewed by John J. McCusker, "British Mercantilist Policies and the American Colonies," in Stanley L. Engerman and Robert E. Gallman, eds., *The Cambridge Economic History of the United States,* vol. 1, *The Colonial Era* (New York: Cambridge University Press, 1996), 337–41, and Peter A. Coclanis, *The Shadow of a Dream: Economic Life and Death in the South Carolina Low Country, 1670–1920* (New York: Oxford University Press, 1989), 15–21.

4. Richard Hakluyt, "Pamphlet for the Virginia Enterprise" (orig. 1585), in E. G. R. Taylor, ed., *The Original Writings & Correspondence of the Two Richard Hakluyts*, vol. 2 (London: The Hakluyt Society, 1935), 330, 331–32, 333.

5. Ibid., 330.

6. Karen Ordahl Kupperman, "Fear of Hot Climates in the Anglo-American Colonial Experience," *William and Mary Quarterly*, 3d ser., 41 (1984), 213–40.

7. Carville Earle, "Why the Puritans Settled in New England: The Problematic Nature of English Colonization in North America, 1580–1700," in *Geographical Inquiry and American Historical Problems* (Stanford, Calif.: Stanford University Press, 1992), 59, 69.

8. David Hackett Fischer, *Albion's Seed: Four British Folkways in America* (New York: Oxford University Press, 1989), 253. Southern political culture is characterized in similar terms in Daniel J. Elazar, *Cities of the Prairie: The Metropolitan Frontier and American Politics* (New York: Basic Books, 1970), 258–66.

9. Earle, "Why the Puritans Settled in New England," 59.

10. David Vickers, "The Northern Colonies: Economy and Society, 1600–1775," in Engerman and Gallman, *Cambridge Economic History*, 210.

11. William Bradford, *Of Plymouth Plantation, 1620–1647*, ed. Samuel Eliot Morison (New York: Alfred A. Knopf, 1970), 129.

12. Fischer, *Albion's Seed*; Elazar, *Cities of the Prairie*.

13. The fullest discussion is Karen Ordahl Kupperman, "The Puzzle of the American Climate in the Early Colonial Period," *American Historical Review* 87 (1982), 1262–89.

14. Carl O. Sauer, "The Settlement of the Humid East," *Climate and Man: Yearbook of Agriculture, 1941* (Washington, DC: U.S. Government Printing Office, 1941), 159.

15. Philip L. Barbour, ed., *The Complete Works of Captain John Smith (1580–1631)*, vol. 1 (Chapel Hill: University of North Carolina Press, 1986), 35, 210.

16. Edmund S. Morgan, "The Labor Problem at Jamestown, 1607–18," *American Historical Review* 76 (1971), 595–611.

17. Barbour, *The Complete Works of Captain John Smith*, vol. 1, 218.

18. Carville Earle, "The Ecological Origins of the Virginia Mortality Crisis," in *Geographical Inquiry and American Historical Problems*, 27–28, 40–41.

19. Bradford, *Of Plymouth Plantation*, 61, 62.

20. Timothy Dwight, *Travels in New England and New York*, vol. 1 (orig. 1821), ed. Barbara Miller Solomon with Patricia M. King (Cambridge, Mass.: Belknap Press of Harvard University Press, 1969), 104.

21. Joyce E. Chaplin, *An Anxious Pursuit: Agricultural Innovation and Modernity in the Lower South, 1730–1815*, (Chapel Hill: University of North Carolina Press, 1993), 144; Converse D. Clowse, *Economic Beginnings in Colonial South Carolina, 1670–1730* (Columbia: University of South Carolina Press, 1971), 8, 32, 58–60.

22. Chaplin, *An Anxious Pursuit*, 158–65.

23. Thomas Jefferson to the marquis de Chastellux, Sept. 2, 1785, in *Thomas Jefferson: Writings* (New York: Library of America, 1984), 827.

24. [James Winthrop], "Letters of Agrippa: XII" (orig. 1788), in Herbert J. Storing, ed., *The Complete Anti-Federalist*, vol. 4 (Chicago: University of Chicago Press, 1981), 93.

25. David Humphreys, "A Poem on the Industry of the United States of America," in *The Miscellaneous Works of David Humphreys* (New York: T. and J. Swords, 1804), 98.

26. Chaplin, *An Anxious Pursuit*, 66–91.

27. Edmund S. Morgan, *American Slavery, American Freedom: The Ordeal of Colonial Virginia* (New York: W. W. Norton, 1975).

28. Arthur Middleton, *Tobacco Coast: A Maritime History of Chesapeake Bay in the Colonial Era* (1953; Baltimore, Md.: The Johns Hopkins University Press, 1984), 111–13.

29. Chaplin, *An Anxious Pursuit*, 227–51; Sam B. Hilliard, "Antebellum Tidewater Rice Cultivation in South Carolina and Georgia," in James R. Gibson, ed., *European Settlement and Development in America: Essays on Geographical Change in Honour and Memory of Andrew Hill Clark* (Toronto: University of Toronto Press, 1978), 91–115.

30. Morgan, *American Slavery, American Freedom*.

31. Rupert Vance, *Human Geography of the South: A Study in Regional*

Resources and Human Adequacy, 2d ed. (Chapel Hill: University of North Carolina Press, 1935), 366; Gary Puckrein, "Climate, Health and Black Labor in the English Americas," *Journal of American Studies* 13 (1979), 179–93.

32. G. Terry Sharrer, "Indigo in Carolina, 1671–1796," *South Carolina Historical Magazine* 72 (1971), 94–103.

33. Lewis Cecil Gray, *History of Agriculture in the Southern United States to 1860*, vol. 2 (Washington, D.C.: The Carnegie Institution, 1933), 673–90.

34. Ibid., 739–40, 744.

35. Carroll W. Pursell, *Early Stationary Steam Engines in America: A Study in the Migration of a Technology* (Washington, D.C.: Smithsonian Institution Press, 1969); Chaplin, *An Anxious Pursuit*, 253–54; Joseph Clarke Ribert, *The Tobacco Kingdom: Plantation, Market, and Factory in Virginia and North Carolina, 1800–1860* (Durham, N.C.: Duke University Press, 1938), 7, 40–44.

36. H. Roy Merrens and George D. Terry, "Dying in Paradise: Malaria, Mortality, and the Perceptual Environment in Colonial South Carolina," *Journal of Southern History* 50 (1984), 533–50.

37. Merrens and Terry, "Dying in Paradise"; Chaplin, *An Anxious Pursuit*; Peter A. Coclanis, *The Shadow of a Dream: Economic Life and Death in the South Carolina Low Country, 1670–1920* (New York: Oxford University Press, 1989), 42–45.

38. Chaplin, *An Anxious Pursuit*, 96–98; Merrens and Terry, "Dying in Paradise"; Carl Bridenbaugh, "Colonial Newport as a Summer Resort," *Rhode Island Historical Society Collections* 26 (1933), 1–26.

39. Darrett B. Rutman and Anita H. Rutman, "Of Agues and Fevers: Malaria in the Early Chesapeake," *William and Mary Quarterly*, 3d ser., 33 (1976), 31–60.

40. *Annals of Congress* I (1789–80), 880, 907.

41. Thomas Jefferson to Albert Gallatin, Sept. 18, 1801, in *The Works of Thomas Jefferson*, vol. 9, ed. Paul Leicester Ford (New York: The Knickerbocker Press, 1905), 306.

42. Edwin Morris Betts and James Adam Bear, Jr., eds., *The Family Letters of Thomas Jefferson* (Columbia: University of Missouri Press, 1966), 111, 179.

43. Middleton, *Tobacco Coast*, 71.

44. David Ludlum, *Early American Hurricanes, 1492–1870* (Boston: American Meteorological Society, 1963), 41–59.

45. Jonathan Fricker, "The Origins of the Creole Raised Plantation House," *Louisiana History* 25 (1984), 137–53; see also Albert Manucy, *The Houses of St. Augustine, 1565–1821* (St. Augustine, Fla.; St. Augustine Historical Society, 1962), 11, 55; Henry Glassie, *Pattern in the Material Folk Culture of the Eastern United States* (Philadelphia: University of Pennsylvania Press, 1968), 185.

46. Glassie, *Pattern in the Material Folk Culture of the United States*, 184.

47. Henry Glassie, *Folk Housing in Middle Virginia* (Knoxville: University of Tennessee Press, 1975), 136

48. Ibid., 137–38; Rhys Isaac, *The Transformation of Virginia, 1740–1790* (Chapel Hill: University of North Carolina Press, 1982), 305.

49. Thomas Jefferson, *Notes on the State of Virginia* (orig. 1787), in *Thomas Jefferson: Writings*, 278.

50. *The Journal of Latrobe, by Benjamin H. Latrobe*, ed. J. H. B. Latrobe (1905; New York: Burt Franklin, 1971), 187, 210.

51. David Ramsay, *History of South Carolina*, vol. 2 (1809; W. J. Mc-Duffie: Newberry, S.C., 1858), 217, 227–28.

52. L. Chalmers, *An Account of the Weather and Diseases of South-Carolina* (London: Edward and Charles Dilly, 1776), 1: 30–31.

53. John W. Reps, *The Making of Urban America: A History of City Planning in the United States* (Princeton, N.J.: Princeton University Press, 1965), 314–17, 321–22.

54. Ibid., 319–20.

55. Carl Bridenbaugh, *Cities in the Wilderness: The First Century of Urban Life in America 1625–1742*, rev. ed. (New York: Alfred A. Knopf, 1960), 169; for discussions of laws to remove trees, see *Philadelphia Gazette and Weekly Advertiser*, Aug. 21, 1782, 1–2; *The Daily Advertiser* (New York), May 31, 1791, 2; March 8, 1792, 152.

56. Charles Caldwell, *Medical and Philosophical Memoirs* (Philadelphia: T. and William Bradford, 1801), 9–14.

57. Benjamin Franklin to Francis Hopkinson, Dec. 24, 1782, in *The Works of Benjamin Franklin*, vol. 10, ed. John Bigelow (New York: The Knickerbocker Press, 1904), 60.

58. Benjamin Franklin to Mary Stevenson, November 1760, in *Benjamin Franklin: Writings* (New York: The Library of America, 1987), 779–81; Timothy Dwight, *Greenfield Hill: A Poem in Seven Parts* (New York: Childs and Swaine, 1794), 529; Timothy Dwight, *Travels in New England and New York* (orig. 1821), vol. 1, ed. Barbara Miller Solomon with Patricia M. King (Cambridge, Mass.: Belknap Press of Harvard University Press, 1969), 60; *A View of the Soil and Climate of the United States of America . . . by C. F. Volney, Translated, With Occasional Remarks, by C. B. Brown* (Philadelphia: J. Conrad & Co., 1804), 108–09.

59. Abbott Lowell Cummings, *The Framed Houses of Massachusetts Bay, 1625–1725* (Cambridge, Mass.: Belknap Press of Harvard University Press, 1979), 134, 141; Allen G. Noble, *Wood, Brick, and Stone: The North American Settlement Landscape*, vol. 1, *Houses* (Amherst: University of Massachusetts Press, 1984), 18, 19.

60. Glassie, *Pattern in the Material Folk Culture of the Eastern United States*, 184.

61. Henry F. French, "How to Keep Your House Warm in the Country," *New England Farmer*, n.s. 8 (1856), 44; George F. Hoar, *Autobiography of Seventy Years*, vol. 1 (New York: Charles Scribner's Sons, 1903), 42.

62. Jane C. Nylander, *Our Own Snug Fireside: Images of the New England Home, 1760–1860* (New Haven, Conn.: Yale University Press, 1993), 94–96.

63. Benjamin Franklin, "An Account of the New Invented Pennsylvania Fire-Places" (orig. 1744), in Leonard W. Labaree, ed., *The Papers of Benjamin Franklin*, vol. 2 (New Haven: Yale University Press, 1960), 428, 429; Samuel Edgerton, "The Myth of the Franklin Stove," *Early American Life* 7, no. 2 (1976), 38–41, 60–62.

64. Michael Williams, *Americans and Their Forests: A Historical Geography* (Cambridge: Cambridge University Press, 1989), 78–80; Gordon G. Whitney, *From Coastal Wilderness to Fruited Plain: A History of Environmental Change in Temperate North America from 1500 to the Present* (New York: Cambridge University Press, 1994), 212–25.

65. Robert E. Cray, Jr., *Paupers and Poor Relief in New York City and its Rural Environs, 1700–1830* (Philadelphia: Temple University Press, 1988), 74–75; Raymond A. Mohl, *Poverty in New York, 1783–1825* (New York: Oxford University Press, 1971), 29, 102, 108–10; John K. Alexander, *Render Them Submissive: Responses to Poverty in Philadelphia, 1760–1800* (Amherst: University of Massachusetts Press, 1980), 14–16; Billy G. Smith, *The "Lower Sort": Philadelphia and its Laboring People, 1750–1800* (Ithaca, N.Y.: Cornell University Press, 1990), 145–46.

66. Henry W. Farnam, *Chapters in the History of Social Legislation in the United States to 1860* (Washington, D.C.: The Carnegie Institution, 1938), 71–72, 93–94, 112–15; Jon C. Teaford, *The Municipal Revolution in America* (Chicago: University of Chicago Press, 1975), 93–100; Martin Bruegel, "Uncertainty, Pluriactivity, and Neighborhood Exchange in the Rural Hudson Valley in the Late Eighteenth Century," *New York History* 77 (1996), 255–56.

67. David N. Johnson, *Sketches of Lynn; or, The Changes of Fifty Years* (Lynn, Mass.: Thomas P. Nichols, 1880), 14; Christopher Clark, *The Roots of Rural Capitalism: Western Massachusetts, 1780–1860* (Ithaca, N.Y.: Cornell University Press, 1990), 82; Dwight, *Travels in New England and New York*, vol. 2, 2; Donald R. Hoke, *Ingenious Yankees: The Rise of the American System of Manufactures in the Private Sector* (New York: Columbia University Press, 1990), 268n8.

68. Mary Beth Norton, *Liberty's Daughters: The Revolutionary Experiences of American Women, 1750–1800* (Boston: Little, Brown, 1980), 12; Clark, *Roots of Rural Capitalism*, 25–26.

69. Winifred B. Rothenberg, "Structural Change in the Farm Labor Force: Contract Labor in Massachusetts Agriculture, 1750–1865," in Claudia Goldin and Hugh Rockoff, eds., *Strategic Factors in Nineteenth Century American Economic History: A Volume to Honor Robert W. Fogel* (Chicago: University of Chicago Press, 1992), 112–13n, 114–21, 124–26; Kenneth L. Sokoloff and David Dollar, "Agricultural Seasonality and the Organization of Manufacturing in Early Industrial Economies: The Contrast Between England and the United States," *Journal of Economic History* 57 (1997), 288–321; Elinor F. Oakes, "A Ticklish Business: Dairying in New England and Pennsylvania, 1750–1812," *Pennsylvania History* 47 (1980), 195–212.

70. Sarah F. McMahon, "A Comfortable Subsistence: The Changing Composition of Diet in Rural New England, 1620–0," *William and Mary Quarterly*, 3d ser., 42 (1985), 26–65; Nylander, *Our Own Snug Fireside*, 96–97. Oscar Edward Anderson, Jr., *Refrigeration in America: A History of a New Technology and Its Impact* (Princeton, N.J.: Princeton University Press, 1953); Joan M. Jensen, *Loosening the Bonds: Mid-Atlantic Farm Women, 1750–1850* (New Haven, Conn.: Yale University Press, 1986), 96–100, 109.

71. Henry G. Pearson, "Frederic Tudor, Ice King," *Massachusetts Historical Society Proceedings* 65 (1933), 175–82.

72. J. Hector St. John de Crèvecoeur, "A Snow-Storm as it Affects the American Farmer," in *Letters from an American Farmer and Sketches of Eighteenth-Century America*, ed. Albert E. Stone (New York: Penguin Books, 1981), 239; James Fenimore Cooper, *The Pioneers; or, The Sources of the Susquehanna* (orig. 1823), in *James Fenimore Cooper: The Leatherstocking Tales*, vol. 1 (New York: The Library of America, 1985), 216; Albert Gallatin, *Report of the Secretary of the Treasury on the Subject of Public Roads and Canals* (1808; New York: Augustus M. Kelley, 1968), 64–65.

73. Bridenbaugh, *Cities in the Wilderness*, 155–58, 315–18; Carl Bridenbaugh, *Cities in Revolution: Urban America, 1743–1776* (London: Oxford University Press, 1955), 28–33, 238–39.

74. Dwight, *Travels in New England and New York*, vol. 1, 170.

75. Henry Adams, *History of the United States During the Administrations of Thomas Jefferson* (1889; New York: The Library of America, 1986), 8–9.

76. Howard I. Chapelle, *The Search for Speed Under Sail, 1700–1855* (New York: Bonanza Books, 1967); Benjamin Franklin to David Le Roy, August 1785, in *The Works of Benjamin Franklin*, vol. 11, ed. John Bigelow (New York: The Knickerbocker Press, 1904), 100.

77. Maris A. Vinovskis, "Mortality Rates and Trends in Massachusetts Before 1860," *Journal of Economic History* 32 (1972), 193, 196; Barbara J. Logue, "In Pursuit of Prosperity: Disease and Death in a Massachusetts Commercial Port, 1660–1850," *Journal of Social History* 25 (1991), 318–20.

78. Franklin to Le Roy, *Works of Benjamin Franklin*, vol. 11, 125–26.

79. Henry H. Hall, "Fire and Marine Insurance," in Chauncey M. Depew, ed., *One Hundred Years of American Commerce*, vol. 1 (New York: D. Hayes, 1895), 88; Douglass C. North, "Sources of Productivity Change in Ocean Shipping, 1600–1850," *Journal of Political Economy* 76 (1968), 958.

80. Franklin to Le Roy, *Works of Benjamin Franklin*, vol. 11, 99, 103, 104.

81. Benjamin Franklin to Horace-Benedict de Saussure, Oct. 8, 1772, in *The Papers of Benjamin Franklin*, vol. 19, ed. William B. Willcox (New Haven: Yale University Press, 1975), 325.

82. Quoted in J. Munsell, *Annals of Albany*, vol. 6 (Albany, N.Y.: J. Munsell, 1855), 20.

83. "Poor Richard, 1738," in *Benjamin Franklin: Writings* (New York. Library of America, 1987). 1207.

84. Susan E. Klepp, "Seasoning and Society: Racial Differences in Mortality in Eighteenth-Century Philadelphia," *William and Mary Quarterly*, 3d ser., 51 (1994), 473–506.

85. Increase Mather, *A Brief History of the War with the Indians in New-England* (orig. 1676), in *So Dreadfull a Judgment: Puritan Responses to King Philip's War, 1676–1677*, ed. Richard Slotkin and James K. Folsom (Middletown, Conn.: Wesleyan University Press, 1978), 89–90, 109–10, 118, 127, 136–37; see generally David D. Hall, "A World of Wonders: The Mentality of the Supernatural in Seventeenth-Century New England," in David D. Hall and David Grayson Allen, eds., *Seventeenth-Century New England* (Boston: The Colonial Society of Massachusetts, 1984), 239–74.

86. John C. Fitzpatrick, ed., *The Writings of George Washington*, vol. 4 (Washington, DC: Government Printing Office, 1931), 433–34.

87. John F. Berens, *Providence & Patriotism in Early America, 1640–1815* (Charlottesville: University Press of Virginia, 1978), 94; John Rodgers, *The Divine Goodness Displayed, in the American Revolution* (New York: Samuel Loudon, 1784), 18n, 20n.

88. Ezra Stiles, "The United States Elevated to Glory and Honor" (orig. 1783), in John Wingate Thornton, ed., *The Pulpit of the American Revolution; or, The Political Sermons of the Period of 1776* (Boston: Gould and Lincoln, 1860), 444.

89. Rodgers, *The Divine Goodness Displayed*, 23n.

90. Benjamin Trumbull, *God Is to Be Praised for the Glory of His Majesty, and for His Mighty Works* (New Haven, Conn.: Thomas and Samuel Green, 1784), 17; Henry Cumings, *A Sermon Preached in Billerica, December 11, 1783* (Boston: T. and J. Fleet, 1784), 27.

91. Lester H. Cohen, *The Revolutionary Histories: Contemporary Narratives of the American Revolution* (Ithaca, N.Y.: Cornell University Press, 1980), 61–67, 76–77.

92. Cecelia Tichi, *New World, New Earth: Environmental Reform in American Literature From the Puritans Through Whitman* (New Haven, Conn.: Yale University Press, 1979), 115.

93. Kenneth R. Ball, "Joel Barlow's 'Canal' and Natural Religion," *Eighteenth-Century Studies* 2 (1968), 238; Joel Barlow, *The Columbiad. A Poem, With the Last Corrections of the Author* (Washington, D.C.: Joseph Milligan, 1825), 346, 347, 358.

94. Samuel Hopkins, *A Treatise on the Millennium* (Boston: Isaiah Thomas and Ebenezer T. Andrews, 1793), 70.

95. Barlow, *The Columbiad*, 40, 45.

96. On this passage, see Tichi, *New World, New Earth*, 144–45.

97. Barlow, *The Columbiad*, 369–70.

98. See especially Kenneth Thompson, "The Question of Climatic Stability in America Before 1900," *Climatic Change* 3 (1981), 227–41.

99. Hugh Williamson, *Observations on the Climate in Different Parts of North America* (New York: T. & J. Swords, 1811), 30; Moses Greenleaf, *A Statistical View of the District of Maine* (Boston: Cummings and Hilliard, 1816), 26–27, 29; *The Daily Advertiser* (New York), June 12, 1790, 2.

100. I. Bernard Cohen, "Prejudice Against the Introduction of Lightning Rods," *Journal of the Franklin Institute* 253 (1952), 393–440; Benjamin Franklin to Cadwallader Colden, April 12, 1753, in Leonard W. Labaree, ed., *The Papers of Benjamin Franklin*, vol. 4 (New Haven: Yale University Press, 1961), 463.

101. Cohen, "Prejudice Against the Introduction of Lightning Rods"; *Columbian Centinel*, Oct. 9 and Oct. 12, 1793.

102. See, e.g., Noah Webster, "On the Supposed Change in the Temperature of Winter" (orig. 1806), in *A Collection of Papers on Political, Literary, and Moral Subjects* (1843; New York: Burt Franklin, 1968); Timothy Dwight, *Travels in New England and New York* (orig. 1821), vol. 1, ed. Bar-

bara Miller Solomon (Cambridge, Mass.: Belknap Press of Harvard University Press, 1969), 40–41, 303.

103. Ball, "Joel Barlow's 'Canal,'" 238.

CHAPTER 2

1. Malcolm Rohrbough, *The Trans-Appalachian Frontier: People, Societies, and Institutions, 1775–1850* (New York: Oxford University Press, 1978), 157.

2. See Richard H. Steckel, "The Economic Foundations of East-West Migration During the Nineteenth Century," *Explorations in Economic History* 20 (1983), 14–36, and Donald F. Schaefer, "A Statistical Profile of Frontier and New South Migrants," *Agricultural History* 59 (1985), 564–65, 571; also William O. Lynch, "The Westward Flow of Southern Colonists Before 1861," *Journal of Southern History* 9 (1943), 305–6; Frank L. Owsley, "The Pattern of Migration and Settlement on the Southern Frontier," *Journal of Southern History* 11 (1945), 166–75; and John C. Hudson, "North American Origins of Middlewestern Frontier Populations," *Annals of the Association of American Geographers* 78 (1988), 395–413.

3. *Congressional Globe*, 35th Congress, 1st session (1858), 1341; *New Orleans Daily Crescent*, Apr. 17, 1860, 4; June 15, 1860, 4.

4. *Boston Evening Transcript*, Nov. 28, 1859, 1.

5. Charles Caldwell, "Thoughts on the Means of Preserving Health, in Hot Climates," *Transylvania Journal of Medicine*, 6 (1833), 361.

6. *Freedom's Journal* 1 (1827), 66, 102, 141–42, 153; *The Liberator* 1 (1831), 107, 110; Thomas R. Dew, *Review of the Debate in the Virginia Legislature of 1831 and 1832* (Richmond, Va.: T. W. White, 1832), 71–72.

7. Steckel, "Economic Foundations."

8. [Frances M. Whitcher], *The Widow Bedott Papers; With an Introduction by Alice B. Neal* (New York: Derby & Jackson, 1856), 171; *"This State of Wonders": The Letters of an Iowa Frontier Family, 1858–1861*, ed. John Kent Folmar (Iowa City: University of Iowa Press, 1986), 34.

9. Lorin Blodget, *Climatology of the United States and of the Temperate Latitudes of the North American Continent* (Philadelphia: J. B. Lippincott, 1857), 257–316.

10. D. W. Meinig, *The Shaping of America: A Geographical Perspective on 500 Years of History,* vol. 2, *Continental America, 1800–1867* (New Haven: Yale University Press, 1993), 238.

11. John S. Wright, *Letters from the West; or, A Caution to Emigrants* (Salem, N.Y.: Dodd & Stevenson, 1819), 42.

12. Meinig, *Continental America*, 239.

13. *The United States Magazine and Democratic Review* n.s. 15 (1844), 183.

14. Solon Robinson, "Cost of a Farm, and Raising Products on the Western Prairies" (orig. 1842), in Herbert Anthony Keller, ed., *Solon Robinson, Pioneer and Agriculturist,* 2 vols. (1936; New York: Da Capo, 1968), 1: 344.

15. Edgar W. Martin, *The Standard of Living in 1860: American Consumption Levels on the Eve of the Civil War* (Chicago: University of Chicago Press, 1942), 267–69.

16. *Genesee Farmer and Gardener's Journal* 1 (1831), 70.

17. Oliver W. Holmes, "The Turnpike Era," in Alexander C. Flick, *History of the State of New York*, vol. 5 (New York: Columbia University Press, 1934), 290–91.

18. Robert F. Hunter, "Turnpike Construction in Antebellum Virginia," *Technology and Culture* 4 (1963), 177–200.

19. *Ohio Cultivator* 6 (1850), 74; on the shortcomings of local management, see also John R. Stilgoe, *Common Landscape of America, 1580 to 1845* (New Haven: Yale University Press, 1982), 128–32.

20. George Wilson Pierson, *Tocqueville in America* (1938; Baltimore, Md.: The Johns Hopkins University Press, 1996), 189, 192, 653.

21. Philip D. Jordan, *The National Road* (Indianapolis: Bobbs-Merrill, 1948).

22. *Gales & Seaton's Register of Debates in Congress* 4 (20th Congress, 1st session, 1828), 110.

23. George Rogers Taylor, *The Transportation Revolution, 1815–1860* (New York: Rinehart, 1951), 21–22.

24. Joseph Durrenberger, *Turnpikes: A Study of the Toll Road Movement in the Middle Atlantic States and Maryland* (1931; Cos Cob, Conn.: John E. Edwards, 1968).

25. Louis C. Hunter, *Studies in the Economic History of the Ohio Valley* (Northampton, Mass.: Smith College Studies in History, vol. 19, no. 1–2, 1934), 11; see also Thomas Senior Berry, *Western Prices Before 1861* (Cambridge, Mass.: Harvard University Press, 1943), 60–67.

26. Louis C. Hunter with Beatrice Jones Hunter, *Steamboats on the Western Rivers: An Economic and Technological History* (Cambridge, Mass.: Harvard University Press, 1949).

27. Hunter, *Studies*, 12.

28. For Ellet's plan, see his *The Mississippi and Ohio Rivers* (Philadelphia: Lippincott, Grambo, 1853); on its history, Gene D. Lewis, *Charles Ellet, Jr.: The Engineer as Individualist* (Urbana: University of Illinois Press, 1968), 133–51.

29. On two canal systems, see Walter S. Sanderson, *The Great National Project: A History of the Chesapeake and Ohio Canal* (Baltimore, Md.: The Johns Hopkins University Press, 1946), 207–8, 211–12; and Paul Fatout, *Indiana Canals* (West Lafayette, Ind.: Purdue University Studies, 1972).

30. Noble E. Whitford, *History of the Canal System of the State of New York* (Albany, N.Y.: Brandow Printing Co., 1906), 959.

31. Blake McKelvey, *Snow in the Cities: A History of America's Urban Response* (Rochester, N.Y.: University of Rochester Press, 1995), 34.

32. William Cronon, *Nature's Metropolis: Chicago and the Great West* (New York: W. W. Norton, 1991), 78; Harold A. Winters, "The Battle that Was Never Fought: Weather and the Union Mud March of January 1863," *Southeastern Geographer* 31 (1991), 36.

33. Isaac Weld, Jr., *Travels Through the States of North America, and the Provinces of Upper and Lower Canada, During the Years 1795, 1796, and 1797* (4th ed.; London: John Stockdale), 1; 1–2, 5; Charles Richard Weld, *A Vacation Tour in the United States and Canada* (London: Longman, Brown, Green, and Longmans, 1855), 7–8, 14, 16.

34. Taylor, *The Transportation Revolution*, 145.

35. Robert Greenhalgh Albion, *Square-Riggers on Schedule: The New York Sailing Packets to England, France, and the Cotton Ports* (Princeton, N.J.: Princeton University Press, 1938), 174–201.

36. Frances Leigh Williams, *Matthew Fontaine Maury: Scientist of the Seas* (New Brunswick, N.J.: Rutgers University Press, 1963), 178–95; Taylor, *The Transportation Revolution*, 110–12, 145–46.

37. Weld, *A Vacation Tour*, 390–91.

38. Alexander Crosby Brown, *Women and Children Last: The Loss of the Steamship 'Arctic'* (London: Frederick Muller Limited, 1961).

39. Brown, *Women and Children Last*, 183–85.

40. *New York Herald*, Oct. 13, 1854, 4.

41. Cedric Ridgley-Nevitt, *American Steamships on the Atlantic* (Newark: University of Delaware Press, 1981), 159.

42. John H. Morrison, *History of American Steam Navigation* (New York: W. F. Sametz, 1903), 574–90.

43. Robert M. Browning, *From Cape Charles to Cape Fear: The North Atlantic Blockading Squadron During the Civil War* (Tuscaloosa: University of Alabama Press, 1993), 234.

44. Robert F. Bennett, *Surfboats, Rockets, and Carronades* (U.S. Department of Transportation: Washington, D.C., Government Printing Office, n.d.), 35–53; Dennis R. Means, "'A Heavy Sea Running': The Formation of the U.S. Life-Saving Service, 1846–1878," *Prologue* 19 (1987), 223–43.

45. Forest G. Hill, *Roads, Rails, and Waterways: The Army Engineers and Early Transportation* (Norman: University of Oklahoma Press, 1957).

46. David Ludlum, *Early American Hurricanes, 1492–1870* (Boston: American Meteorological Society, 1963), 91; Samuel Eliot Morison, *The Maritime History of Massachusetts, 1783–1860* (Boston: Houghton Mifflin, 1921), 311; Wayne M. O'Leary, "The Maine Sea Fisheries, 1830–1890: The Rise and Fall of a Native Industry," Ph.D. dissertation, University of Maine, 1981, 335.

47. G. Brown Goode and J. W. Collins, "The Fresh-Halibut Fishery," in George Brown Goode, ed., *The Fisheries and Fishery Industries of the United States: Section V: History and Methods of the Fisheries* (Washington, D.C.: Government Printing Office, 1887), 1: 20.

48. O'Leary, "The Maine Sea Fisheries," 342–46; W. M. P. Dunne, *Thomas F. McManus and the American Fishing Schooners* (Mystic, Conn.: Mystic Seaport Museum, 1994), 41, 52–53, 97–99.

49. Weld, *A Vacation Tour*, 191.

50. James D. Reid, *The Telegraph in America: Its Founders, Promoters, and Noted Men* (1879; New York: Arno Press, 1974), 214–16.

51. Philip Dorf, *The Builder: A Biography of Ezra Cornell* (New York: Macmillan, 1952), 60–62.

52. Weld, *A Vacation Tour*, 237–38. For numerous examples, see Reid, *The Telegraph in America*; Robert L. Thompson, *Wiring a Continent: The History of the Telegraph Industry in the United States, 1832–1866* (Princeton, N.J.: Princeton University Press, 1947); and Alvin F. Harlow, *Old Wires and New Waves* (1936; New York: Arno Press, 1971).

53. Martin, *The Standard of Living in 1860*, 272n, 275.

54. *DeBow's Commercial Review* 1 (1846), 136.

55. James P. Delgado, *To California by Sea: A Maritime History of the California Gold Rush* (Columbia: University of South Carolina Press, 1990), 167–70; Norman E. Klare, *The Final Voyage of the Central America* (Spokane, Wash.: Arthur H. Clark, 1992).

56. Samuel Carter III, *Cyrus Field: Man of Two Worlds* (New York: G. P. Putnam's Sons, 1968), 115, 149, 154, 155.

57. Joseph Henry, "On the Application of the Telegraph to the Premonition of Weather Changes" (orig. 1859), in *Scientific Writings of Joseph Henry*, vol. 2 (Washington, D.C.: Smithsonian Institution, 1886), 440.

58. On Redfield and Espy, see James Rodger Fleming, *Meteorology in America, 1800–1870* (Baltimore, Md.: The Johns Hopkins University Press, 1990).

59. Elias Loomis, "Report on the Meteorology of the United States," Appendix 2, Senate Miscellaneous Document 23, 30th Congress, 1st session (1848), 203; W. C. Redfield, "On Three Several Hurricanes of the American Seas and their Relations to the Northers, So Called, of the Gulf of Mexico and the Bay of Honduras," *American Journal of Science*, 2nd ser., 2 (1846), 334.

60. Quoted in Diana Fontaine Corbin, *A Life of Matthew Fontaine Maury, Compiled by His Daughter, Diana Fontaine Maury Corbin* (London: S. Low, Marston, Searle & Rivington, 1888), 85–86.

61. Frances Leigh Williams, *Matthew Fontaine Maury: Scientist of the Seas* (New Brunswick, N.J.: Rutgers University Press, 1963) 309–26; Harold L. Burstyn, "Seafaring and the Emergence of American Science," in Benjamin W. Labaree, ed., *The Atlantic World of Robert G. Albion* (Middletown, Conn.: Wesleyan University Press, 1975), 76–109.

62. Corbin, *Life of Matthew Fontaine Maury*, 86; Henry quoted in Williams, *Matthew Fontaine Maury*, 317.

63. J. Cecil Alter, "National Weather Service Origins," *Bulletin of the Historical and Philosophical Society of Ohio* 7 (1948), 146–47, 150–51.

64. Henry, "On the Application of the Telegraph," 441.

65. *Southern Planter* 17 (1857), 136–39.

66. *The Farmers' Register* 1 (1833), 447.

67. Corbin, *Life of Matthew Fontaine Maury*, 88.

68. Richard B. DuBoff, "The Telegraph and the Structure of Markets in the United States, 1845–1860," *Research in Economic History* 8 (1983), 257, 259–61.

69. *The Farmers' Register* 4 (1836), 754–55.

70. C[aroline] M. Kirkland, "Western Sketches.—No. 7. The Hard Winter," *The Union Magazine of Literature and Art* 2 (1848), 43.

71. William L. Barney, *The Secessionist Impulse: Alabama and Mississippi in 1860* (Princeton, N.J.: Princeton University Press, 1974), 153–63.

72. Paul W. Gates, *Agriculture and the Civil War* (New York: Alfred A. Knopf, 1965).

73. Joseph B. Hoyt, "The Cold Summer of 1816," *Annals of the Association of American Geographers* 48 (1958), 122–23; John D. Post, *The Last Great Subsistence Crisis in the Western World* (Baltimore, Md.: The Johns Hopkins University Press, 1977), 12–13; and Henry Stommel and Eliza-

beth Stommel, *Volcano Weather: The Story of 1816, the Year Without a Summer* (Newport, R.I.: Seven Seas Press, 1983), 73–75. On the unusual success of the wheat crop, see also *Memoirs of the Philadelphia Society for Promoting Agriculture* 4 (1818), xi, 113–14, 128, 130, 156, 194, 195.

74. Price movements are documented by Hoyt, "The Cold Summer of 1816," 125–26, and Stommel and Stommel, *Volcano Weather*, 83–85.

75. Post, *The Last Great Subsistence Crisis*, 89.

76. This account follows Post, *The Last Great Subsistence Crisis*, 153–55.

77. Adam Hodgson, *Remarks During a Trip Through North America in the Years 1819, 1820, and 1821* (1823; Westport, Conn.: Negro Universities Press, 1970), 32.

78. Walter Buckingham Smith and Arthur Harrison Cole, *Fluctuations in American Business, 1790–1860* (Cambridge, Mass.: Harvard University Press, 1935), 98–99; James L. Huston, *The Panic of 1857 and the Coming of the Civil War* (Baton Rouge: Louisiana State University Press, 1987).

79. Peter A. Coclanis, "Distant Thunder: The Creation of a World Market in Rice and the Transformations It Wrought," *American Historical Review* 98 (1993), 1056, 1060, 1066, 1071.

80. J. Carlyle Sitterson, *Sugar Country: The Cane Sugar Industry in the South, 1753–1950* (Lexington: University of Kentucky Press, 1953), 175–77.

81. *Congressional Globe*, 35th Congress, 1st session (1858), Appendix, 274–75.

82. See, for example, *Congressional Globe*, 33rd Congress, 1st session (1854), Appendix, 212, 318, 375, 539; James C. Malin, "Kansas: Some Reflections on Culture Inheritance and Originality" (orig. 1961), in Malin, *History & Ecology: Studies of the Grassland*, ed. Robert P. Swierenga (Lincoln: University of Nebraska Press, 1984), 238–57.

83. Lawrence J. Jelinek, *Harvest Empire: A History of California Agriculture* (San Francisco: Boyd & Fraser, 1979), 32–37; Paul W. Gates, *California Ranchos and Farmers, 1846–1862* (Madison: State Historical Society of Wisconsin, 1967).

84. Leonard J. Arrington, *Great Basin Kingdom: An Economic History of the Latter-Day Saints, 1830–1900* (Cambridge, Mass.: Harvard University Press, 1958), 48–50, 52–53, 57–63, 148–56; Paul W. Gates, *The Farmer's Age: Agriculture, 1815–1860* (New York: Holt, Rinehart and Winston, 1960), 383–86.

85. Allan G. Bogue, *From Prairie to Corn Belt: Farming on the Illinois and Iowa Prairies in the Nineteenth Century* (Chicago: University of Chicago Press, 1963), 135–37; John C. Hudson, *Making the Corn Belt: A Geographical History of Middle-Western Agriculture* (Bloomington: Indiana University Press, 1994), 152–54; David C. Smith, Harold W. Borns, W. R. Baron, and Anne E. Bridges, "Climatic Stress and Maine Agriculture, 1785–1885," in T. M. L. Wigley, M. J. Ingram, and G. Farmer, eds., *Climate and History: Studies in Past Climates and their Impact on Man* (Cambridge: Cambridge University Press, 1981), 457, 459–61; David Demeritt, "Climate, Cropping, and Society in Vermont, 1820–1850," *Vermont History* 59 (1991), 133–65; James S. Lippincott, "The Fruit Regions of the Northern United States and their Local Climates," *Report of the Commissioner of Agriculture for the Year 1866* (Washington, D.C.: Government Printing Office, 1867), 137–90.

86. For representative catalogues of weather signs, see *Southern Agriculturist and Register of Rural Affairs* 11 (1838), 290–97; *American Agriculturist* 2 (1843), 101–2, 270–72; *Ohio Cultivator* 3 (1847), 7, 71, 91.

87. *Ohio Cultivator* 3 (1847), 22.

88. Leo Rogin, *The Introduction of Farm Machinery and its Relation to the Productivity of Labor in the Agriculture of the United States During the Nineteenth Century* (Berkeley: University of California Press, 1931).

89. Herbert A. Kellar, "The Reaper as a Factor in the Development of the Agriculture of Illinois, 1834–1865," *Transactions of the Illinois State Historical Society for the Year 1927*, 112; William T. Hutchinson, *Cyrus Hall McCormick*, vol. 1 (New York: Century, 1930), 69, 74.

90. Bogue, *From Prairie to Corn Belt*, 125; Gates, *The Farmer's Age*, 260; Henry F. French, *Farm Drainage* (New York: C. M. Saxton, Barket, 1860), 261–63, 271–74; Howard S. Russell, *A Long Deep Furrow: Three Centuries of Farming in New England* (Hanover, N.H.: University Press of New England, 1976), 374–77; B. T. Galloway, "Progress of Commercial Growing of Plants Under Glass," *Yearbook of the United States Department of Agriculture, 1899* (Washington, D.C.: Government Printing Office, 1900), 577–81.

91. William Dusinberre, *Them Dark Days: Slavery in the American Rice Swamps* (New York: Oxford University Press, 1996), 71–74.

92. Merton M. Sealts, ed., *The Journals and Miscellaneous Notebooks of Ralph Waldo Emerson*, vol. 4, *1835–1838* (Cambridge, Mass.: The Belknap Press of Harvard University Press, 1965), 301.

93. Jacob Bigelow, "Inaugural Address," *North American Review* 4 (1817), 75.

94. A point stressed long ago by Louis C. Hunter, "Seasonal Aspects of Industry and Commerce Before the Age of Big Business," in *Studies in the Economic History of the Ohio Valley* (Northampton, Mass.: Smith College Studies in History, 19, no. 1–2, 1934), 5–49.

95. Ibid., 32–41; Louis C. Hunter, *A History of Industrial Power in the United States, 1780–1930*, vol. 1, *Waterpower in the Age of the Steam Engine* (Charlottesville: University Press of Virginia, 1979).

96. Hunter, *Waterpower*, 142–52; Theodore Steinberg, *Nature Incorporated: Industrialization and the Waters of New England* (New York: Cambridge University Press, 1991).

97. Hunter, *Waterpower*, 292–342.

98. Quoted in Philip Scranton, *Proprietary Capitalism: The Textile Manufactures of Philadelphia, 1800–1885* (Cambridge: Cambridge University Press, 1983), 224.

99. Louis C. Hunter, *A History of Industrial Power in the United States, 1780–1930*, vol. 2, *Steam Power* (Charlottesville: University Press of Virginia, 1985), 75, 85–87; Jeremy Atack, "Fact in Fiction? The Relative Costs of Steam and Water Power: A Simulation Approach," *Explorations in Economic History* 16 (1979), 409–30.

100. *Frank Leslie's Illustrated Newspaper*, 4 (Aug. 8, 1857), 151–52; Joshua V. H. Clark, *Onondaga; or, Reminiscences of Earlier and Later Times* (Syracuse, N.Y.: Stoddard and Babcock, 1846), 2: 32; *Hunt's Merchants Magazine* 34 (1856), 510; 37 (1857), 245; Edward W. Parker, "Salt," in *Census Reports, Vol. 9, Twelfth Census, Manufactures, Part III: Special Reports*

in Selected Industries (Washington, D.C.: United States Census Office, 1902), 536.

101. Hunter, "Seasonal Aspects," 41–48; Margaret Walsh, *The Rise of the Midwestern Meat Packing Industry* (Lexington: University Press of Kentucky, 1982), 24–25; William G. Panschar, *Baking in America* (Evanston, Ill.: Northwestern University Press, 1956), 1: 38; Francis G. Couvares, *The Remaking of Pittsburgh: Class and Culture in an Industrializing City* (Albany: State University of New York Press, 1984), 15; "Report of the Committee on the Machinery of the United States" (orig. 1855), in Nathan Rosenberg, ed., *The American System of Manufactures* (Edinburgh: Edinburgh University Press, 1969), 112; Pearce Davis, *The Development of the American Glass Industry* (Cambridge, Mass.: Harvard University Press, 1949), 127–28.

102. Joseph D. Weeks, *Report on the Statistics of Wages in the Manufacturing Industries* (Washington, D.C.: Government Printing Office, 1886), 28, 30, 32, 33, 257–58, 260, 262–63, 283, 297, 461.

103. Bruce Laurie, "'Nothing on Compulsion': Life Styles of Philadelphia Artisans, 1820–1850," *Labor History* 15 (1974), 391–94; Carville Earle and Ronald Hoffman, "The Industrial Revolution as a Response to Cheap Labor and Agricultural Seasonality, 1790–1860: A Reexamination of the Habakkuk Thesis," in Carville Earle, *Geographical Inquiry and American Historical Problems* (Stanford, Calif.: Stanford University Press, 1992), 173–225.

104. Peter Way, *Common Labour: Workers and the Digging of North American Canals, 1780–1860* (New York: Cambridge University Press, 1993), 81–82, 108–11, 116.

105. David E. Schob, *Hired Hands and Plowboys: Farm Labor in the Midwest, 1815–1860* (Urbana: University of Illinois Press, 1975), 150–72.

106. Robert Ozanne, *Wages in Practice and Theory: McCormick and International Harvester, 1860–1960* (Madison: University of Wisconsin Press, 1968), 17.

107. Oscar Edward Anderson, *Refrigeration in America: The History of a New Technology and Its Impact* (Princeton, N.J.: Princeton University Press, 1953), 28–29, 33–35; Hunter, "Seasonal Aspects," 43–44, 46–47.

108. Anderson, *Refrigeration in America*, 22–36; Martin, *The Standard of Living in 1860*, 46–48; Joe B. Frantz, *Gail Borden: Dairyman to a Nation* (Norman: University of Oklahoma Press, 1951)

109. Shelby Foote, *The Civil War: A Narrative*, vol. 1: *Fort Sumter to Perryville* (1958; New York: Vintage Books, 1986), 178; *Manufactures of the United States in 1860; Compiled from the Original Reports of the Eighth Census* (Washington, D.C.: Government Printing Office, 1865), cxlix, 737; Cyril Ehrlich, *The Piano: A History*, rev. ed. (Oxford: Clarendon Press, 1990), 32–33, 49.

110. *Manufactures of the United States in 1860*, lxxvi; P. W. Barker, *Charles Goodyear: Connecticut Yankee and Rubber Pioneer* (Boston, Mass.: Godfrey L. Cabot, 1940).

111. Charles Goodyear, *Gum-Elastic and Its Varieties*, vol. 2, *The Applications and Uses of Vulcanized Gum-Elastic; with Descriptions and Directions for Manufacturing Purposes* (New Haven, Conn.; the author, 1853), 33, 47–48, 49, 50, 54, 55, 57–58, 67, 91, 141–45, 147, 154, 280, 305–24, 351–52, 359–66.

112. *Hunt's Merchants' Magazine* 30 (1854), 378–79.

113. Lois Banner, *American Beauty* (New York; Alfred A. Knopf, 1983), 46, 48.

114. Dr. W. W. Hall, *Health and Disease: A Book for the People* (New York: H. B. Price, 1859), 147; Orville Dewey, *The Old World and the New* (New York, Harper & Brothers, 1836), vol. 1, 134.

115. Gayle Veronica Fischer, "Who Wears the Pants? Women, Dress Reform, and Power in the Mid-Nineteenth-Century United States," Ph.D. dissertation, Indiana University, 1995, and Robert E. Riegel, "Women's Clothes and Women's Rights," *American Quarterly* 25 (1963), 390–401 focus on the feminist dress reformers.

116. *Boston Medical and Surgical Journal* 55 (1856), 392–93 and 56 (1856), 518; *New-York Mirror* 19 (1841), 75; *The Water-Cure Journal and Herald of Reforms* 8 (1849), 184.

117. Martin, *The Standard of Living in 1860,* 205–10; Zerah Hawley, *A Journal of a Tour Through Connecticut, Massachusetts, New-York, the Northern Part of Pennsylvania and Ohio, Including a Year's Residence in that Part of the State of Ohio, Styled the New Connecticut, or Western Reserve* (New Haven, Conn.: S. Converse, 1822), 35, 42–43; Bell Irvin Wiley, *The Life of Johnny Reb: The Common Soldier of the Confederacy* (Indianapolis: Bobbs-Merrill, 1943), 112–22; Mary Elizabeth Massey, *Ersatz in the Confederacy* (Columbia: University of South Carolina Press, 1952), 79–98.

118. [Eliza W. R. Farrar], *The Young Lady's Friend. By a Lady* (Boston: American Stationers', 1836), 110.

119. Banner, *American Beauty*, 54.

120. See, e.g., Farrar, *The Young Lady's Friend*, 100; Frances Trollope, *Domestic Manners of the Americans* (1832: New York: Alfred A. Knopf, 1949), 300; Frances Wright, *Views of Society and Manners in America* (1821; Cambridge, Mass.: Belknap Press of Harvard University Press, 1963), 245–46; Catherine Beecher, *A Treatise on Domestic Economy* (New York: Marsh, Capen, Lyon, and Webb, 1841), 95–96; *Boston Medical and Surgical Journal* 19 (1839), 428; John F. Watson, *Annals of Philadelphia and Pennsylvania, in the Olden Time*, 2 vols. (Philadelphia: Carey and Hart, 1845), 1: 195.

121. R. Turner Wilcox, *Five Centuries of American Costume* (New York: Charles Scribner's Sons, 1963), 145; Banner, *American Beauty*, 94, 97–98; Fischer, "Who Wears the Pants?," 41.

122. Banner, *American Beauty*, 233–34; *New York Journal of Medicine*, 3d series, 7 (1859), 72; *The Water-Cure Journal and Herald of Reforms* 15 (1853), 60.

123. Walt Whitman, "[Song of Myself]" (orig. 1855), in John Hollander, ed., *American Poetry: The Nineteenth Century* (New York: Library of America, 1993), 1: 777; Banner, *American Beauty*, 46; *Godey's Lady's Book* 39 (1849), 228.

124. *New York Journal of Medicine*, 3d series, 7 (1859), 71–72.

125. Mary E. Fry, "Let Us Have a National Costume," *The Ladies' Repository* 16 (1856), 736–37.

126. Eliza W. Farnham, *Life in Prairie Land* (New York: Harper & Brothers, 1846), 199; Solon Robinson, "To Western Emigrants" (orig.

1840), in Herbert Anthony Keller, ed., *Solon Robinson: Pioneer and Agriculturist* (1936; New York: Da Capo, 1968), 1: 159.

127. *Scientific American* 8 (1852), 173; *New York Times*, July 15, 1853, 2.

128. Roger G. Kennedy, *Greek Revival America* (New York: Stewart, Tabori & Chang, 1989), 204; James C. Bonner, "Plantation Architecture of the Lower South on the Eve of the Civil War," *Journal of Southern History* 11 (1945), 380.

129. Andrew Jackson Downing, *Cottage Residences* (1842; Watkins Glen, N.Y.: Century House, 1967), 22; Calvert Vaux, "Hints for Country House Builders," *Harper's New Monthly Magazine* 11 (1855), 763, 771–72.

130. Orson S. Fowler, *A Home for All* (1853; reprinted as *The Octagon House: A Home for All*, New York: Dover Publishers, Inc., 1973), 75, 147; *The Prairie Farmer* 15 (1855), 60–61.

131. See, e.g., *Genesee Farmer and Gardener's Journal* 8 (1838), 189; Wright, *Views of Society and Manners in America*, 102; William E. Baxter, *America and the Americans* (London: Geo. Rutledge, 1855), 21; on the dangers of trees near houses, Lewis F. Allen, *Rural Architecture* (New York: C. M. Saxton, 1852), 35; Stilgoe, *Common Landscape of America, 1580 to 1845*, 165.

132. Andrew Jackson Downing, *The Architecture of Country Houses* (New York: D. Appleton, 1850), 23.

133. Thomas Colley Grattan, *Civilized America*, vol. 1 (London: Bradbury and Evans, 1859), 105; Captain [Lauchlan] MacKinnon, *Atlantic and Transatlantic Sketches* (New York: Harper and Brothers, 1852), 16; William Chambers, *Things as They Are in America* (London: W. and R. Chambers, 1854), 317; Marianne Finch, *An Englishwoman's Experience in America* (London: Richard Bentley, 1853), 188.

134. James Fenimore Cooper, *Gleanings in Europe: England*, ed. Donald A. Ringe and Kenneth W. Staggs (Albany, N.Y.: State University of New York Press, 1982), 85–86; Henry Colman, *European Life and Manners; In Familiar Letters to Friends*, 2 vols. (Boston: Little and Brown, 1849), 1: 319; [Stephen Fiske], *English Photographs, by an American* (London: Tinsley Brothers, 1869), 192, 196.

135. Noah Webster, "Domestic Economy," *Connecticut Courant*, Apr. 22, 1817, 2.

136. A. William Hoglund, "Forest Conservation and Stove Inventors–1789–1850," *Journal of Forest History* 5, no. 4 (1962), 2–8; Gordon G. Whitney, *From Coastal Wilderness to Fruited Plain: A History of Environmental Change in Temperate North America, 1500 to the Present* (New York: Cambridge University Press, 1994), 212–16; Michael Williams, *Americans and Their Forests: A Historical Geography* (Cambridge: Cambridge University Press, 1989), 133–39.

137. They did not appear widely in New England, for example, until the late 1820s: Frank G. White, "Stoves in Nineteenth-Century New England," *Antiques* 116 (1979), 592–93.

138. Frederick Moore Binder, *Coal Age Empire: Pennsylvania Coal and Its Utilization to 1860* (Harrisburg, Penn.: Pennsylvania Historical and Museum Commission, 1974), 3–19; Alfred D. Chandler, Jr., "Anthracite Coal

and the Beginnings of the Industrial Revolution in the United States," *Business History Review* 46 (1972), 152–56.

139. Eliot Jones, *The Anthracite Coal Combination in the United States* (Cambridge, Mass.: Harvard University Press, 1914), 223–24.

140. Binder, *Coal Age Empire*, 22–24.

141. *First Report of the Committee on Public Hygiene of the American Medical Association* (Philadelphia: T. K. and P. G. Collins, 1849), 446, 452, 457, 466, 475–76, 565–66, 620; *Farmers' Register* 8 (1840), 212.

142. Ruth Schwartz Cowan, *More Work for Mother: The Ironies of Household Technology from the Open Hearth to the Microwave* (New York: Basic Books, 1983), 56–57, 61–62, 163–64; *Manufactures of the United States in 1860; Compiled from the Original Reports of the Eighth Census* (Washington, D.C.: Government Printing Office, 1865), 735.

143. *The Cultivator* n.s. 1 (1847), 75–76; [Susan Fenimore Cooper], *Rural Hours; By a Lady* (New York: G. P. Putnam, 1851), 295–96.

144. Webster, "Domestic Economy," 2; *The Cultivator* 7 (1840), 62.

145. *First Report of the Committee on Public Hygiene*, 585.

146. Benjamin L. Walbert, III, "The Infancy of Central Heating in the United States: 1803 to 1845," *Association for Preservation Technology Bulletin* 3, no. 4 (1971), 76–87; Eugene S. Ferguson, "An Historical Sketch of Central Heating: 1800–1860," in Charles E. Peterson, ed., *Building Early America: Contributions toward the History of a Great Industry* (Radnor, Penn.: Chilton, 1976), 165–85; Martin, *The Standard of Living in 1860*, 93.

147. *A Philadelphia Perspective: The Diary of Sidney George Fisher During the Years 1834–1871*, ed. Nicholas B. Wainwright (Philadelphia: The Historical Society of Pennsylvania, 1967), 314.

148. "Warming Houses," *Journal of Health* 2 (1831), 80–81.

149. For typical objections, see *Genesee Farmer and Gardeners Journal* 6 (1836), 401; *Maine Farmer* 5 (1837), 337; Jacob Bigelow, *The Useful Arts; Considered in Connection with the Applications of Science*, vol. 1, (1840; New York: Harper & Brothers, 1855), 324, 330; *New England Farmer* 21 (1842), 190; 22 (1843), 147; 23 (1844), 160; n.s. 1 (1849), 365; *The Union Agriculturist and Western Prairie Farmer* 6 (1846), 98–99; 7 (1847), 85; *Ohio Cultivator* 8 (1852), 282–83.

150. Lady Emmeline Stuart Wortley, *Travels in the United States, etc., During 1849 and 1850* (New York: Harper & Brothers, 1851), 80.

151. Charles Dickens, *American Notes and Pictures from Italy* (1842 and 1846; London: Oxford University Press, 1970), 49; Anthony Trollope, *North America* (New York: Harper & Brothers, 1862), 133, 170, 203.

152. Frederick Law Olmsted, *A Journey in the Seaboard Slave States, With Notes on Their Economy* (New York: Dix & Edwards, 1856), 409–10.

153. Ibid., 3–5, 305–6, 334, 336; Frederick Law Olmsted, *A Journey Through Texas* (London: Sampson Low, Son & Co., 1857), 61, 66–67, 93, 100, 101–2, 103, 107, 111, 116, 122; Frederick Law Olmsted, *A Journey in the Back Country* (New York: Mason Brothers, 1860), 230–31, 235.

154. Olmsted, *A Journey Through Texas*, 143–44, 177, 184, 189.

155. John Bassett Moore, ed., *The Works of James Buchanan*, vol. 2, *1830–1836* (Philadelphia: J. B. Lippincott, 1908), 199, 243, 333; George W.

Curtis, ed., *The Correspondence of John Lothrop Motley*, vol. 1 (New York: Harper & Brothers, 1889), 79; Robert Sears, *An Illustrated Description of the Russian Empire* (New York: Robert Sears, 1855), 386–87; Nathan Appleton, *Russian Life and Society as Seen in 1866–'67 by Appleton and Longfellow* (Boston: Murray and Emery, 1904), 150.

156. Kathleen Tillotson, ed., *The Letters of Charles Dickens*, vol. 4, *1844–1846* (Oxford: Clarendon Press, 1977), 222, 252.

157. Nathaniel Hawthorne, *The French and Italian Notebooks*, ed. Thomas Woodson (Columbus: Ohio State University Press, 1980), 53–54; William Dean Howells, *Venetian Life* (1866; New York: Hurd and Houghton, 1867), 40, 43.

158. Ezra C. Seaman, *Essays on the Progress of Nations* (New York: Charles Scribner, 1852), 184; John W. Draper, *History of the American Civil War* (New York: Harper & Brothers, 1868), 1: 105.

159. William B. Meyer, "Urban Heat Island and Urban Health: Early American Perspectives," *The Professional Geographer* 43 (1991), 41.

160. *New York Times*, July 16, 1868, 8

161. *New York Herald*, Aug. 14, 1853, 4; Aug. 15, 1853, 1; Aug. 16, 1853, 1; Aug. 17, 1853, 4; *New York Times*, Aug. 22, 1853, 4; Aug. 24, 1853, 4; *New York Tribune*, Aug. 15, 1853, 4; Aug. 22, 1853, 4.

162. David M. Ludlum, *Early American Winters I: 1821–1870* (Boston: American Meteorological Society, 1968), 53–57, 62–69; effects calculated from weekly mortality reports, *New York Tribune* and *Boston Medical and Surgical Journal*, various dates, 1850s.

163. *First Report of the Committee on Public Hygiene*, 497. The fullest treatment of the phenonemon, though it focuses on the postbellum years, is Harold Roy Lentzner, "Seasonal Patterns of Infant and Child Mortality in New York, Chicago, and New Orleans: 1870–1919," Ph.D. dissertation, University of Pennsylvania, 1987.

164. See, e.g., Gouverneur Emerson, "Vital Statistics of Philadelphia, for the Decennial Period from 1830 to 1840," *American Journal of the Medical Sciences* 31 (1848), 2–33; Lemuel Shattuck, comp., *Bills of Mortality, 1810–1849, City of Boston, With an Essay on the Vital Statistics of Boston from 1810 to 1841* (Boston: Registry Department, 1893); *Annual Report of the City Inspector of the City of New York*, various years, 1850s. The peak in the rural North occured in the fall.

165. On the nature, causes, and treatment of cholera infantum as understood at the time: Edward Hallowell, "On the Endemic Gastro-follicular Enteritis, or 'Summer Complaint' of Children, as it Prevails in the United States," *American Journal of Medical Sciences*, n.s. 14 (1947), 40–67; D. Francis Condie, *A Practical Treatise on the Diseases of Children*, 4th ed. (Philadelphia: Blanchard and Lea, 1853), 232–42.

166. William E. Horner, "An Inquiry into the Anatomical Characters of Infantile Follicular Inflammation of the Gastro-Intestinal Mucous Membrane, and into its Probable Identity with Cholera Infantum," *American Journal of the Medical Sciences* 3 (1829), 249; J. Lewis Smith, "Report of the Post-Mortem Appearances in Eleven Cases of Cholera Infantum," *The New York Journal of Medicine*, 3d ser., 5 (1858), 32.

167. "The Summer Complaint of Children," *Journal of Health* 1 (1830)

22–24; Robley Dunglison, *Human Health*, 2d ed. (Philadelphia: Lea & Blanchard, 1844), 114–15; Condie, *A Practical Treatise*, 238, 239.

168. *American Ladies' Magazine* 1 (1828), 536

169. Richard Henry Dana, Jr. *Two Years Before the Mast* (New York: Modern Library, 1936), 321; John Disturnell, *Springs, Water-falls, Sea-bathing Resorts, and Mountain Scenery of the United States and Canada* (New York: J. Disturnell, 1855).

170. *A Philadelphia Perspective: The Diary of Sidney George Fisher Covering the Years 1834–1871*, ed. Nicholas B. Wainwright (Philadelphia: The Historical Society of Pennsylvania, 1967), 55.

171. Alex. Mackay, *The Western World; or, Travels in the United States in 1846–'47*, vol. 1, 2d ed. (London: Richard Bentley, 1849), 135–36; Sarah Mytton Maury, *An Englishwoman in America* (London: Thomas Richardson and Sons, 1848), 201.

172. Meyer, "Urban Heat Island," 44; John Duffy, *The Sanitarians: A History of American Public Health* (Urbana, Ill.: University of Illinois Press, 1990); Stanley K. Schultz, *Constructing Urban Culture: American Cities and City Planning, 1800–1920* (Philadelphia: Temple University Press, 1989), 122–39.

173. *Congressional Globe*, 29th Congress, 2d session (1847), 370; Samuel Forry, *The Climate of the United States and Its Endemic Influences* (New York: J. and H. G. Langley, 1842), 347–49, 367–68; *The Medical and Surgical History of the War of the Rebellion. Part III. Volume 1. Medical History. Being the Third Medical Volume. Prepared by Charles Smart* (Washington, D.C.: Government Printing Office, 1888), 23.

174. Richard H. Steckel, "Slave Mortality: Analysis of Evidence from Plantation Records," *Social Science History* 3, no. 3–4 (1979), 107–9, and "A Dreadful Childhood: The Excess Mortality of American Slaves," *Social Science History* 10 (1986), 442.

175. *The Knickerbocker; or New-York Monthly Magazine*, 21 (1843), 224; Disturnell, *Springs, Water-falls*.

176. Such defenses are surveyed by J. H. Cassedy, "Medical Men and the Ecology of the Old South," in Ronald L. Numbers and Todd L. Savitt, eds., *Science and Medicine in the Old South* (Baton Rouge, La.: Louisiana State University Press, 1989), 106–38.

177. John M. Gorrie, "Refrigeration and Ventilation of Cities," *Southern Quarterly Review* 1 (1842) 413–46. On Gorrie's career, see Gloria Jahoda, *The Other Florida* (New York: Charles Scribner's Sons, 1967), 85–105.

178. On Southern sanitary reformers, see Margaret H. Warner, "Public Health in the Old South," in Ronald L. Numbers and Todd L. Savitt, eds., *Science and Medicine in the Old South* (Baton Rouge, La.: Louisiana State University Press, 1989), 226–55.

179. John William Draper, *Human Physiology, Statistical and Dynamical*, 2d ed. (New York: Harper Brothers, 1858), 181.

180. Gorrie, "Refrigeration and Ventilation of Cities," 444.

181. Henry David Thoreau, "Paradise (To Be) Regained" (orig. 1843), in Wendell Glick, ed., *The Writings of Henry David Thoreau: Reform Papers* (Princeton, N.J.: Princeton University Press, 1973), 20, 21.

182. James P. Espy, *To the Friends of Science* (n.p., 1845), 5.

183. *Ohio Cultivator* 1 (1845), 143; *The United States Magazine and Democratic Review*, n.s. 9 (1841), 422.

184. Thoreau, "Paradise," 21.

185. Clark C. Spence, *The Rainmakers: American "Pluviculture" to World War II* (Lincoln: University of Nebraska Press, 1980).

186. On Espy's meteorology, see especially his *The Philosophy of Storms* (Boston: Little and Brown, 1841) and Fleming, *Meteorology in America.*

187. James P. Espy, "For the National Gazette" [open letter], *National Gazette and Literary Register* [Philadelphia], Apr. 6, 1839, 2.

188. Espy, *To the Friends of Science*; for later statements, see James P. Espy, *Second Report on Meteorology*, Senate Executive Document no. 39, 31st Congress, 1st session (1849) and *Fourth Report on Meteorology*, Senate Executive Document no. 65, 34th Congress, 3d session (1857).

189. *Columbian Centinel* (Boston), Dec. 22, 1838, 2.

190. Joseph Henry, "Meteorology in Its Connection with Agriculture," in *Report of the Commissioner of Patents for the Year 1858: Agriculture*, Senate Executive Document no. 47, 35th Congress, 2d session (1859), 493.

191. Nathaniel Hawthorne, "The Hall of Fantasy" (orig. 1843), in *Tales and Sketches* (New York: The Library of America, 1982), 739; *Boston Quarterly Review* 4 (1841), 520.

192. For especially energetic defenses of Espy in this vein, see editorials in *National Gazette and Literary Register* [Philadelphia], Apr. 6, 1838, 2; *Public Ledger* [Philadelphia], Oct. 13, 1842, 2.

193. *Congressional Globe*, 30th Congress, 1st session (1848), 826.

194. Ibid., 7 (1838), 42.

195. Ibid., 30th Congress, 1st session (1848), 826–27.

196. Ibid., 33rd Congress, 1st session (1854), 360–61; 34th Congress, 1st session (1856), 1726; see also 33rd Congress, 2d session (1855), 612; 34th Congress, 3d session (1857), 638. For the horrified reaction of an earlier South Carolina senator, see Ben. Perley Poore, *Perley's Reminiscences of Sixty Years in the National Metropolis*, vol. 1 (Philadelphia: Hubbard Brothers, 1886), 226.

197. Miss [Eliza] Leslie, "The Rain King; or, A Glance at the Next Century," *Godey's Lady's Book and Ladies' American Magazine* 25 (1842), 7–11.

198. *The Water-Cure Journal and Herald of Reforms* 19 (1855), 27.

CHAPTER 3

1. John William Draper, *Thoughts on the Future Civil Policy of America* (New York: Harper & Brothers, 1865), 166.

2. Henry Gannett, *The Building of a Nation* (New York: Henry T. Thomas, 1895), 58.

3. Richard H. Steckel, "The Economic Foundations of East-West Migration During the Nineteenth Century," *Explorations in Economic History* 20 (1983), 31; Lowell E. Gallaway and Richard K. Vedder, "Mobility of Native Americans," *Journal of Economic History* 31 (1971), 639.

4. *Congressional Globe*, 40th Congress, 2d session (1868), 1874; ibid.,

Appendix, 454; "Speech in the Senate, On His San Domingo Resolutions" (orig. 1871), in *The Works of Charles Sumner*, vol. 14 (Boston: Lee and Shepard, 1883), 247–48.

5. *Congressional Record*, 45th Congress, 3d session (1879), 1223; Francis Paul Prucha, *The Great Father; The United States Government and the American Indians*, vol. 1 (Lincoln, Neb.: University of Nebraska Press, 1984), 565–80; Senate Miscellaneous Document no. 53, 45th Congress, 3d session (1879), 279, 280.

6. On the Exodus generally, see Robert G. Athearn, *In Search of Canaan: Black Migration to Kansas, 1879–80* (Lawrence, Kan.: The Regents Press of Kansas, 1978), and Nell Irvine Painter, *Exodusters: Black Migration to Kansas after Reconstruction* (New York: Alfred A. Knopf, 1977).

7. Senate Report no. 693, 46th Congress, 2d session (1880), 1: 273; 2: 423, 540, 579, 582.

8. Ibid., 1: 361; also 3: 40, 373; Arna Bontemps and Jack Conroy, *Anywhere But Here* (New York: Hill and Wang, 1966), 53.

9. Frederick Douglass, "The Negro Exodus from the Gulf States" (orig. 1879), John W. Blassingame and John R. McKivigan, eds., *The Frederick Douglass Papers: Series One: Speeches, Debates, and Interviews,* vol. 4, *1864–80* (New Haven, Conn.: Yale University Press, 1991), 530.

10. Athearn, *In Search of Canaan*, 243–44, 256; Painter, *Exodusters*, 191, 198.

11. Bradley H. Baltensperger, "Plains Promoters and Plain Folk: Pre-Migration and Post-Settlement Images of the Central Great Plains," Ph.D. dissertation, Clark University, 1974, 84–85, 128, 149–50, 167–68, 189–90, 207, 211, 217.

12. The phrase "sawed house" is from James C. Malin, "The Grassland of North America: Its Occupance and the Challenge of Continuous Reappraisals," in William L. Thomas, Jr., ed., *Man's Role in Changing the Face of the Earth* (Chicago: University of Chicago Press, 1956), 360.

13. Josephine H. Peirce, *Fire on the Hearth: The Evolution and Romance of the Heating-Stove* (Springfield, Mass.: Pond-Ekberg, 1951), 192–96; Isaiah Bowman, *The Pioneer Fringe* (New York: American Geographical Society, 1931), 116.

14. Walter Prescott Webb, *The Great Plains* (Boston: Ginn and Company, 1931), 19n.

15. John Wesley Powell, *Report on the Arid Lands of the United States, With a More Detailed Account of the State of Utah* (orig. 1878), ed. Wallace Stegner (Cambridge, Mass.: Belknap Press of Harvard University Press, 1962), 12–13, 20–28.

16. A school of thought named and analyzed by Walter and Joanna Kollmorgen, "Landscape Meteorology in the Plains Area," *Annals of the Association of American Geographers* 63 (1973), 424–41.

17. The fullest account is Charles Robert Kutzleb, "Rain Follows the Plow: The History of an Idea," Ph.D. dissertation, University of Colorado, 1968 (on Wilber, see pp. 122–24).

18. For example, Mark W. Harrington, "Is the Rain-fall Increasing on the Plains?," *American Meteorological Journal* 4 (1887), 369–73; A. W. Greely, *American Weather* (New York: Dodd, Mead, 1888), 155–58; 1888.

On railroad and territorial promotion, Kutzleb, "Rain Follows the Plow" and David M. Emmons, *Garden in the Grassland: Boomer Literature of the Central Great Plains* (Lincoln: University of Nebraska Press, 1971).

19. Powell, *Report on the Arid Lands of the United States,* 105; Kutzleb, "Rain Follows the Plow," 126–27, 156–57, 179, 197, 201–2, 204.

20. Wheeler, David L. "Winter on the Cattle Range: Western Kansas, 1884–1886," *Kansas History* 15 (1992), 2–17.

21. Gilbert C. Fite, *The Farmers' Frontier, 1865–1900* (New York: Holt, Rinehart and Winston, 1966), 108–9, 127–30; W. C. Holden, "West Texas Drouths," *The Southwestern Historical Quarterly* 32 (1928), 113–16.

22. In re House Roll 284, 31 Neb 505, 511 (1891).

23. Richard A. Warrick, "Drought in the Great Plains: A Case Study of Research on Climate and Society in the USA," in Jesse Ausubel and A. K. Biswas, eds., *Climatic Constraints and Human Activities* (Oxford: Pergamon Press, 1980), 107.

24. On the early irrigation movement, see Donald J. Pisani, *To Reclaim a Divided West: Water, Law, and Public Policy, 1848–1902* (Albuquerque: University of New Mexico Press, 1992).

25. D. W. Meinig, *The Great Columbia Plain: A Historical Geography, 1805–1910* (Seattle: University of Washington Press, 1968), 307–15, 415–16.

26. Bradley H. Baltensperger, "Agricultural Change among Great Plains Russian Germans," *Annals of the Association of American Geographers* 73 (1983), 75–88.

27. James C. Malin, *Winter Wheat in the Golden Belt of Kansas* (Lawrence: University of Kansas Press, 1944).

28. Mary W. M. Hargreaves, *Dry Farming in the Northern Great Plains: 1900–1925* (Cambridge, Mass.: Harvard University Press, 1957), 117.

29. Quoted in ibid., 117.

30. Timothy John Rickard, "Perceptions and Results of the Irrigation Movement in the Western United States," Ph. D. dissertation, University of Kansas, 1974.

31. Pisani, *To Reclaim a Divided West,* 104.

32. On these developments, see especially Pisani, *To Reclaim a Divided West.*

33. Rickard, "Perceptions and Results," esp. ch. 10, "The Cost of Reclamation," 338–99.

34. Billy M. Jones, *Health-Seekers in the Southwest, 1817–1900* (Norman: University of Oklahoma Press, 1967), 200–01; John E. Baur, *The Health Seekers of Southern California, 1870–1900* (San Marino: The Huntington Library, 1959), 54–79.

35. Jones, *Health-Seekers,* 188–90; Baur, *The Health Seekers,* 174–75.

36. J. P. Widney, M.D., "The Colorado Desert," *The Overland Monthly* 10 (1873), 44–50.

37. John Wesley Powell, "The New Lake in the Desert," *Scribner's Magazine* 10 (1891), 467; *Los Angeles Times,* Aug. 22, 1891, 4; Sept. 7, 1891, 4; Sept. 21, 1891, 4; April 4, 1892, 4.

38. Sherwood D. Burgess, "Oakland's Water War," *California History* 64 (1985), 34–41; Lyle W. Dorsett, *The Queen City: A History of Denver* (Boulder, Colo.: Pruett, 1977), 79.

39. William L. Kahrl, *Water and Power: The Conflict over Los Angeles' Water Supply in the Owens Valley* (Berkeley: University of California Press, 1982); Norris Hundley, Jr., *The Great Thirst: Californians and Water, 1770s–1990s* (Berkeley: University of California Press, 1992).

40. Donald J. Pisani, *Water, Land, and Law in the West: The Limits of Public Policy, 1850–1920* (Lawrence: University Press of Kansas, 1996), 129–30.

41. *Massachusetts Weekly Spy* (Worcester), May 3, 1878, 2.

42. *New York Tribune*, Jan. 12, 1882, 5.

43. See generally Nelson M. Blake, *Water for the Cities: A History of the Urban Water Supply Problem in the United States* (Syracuse, N.Y.: Syracuse University Press, 1956).

44. Charles H. Weidner, *Water for a City: A History of New York City's Problem from the Beginning to the Delaware River System* (New Brunswick, N.J.: Rutgers University Press, 1974), 52–53, 56–57

45. *New York Tribune*, Oct. 24, 1881, 4; Oct. 28, 8; Oct. 29, 8; Nov. 15, 1891, 1, 4.

46. James B. Francis, Theodore G. Ellis, and William E. Worthen, "The Failure of the Mill River Dam," *Transactions of the American Society of Civil Engineers* 3 (1875), 118; David G. McCullough, *The Johnstown Flood* (New York: Simon and Schuster, 1968).

47. W J McGee, "The Flood Plains of Rivers," *Forum* 11 (1891), 221–22.

48. Gordon B. Dodds, "The Stream-Flow Controversy: A Conservation Turning Point," *Journal of American History* 56 (1969), 59–69.

49. H. M. Chittenden, in "Discussion: Forests, Reservoirs, and Stream Flow," *Transactions of the American Society of Civil Engineers* 62 (1909), 501; A. Miller Todd, in ibid., 340; for a review of the chief studies and the debate over them, see Dodds, "The Stream-Flow Controversy," 64–65.

50. McGee, "The Flood Plains of Rivers," 229.

51. H. M. Chittenden, in "Discussion: Forests, Reservoirs, and Stream Flow," 501.

52. Robert L. Brandfon, *Cotton Kingdom of the New South: A History of the Yazoo Mississippi Delta from Reconstruction to the Twentieth Century* (Cambridge, Mass.: Harvard University Press, 1967).

53. Mary G. McBride and Ann M. McLaurin, "The Origin of the Mississippi River Commission," *Louisiana History* 36 (1995), 389–411.

54. *Congressional Record*, 47th Congress, 1st session (1882), Appendix, 317.

55. *Chicago Tribune*, March 14, 1882, 4

56. *Congressional Record*, 47th Congress, 1st session (1882), 3141.

57. Arthur DeWitt Frank, *The Development of the Federal Program of Flood Control on the Mississippi River* (New York: Columbia University Press, 1930).

58. *Congressional Record*, 47th Congress, 1st session (1882), 3142, 3216.

59. For a list of such appropriations, see Gilbert Fowler White, *Human Adjustment to Floods: A Geographical Approach to the Flood Problem in the United States*, University of Chicago Department of Geography Research Paper No. 29 (1945), 27–29.

60. See, for example, *Congressional Record*, 48th Congress, 1st session (1884), 1032–40.

61. Foster Rhea Dulles, *The American Red Cross: A History* (New York: Harper & Brothers, 1950), 27–29; Elizabeth Brown Pryor, *Clara Barton: Protestant Angel* (Philadelphia: University of Pennsylvania Press, 1987), 219–22, 232–37.

62. Donald R. Whitnah, *A History of the United States Weather Bureau* (Urbana: University of Illinois Press, 1961).

63. David W. Francis, "Marine Casualties on the Great Lakes 1863–1873: An Analysis," *Inland Seas* 42 (1986), 261–69; Patrick Hughes, *A Century of Weather Service; A History of the Birth and Growth of the National Weather Service, 1870–1970* (New York: Gordon and Breach, 1970), 38.

64. Erik Daniel Craft, "The Provision and Value of Weather Information Services in the United States During the Founding Period of the Weather Bureau with Special Reference to Transportation on the Great Lakes," Ph.D. dissertation, University of Chicago, 1995.

65. Quoted in *Monthly Weather Review* 26 (1898), 4.

66. T. H. Eames, "The Wreck of the Steamer 'Portland,'" *New England Quarterly* 13 (1940), 191–206; *Monthly Weather Review* 26 (1898), 494–95.

67. *Cleveland Press*, Nov. 17, 1913, 1; *Detroit News*, Nov. 19, 1913, 4; *Cleveland Plain Dealer*, Nov. 20, 1913, 1.

68. Charles F. von Herrmann, "How Farmers May Utilize the Special Warnings of the Weather Bureau," *Yearbook of the United States Department of Agriculture, 1909* (Washington, D.C.: Government Printing Office, 1910), 387–98.

69. Mark Harrington, "Report of the Chief of the Weather Bureau," in *Report of the Secretary of Agriculture, 1891* (Washington, D.C.: Government Printing Office, 1892), 546.

70. Herbert J. Webber, "The Two Freezes of 1894–95 in Florida, and What They Teach," *Yearbook of the U.S. Department of Agriculture, 1895* (Washington, D.C.: Government Printing Office, 1896), 159–74; Sigismond deR. Diettrich, "Florida's Climatic Extremes: Cold Spells and Freezes," *Economic Geography* 25 (1949), 73.

71. Alvin T. Burrows, "Hot Waves and Their Effects," *Yearbook of the United States Department of Agriculture, 1900* (Washington, D.C.: Government Printing Office, 1901), 325–36; Robert DeCourcy Ward, "Some Economic Aspects of the Heat and Drought of July, 1901 in the United States," *Bulletin of the American Geographical Society* 33 (1901), 338–47.

72. Whitnah, *A History of the United States Weather Bureau*, 96; Snowden Flora, *Tornadoes of the United States* (Norman: University of Oklahoma Press, 1953), 37–38.

73. Dulles, *The American Red Cross*, 31–33; Pryor, *Clara Barton*, 274–79, 327–30.

74. Mary Cable, *The Blizzard of 1888* (New York: Atheneum, 1988), 16; Whitnah, *A History of the United States Weather Bureau*, 122–23.

75. Compare, e.g., *Springfield Daily Republican*, March 15, 1888, 4; *Hartford Daily Courant*, March 14, 1888, 4 with *New York Times*, March 13, 1888, 4; Feb. 16, 1899, 6.

76. *Manufacturer and Builder* 13 (1881), 27, 74–75; *The Times* (London), Jan. 20, 1881.

77. *Electrical Review and Western Electrician* 64 (1914), 546; *New York Times*, March 4, 1914, 2.

78. *The Electrical World* 29 (1907), 16–17.

79. Joseph Brady, "The Magnetic Telegraph," *The Ladies' Repository* 10 (1850), 61–62.

80. Carolyn Marvin, *When Old Technologies Were New: Thinking About Electric Communication in the Late Nineteenth Century* (New York: Oxford University Press, 1988), 119–21; David E. Nye, *Electrifying America: Social Meanings of a New Technology, 1880–1940* (Cambridge, Mass.: MIT Press, 1990), 290.

81. Claude S. Fischer, *America Calling: A Social History of the Telephone* (Berkeley: University of California Press, 1992), 92–100; Willis L. Moore, "Report of the Chief of the Weather Bureau," in *Annual Reports of the Department of Agriculture for the Fiscal Year Ended June 30, 1906* (Washington, D.C.: Government Printing Office, 1907), 106.

82. *New York Times*, Jan 27, 1909, 1; Susan J. Douglas, *Inventing American Broadcasting, 1899–1922* (Baltimore, Md.: The Johns Hopkins University Press, 1987), 200.

83. Robert Friedel and Paul Israel with Bernard S. Finn, *Edison's Electric Light: Biography of an Invention* (New Brunswick, N.J.: Rutgers University Press, 1986), 178.

84. Ronald R. Kline, *Steinmetz: Engineer and Socialist* (Baltimore, Md.: The Johns Hopkins University Press, 1992), 98–99, 138–46; Thomas P. Hughes, *Networks of Power: Electrification in Western Society, 1880–1930* (Baltimore, Md.: The Johns Hopkins University Press, 1983), 381–84.

85. Forrest McDonald, *Let There Be Light: The Electric Utility Industry in Wisconsin, 1881–1955* (Madison, Wis.: The American History Research Center, 1957), 111–14; Louis C. Hunter and Lynwood Bryant, *A History of Industrial Power in the United States, 1780-1930*, vol. 3, *The Transmission of Power* (Cambridge, Mass.: MIT Press, 1991), 362.

86. Forrest McDonald, *Insull* (Chicago: University of Chicago Press, 1962), 63.

87. *Electrical World* 59 (1912), 441–42.

88. Samuel Insull, "The Production and Distribution of Energy" (orig. 1913), in William Eugene Keily, *Central-Station Electric Service: Its Commercial Development and Economic Significance as Set Forth in the Public Addresses (1897–1914) of Samuel Insull* (Chicago: privately printed, 1915), 361; McDonald, *Insull* 137–42.

89. Walter Buckingham Smith and Arthur Harrison Cole, *Fluctuations in American Business, 1790–1860* (Cambridge, Mass.: Harvard University Press, 1935), 139.

90. Jeffrey A. Miron, "Financial Panics, the Seasonality of the Nominal Interest Rate, and the Founding of the Fed," *American Economic Review* 76 (1986), 125–40; Catherine M. Chambers and James S. Fackler, "A Multivariate Analysis of Interest Rate Seasonality at the Time of the Founding of the Federal Reserve," *Southern Economic Journal* 61 (1995), 654–63.

91. A. Piatt Andrew, "The Influence of the Crops Upon Business in

America," *Quarterly Journal of Economics* 20 (1906), 323–53; James Y. Simms, Jr., "Impact of Russian Famine, 1891 and 1892, Upon the United States," *Mid-America* 60 (1978), 171–84.

92. Charles A. Jenkins, *Report on the Insurance Business in the United States at the Eleventh Census: 1890, Part I, Fire, Marine, and Inland Insurance* (Washington, D.C.: Government Printing Office, 1894), 1101–03; William Gardner Rees, "Weather Insurance," *Monthly Weather Review* 44 (1916), 575–80.

93. Henry C. Emery, *Speculation on the Stock and Produce Exchanges of the United States* (New York: Columbia University Press, 1896); Harrison H. Brace, *The Value of Organized Speculation* (Boston: Houghton Mifflin, 1913).

94. William Cronon, *Nature's Metropolis: Chicago and the Great West* (New York: W. W. Norton, 1991), 230–35; Oscar Edward Anderson, Jr., *Refrigeration in America: A History of a New Technology and its Impact* (Princeton: Princeton University Press, 1953), 168–70; Edward Wiest, *The Butter Industry in the United States: An Economic Study of Butter and Oleomargarine* (New York: Columbia University Press, 1916).

95. Anderson, *Refrigeration in America*, 155; James L. McCorkle, Jr., "Moving Perishables to Market: Southern Railroads and the Nineteenth-Century Origins of Southern Truck Farming," *Agricultural History* 66, no. 1 (1992), 42–62.

96. Carleton H. Parker, "The California Casual and His Revolt," *Quarterly Journal of Economics* 30 (1915), 122; Lawrence J. Jelinek, *Harvest Empire: A History of California Agriculture* (San Francisco: Boyd & Fraser, 1979), 35–37, 47–52, 55–60; Cletus E. Daniel, *Bitter Harvest: A History of California Farmworkers, 1870–1941* (Ithaca, N.Y.: Cornell University Press, 1981).

97. Toby Higbie, "Indispensable Outcasts: Harvest Laborers in the Wheat Belt of the Middle West, 1890–1925," *Labor History* 38 (1997), 393–412.

98. Karen Sawislak, *Smoldering City: Chicagoans and the Great Fire, 1871–1874* (Chicago: University of Chicago Press, 1995), 169.

99. *Manufactures 1909: Reports for Principal Industries, vol. 10, Thirteenth Census of the United States* (Washington, D.C.: Government Printing Office, 1913), 640.

100. *The American Architect and Building News* 9 (1881), 57; 8 (1880), 266; Carl W. Condit, *American Building Art: The Nineteenth Century* (New York: Oxford University Press, 1960), 238.

101. R. W. Powell, "Glue," in *Report on Manufacturing Industries in the United States at the Eleventh Census: 1890, Part 3, Selected Industries* (Washington, D.C.: Government Printing Office, 1895), 377.

102. Philip T. Silva, Jr., "The Position of Workers in an Industrial Community: Fall River in the Early 1880s," *Labor History* 16 (1975), 239–40, 240n15; Agnes M. Larson, *History of the White Pine Industry in Minnesota* (Minneapolis: University of Minnesota Press, 1949), 349–50, 354–55.

103. Gail Cooper, *Air-Conditioning America: Engineers and the Controlled Environment* (Baltimore, Md.: The Johns Hopkins University Press, 1998).

104. George F. Swain, "Statistics of the Water Power Employed in Manufacturing in the United States," *Publications of the American Statistical Association*, n.s. 1 (1888), 36; Louis C. Hunter, *A History of Industrial Power in the United States, 1780–1930*, vol. 1, *Waterpower in the Age of the Steam Engine* (Charlottesville: University Press of Virginia, 1979), 399–400, 480, 483.

105. Anderson, *Refrigeration in America*.

106. Alexander Keyssar, *Out of Work: The First Century of Unemployment in Massachusetts* (New York: Cambridge University Press, 1986), 60–61.

107. Ibid., 63; see also Stanley Engerman and Claudia Goldin, "Seasonality in Nineteenth-Century Labor Markets," in Thomas Weiss and Donald Schaefer, eds., *American Economic Development in Historical Perspective* (Stanford, Calif.: Stanford University Press, 1994), 99–126.

108. Keyssar, *Out of Work*, 67.

109. Timothy J. Hatton and Jeffrey G. Williamson, "Unemployment, Employment Contracts, and Compensating Wage Differentials: Michigan in the 1890s," *Journal of Economic History* 51 (1991), 605–32.

110. Data on strike patterns are collected in *Third Annual Report of the Commissioner of Labor. 1887. Strikes and Lockouts* (Washington, D.C.: Government Printing Office, 1888) and *Tenth Annual Report of the Commissioner of Labor. 1894. Strikes and Lockouts* (Washington, D.C.: Government Printing Office, 1896).

111. *Electrical Review and Western Electrician* 61 (1912), 147; *Electrical World* 70 (1917), 422–25; Louis C. Hunter and Lynwood Bryant, *A History of Industrial Power in the United States, 1780–1930*, vol. 3, *The Transmission of Power* (Cambridge, MA: MIT Press, 1991), 275–83.

112. McDonald, *Insull*; Thomas Parke Hughes, *Networks of Power: Electrification in Western Society, 1880–1930* (Baltimore, Md.: The Johns Hopkins University Press, 1983).

113. Mary H. Blewett, *Men, Women, and Work: Class, Gender, and Protest in the New England Shoe Industry, 1780–1910* (Urbana: University of Illinois Press, 1988), 163–65.

114. Arthur van Harlingen, "The Care of the Person," in Albert H. Buck, ed., *A Treatise on Hygiene and Public Health* (New York: William Wood, 1879), 1: 379; Thorstein Veblen, *The Theory of the Leisure Class: An Economic Study of Institutions* (1899; New York: The Modern Library, 1931), 167–68.

115. Daniel Scott-Smith, "A Higher Quality of Life for Whom? Mouths to Feed and Clothes to Wear in the Families of Late Nineteenth-Century American Workers," *Journal of Family History* 19 (1994), 24–27.

116. Veblen, *The Theory of the Leisure Class*, 168.

117. Harry E. Barbour, "Rubber Boots and Shoes," in *Manufactures, Part 3: Special Reports on Selected Industries, Census Reports vol. 9, Twelfth Census of the United States, Taken in the Year 1900* (Washington, D.C.: United States Census Office, 1902), 771.

118. Estelle Ansley Worrell, *American Costume: 1840 to 1920* (Harrisburg, Penn.: Stackpole Books, 1979), 87, 126.

119. Henry James, *The Bostonians* (orig. 1886), in *Novels, 1881–1886*

(New York: The Library of America, 1985), 855, 894, 905, 1179, 1209; William Dean Howells, *Annie Kilburn* (orig. 1888), in *Novels, 1886–1888* (New York: The Library of America, 1989), 666.

120. *New York Times*, Dec. 1, 1889, 13.

121. *The India Rubber World* 4 (1891), 218.

122. *The India Rubber World and Electrical Trades Review* 1 (1890), 128.

123. *The Boston Post*, Aug. 8, 1891, 1; *The Woman's Journal*, 22 (1891), 270.

124. E. Alexander Powell, *Gone Are the Days* (Boston: Little, Brown, 1938), 160; Worrell, *American Costume*, 109, 111.

125. Henry Cuyler Bunner, "The Two Churches of 'Quawket" (orig. 1890), in *The Stories of Henry Cuyler Bunner: 'Short Sixes' and The Suburban Sage* (New York: Charles Scribner's Sons, 1917), 46.

126. Bruce Price, "The Suburban Home," *Scribner's Magazine* 8 (1890), 6.

127. *The Manufacturer and Builder* 13 (1881), 212.

128. Edward Atkinson, "Crazy Roofs and Roofs Sensible," *The American Architect and Building News* 17 (1885), 261.

129. William Cronon, "Inconstant Unity: The Passion of Frank Lloyd Wright," in Terence Riley and Peter Reed, eds., *Frank Lloyd Wright: Architect* (New York: The Museum of Modern Art, 1994), 8, 24–25; Brendan Gill, *Many Masks: A Life of Frank Lloyd Wright* (New York: G. P. Putnam's Sons, 1987), 195.

130. Charles de Kay, "Villas All Concrete," *Architectural Record* 17 (1905), 95–96.

131. Michael Peterson, "Thomas Edison's Concrete Houses," *American Heritage of Invention and Technology* 11, no. 3 (Winter 1996), 50–56.

132. Jacob A. Riis, *How the Other Half Lives: Studies Among the Tenements of New York City* (1901; New York: Dover Publications, 1971), 126.

133. G. M. Shattuck and Margaret Hilferty, "Causes of Death from Heat in Massachusetts," *New England Journal of Medicine* 209 (1933), 319–29; Stanley A. Changnon, Kenneth E. Kunkel, and Beth C. Reinke, "Impacts and Responses to the 1995 Heat Wave: A Call to Action," *Bulletin of the American Meteorological Society* 77 (1996), 1498; *New York Tribune*, Aug 16, 1896, 7.

134. William B. Meyer, "The Worst Weather Disaster in New England History," *Yankee* 61, no. 1 (1997), 48–53, 118.

135. Compare *Chicago Tribune*, July 5, 1901, 12, and Stephen Smith, "Vegetation a Remedy for the Summer Heat of Cities," *Popular Science Monthly* 54 (1899), 441 (quotation) with Philadelphia *Evening Bulletin*, Aug. 12, 1891, 4, and *New York Tribune*, Aug. 10, 1896, 2.

136. William Dean Howells, *A Traveller from Altruria* (orig. 1894), in *The Altrurian Romances*, ed. Clara and Rudolf Kirk (Bloomington: Indiana University Press, 1968), 65.

137. Oliver Wendell Holmes, *A Mortal Antipathy* (1885; Boston: Houghton, Mifflin, 1898), 171.

138. Harold Roy Lentzner, "Seasonal Patterns of Infant and Child Mortality in New York, Chicago, and New Orleans: 1870–1919," Ph.D. dissertation, University of Pennsylvania, 1987; Rose A. Cheney, "Seasonal

Aspects of Infant and Childhood Mortality: Philadelphia, 1865–1920," *Journal of Interdisciplinary History* 14 (1984), 561–85.

139. Lester Frank Ward, *The Psychic Factors of Civilization* (1893; Boston: Ginn & Company, 1901), 258.

140. David McCullough, *The Path Between the Seas: The Creation of the Panama Canal, 1870–1914* (New York: Simon and Schuster, 1977), 581–82.

141. Lentzner, "Seasonal Patterns of Infant and Child Mortality"; Cheney, "Seasonal Aspects."

142. Anne Gertrude Sneller, *A Vanished World* (Syracuse, N.Y.: Syracuse University Press, 1964), 155.

143. *New York Tribune*, Dec. 13, 1892, 6; Apr. 30, 1891, 6; Arnold Bennett, *Those United States* (London: Martin Secker, 1912), 147–48; George W. E. Russell, ed., *Letters of Matthew Arnold, 1848–1888*, vol. 3 (1903–4; New York: AMS Press, 1970), 168, 172.

144. D. F. Lincoln, "The Atmosphere," in Albert H. Buck, ed., *A Treatise on Hygiene and Public Health* (New York: William Wood, 1879), 1: 678; Theodore Dreiser, *A Traveler at Forty* (New York: Century, 1913), 47–48; Elizabeth Cady Stanton, *Eighty Years and More: Reminiscences, 1815–1897* (New York: Fisher Unwin, 1898), 367; Rupert Hart-Davis, *Max Beerbohm's Letters to Reggie Turner* (Philadelphia: J. B. Lippincott, 1965), 99; Rudyard Kipling, *From Tideway to Tideway* (orig. 1892), in *A Diversity of Creatures and Letters of Travel, 1892–1913* (Garden City, N.Y.: Doubleday, Page, 1925), pt. 2, 3; Joseph Hatton, *Henry Irving's Impressions of America; Narrated in a Series of Sketches, Chronicles, and Conversations* (Boston: J. R. Osgood, 1884), 1: 252.

145. For a good description of the advantages of electric heating, see *The Electrical World* 18 (1891), 255–57.

146. Quoted in Spencer Klaw, *Without Sin: The Life and Death of the Oneida Community* (New York: Allen Lane/The Penguin Press, 1993), 84.

147. Baur, *The Health Seekers of Southern California*, 36–37; Ruth Kedzie Wood, *The Tourist's California* (New York: Dodd, Mead, 1914), 28–29.

148. Harriet Beecher Stowe, *Palmetto Leaves* (Boston: James R. Osgood, 1873), 32–33, 124–25, 131.

149. Louise Boland Morse, *Wage-Earners' Budgets: A Study of Standards and Cost of Living in New York City* (New York: Henry Holt, 1907), 40–41; Robert Coit Chapin, *The Standard of Living Among Workingmen's Families in New York City* (New York: Russell Sage Foundation, Charities Publication Committee, 1909), 115.

150. Eliot Jones, *The Anthracite Coal Combination in the United States; With Some Account of the Early Development of the Anthracite Industry* (Cambridge, Mass.: Harvard University Press, 1914).

151. Robert J. Cornell, *The Anthracite Coal Strike of 1902* (1957; New York: Russell & Russell, 1971), 182.

152. *New York Tribune*, Jan. 18, 1903, 6; Jan. 27, 6; *Chicago Tribune*, Jan, 11, 1903, 3; Jan. 13, 1.

153. James P. Johnson, "The Wilsonians as Crisis Managers: Coal and the 1917–18 Winter Crisis," *Prologue* 9 (1977), 193–208; John G. Clark, *Energy and the Federal Government: Fossil Fuel Policies, 1900–1966* (Urbana: University of Illinois Press, 1987), 68–74, 78–80.

154. Harold G. Moulton, *Waterways Versus Railways* (Boston: Houghton Mifflin, 1912), 70, 72–73.

155. Ibid., 51–52, 54–60.

156. James D. Richardson, ed., *A Compilation of the Messages and Papers of the Presidents*, vol. 6 (New York: Bureau of National Literature, Inc., 1897), 2310–16; a classic account is Albert Bushnell Hart, "The Biography of a River and Harbor Bill," *Papers of the American Historical Association* 3 (1888), 180–96.

157. B. B. Adams, Jr., "The Every-Day Life of Railroad Men," *Scribner's Magazine* 4 (1888), 548, 551; Thomas M. Cooley and Charles H. Cooley, "Transportation" in N. S. Shaler, ed., *The United States of America* (New York: D. Appleton, 1894), 2: 788.

158. Walter Licht, *Working for the Railroad* (Princeton, N.J.: Princeton University Press, 1983), 181–85, 188–90.

159. Guy H. Burnham, "The Weather Element in Railroading," *Monthly Weather Review* 50 (1922), 1–7; Robert DeC. Ward, "The Railroads Versus the Weather," *Proceedings of the American Philosophical Society* 70 (1931), 137–66; Bernard Mergen, *Snow in America* (Washington, D.C.: Smithsonian Institution Press, 1997), 41–50.

160. George E. Waring, comp., *Report on the Social Statistics of Cities, Part 1, The New England and the Middle States, Tenth Census of the United States, vol. 18* (Washington: Government Printing Office, 1886).

161. Cooley and Cooley, "Transportation," 792.

162. Charles L. Dearing, *American Highway Policy* (Washington, D.C.: The Brookings Institution, 1941), 40–45; Hal S. Barron, "And the Crooked Shall Be Made Straight: Public Road Administration and the Decline of Localism in the Rural North, 1870–1930," *Journal of Social History* 26 (1992), 81–103.

163. Stanley K. Schultz, *Constructing Urban Culture: American Cities and City Planning, 1800–1920* (Philadelphia: Temple University Press, 1989), 80, 177.

164. See, e.g., M. K. Whittlesey, "What's the Use?," *Good Roads* 2 (1892), 317–24; N. G. Spalding, "Profit and Loss to the Farmer," *Good Roads* 4 (1893), 185–91.

165. Quoted in Allan Nevins with Frank Ernest Hill, *Ford: The Times, the Man, the Company* (New York: Charles Scribner's Sons, 1954), 256.

166. Henry Ford with Samuel Crowther, *My Life and Work* (Garden City, N.Y.: Doubleday, Page, 1923), 68.

167. Dearing, *American Highway Policy*, 45–58, 219–65; Barron, "And the Crooked Shall Be Made Straight," 87–93.

168. Dearing, *American Highway Policy*, 266.

169. Sinclair Lewis, *Main Street* (orig. 1920), in *Main Street & Babbitt* (New York: Library of America, 1992), 38, 91, 152, 154, 213.

170. Jeff Rosenfeld, "Cars vs. the Weather: A Century of Progress," *Weatherwise* 49, no. 5 (Oct./Nov. 1996), 16–17; T. P. Newcomb and R. T. Spurr, *A Technical History of the Motor Car* (Bristol: Adam Hilger, 1989).

171. George Wise, "Technological Prediction, 1890–1940," Ph.D. dissertation, Boston University, 1976, 148, 150.

172. J. M. Rusk, "American Farming a Century Hence," *North American Review* 156 (1893), 261.

173. Some examples are described in William B. Meyer, "The Life and Times of U.S. Weather: What Can We Do About It?," *American Heritage* 37, no. 4 (1986), 38–48.

174. William Dean Howells, *The Altrurian Romances*, ed. Clara and Rudolf Kirk (Bloomington: Indiana University Press, 1968), 155–57.

175. For examples, see J. C. Goodridge, Jr., "Can the Temperature of the Atlantic States Be Changed?," *Scientific American*, Oct. 31, 1885, 280–81; and "Modifying the Climate by Closing the Straits of Belle Isle," May 29, 1886, 344; *Concord* (N.H.) *Daily Monitor*, July 30, 1879, 2; N. S. Shaler, "How to Change the North American Climate," *Atlantic Monthly* 40 (1877), 724–31; *New York Herald*, Feb. 1, 1876, 8.

176. J. P. Widney, "The Colorado Desert," *The Overland Monthly* 10 (1873), 44–50; *Scientific American*, March 28, 1874, 193; May 24, 1879, 324; *New York Herald*, April 13, 1879, 10; Senate Miscellaneous Document no. 84, 43rd Congress, 1st session; *The Daily Picayune* (New Orleans), April 15, 1887, 4; John Hay, "Irrigation," *Mid-Continental Review* 3 (1891), 109–28.

177. Mark Twain, *The American Claimant* (New York: Charles L. Webster, 1892), 271–73; Carroll Livingston Riker, *Power and Control of the Gulf Stream: How It Regulates the Climates, Heat, and Light of the World* (New York, 1912); R. G. Skerrett, "Warming the North Atlantic Coast," *Technical World* 19 (March, 1913), 62; *Scientific American*, Feb. 15, 1913, 150; *Literary Digest*, Aug. 30, 1913, 316.

178. Edward Powers, *War and the Weather, Artificial Production of Rain* (Chicago: S. C. Griggs, 1871).

179. Ibid., 43.

180. Ibid., 112.

181. On the experiments and the debate over their success, see Clark C. Spence, "The Dyrenforth Rainmaking Experiments: A Government Venture in 'Pluviculture,'" *Arizona and the West* 3 (1961), 205–32; and Kutzleb, "Rain Follows the Plow," 293–318.

182. *The Nation* 53 (1891), 253–54; Robert DeC. Ward, "How Far Can Man Change His Climate?," *Scientific Monthly* 30 (1930), 13; N. F. Fyodorov, "Razoruzhenie: Kak orudie razrusheniia obratit' v orudie spaseniia" (orig. 1898), in *Filosofiia obshchego dela: Stat'i, mysli, pis'ma*, vol. 1 (Moscow: Verniy, 1906), 664; "K stat'e 'Razoruzhenie'" (orig. 1898), *ibid.*, vol. 2 (Moscow, 1913), 280.

183. *Birmingham Age-Herald*, Aug. 22, 1891, 4.

184. *The Evening News* (Detroit), August 22, 1891, 4; *Houston Daily Post*, Aug. 31, 1891, 4; *St. Louis Post-Dispatch*, Aug. 12, 1891, 4.

185. Louisville *Courier-Journal*, Aug. 17, 1891, 4; for two other searching discussions of government rainmaking, see *New York Times*, Feb. 14, 1880, 4 and *The Morning News* (Savannah), Sept. 11, 1891, 4.

186. *Congressional Record*, 52nd Congress, 1st session (1892), 5153–58.

187. Hamlin Garland, *Roadside Meetings* (New York: Macmillan, 1930), 216–17; for other descriptions of Miller's apparatus, see *New York Tribune*, Nov. 8, 1896, 5; *New York Times Saturday Review*, Nov. 19, 1898, 784; Maynard Shipley, "California's Great Poet," *The Overland Monthly*, 2d

ser., 35 (1920), 476; George Sterling, "Joaquin Miller," *The American Mercury* 7 (1926), 229.

188. Joaquin Miller, *The Building of the City Beautiful* (Cambridge and Chicago: Stone and Kimball, 1893), 44, 111.

CHAPTER 4

1. Ellen Churchill Semple, *Influences of Geographic Environment* (New York: Henry Holt, 1911), 37, 619, 625–26.

2. Good modern accounts of the migration and its timing include Jack Temple Kirby, "The Southern Exodus, 1910–1960: A Primer for Historians," *Journal of Southern History* 49 (1983), 585–600; James R. Grossman, *City of Hope: Chicago, Black Southerners, and the Great Migration* (Chicago: University of Chicago Press, 1989), chaps. 1–4; and William J. Collins, "When the Tide Turned: Immigration and the Delay of the Great Black Migration," *Journal of Economic History* 57 (1997), 607–32.

3. Emmett J. Scott, *Negro Migration During the War* (1920; New York: Arno Press, 1969), 31, 79, 171–72.

4. *Saturday Evening Post* 198, no. 27 (Jan. 2, 1926), 12.

5. *Florida Old & New: The Year-Book of Florida, 1925–1926* (Orlando: Rufus R. Wilson, 1926), xx, 59, 79, 83, 156, 177, 208–9; *Florida News*, Sept. 14, 1925, 2.

6. Frank P. Stockbridge, "The Florida Rush of 1925," *Current History* 23 (1925), 178–85; *Florida News*, Dec. 14, 1925, 15.

7. Homer B. Vanderblue, "The Florida Land Boom," *Journal of Land and Public Utility Economics* 3 (1927), 113–31, 252–69.

8. Reinhold Paul Wolff, *Miami: Economic Patterns of a Resort Area* (Coral Gables: University of Miami, 1945), 117; Robe B. Carson, "The Florida Tropics," *Economic Geography* 27 (1951), 322.

9. Carey McWilliams, *Southern California Country: An Island on the Land* (New York: Dell, Sloan & Pearce, 1946), 135.

10. Clark Davis, "From Oasis to Metropolis: Southern California and the Changing Context of American Leisure," *Pacific Historical Review* 61 (1992), 358–60, 362, 365–72.

11. *Saturday Evening Post* 194, no. 44 (Apr. 29, 1922), 8.

12. "Florida or California," *Current History* 48, no. 3 (March, 1938), 74.

13. Quoted in Lucinda Eddy, "Visions of Paradise: The Selling of San Diego," *Journal of San Diego History* 41 (1995), 185.

14. C. Warren Thornthwaite with Helen I. Slentz, *Internal Migration in the United States* (Philadelphia: University of Pennsylvania Press, 1934), 18.

15. *Good Housekeeping* 68, no. 6 (1919), 80, 169; 73, no. 1 (1921), 88; *New York Times Magazine*, July 7, 1929, 12.

16. Andrew McClary, "Sunning for Health: Heliotherapy as Seen by Professionals and Popularizers, 1920–1940," *Journal of American Culture* 5, no. 1 (1982), 65–68.

17. *Popular Science Monthly* 114, no. 4 (1929), 27; Barbara Keesling and Howard S. Friedman, "Psychosocial Factors in Sunbathing and Sunscreen Use," *Health Psychology* 6 (1987), 479; Ruth P. Rubinstein, *Dress Codes:*

Meanings and Messages in American Culture (Boulder, Colo.: Westview Press, 1995), 185–86.

18. *Scientific Monthly* 19 (1924), 335.

19. Paul H. Nystrom, *Economics of Fashion* (New York: The Ronald Press, 1928), 154.

20. Stuart Chase with Marian Tyler, *Mexico: A Study of Two Americas* (New York: Macmillan, 1931), 163; Nystrom, *Economics of Fashion*, 155–56.

21. Robert S. Lynd and Helen Merrell Lynd, *Middletown: A Study in American Culture* (New York: Harcourt, Brace and Company, 1929), 159; C. P. Yaglou and Philip Drinker, "The Summer Comfort Zone: Climate and Clothing," *Journal of Industrial Hygiene* 10 (1928), 361–62; H. Feldman, *The Regularization of Employment: A Study in the Prevention of Unemployment* (New York: Harper & Brothers, 1925), 178.

22. Feldman, *The Regularization of Employment*, 178–79.

23. E. E. Free and Travis Hoke, *Weather* (New York: National Travel Club, 1928), 326.

24. C. P. Yaglou and Anne Mesmer, "The Importance of Clothing in Air Conditioning," *Journal of the American Medical Association* 117 (1941), 1261–62.

25. For example, G. K. Chesterton, *What I Saw in America* (New York: Dodd, Mead and Company, 1922), 277; Clare Sheridan, *My American Diary* (New York: Boni and Liveright, 1922), 15, 17–18; Sir Charles Igglesden, *A Mere Englishman in America* (Ashford: Kentish Express, 1930), 23–25; Sondra J. Stang and Karen Cochran, eds., *The Correspondence of Ford Madox Ford and Stella Bowen* (Bloomington: Indiana University Press. 1993), 254, 276, 309.

26. John Peale Bishop, "The South Revisited" (orig. 1939), in Edmund Wilson, ed., *The Collected Essays of John Peale Bishop* (New York: Charles Scribner's Sons, 1948), 452

27. Pitirim Sorokin, *Contemporary Sociological Theories* (New York: Harper & Brothers, 1928), 110.

28. Harold K. Kanarek, "The Pennsylvania Anthracite Strike of 1922," *Pennsylvania Magazine of History and Biography* 99 (1975), 207–25; and "Disaster for Hard Coal: The Anthracite Strike of 1925–1926," *Labor History* 15 (1974), 44–62; Robert H. Zieger, "Pennsylvania Coal and Politics: The Anthracite Strike of 1925–1926," *Pennsylvania Magazine of History and Biography* 93 (1969), 244–62.

29. H. F. Williamson, R. L. Andreano, A. R. Daum, and G. C. Klose, *The American Petroleum Industry: The Age of Energy, 1899–1959* (Evanston: Northwestern University Press, 1963), 492.

30. Mark Rose, *Cities of Light and Heat: Domesticating Gas and Electricity in Urban America* (University Park: Pennsylvania State University Press, 1995), 117–23.

31. *Sixteenth Census of the United States: 1940, Housing, vol. 2: General Characteristics* (Washington, D.C.: Government Printing Office, 1943), 99–101.

32. Gail Ann Cooper, "Manufactured Weather: A History of Air Conditioning in the United States, 1902–1955," Ph.D. dissertation, University

of California at Santa Barbara, 1987; Robert Friedman, "The Air-Conditioned Century," *American Heritage* 35, no. 5 (1984), 28–29; Raymond Arsenault, "The End of the Long Hot Summer: The Air Conditioner and Southern Culture," *Journal of Southern History* 50 (1984), 605; *Fortune* 17, no. 4 (1938), 87.

33. Bob Cunningham, "The Box That Broke the Barrier: The Swamp Cooler Comes to Southern Arizona," *The Journal of Arizona History* 26 (1985), 163–74.

34. Robert S. Lynd and Helen Merrell Lynd, *Middletown in Transition: A Study in Cultural Conflicts* (New York: Harcourt, Brace and Company, 1937), 195.

35. *The Farm-Housing Survey* (Washington, D.C.: U.S. Department of Agriculture Miscellaneous Publication No. 323, 1939), 11, 15, 20–21; Carle C. Zimmerman and Merle E. Frampton, *Family and Society: A Study of the Sociology of Reconstruction* (New York: D. Van Nostrand, 1935), 197–98, 232, 245, 258; Lynd and Lynd, *Middletown in Transition*, 195.

36. Vividly described in Robert A. Caro, *The Path to Power* (New York: Vintage Books, 1983), 510–11.

37. L. H. Newburgh, "Preface," in L. H. Newburgh, ed., *Physiology of Heat Regulation and the Science of Clothing* (Philadelphia: W. B. Saunders, 1949), v.

38. John Garretson Clark, *Energy and the Federal Government* (Urbana: University of Illinois Press, 1987), 338, 342–43.

39. *Journal of the American Medical Association* 120 (1942), 370–72.

40. W. H. Forbes, "Laboratory and Field Studies," in Newburgh, *Physiology of Heat Regulation*, 329; Douglas H. K. Lee and Hoyt Lemons, "Clothing for Global Man," *Geographical Review* 39 (1949), 181.

41. Arnold Court, "Wind Chill," *Bulletin of the American Meteorological Society* 29 (1948), 493.

42. T. P. Newcomb and R. T. Spurr, *A Technical History of the Motor Car* (Bristol: Adam Hilger, 1989), 50–51, 411; Michael Lamm, "Postfix: South Wind," *American Heritage of Invention and Technology* 10, no. 4 (1995), 64; John H. White, Jr., *The American Railroad Passenger Car* (Baltimore, Md.: The Johns Hopkins University Press, 1978), 407–9.

43. Vera Brittain, *Thrice a Stranger* (New York: The Macmillan Company, 1938), xv.

44. Jeff Rosenfeld, "Cars vs. the Weather: A Century of Progress," *Weatherwise* 49, no. 5 (1996), 14–23.

45. Allan Nevins and Frank Ernest Hill, *Ford: Expansion and Challenge, 1915–1933* (New York: Charles Scribner's Sons, 1957).

46. Lynd and Lynd, *Middletown*, 255.

47. Blake McKelvey, *Snow in the Cities: A History of America's Urban Response* (Rochester, N.Y.: University of Rochester Press, 1995), 99–100, 104, 115–16; Bernard Mergen, *Snow in America* (Washington, D.C.: Smithsonian Institution Press, 1997), 58–65.

48. Charles Donald Fox, *The Truth About Florida* (New York: Charles Renard, 1925), 143; Ruth Kedzie Wood, *The Tourist's California* (New York: Dodd, Mead and Company, 1914), 21.

49. John D. Sumner, "An Analysis of Mississippi River Traffic, 1918–

1930," *Journal of Land and Public Utility Economics* 8 (1931), 355–66; Harold G. Moulton and others, *The American Transportation Problem* (Washington, D.C.: The Brookings Institute, 1933).

50. Thomas F. Barton, "Twenty-Five Years' Use of the 9-Foot Ohio River Channel," *Economic Geography* 33 (1957), 41–49.

51. Harold G. Moulton, Charles S. Morgan, and Adah L. Lee, *The St. Lawrence Navigation and Power Project* (Washington, D.C.: The Brookings Institute, 1929), 69; Florence Whitbeck, "New York Barge Canal–Expectations and Realizations," *Economic Geography* 4 (1928), 196–206.

52. *New York Times*, Aug. 19, 1934, 3: 10; Richard F. Palmer, "Last of the Great Lakes Schooners: The *Lyman M. Davis*," *Inland Seas* 51, no. 1 (Spring, 1995), 2–15.

53. Harold Waters, *Smugglers of Spirits: Prohibition and the Coast Guard Patrol* (New York: Hastings House, 1971), 134.

54. Richard P. Hallion, *Legacy of Flight: The Guggenheim Contribution to American Aviation* (Seattle: University of Washington Press, 1977), 11–13, 16–17.

55. Moulton, *American Transportation Problem*, 732–33.

56. Hallion, *Legacy of Flight*, 101–27; Roger E. Bilstein, *Flight Patterns: Trends of Aeronautical Development in the United States, 1918–1929* (Athens: University of Georgia Press, 1983), 117–23.

57. Henry Ladd Smith, *Airways: A History of Commercial Aviation in the United States* (1942; Washington, D.C.: Smithsonian Institution Press, 1991); Carl Solberg, *Conquest of the Skies: A History of Commercial Aviation in America* (Boston: Little, Brown, 1979), 202–5.

58. Solberg, *Conquest of the Skies*, 179–89.

59. Hallion, *Legacy of Flight*, 91–100; Donald R. Whitnah, *A History of the United States Weather Bureau* (Urbana: University of Illinois Press, 1961), 167–200.

60. *New York Times*, March 26, 1933, 9: 8; Clark C. Spence, *The Rainmakers: American "Pluviculture" to World War II* (Lincoln: University of Nebraska Press, 1980), 116.

61. Reynold M. Wik, "The Radio in Rural America during the 1920s," *Agricultural History* 55 (1981), 341–43.

62. Charles C. Bates and John F. Fuller, *America's Weather Warriors, 1814–1985* (College Station: Texas A&M University Press, 1986).

63. Henry Guerlac, *Radar in World War II*, 2 vols. (New York: American Institute of Physics, 1987).

64. Whitnah, *A History of the United States Weather Bureau*, 203–5; *New York Times*, Dec. 17, 1941, 33.

65. *New York Times*, Dec. 17, 1941, 26.

66. *Fortune* 21, no. 4 (April 1940), 58–59.

67. Mergen, *Snow in America*, 94–108.

68. *Recent Social Trends in the United States: Report of the President's Research Committee on Social Trends* (New York: Whittlesey House, 1934), 912–57.

69. Andrew H. Palmer, "Weather Insurance," *Bulletin of the American Meteorological Society* 3 (1922), 68, and "Recent Developments in Weather Insurance," *Bulletin of the American Meteorological Society*, 6 (1925), 68–70.

70. *New York Times*, Oct. 30, 1921, 2: 3.

71. Joseph P. Beaton, "Why the Movies Chose Hollywood," *Journal of Cultural Geography* 4, no. 1 (1983), 100, 105; Richard Schickel, *D. W. Griffith: An American Life* (New York: Simon and Schuster, 1984), 429–33, 516–17; *The American Cinematographer* 6, no. 10 (1926), 13; Aldous Huxley, "Los Angeles: A Rhapsody" (orig. 1926), in *Aldous Huxley's Stories, Essays, & Poems* (London: Dent, 1937), 224.

72. *Seasonal Operation in the Construction Industries* (New York: McGraw-Hill, 1924); "Causes of Seasonal Fluctuations in the Construction Industry," *Monthly Labor Review* 33, no. 3 (Sept., 1931), 6–33.

73. Simon Kuznets, *Seasonal Variations in Industry and Trade* (New York: National Bureau of Economic Research, 1933), 150–51.

74. John I. Griffin, *Strikes: A Study in Quantitative Economics* (New York: Columbia University Press, 1939), 53, 147, 149.

75. Kuznets, *Seasonal Variations in Industry and Trade*, 362–63, 365–66; see also J. Maurice Clark, *Studies in the Economics of Overhead Costs* (Chicago: University of Chicago Press, 1923), 149–53, 159–66.

76. Oscar Edward Anderson, Jr., *Refrigeration in America: The History of a New Technology* (Princeton, N.J.: Princeton University Press, 1953), 109–10, 213–15; W. S. Woytinsky, *Seasonal Variations in Employment in the United States* (Washington, D.C.: Committee on Social Security, Social Science Research Council, 1939), 47.

77. Edwin S. Smith, *Reducing Seasonal Unemployment: The Experience of American Manufacturing Concerns* (New York: McGraw-Hill, 1931), 256–76; Kuznets, *Seasonal Variations*, 135–36.

78. Smith, *Reducing Seasonal Unemployment*, 46; Woytinsky, *Seasonal Variations in Employment*, 47.

79. A good review of the issues involved is Robert J. Myers, "Seasonal Unemployment Insurance," *American Economic Review* 21 (1931), 416–26.

80. Samuel Insull, "Production and Distribution of Electric Energy in the Central Portion of the Mississippi Valley" (orig. 1921), in William E. Keily, ed., *Public Utilities in Modern Life: Selected Speeches by Samuel Insull* (Chicago: privately printed, 1924), 284.

81. Feldman, *The Regularization of Employment,* 93, 97, 136–37, 137–38; Smith, *Reducing Seasonal Unemployment*, 89–94.

82. Robert DeCourcy Ward, "How Far Can Man Control His Climate?," *Scientific Monthly* 30 (1930), 8; Kuznets, *Seasonal Variations*, 270.

83. Gail Cooper, *Air-Conditioning America: Engineers and the Controlled Environment* (Baltimore, Md.: The Johns Hopkins University Press, 1998), 85–87; Friedman, "The Air-Conditioned Century," 27–28; *Popular Science Monthly* 120, no. 4 (April, 1932), 122.

84. "Now We Have No Summer Slump," *System* 45 (1924), 713–14.

85. Feldman, *The Regularization of Employment*, 177–79; Mark Pendergast, *For God, Country and Coca-Cola* (New York: Charles Scribner's Sons, 1993), 148.

86. Gertrude Berta Grieg, *Seasonal Fluctuations in Employment in the Women's Clothing Industry* (New York: Columbia University Press, 1949); Feldman, *The Regularization of Employment*, 138–47; Smith, *Reducing Seasonal Unemployment*, 41–43.

87. "Three Ways to Double Summer Sales," *System* 48 (1925), 49.

88. Joyce Shaw Peterson, *American Automobile Workers, 1900–1933* (Albany: State University of New York Press, 1987), 134–35; *New York Times*, Jan. 10, 1932, 10: 6.

89. *Electrical World* 108 (1937), 1710; see also 107 (1937), 728–29; 109 (1938), 716.

90. Cletus E. Daniel, *Bitter Harvest: A History of California Farm Workers, 1870–1941* (Ithaca, N.Y.: Cornell University Press, 1981); Carey McWilliams, *Factories in the Field: The Story of Migratory Farm Labor in California* (Boston: Little, Brown, 1940).

91. John Steinbeck, *The Harvest Gypsies* (1936; Berkeley: Heyday Books, 1988), 20.

92. Cindy Hahamovitch, *The Fruits of their Labor: Atlantic Coast Farmworkers and the Making of Rural Poverty, 1870–1945* (Chapel Hill: University of North Carolina Press, 1997); Carey McWilliams, *Ill Fares the Land: Migrants and Migratory Labor in the United States* (Boston: Little, Brown, 1942).

93. Will D. Swearingen, *Moroccan Mirages: Agricultural Dreams and Deceptions, 1912–1986* (Princeton, N.J.: Princeton University Press, 1987).

94. Charles C. Colby, "The California Raisin Industry: A Study in Geographic Interpretation," *Annals of the Association of American Geographers* 14 (1924), 88, 90–91, 107–8.

95. John E. Dalton, *Sugar: A Case Study of Government Control* (New York: The Macmillan Company, 1937).

96. R. P. Teele, "The Federal Subsidy in Land Reclamation," *Journal of Land and Public Utility Economics* 3 (1927), 338–42.

97. Gilbert C. Fite, "Great Plains Farming: A Century of Change and Adjustment," *Agricultural History* 51 (1977), 249–52.

98. Neil Fligstein, *Going North: Migration of Blacks and Whites from the South, 1900–1950* (New York: Academic Press, 1981), 102–5, 137–38.

99. The fullest account is Nan Elizabeth Woodruff, *As Rare as Rain: Federal Relief in the Great Southern Drought of 1930–31* (Urbana: University of Illinois Press, 1985).

100. Ibid.; David E. Hamilton, "Herbert Hoover and the Great Drought of 1930," *Journal of American History* 68 (1982), 850–75.

101. Foster Rhea Dulles, *The American Red Cross: A History* (New York: Harper & Brothers, 1950), 280–88; Woodruff, *As Rare as Rain*.

102. Woodruff, *As Rare as Rain*, 140–57 (quotation from 140).

103. Useful accounts include Paul Bonnifield, *The Dust Bowl: Men, Dirt, and Depression* (Albuquerque: University of New Mexico Press, 1979); R. Douglas Hurt, *The Dust Bowl: An Agricultural and Social History* (Chicago: Nelson-Hall, 1981); Pamela Riney-Kehrberg, *Rooted in Dust: Surviving Drought and Depression in Southwest Kansas* (Lawrence: University Press of Kansas, 1994).

104. Martyn J. Bowden et al., "The Effects of Climate Fluctuations on Human Populations: Two Hypotheses," in T. M. L. Wigley, M. J. Ingram, and G. Farmer, eds., *Climate and History* (Cambridge: Cambridge University Press, 1981), 479–513; Richard A. Warrick, "Drought in the U.S. Great Plains: Shifting Social Consequences?," in Kenneth Hewitt, ed., *Interpretations of Calamity* (Boston: Allen and Unwin, 1983), 67–82.

105. The program was cautiously presented in *The Future of the Great Plains: Report of the Great Plains Committee* (Washington, D.C.: U.S. Government Printing Office, 1937); regional opposition is chronicled in Bonnifield, *The Dust Bowl*.

106. M.-L. Quinn, "Federal Drought Planning in the Great Plains: A First Look," *Climatic Change* 4 (1982), 285–87.

107. Randall A. Kramer, "Federal Crop Insurance, 1938–1982," *Agricultural History* 57 (1983), 186–88.

108. Henry A. Wallace, *New Frontiers* (New York: Reynal and Hitchcock, 1934), 203–4.

109. Henry A. Wallace, "The New Farm Act," *Vital Speeches of the Day* 4 (1938), 338–40.

110. Theodore Saloutos, *The American Farmer and the New Deal* (Ames: The Iowa State University Press, 1982).

111. Richard B. Craig, *The Bracero Program: Interest Groups and Foreign Policy* (Austin: University of Texas Press, 1971).

112. McWilliams, *Ill Fares the Land*, 187.

113. Notably Walter J. Stein, *California and the Dust Bowl Migration* (Westport, Conn.: Greenwood Press, 1973); James N. Gregory, *American Exodus: The Dust Bowl Migration and Okie Culture in California* (New York: Oxford University Press, 1989); Charles J. Shindo, *Dust Bowl Migrants in the American Imagination* (Lawrence: University Press of Kansas, 1997).

114. Pete Daniel, *Deep'n as It Comes: The 1927 Mississippi River Flood* (New York: Oxford University Press, 1977), 9.

115. John M. Barry, *Rising Tide: The Great Mississippi Flood of 1927 and How It Changed America* (New York: Simon and Schuster, 1997).

116. Robert Kelley, *Battling the Inland Sea: American Political Culture, Public Policy, and the Sacramento Valley, 1850–1986* (Berkeley: University of California Press, 1989).

117. Foster Rhea Dulles, *The American Red Cross: A History* (New York: Harper, 1950); Pete Daniel, *The Shadow of Slavery: Peonage in the South, 1901–1969* (Urbana: University of Illinois Press, 1972), 149–69.

118. William Edward Leuchtenberg, *Flood Control Politics: The Connecticut River Problem, 1927–1950* (Cambridge, Mass.: Harvard University Press, 1953).

119. Arthur Maass, *Muddy Waters: The Army Corps of Engineers and the Nation's Rivers* (Cambridge, Mass.: Harvard University Press, 1951).

120. Donald Davidson, *The Tennessee,* vol. 2, *The New River: Civil War to TVA* (New York: Rinehart & Company, 1948), 237; Leuchtenberg, *Flood Control Politics*.

121. L. Segoe, "Flood Control and the Cities," *The American City* 52, no. 3 (March, 1937), 55–56 (emphases omitted).

122. Gilbert Fowler White, *Human Adjustment to Floods: A Geographical Approach to the Flood Problem in the United States*, University of Chicago Department of Geography Research Paper No. 29 (1945), 2, 33, 200–04.

123. *New York-New England Hurricane and Floods, 1938: Official Report of Relief Operations* (Washington, D.C.: American National Red Cross,

1939), 8, 39–42, 63–64; Alfred V. Kidder, "Looking Backward," *Proceedings of the American Philosophical Society* 83 (1940), 532.

124. Smith, *Airways,* 351; Ernest M. Gould, Jr., "Fifty Years of Management at the Harvard Forest" (orig. 1960), in Ian Burton and Robert W. Kates, eds., *Readings in Resource Management and Conservation* (Chicago: University of Chicago Press, 1965), 308–26.

125. Theodore Steinberg, "Do-it-Yourself Deathtrap: The Unnatural History of Natural Disaster in South Florida," *Environmental History* 2 (1997), 418–21 (1926), 412–23 (1928), 423–25 (1935); Jay Barnes, *Florida's Hurricane History* (Chapel Hill: University of North Caolina Press, 1998), 111–26, 127–40, 144–59.

126. Hans Christian Adamson and George Francis Kosco, *Halsey's Typhoons* (New York: Crown Publishers, Inc., 1967); C. Raymond Calhoun, *Typhoon: The Other Enemy* (Annapolis, MD: Naval Institute Press, 1981).

127. Robert DeCourcy Ward, "How Far Can Man Control His Climate?" *Scientific Monthly* 30 (1930), 5–18 (quotation from p. 18); Willis Luther Moore, *The New Air World: The Science of Meteorology Simplified* (Boston: Little, Brown, 1922); Charles Fitzhugh Talman, *Meteorology: The Science of the Atmosphere* (New York: P. F. Collier & Son Company, 1922), 332–45; W. J. Humphreys, *Rain Making and Other Vagaries* (Baltimore, Md.: The Williams and Wilkins Company, 1926), and *Ways of the Weather: A Cultural Survey of Meteorology* (Lancaster, Penn.: The Jacques Cattell Press, 1942), 323–35.

128. "Does Prayer Change the Weather?," *The Christian Century* 47 (Sept. 10, 1930), 1084.

129. Elizabeth Madox Roberts, *Jingling in the Wind* (New York: The Viking Press, 1928), 21–23, 26–30.

130. Stephen S. Visher, "Climatic Effects of the Proposed Wooded Shelter Belt on the Great Plains," *Annals of the Association of American Geographers* 25 (1935), 63–73.

131. Raphael Zon, "How the Forests Feed the Clouds," in Otis W. Caldwell and Edwin E. Slosson, eds., *Science Remaking the World* (Garden City, N.Y.: Doubleday, Page, 1925), 212–22; *Forests and Water in the Light of Scientific Investigation* (Washington, D.C.: U.S. Government Printing Office, 1927); "Shelterbelts: Futile Dream or Workable Plan," *Science* 81 (1935), 391, 392.

132. Ward, "How Far Can Man Control His Climate?" 6.

133. For a generally favorable estimate, see Geoffrey J. Martin, *Ellsworth Huntington: His Life and Thought* (Hamden, Conn.: Archon Books, 1973); for a highly critical one, James Rodger Fleming, *Historical Perspectives on Climate Change* (New York: Oxford University Press, 1998), 95–106.

134. Ellsworth Huntington, *Civilization and Climate*, 3d ed. (New Haven, Conn.: Yale University Press, 1924), 36, 403, 408.

135. Clarence A. Mills, *Climate Makes the Man* (New York: Harper & Brothers, 1942); Clarence A. Mills and James T. Heady, *Living With the Weather* (Cincinnati: Caxton Press, 1934), 134.

136. Preston E. James, "The Contribution of Geography to the Social

Studies" (orig. 1941), in D. W. Meinig, ed., *On Geography: Selected Writings of Preston E. James* (Syracuse, N.Y.: Syracuse University Press, 1971), 330.

137. Isaiah Bowman, *Geography in Relation to the Social Sciences* (New York: Charles Scribner's Sons, 1934), 37.

CHAPTER 5

1. Edward L. Ullman, "Amenities as a Factor in Regional Growth," *Geographical Review* 44 (1954), 119–32.

2. Marion Clawson, "The Influence of Weather on Outdoor Recreation," in W. R. Derrick Sewell, ed., *Human Dimensions of Weather Modification*, University of Chicago Department of Geography Research Paper No. 105 (1966), 191–92.

3. Edward T. Price, "The Geography of California's Southland," *Annals of the Association of American Geographers* 49 (1959), 101.

4. David Savageau and Geoffrey Loftus, *Places Rated Almanac*, 5th ed. (New York: Macmillan, 1997), 176–77.

5. *Congressional Record*, 55th Congress, 2d session (1898), Appendix, 616; Edward L. Ullman, "Rivers as Regional Bonds," *Geographical Review* 41 (1951), 224.

6. The earlier literature is reviewed by Larry M. Svartz, "Environmental Preference Migration: A Review," *Geographical Review* 66 (1976), 314–30, later work by Mary M. Kritz, "Climate Change and Migration Adaptations," 1990 Working Paper Series 2.16, Population and Development Program, Department of Rural Sociology, Cornell University. A recent study reaching similar conclusions is P. E. Mueser and P. E. Graves, "Examining the Role of Economic Opportunity and Amenities in Explaining Population Redistribution," *Journal of Urban Economics* 37 (1995), 176–200.

7. H. W. Martin, S. K. Hoppe, C. L. Larson, and R. L. Leon, "Texas Snowbirds: Seasonal Migrants to the Rio Grande Valley," *Research on Aging* 9 (1987), 141; Timothy D. Hogan, "Determinants of the Seasonal Migration of the Elderly to Sunbelt States," *Research on Aging* 9 (1987), 115–33; Donald N. Steinnes and Timothy D. Hogan, "Take the Money and Sun: Elderly Migration as a Consequence of Gains in Unaffordable Housing Markets," *Journal of Gerontology* 47 (1992), S197–203; Patricia Gober and R. C. Mingis, "A Geography of Non-Permanent Residence in the U.S.," *Professional Geographer* 36 (1984), 164–73; William J. Craig, "Seasonal Migration of the Elderly: Minnesota Snowbirds," *Southeastern Geographer* 32 (1992), 38–50.

8. Philip J. Gersmehl, "Putting Information in Perspective," *Journal of Geography* 96 (1997), 235–42.

9. Paul F. Starrs and John B. Wright, "Great Basin Growth and the Withering of California's Pacific Idyll," *Geographical Review* 85 (1995), 417–35.

10. *New York Times*, Feb. 14, 1993, 1: 47.

11. Edward A. Ackerman and George O. G. Löf with Conrad Seipp, *Technology and American Water Development* (Baltimore, Md.: The Johns Hopkins University Press for Resources for the Future, 1959), 143–45.

12. United States Department of Energy, *Monthly Energy Review*.

13. The classic work is P. O. Fanger, *Thermal Comfort: Analysis and Applications in Environmental Engineering* (New York: McGraw-Hill, 1970).

14. For reviews of the literature and issues, see, e.g., Donald A. McIntyre, "Chamber Studies: Reductio ad absurdum?," *Energy and Buildings* 5 (1982), 89–96; Wim Heijs and Peter Stringer, "Research on Residential Thermal Comfort: Some Considerations for Environmental Psychologists," *Journal of Environmental Psychology* 8 (1988), 235–47; Baruch Givoni, *Climate Considerations in Building and Urban Design* (New York: Van Nostrand Reinhold, 1998), 3–36; Gail S. Brager and Richard J. de Dear, "Thermal Adaptation in the Built Environment: A Literature Review," *Energy and Buildings* 27 (1998), 83–96.

15. Vladimir Nabokov, *Pale Fire* (orig. 1962), in *Novels, 1955–1962* (New York: The Library of America, 1996), 447–48; also *Pnin* (orig. 1957), in *ibid.*, 311, 320–21, 322, 342, 402.

16. *New York Times*, Dec. 31, 1948, 10; see also Evelyn Waugh, "Kicking Against the Goad" (orig. 1949), in Donat Gallagher, ed., *The Essays, Articles and Reviews of Evelyn Waugh* (Boston: Little, Brown, 1983), 371–72.

17. Leslie James, *Americans in Glasshouses* (New York: Henry Schuman, 1952), 76; Jack Pitman, *England Ebbing* (New York: Stein & Day, 1987), 106.

18. Donald A. McIntyre, *Indoor Climate* (London: Applied Science Publishers, 1980), 202.

19. Elizabeth Shove, Loren Lutzenhuiser, Simon Guy, Bruce Hackett, and Harold Wilhite, "Energy and Social Systems," in Steve Rayner and Elizabeth Malone, eds., *Human Choice and Climate Change*, vol. 2, *Resources and Technology* (Columbus, Ohio: Battelle Press, 1998), 315.

20. Raymond Arsenault, "The End of the Long Hot Summer: The Air Conditioner and Southern Culture," *Journal of Southern History* 50 (1984)

21. John A. Burns, *Energy-Conserving Features Inherent in Older Homes* (Washington, D.C.: U.S. Department of Housing and Urban Development, Office of Policy Development and Research, Dvision of Building Technology, 1982).

22. Gail Ann Cooper, "Manufactured Weather: A History of Air Conditioning in the United States, 1902–1955," Ph.D. dissertation, University of California at Santa Barbara, 1987, 227–33.

23. James Marston Fitch, *Architecture and the Esthetics of Plenty* (New York: Columbia University Press, 1961), 244–45.

24. Paul D. Luyben, "Prompting Thermostat Setting Behavior: Public Response to a Presidential Appeal for Conservation," *Environment and Behavior* 14 (1982), 113–28.

25. S. Meyers, "Energy Consumption and Structure of the U.S. Residential Sector: Changes Between 1970 and 1985," *Annual Review of Energy* 12 (1987), 92–93.

26. Paul C. Stern et al., "The Effectiveness of Incentives for Residential Energy Consumption," *Evaluation Review* 10 (1986), 147–76.

27. *New York Times*, Jan. 29, 1977, 19.

28. Andrew G. Glass and Robert N. Hooker, "The Emerging Epidemic of Melanoma and Squamous Cell Skin Cancer," *Journal of the*

American Medical Association 262 (1989), 2097–2100; on totals, Martin A. Weinstock, "Ultraviolet Radiation and Skin Cancer: Epidemiological Data From the United States and Canada," in Antony R. Young et al., eds., *Environmental UV Photobiology* (New York: Plenum Press, 1993); Mark R. Leary and Jody L. Jones, "The Social Psychology of Tanning and Sunscreen Use: Self-Presentational Motives as a Predictor of Health Risk," *Journal of Applied Social Psychology* 23 (1993), 1390–1406.

29. Eva Jacobs and Stephanie Shipp, "How Family Spending Has Changed in the United States," *Monthly Labor Review* 113, no. 3 (1990), 22.

30. As proposed by Valerie Steele, "Appearance and Identity," in Claudia Brush Kidwell and Valerie Steele, eds., *Men and Women: Dressing the Past* (Washington, D.C.: Smithsonian Institution, 1989), 24, and Judith Waldrop with Marcia Magelonsky, *The Seasons of Business: The Marketer's Guide to Consumer Behavior* (Ithaca, NY: American Demographics Books, 1992), 64.

31. Marshall Sahlins, *Culture and Practical Reason* (Chicago: University of Chicago Press, 1976), 183n15; Anthony Leeds, "Clothing," in David E. Hunter and Phillip Whitten, eds., *Encyclopedia of Anthropology* (New York: Harper & Row, 1976), 75–76.

32. Catherine A. Lutz and Jane L. Collins, *Reading National Geographic* (Chicago: University of Chicago Press, 1993), 233.

33. Patrick Hughes and Richard Wood, "Hail: The White Plague," *Weatherwise* 46, no. 2 (April/May, 1993), 21; Carolinda Hall, "Mayday," *ibid.,* 49, no. 3 (June-July, 1996), 25–28.

34. Lynn A. Sheretz and B. C. Farhar, "An Analysis of the Relationship Between Rainfall and the Occurrence of Traffic Accidents," *Journal of Applied Meteorology* 17 (1978), 711–15; S. A. Changnon, "Effects of Summer Precipitation on Urban Transportation," *Climatic Change* 32 (1996), 481–94.

35. *Proceedings, Special Public Hearing, Fog Accidents on Limited Access Highways*, PB92-917001, NTSB/RP-92/01, 4–6.

36. Ibid., 1; Harry A. Smith, "Pavement Contributions to Wet-Weather Skidding Accident Reductions," in *Skidding Accidents: Pavement Characteristics*, Transportation Research Record #622 (Washington, D.C.: National Academy of Sciences, 1976), 51; National Transportation Safety Board, "Special Study: Fatal Highway Accidents on Wet Pavement," Report NTSB-HSS-80-1, NTSB Bureau of Technology, Washington, DC, 1980.

37. Jeff Rosenfeld, "Cars vs. the Weather: A Century of Progress," *Weatherwise* 49, no. 5 (Oct./Nov., 1996), 14–23; T. P. Newcomb and R. T. Spurr, *A Technical History of the Motor Car* (Bristol: Adam Hilger, 1989).

38. Rosenfeld, "Cars vs. the Weather," 23.

39. Rashad M. Hanbali and Daniel A. Kuemmel, "Traffic Volume Reductions Due to Winter Storm Conditions," *Snow Removal and Ice Control Technology*, Transportation Research Record #1387 (Transportation Research Board, National Research Council, 1993), 159–64.

40. John F. Rooney, Jr., "The Urban Snow Hazard in the United States: An Appraisal of Disruption," *Geographical Review* 57 (1967), 538.

41. *Highway Deicing: Comparing Salt and Calcium Magnesium Acetate* (Washington, D.C.: National Research Council, 1991), 18.

42. Ibid., 27, 34–39.

43. Peter Rogers, "Hydrology and Water Quality," in William B. Meyer and B. L. Turner II, eds., *Changes in Land Use and Land Cover: A Global Perspective* (New York: Cambridge University Press, 1994), 254.

44. A. J. Haagen-Smit, "The Control of Air Pollution," *Scientific American* 210, no. 1 (January 1964), 27.

45. Jane V. Hall, Arthur M. Winer, Michael T. Kleinman, Frederick W. Lurmann, Victor Brajer, and Steven D. Colome, "Valuing the Health Benefits of Clean Air," *Science* 255 (1992), 815.

46. Carl Solberg, *Conquest of the Skies: A History of Commercial Aviation in America* (Boston: Little, Brown, 1979), 363–64.

47. Roger A. Pielke, Jr., "Asking the Right Questions: Atmospheric Sciences Research and Societal Needs," *Bulletin of the American Meteorological Society* 78 (1997), 260–61.

48. Jan Bertness, "Rain-Related Impacts on Selected Transportation Activities and Utility Services in the Chicago Area," *Journal of Applied Meteorology* 19 (1980), 545–56; Changnon, "Effects of Summer Precipitation on Urban Transportation."

49. Edwin Kiesler, Jr., "The Dominoes Are Falling," *Smithsonian* 29, no. 7 (1998), 50, 56.

50. Charles Perrow, *Normal Accidents: Living With High-Risk Technologies* (New York: Basic Books, 1984), 204, 224.

51. William Koellner, "Climate Variability and the Mississippi River Navigation System," in Michael H. Glantz, ed., *Societal Responses to Regional Climatic Change: Forecasting by Analogy* (Boulder, Colo.: Westview Press, 1988), 257.

52. Ronald L. Heilmann, Harold M. Mayer, and Eric Schenker, *Great Lakes Transportation in the Eighties* (Madison: University of Wisconsin Sea Grant Institute, 1986), 75–77; Mark L. Thompson, *Steamboats and Sailors of the Great Lakes* (Detroit, Mich.: Wayne State University Press, 1991), 183–93.

53. Marty Jezer, *Abbie Hoffman: American Radical* (New Brunswick, N.J.: Rutgers University Press, 1992), 267–74.

54. Stanley A. Changnon, "The 1988 Drought, Barges, and Diversion," *Bulletin of the American Meteorological Society* 70 (1989), 1092–1104.

55. *St. Louis Post-Dispatch*, Sept. 18, 1988, F:1, 8; Walter M. Kollmorgen, "Settlement Control Beats Flood Control," *Economic Geography* 29 (1953), 213–14.

56. Kenneth D. Frederick, "Climate Change Impacts on Water Resources and Possible Responses in the MINK Region," *Climatic Change* 24 (1993), 107–08.

57. John E. Thorson, *River of Promise, River of Peril: The Politics of Managing the Missouri River* (Lawrence: University Press of Kansas, 1994), 77–78; Sarah F. Bates, David H. Getches, Lawrence J. MacDonnell, and Charles F. Wilkinson, *Searching Out the Headwaters: Change and Rediscovery in Western Water Policy* (Washington, D.C.: Island Press, 1993),

126–27; *St. Louis Post-Dispatch*, March 7, 1995, B2; *Chicago Tribune*, Aug. 15, 1991, 3, 1, 2.

58. Daniel Schaffer, "Managing the Tennessee: Principles, Practice, and Change," *The Public Historian* 12, no. 2 (Spring, 1990), 8–9, 27–28.

59. Jeffrey Englin, "Estimating the Amenity Value of Rainfall," *Annals of Regional Science* 30 (1996), 273–83.

60. Nelson M. Blake, *Water for the Cities: A History of the Urban Water Supply Problem in the United States* (Syracuse, N.Y.: Syracuse University Press, 1956), 280–85; Charles H. Weidner, *Water for a City: A History of New York City's Problem from the Beginning to the Delaware River System* (New Brunswick, N.J.: Rutgers University Press, 1974).

61. Robert A. Weisman, "The 1980–81 Drought in Southeastern New York," *Bulletin of the American Meteorological Society* 66 (1985), 788–94.

62. Described by Clifford S. Russell, D. G. Arey, and Robert W. Kates, *Drought and Water Supply: Implications of the Massachusetts Experience for Municipal Planning* (Baltimore, Md.: The Johns Hopkins University Press for Resources for the Future, 1970), and William E. Riebsame, "Adjusting Water Resources Management to Climate Change," *Climatic Change* 13 (1988), 69–97.

63. *New York Times*, Sept. 2, 1965, 28.

64. Norris Hundley, *The Great Thirst: Californians and Water, 1770s–1990s* (Berkeley: University of California Press, 1992); William Kahrl, *Water and Power: The Conflict over Los Angeles' Water Supply in the Owens Valley* (Berkeley: University of California Press, 1982).

65. Hundley, *The Great Thirst*, 385; Marc Reisner and Sarah Bates, *Overtapped Oasis: Reform or Revolution for Western Water* (Washington, D.C.: Island Press, 1990), 32–34; Vernon W. Ruttan, *The Economic Demand for Irrigated Acreage: New Methodology and Some Preliminary Projections, 1954–1980* (Baltimore, Md.: The Johns Hopkins University Press for Resources for the Future, 1965).

66. Peter Rogers, "Assessing the Socioeconomic Consequences of Climate Change on Water Resources," *Climatic Change* 28 (1994), 199–202.

67. See especially National Research Council, *Water Transfers in the West: Efficiency, Equity, and the Environment* (Washington, D.C.: National Academy of Sciences Press, 1992).

68. Kahrl, *Water and Power*, describes both controversies.

69. Lloyd S. Dixon, Nancy H. Moore, and Susan W. Schrechter, *California's 1991 Drought Water Bank: Economic Impacts in the Selling Regions* (RAND, 1993).

70. Martyn J. Bowden et al., "The Effects of Climate Fluctuations on Human Populations: Two Hypotheses," in T. M. L. Wigley, M. J. Ingram, and G. Farmer, eds., *Climate and History* (Cambridge: Cambridge University Press, 1981), 479–513; Richard A. Warrick, "Drought in the U.S. Great Plains: Shifting Social Consequences?," in Kenneth Hewitt, ed., *Interpretations of Calamity* (Boston: Allen and Unwin, 1983), 67–82.

71. D. G. Baker, D. L. Ruschy, and R. H. Skaggs, "Agriculture and the Recent 'Benign Climate' in Minnesota," *Bulletin of the American Meteorological Society* 74 (1993), 1035–40; *Preparing U.S. Agriculture for Climate*

Change, Council on Agricultural Science and Technology, Report 119, Ames, Iowa, 1992, 25, 28.

72. Vaclav Smil, *Energy, Food, Environment* (Oxford: Oxford University Press, 1987), 241–42.

73. Donald A. Wilhite, "Government Response to Drought in the United States, with Particular Reference to the Great Plains," *Journal of Climate and Applied Meteorology* 22 (1983), 45–47.

74. Randall A. Kerr, "Federal Crop Insurance, 1938–1982," *Agricultural History* 57 (1983), 181–200.

75. Darrell L. Hueth and William R. Furtan, eds., *Economics of Agricultural Crop Insurance: Theory and Evidence* (Boston: Kluwer Academic Publishers, 1994).

76. Philip L. Martin and David A. Martin, *The Endless Quest: Helping America's Farm Workers* (Boulder, Colo.: Westview Press, 1994), 161–63, 168–74.

77. David Griffith and Ed Kissam, *Working Poor: Farmworkers in the United States* (Philadelphia: Temple University Press, 1995).

78. Lester B. Lave, "The Value of Better Weather Information to the Raisin Industry," *Econometrica* 31 (1963), 151–64; Bruce Babcock, "The Value of Weather Information in Market Equilibrium," *American Journal of Agricultural Economics* 72 (1990), 63–72.

79. Elizabeth Brooks and Jacque Emel, "The Llano Estacado of the American Southern High Plains," in Jeanne X. Kasperson, Roger E. Kasperson, and B. L. Turner II, eds., *Regions at Risk: Comparisons of Threatened Environments* (Tokyo: United Nations University Press, 1995), 275–80.

80. For a detailed study, see Rolando V. Garcia, *Nature Pleads Not Guilty* (Oxford: Pergamon Press, 1981).

81. Kathleen A. Miller and Michael H. Glantz, "Climate and Economic Competitiveness: Florida Freezes and the Global Citrus Processing Industry," *Climatic Change* 12 (1988), 135–64.

82. *Preparing U.S. Agriculture for Climate Change*, 24.

83. J. K. Lewandrowski and R. J. Brazee, "Farm Programs and Climate Change," *Climatic Change* 23 (1993), 1–20.

84. Willis H. Carrier et al., *Modern Air Conditioning, Heating, and Ventilation*, 3d edition (New York: Pitman, 1959), 403.

85. Leo G. Rydzewski, William G. Dennis, and Philip L. Rones, "Seasonal Employment Patterns Over the Past Three Decades," *Monthly Labor Review* 116, no. 7 (1993), 8–9.

86. John Tschetter and John Lukasiewicz, "Employment Changes in Construction: Secular, Cyclical, and Seasonal," *Monthly Labor Review* 106, no. 3 (1983), 14–15; M. T. Cammarota, "The Impact of Unseasonable Weather on Housing Starts," *Journal of the American Real Estate and Urban Economics Association* 17 (1989), 300–13.

87. Kenneth T. Rosen, *Seasonal Cycles in the Housing Market: Patterns, Costs, and Policies* (Cambridge, Mass.: MIT Press, 1979), 125.

88. For many examples, see Waldrop with Magelonsky, *The Seasons of Business*.

89. Rydzewski et al., "Seasonal Employment Patterns."

90. W. J. Maunder, *The Value of the Weather* (London: Methuen, 1970), 146–57.

91. Victor Gruen and Larry Smith, *Shopping Towns USA: The Planning of Shopping Centers* (New York: Reinhold, 1960), 49.

92. Edgar Lion, *Shopping Centers: Planning, Development, and Administration* (New York: John Wiley & Sons, 1976), 171.

93. "Chasing the Wind," *American Cinematographer* 77, no. 5 (May 1996), 36–38, 40, 42, 44 and "*Twister* Kicks Up a Storm," ibid., 77, no. 12 (December 1996), 76–78, 80–81; *Time*, Nov. 24, 1997, 77; *Boston Globe*, Dec. 9, 1997, A1.

94. Leigh Henry, "Let it Rain," *New York Times Magazine*, Dec. 1, 1946, 51.

95. Michael Gershman, *Diamonds: The Evolution of the Ballpark* (Boston: Houghton Mifflin, 1993), 192–94.

96. Bernard Mergen, *Snow in America* (Washington, D.C.: Smithsonian Institution Press, 1997), 109–112.

97. As noted by Robert L. A. Adams, "Weather, Weather Information, and Outdoor Recreation Decisions: A Case Study of the New England Beach Trip," Ph.D. dissertation, Clark University, 1971, 21.

98. George A. Barnett, Hsin-Jung Chang, Edward L. Fink, and William D. Richards, Jr., "Seasonality in Television Viewing: A Mathematical Model of Cultural Processes," *Communication Research* 18 (1991), 755–72; George A. Barnett and Sung Ho Cho, "Predicting Television Viewing: Cycles, the Weather, and Social Events," in James H. Watt and C. Arthur VanLear, eds., *Dynamic Patterns in Communication Processes* (Thousand Oaks, Calif.: Sage Publications, 1996), 231–54.

99. K. Smith, "The Influence of Weather and Climate on Recreation and Tourism," *Weather* 48 (1993), 398–404.

100. Bryan H. Farrell, *Hawaii: The Legend That Sells* (Honolulu: University of Hawaii Press, 1982), 16–17; Hal K. Rothman, *Devil's Bargains: Tourism in the Twentieth-Century American West* (Lawrence: University Press of Kansas, 1998), 4–5.

101. Rothman, *Devil's Bargains*, 348–49.

102. U.S. Department of Energy, *Monthly Energy Review*; Energy Information Agency, "Assessment of Summer 1997 Motor Gasoline Price Increase," DOE/EIA-0621 (1998), 3–4.

103. Jeffrey A. Miron, *The Economics of Seasonal Cycles* (Cambridge, Mass.: MIT Press, 1996), 40–41, 45.

104. Carl F. Kaestle, *Pillars of the Republic: Common Schools and American Society, 1780–1860* (New York: Hill and Wang, 1983), 15, 19–20, 111, 125, 132.

105. Michael J. Barrett, "The Case for More School Days," *Atlantic Monthly* 266, no. 5 (1990), 80.

106. *Monthly Energy Review*, various issues.

107. Stanley A. Changnon, Joyce M. Changnon, and David Changnon, "Uses and Applications of Climate Forecasting for Power Utilities," *Bulletin of the American Meteorological Society* 76 (1995), 711–20.

108. Lee R. Hoxit, Herbert S. Leib, Charles F. Chappell, and

H. Michael Mogil, "Disaster by Flood," in Edwin Kessler, ed., *The Thunderstorm in Human Affairs*, 2d ed. (Norman: University of Oklahoma Press, 1983), 19.

109. Stanley A. Changnon, "Changes in Climate and Levels of Lake Michigan: Shoreline Impacts at Chicago," *Climatic Change* 23 (1993), 218–19, 227; Harun Rashid and James Hufferd, "Hazards of Living on the Edge of Water: The Case of Minnesota Point, Duluth, Minnesota," *Human Ecology* 17 (1989), 85–100; D. M. Bush, O. H. Pilkey, Jr., and W. J. Neal, *Living By the Rules of the Sea* (Durham, N.C.: Duke University Press, 1996), 1–5.

110. Roger A. Pielke, Jr. and Roger A. Pielke, Sr., *Hurricanes: Their Nature and Impacts on Society* (Chichester: John Wiley & Sons, 1997), 164.

111. Roger A. Pielke, Jr., "Reframing the U.S. Hurricane Problem," *Society & Natural Resources* 10 (1997), 485.

112. Theodore Steinberg, "Do-It-Yourself Deathtrap: The Unnatural History of Natural Disaster in South Florida," *Environmental History* 2 (1997), 431–32; Ronald A. Cook and Mehrdad Soltani, *Hurricanes of 1992: Lessons Learned and Implications for the Future* (New York: American Society of Civil Engineers, 1992).

113. Steven Whitman, Glenn Good, Edmund R. Donoghue, Nanette Benbow, Wenyuan Shou, and Shanxuan Mou, "Mortality in Chicago Attributed to the July 1995 Heat Wave," *American Journal of Public Health* 87 (1997), 1515–18.

114. Stanley A. Changnon, Kenneth E. Kunkel, and Beth C. Reinke, "Impacts and Responses to the 1995 Heat Wave: A Call to Action," *Bulletin of the American Meteorological Society* 77 (1996), 1497–1506; T. S. Jones et al., "Mortality and Morbidity Associated With the July 1980 Heat Wave in St. Louis and Kansas City," *Journal of the American Medical Association* 247 (1982), 3327–30.

115. Henry C. Hart, *The Dark Missouri* (Madison: University of Wisconsin Press, 1957), 89, 149, 151.

116. Gilbert F. White, Wesley C. Calef, James W. Hudson, Harold M. Mayer, John R. Sheaffer, and Donald J. Volk, *Changes in Urban Occupance of Flood Plains in the United States*, Department of Geography Research Paper No. 57, University of Chicago, 1958.

117. Rutherford H. Platt, "Floods and Man: A Geographer's Agenda," in Robert W. Kates and Ian Burton, eds., *Geography, Resources, and Environment,* vol. 2, *Themes from the Work of Gilbert F. White* (Chicago: University of Chicago Press, 1986), 51–61.

118. P. S. Showalter, W. E. Riebsame, and M. F. Myers, *Natural Hazard Trends in the United States: A Preliminary Review for the 1990s*, Natural Hazards Working Paper No. 82, Institute of Behavioral Science, University of Colorado, Boulder, 1990, 34.

119. Jon Kusler and Larry Larson, "Beyond the Ark: A New Approach to U.S. Floodplain Policy," *Environment* 35, no. 5 (1993), 9.

120. Robert Henson, *Television Weathercasting: A History* (Jefferson, N.C.: McFarland, 1990), 104–19; William E. Riebsame, Henry F. Diaz, Todd Moses, and Martin Price, "The Social Burden of Weather and Climate Hazards," *Bulletin of the American Meteorological Society* 67 (1986),

1380–81; Snowden D. Flora, *Tornadoes of the United States* (Norman: University of Oklahoma Press, 1953), 38–39.

121. Thomas R. Stewart, "Forecast Value: Descriptive Decision Studies," in Richard W. Katz and Allan H. Murphy, eds., *Economic Value of Weather and Climate Forecasts* (New York: Cambridge University Press, 1997), 147–81.

122. Robert L. A. Adams, "Weather, Weather Information, and Outdoor Recreation Decisions: A Case Study of the New England Beach Trip," Ph.D. dissertation, Clark University, 1971.

123. Robert L. A. Adams, "Uncertainty in Nature, Cognitive Dissonance, and the Perceptual Distortion of Environmental Information: Weather Forecasts and the New England Beach Trip," *Economic Geography* 49 (1973), 296–97; on the shortcomings of information alone as a means of reducing hazard impacts, see also John H. Sims and Duane D. Baumann, "Educational Programs and Human Response to Natural Hazards," *Environment and Behavior* 15 (1983), 165–89.

124. Herbert J. Gans, *Deciding What's News: A Study of CBS Evening News, NBC Nightly News, Newsweek, and Time* (New York: Pantheon Books, 1979), 58.

125. Sarah Lichtenstein, Paul Slovic, Baruch Fischoff, Mark Layman, and Barbara Combs, "Judged Frequency of Lethal Events," *Journal of Experimental Psychology: Human Learning and Memory* 4 (1978), 551–78.

126. *New York Times*, Sept. 22, 1994, C2.

127. Horace Byers, "History of Weather Modification," in W. N. Hess, ed., *Weather and Climate Modification* (New York: John Wiley & Sons, 1974), 9–12.

128. Ibid., 13–21; Georg Breuer, *Weather Modification: Prospects and Problems*, trans. H. Morth (Cambridge, England: Cambridge University Press, 1980), 29–35.

129. Edward A. Morris, "The Law and Weather Modification," *Bulletin of the American Meteorological Society* 46 (1965), 620.

130. Byers, "History of Weather Modification," 14–15.

131. *New York Times* Feb. 25, 1950, 12; March 23, 1; June 5, 25; July 27, 24; Aug. 23, 31; Aug. 27, IV: 8; Feb. 17, 1951, 8; Feb. 20, 27; Dean E. Mann, "The Yuba City Flood: A Case Study of Weather Modification Litigation," *Bulletin of the American Meteorological Society* 49 (1968), 690–714; Wallace E. Howell, "Cloud Seeding and the Law in the Blue Ridge Area," *Bulletin of the American Meteorological Society* 46 (1965), 328–32; Theodore Steinberg, "Cloudbusting in Fulton County" (orig. 1993), in *Slide Mountain; or, The Folly of Owning Nature* (Berkeley: University of California Press, 1995), 106–34. For additional cases of conflict, see J. Eugene Haas, "Sociological Aspects of Weather Modification," in Hess, *Weather and Climate Modification*, 788–92, and Jeff Townsend, *Making Rain in America: A History* (Lubbock, Tex.: ICASALS Publication 75–3, 1975), chaps. 6–10.

132. James C. Malin, "The Grassland of North America: Its Occupance and the Challenge of Continuous Reappraisals," in W. L. Thomas, Jr., ed., *Man's Role in Changing the Face of the Earth* (Chicago: University of Chicago Press, 1956), 352.

133. Matthew Holden, Jr., "Politics and Weather Modification," in

W. R. D. Sewell et al., *Modifying the Weather: A Social Assessment*, Western Geographical Series, vol. 9, Department of Geography, University of Victoria, 1973, 292–96.

134. John Fraser Hart, "The Highest Form of the Geographer's Art," *Annals of the Association of American Geographers* 72 (1982), 7.

135. Erhard Rostlund, "Twentieth-Century Magic" (orig. 1956), in Philip L. Wagner and Marvin W. Mikesell, eds., *Readings in Cultural Geography* (Chicago: University of Chicago Press, 1962), 53.

136. W. R. D. Sewell, Robert W. Kates, and Lee E. Phillips, "Human Response to Weather and Climate: Geographical Contributions," *Geographical Review* 58 (1968), 262–80.

137. Gilbert F. White, "Approaches to Weather Modification," in W. R. D. Sewell, ed., *Human Dimensions of Weather Modification*, University of Chicago Department of Geography Research Paper 105, 1966, 20; Edward A. Ackerman, "Economic Analysis of Weather: An Ideal Weather Pattern Model," in ibid., 66–75.

138. Ian Burton, "Issues in the Design of Social Research for the Management of Atmospheric Resources," in W. R. D. Sewell et al., *Modifying the Weather: A Social Assessment*, Western Geographical Series, vol. 9, Department of Geography, University of Victoria, 1973, 69–73.

139. But see Steve Rayner and Elizabeth Malone, eds., *Human Choice and Climate Change,* 4 vols. (Columbus, Ohio: Battelle Press, 1998).

CONCLUSION

1. Daniel J. Boorstin, *The Americans: The Democratic Experience* (New York: Random House, 1973), 407–8.

2. See, e.g., Jesse H. Ausubel, "Does Climate Still Matter?," *Nature* 350 (1991), 649–52.

3. Gilbert F. White and J. Eugene Haas, *Assessment of Research on Natural Hazards* (New York: Oxford University Press, 1975), 1; for a more recent stocktaking, see Dennis Mileti, *Disasters by Design: A Reassessment of Natural Hazards in the United States* (Washington, D.C.: Joseph Henry Press, 1999).

4. Boorstin, *The Americans,* 408.

Index